# THE FUTURE OF THE LAW

# MARKETS AND THE LAW

*Series Editor:*
Geraint Howells, City University of Hong Kong

*Series Advisory Board:*
Stefan Grundmann – Humboldt University of Berlin, Germany, and
European University Institute, Italy
Hans Micklitz – Bamberg University, Germany
James P. Nehf – Indiana University, USA
Iain Ramsay – Kent Law School, UK
Charles Rickett – Auckland University of Technology, New Zealand
Reiner Schulze – Münster University, Germany
Jules Stuyck – Katholieke Universiteit Leuven, Belgium
Stephen Weatherill – University of Oxford, UK
Thomas Wilhelmsson – University of Helsinki, Finland

Markets and the Law is concerned with the way the law interacts with the market through regulation, self-regulation and the impact of private law regimes. It looks at the impact of regional and international organizations (e.g., EC and WTO) and many of the works adopt a comparative approach and/or appeal to an international audience. Examples of subjects covered include trade laws, intellectual property, sales law, insurance, consumer law, banking, financial markets, labour law, environmental law and social regulation affecting the market as well as competition law. The series includes texts covering a broad area, monographs on focused issues, and collections of essays dealing with particular themes.

*Other titles in the series*

**The European Unfair Commercial Practices Directive**
Impact, Enforcement Strategies and National Legal Systems
*Edited by Willem van Boom, Amandine Garde and Orkun Akseli*
ISBN 978-1-4724-2340-5

**The Law and Economics of Enforcing European Consumer Law**
A Comparative Analysis of Package Travel and Misleading Advertising
*Franziska Weber*
ISBN 978-1-4724-1704-6

**Consumer Protection, Automated Shopping Platforms and EU Law**
*Christiana N. Markou*
ISBN 978-1-4724-2427-3

**Private Law, Nudging and Behavioural Economic Analysis**
The Mandated-Choice Model
*Antonios Karampatzos*
ISBN 978-0-367-41032-2

**The Future of the Law of Contract**
*Edited by Michael Furmston*
ISBN 978-0-367-17403-3

www.routledge.com/Markets-and-the-Law/book-series/ASHSER1252

# THE FUTURE OF THE LAW OF CONTRACT

EDITED BY

MICHAEL FURMSTON

**informa** law
from Routledge

First published in paperback 2024

First published 2020
by Informa Law from Routledge
4 Park Square, Milton Park, Abingdon, Oxon OX14 4RN

and by Informa Law from Routledge
605 Third Avenue, New York, NY 10158

*Informa Law from Routledge is an imprint of the Taylor & Francis Group, an informa business*

Publisher's Note
The publisher has gone to great lengths to ensure the quality of this reprint but points out that some imperfections in the original copies may be apparent.

*British Library Cataloguing-in-Publication Data*
A catalogue record for this book is available from the British Library

*Library of Congress Cataloging-in-Publication Data*
Names: Furmston, M. P., editor.
Title: The future of the law of contract / edited by Michael Furmston
Description: Abingdon, Oxon ; New York, NY : Routledge, 2020. |
Series: Markets and the law | Includes bibliographical references
and index.
Identifiers: LCCN 2019054055 (print) | LCCN 2019054056 (ebook) |
ISBN 9780367174033 (hardback) | ISBN 9780429056550 (ebook)
Subjects: LCSH: Contracts–English-speaking countries.
Classification: LCC K840 .F88 2020 (print) | LCC K840 (ebook) |
DDC 346.02/2–dc23
LC record available at https://lccn.loc.gov/2019054055
LC ebook record available at https://lccn.loc.gov/2019054056

ISBN: 978-0-367-17403-3 (hbk)
ISBN: 978-1-03-292477-9 (pbk)
ISBN: 978-0-429-05655-0 (ebk)

DOI: 10.4324/9780429056550

Typeset in Times New Roman
by Swales & Willis, Exeter, Devon, UK

# CONTENTS

# DETAILED CONTENTS

# CONTRIBUTORS

**Mukarrum Ahmed** is lecturer in business law at Lancaster University, UK, and a barrister of Lincoln's Inn. He is a specialist UK editor of *conflictoflaws.net*, the world's foremost blog on private international law. His articles have appeared in the leading international and European law journals including the *Journal of Private International Law.*

**Roger Brownsword** is a professor of law at King's College London, UK, and has been an academic lawyer for around 50 years. He has published about 20 books, and more than 250 chapters and articles. He has been a member of working parties in the Academy of Medical Sciences (on 'drugs futures') and the Royal Society (on neuroscience and the law, and on machine learning); and he has acted as a specialist adviser to parliamentary committees on stem cell research and cloning, and on research using hybrid embryos.

**J. W. Carter** holds BA and LLB qualifications from the University of Sydney and was awarded a PhD by the University of Cambridge for his thesis on breach of contract. He took up a position at the University of Sydney in 1981 and in 1995 was awarded a Personal Chair in Commercial Law. On his retirement in 2014 John was made Professor Emeritus. John is General Editor of the *Journal of Contract Law*, a consultant to the international law firm Herbert Smith Freehills and a Fellow of the Australian Academy of Law. John's recent books include *Carter's Breach of Contract*, 2nd edn, 2018 and *Contract Law in Australia*, 7th edn, Sydney, 2018.

**Cirami Mastura Drahaman** qualified in the UK and was called to the Bar of England and Wales by the Honourable Society of Gray's Inn in 1996. She was also called to the Bar in Malaysia and practised for a number of years as an advocate and solicitor of the High Court of Malaya. She is currently a lecturer at Sunway University, Malaysia, attached to the Centre for Commercial Law & Justice at Sunway University Business School. Her areas of research include contract law, media law, information technology, intellectual property, privacy and entertainment law.

**Michael Furmston** is an internationally acknowledged authority on contract and commercial law. His published work extends to over 20 books and many dozens of articles, chapters and other contributions. An eminent academic, he has taught at the University of Oxford, UK, where he was a fellow of Lincoln College; at the University of Bristol, UK, where he was Dean of the Faculty of Law and Pro Vice-Chancellor; and also at other institutions of international standing. He was appointed emeritus professor at Bristol in 1998 and Dean and professor at Singapore Management University's School of Law in 2007. He was called to the English Bar in 1960 (Gray's Inn) and has been a Bencher of Gray's Inn since 1989. He has acted as consultant to many clients, owners, contractors and consultants on commercial and construction law.

**Howard Hunter** is emeritus professor of law at, and former Dean of, Emory University School of Law, USA, and emeritus professor of law and former President at Singapore Management University. He is on the International Academic Advisory Board at Alliance University Bangalore and is on the Board of Directors for the American Arbitration Association.

**Loganathan Krishnan** was in legal practice for over two years in London, UK, and then in academia for over 26 years. He lectures business and company law to undergraduate and postgraduate students, and is a chief examiner and external moderator for these subjects. He has presented his research findings at national and international conferences and published papers in many scholarly journals. His research expertise is in the areas of business law, company law and constitutional law. He is an active member of the ASEAN Law Association of Malaysia, committee member of the Constitutional and Human Rights Committee, and the Corporate Securities and Investment Committee, LAWASIA.

**Eliza Mik** has taught courses in contract law and in the law of e-commerce at the Singapore Management University and the University of Melbourne, Australia, as well as courses in FinTech and Blockchain at Bocconi University in Milan, Italy. In parallel with a line of research focused on distributed ledger technologies and smart contracts, she is involved in multiple projects relating to the legal implications of automation, the deployment of 'intelligent agents' in transactional environments, as well as the burgeoning area of 'legal design'. Before joining academia, she worked in-house in a number of software companies, Internet start-ups and telecommunication providers in Australia, Poland, Malaysia and in the United Arab Emirates, where she advised on technology procurement, payment systems and software licensing.

**Sri Bala Murugan** is a lecturer in business law and company law at the Centre for Commercial Law and Justice at Sunway University Business School, Malaysia. He is also a freelance corporate trainer in the field of law. His specialities are the law of attraction, commercial law and anti-money laundering regulations.

**Adnan Trakic** is a senior lecturer with the Department of Business Law and Taxation in the School of Business at Monash University Malaysia. He has taught and researched in the fields of conventional and Islamic finance law, business law and dispute resolution. A co-author of several books, his published work extends to numerous articles, book chapters and other contributions.

**Stephen Waddams** is Goodman/Schipper Professor of Law at the University of Toronto, Canada. He is an author of articles, notes, reviews and essays, mainly on contract law, and of several books. In 1987, he was co-winner of the Owen Prize; in 1989, he was awarded the Canadian Association of Law Teachers/Law Reform Commission of Canada Award for Outstanding Contribution to Legal Research and Law Reform; and, in 1996, he received the David W. Mundell medal for contributions to Law and Letters.

**Cheah You Sum** is an associate professor at the Centre for Commercial Law and Justice of the Sunway University Business School, Malaysia. He has many years of experience in the financial services industry and in academia – he has taught law and business modules with specific research interest in financial services law, corporate governance and strategic management. He is a fellow of the Chartered Insurance Institute (FCII), fellow of The Institute of Chartered Secretaries and Administrator (FCIS), a member of the Chartered Institute of Arbitrators (MCIArb) and an associate of the Asian Institute of Chartered Bankers (AA-ICB). He is currently appointed as an independent director for FWD Takaful Berhad and is the chair to the Nominations and Remuneration Committee of the Board.

# TABLE OF CASES

# TABLE OF LEGISLATION

# LIST OF ARTICLES

## CHAPTER 1

# An overview

## Michael Furmston

### Introduction

**1.1** I gave my first lecture on the law of contract at the University of Birmingham in October 1958, the beginning of my second year there. In nearly all the subsequent 60 years I have taught some parts of the law of contract either at British universities (Birmingham, Belfast, Oxford and Bristol) or more recently at Singapore Management University and Sunway University, Malaysia. During periods of leave I have taught at the National University of Singapore, in Australia (at Sydney, Melbourne, Adelaide and the University of Western Australia) and in Sri Lanka and in Hong Kong. I have taught the common law of contract in civil law countries (at Leuven in Belgium (four times) and Bolzano in Italy). I have also spoken at conferences in Toronto and Chicago. For the first 20 years I also taught the Roman law of contract.

**1.2** One point of this historical reminiscence is that my view of the next 25 years must, for good or ill, be affected by my experience of the last 60 years. The second is that it is not limited to any one system. We are trying in this book to look forward to developments across the common law of contract. The team includes authors from Australia, Canada, the UK, Malaysia and the United States (alphabetical order here and elsewhere). In addition, three of us have taught in Singapore.

### Diversity and unity

**1.3** When I started teaching contract in 1958 I knew that the American law of contract was different. The library had copies of Williston and Corbin and the Restatement but I assumed the Australian and Canadian contract law were the same as English. I had tutorials in Oxford in contract from Otto Lang, who was doing the Bachelor of Civil Law (BCL) and went on to become a professor at the University of Saskatchewan and then a successful national politician. I do not remember any suggestion that the Canadian law of contract was different.

**1.4** This is not the case today. There are books entitled *Australian Law of Contract, Canadian Law of Contract, Malaysian Law of Contract, New Zealand Law of Contract, Singapore Law of Contract*, and so on. I do not think there are any books entitled *American Law of Contract* or *English Law of Contract*. The systems are different but they are not very different.

**1.5** The relationship is illustrated by the recent decision of the UK Supreme Court in *Patel v Mirza*.[1] In this case the court sat exceptionally with nine judges in an attempt to grapple with the difficulties posed by illegality in the law of contract. Six judgments were delivered. All agreed in the result but three disagreed fundamentally on the reasons. Six judgments were delivered and all cited with approval the impressive judgment of the Canadian Supreme Court in *Hall v Hebert*.[2] The Court was agreed on the result but deeply divided on the reasons. The majority view was that the existing law should be replaced by an approach which involved considering and balancing a range of factors.

**1.6** The decision of the Supreme Court was considered and rejected by an enlarged five judge Court of Appeal in Singapore in *Ochroid Trading Ltd v Chua Sion Lui*.[3] It is also receiving anxious consideration in Malaysia where it was cited in *Pang Mun Chung v Cheung Huey Chuen*.[4]

## Doctrine

**1.7** If I had been asked in 1958 about a requirement that contracts should be performed in good faith, I would perhaps have talked about *bona fides* in the four consensual contracts of Roman law (Sale, Hire Partnership and Mandate). The position would be very different today. The requirement that contracts should be performed in good faith has been a feature of American law for some time and has recently been adopted by the Supreme Court of Canada. These developments are discussed in Chapters 2 and 3 by Howard Hunter and Stephen Waddams. There must be a serious possibility that this notion will be adopted in other common law jurisdictions. There have been a number of decisions of the New South Wales Court of Appeal to this effect but not yet any decision either way of the High Court of Australia. At the moment England and Singapore stand at the opposite end of the spectrum.[5] It is clear that jurisdictions which have adopted the notion of good faith performance do not apply it in exactly the same way but the present tendency is to expand rather than to contract its scope.

**1.8** A quite different manifestation of good faith is to be found in insurance law, where it has been held since 1775 that those entering into insurance contracts have a duty of good faith to disclose to the other party information which is material to that party's decision to enter into the contract. Here the path of evolution is in the opposite direction. Both English and Malaysian law have passed legislation significantly limiting the duty of disclosure of a consumer insured. There are important possibilities of development here which are discussed by Cheah You Sum in Chapter 4.

---

1 [2016] UKSC 42.
2 [1993] 2 SCR 159.
3 [2018] SGCA 5.
4 [2018] 8 CLJ 683.
5 There is a general survey of good faith in Commonwealth countries in Michael Furmston and JW Carter, *Eppur Si Muove: The Age of Uniform Law, Essays in Honour of Michael Joachim Bonnell to Celebrate his 70th Birthday* (UNIDROIT 2016).

**1.9** A quite different but also important doctrinal question concerns the place of objectivity. Conventional accounts tend to say that the common law adopts an objective test both of whether a contract exists and as to its content and meaning. This is not wrong but it is incomplete. There are cases where it is also necessary to apply a subjective approach. It is also essential to be clear what we mean by the subjective and objective tests. This is not always simple as John Carter and I seek to show in Chapter 5.

### Evolution and revolution

**1.10** Anyone who has sought to edit a book on the law of contract will know that the law this year is not the same as the law last year. That is why new editions regularly appear. To some extent this is a natural evolution of a case law system. There can be questions which have not come to court before and judges have to decide the correct answer.

**1.11** A rather larger group will consist of cases which are the product of an earlier case. So in *Patel v Mirza*[6] the majority of the Supreme Court completely changed the law as to the effect of illegality on contracts by introducing a test based on the evaluation of a range of factors. It is completely certain that there will be cases which the court has to answer by applying this approach and that there will be disputes about the process which lead to presently unforeseeable decisions.

**1.12** Sometimes courts generate a new discussion of their own motion. A striking example is the question whether a clause providing how damages for breach of contract should be calculated should be struck down as a penalty. For 100 years this has been treated as a straightforward question governed by the speech of Lord Dunedin in *Dunlop Pneumatic Tyre Co Ltd v New Garage Motor Co Ltd*.[7] This case was reconsidered and its effect significantly modified by the Supreme Court in *Cavendish Square Holdings v Talal El Mahdessi*.[8] By a striking coincidence the question was also considered by the High Court of Australia in *Andrews v Australia and New Zealand Banking Group*[9] which took a different view of the law, particularly as to whether the penalty doctrine could have been applied to an event which was not a breach of contract.

**1.13** It is clear that changes in the way people contract may foreseeably lead to particular kinds of dispute. So, some of the law relating to offer and acceptance was stimulated by the development of an efficient post in England. Similarly the 'ticket cases' arose out of the development of the railway system in England in the mid-nineteenth century.

---

6 See n 1.

7 [1915] AC 79. For fuller discussion see my article 'New Zealand Illegal Contracts Act 1970 – an English View' (1972) 5 New Zealand Universities Law Review 151.

8 [2015] UKSC 67.

9 2012 HCA 30. Elaborately criticized by no fewer than five leading Australian contract lawyers at (2013) 30 Journal of Contract Law 99.

**1.14** It is clear that we are undergoing very substantial changes in the way we do business. Electronic developments mean that there are contracting parties who can reach millions of possible partners at the same time and that anyone on the internet is liable to receive many offers all the time. The possible consequences are considered by Roger Brownsword in Chapter 6 and Eliza Mik in Chapter 7.

**1.15** A completely new type of situation is that electronic communication has made it possible for organizations to contract with billions of people at the same time. This is the position for instance with Facebook. It is clear that things can go wrong here and there has been extensive government action across the world. There are important and difficult questions as to the rights of individuals receiving messages from Facebook. Most of them are not paying but the transaction is hardly gratuitous as can be seen from Facebook's bank balance. The problems which arise here are considered by Cirami Mastura Drahaman in Chapter 8.

**1.16** An allied but older problem is the control of exemption clauses. In some form this has been troubling common law courts for 150 years. The common law evolved extensive controls which in many countries were thought not to go far enough, so that legislation has been added, in many cases extensive in effect. It seems unlikely this process has come to an end and this is discussed by Loganathan Krishnan in Chapter 9.

**1.17** Perhaps we may add a footnote here. Slogans which regularly appear in this context are consumer protection and inequality of bargaining power. It is important to remind ourselves that these notions are distinct. A Supreme Court justice buying a second-hand car is undoubtedly a consumer but is not lacking bargaining power or skill. A supplier whose principal customer is Amazon is not a consumer but in nearly all cases will lack bargaining power.

**1.18** The question of the extent to which the law should attempt to minimize the effective inequality of bargaining power is a major question to which it seems clear that no system has yet found a wholly satisfactory answer. This is discussed by Sri Bala Murugan in Chapter 10.

**1.19** One of the features of contract law to which this book testifies is that there are a number of similar but not identical systems. A vast common law empire which we have, alas, not been able to discuss is on the Indian subcontinent, but the common law area only embraces part of the world. Most of the rest of the world is part of the civil law area, a system based historically on either French or German law. This gives rise to serious practical problems in international contract transactions. It will often be the case that each party is reluctant to contract on the law of the other party. One solution is for the parties to choose a neutral contract law and court. This is good for lawyers in London, New York and Singapore where there is a good supply of good lawyers and competent judges. It has been found necessary however to agree controls for the choice of court. This is the subject of the important discussion by Mukarrum Ahmed in Chapter 11.

**1.20** When in the Middle Ages the common law of contract began to develop it would have been in a society where virtually everyone professed to be a

Christian. That has not been true even in England for some time. In the common law world there are in the Indian subcontinent vast number of Hindus and Muslims.

**1.21** This has only recently given rise to difficulties which arise from the fact that Islamic law prohibits charging interest for financial transactions. There are cases both in England and Malaysia which are examined by Adnan Trakic in Chapter 12. The English cases turn largely on construction, on the facts an effective prohibition on interest not being agreed. Malaysia handles the problem in a different way. The country is multi-racial and the Malay majority very largely are Muslim.

**1.22** It is clear that in 25 years' time the common law of contract will be different from today. It seems almost certain that there will still be a number of similar but not identical versions. One can reasonably hope that the highest court in each jurisdiction will pay careful attention to what is happening in other common law jurisdictions. Recent electronic developments mean that this information is readily available throughout the common law world.

## CHAPTER 2

# The implied obligation of good faith

*Howard Hunter*

## Introduction

**2.1** The legal meaning of two simple words, 'good faith', has been debated in scores of cases arising from contract disputes for more than a century.[1] In theory, an agreement made in a common law jurisdiction is defined by the words of the agreement itself. The parties may have discussed a variety of issues, but the scope of the contract between them does not extend beyond the specific matters upon which they have reached mutual agreement. That 'bargain' is the deal, and a court is not expected to add or subtract terms or impose conditions upon which the parties have not agreed. The role of the court is to recognize and enforce the private law of the agreement that has been privately negotiated. This chapter examines the concept of an implied duty of good faith and how that concept may affect a court's analysis of a privately negotiated bargain in common law jurisdictions.

**2.2** External factors already play a substantial role in the enforcement of many private agreements, and those factors may modify the terms of the contract. Many of those external factors derive from statutes or regulations that have been adopted by a government for policy reasons. Insurance contracts are good examples. Policies of insurance are useful mechanisms for the socialization of the costs associated with a variety of risks. Public authorities in all common law countries impose obligations on both insurers and insureds to act responsibly toward one another. Trust agreements provide more examples. A trustee is expected to act as a fiduciary with respect to the beneficiaries of the trust whether the governing documents say anything about fiduciary obligations or not. Consumer protection laws impose other regulations on a wide range of consumer contracts. These kinds of externalities are treated much the same as other legislative or administrative acts and do not pose any particularly difficult problems for common law courts in the consideration of disputes arising from a contract. The meaning of a specific statutory provision or administrative regulation may be debatable, but the application of such a provision or

---

1 To be precise, the concept of good faith has its origins in the influence of the ecclesiastical law on the development of contract doctrines in the common law. The history is outlined in Hamilton, 'The Ancient Maxim Caveat Emptor', 40 Yale Law Journal 1133 (1931) in which the author cites and relies upon a number of sources from as early as the fifteenth century.

regulation to a contract is simply another example of the relationship between the 'pure' common law of judicial decisions and the law derived from legislative or executive actions.

**2.3** The focus of this chapter is specifically on the implied obligation of good faith which is not based upon an external factor, such as legislation, but which is integral to the agreement itself although not expressly stated in the communications between the parties. A famous and highly regarded American judge, Benjamin Cardozo, stated more than a century ago that every contract is 'instinct with an obligation, imperfectly expressed, of good faith' in performance.[2] The contract at issue was a simple one. Lucy, Lady Duff-Gordon, was a designer of fashionable hats and associated items for ladies. She wanted to expand her business beyond London and contracted with a New Yorker for him to have an exclusive right to sell her goods in that city. A dispute arose between Lady Duff-Gordon and the New York seller. One question was whether the contract was too vague to be enforceable and therefore was a nullity because of the absence of clear and definite terms. Judge Cardozo reasoned that the contract itself was sufficiently clear because there was an unspoken understanding that each party would seek to make it successful. Success itself was not required. The New York representative might not sell a single hat, but it was reasonably expected that he would try to sell Lady Duff-Gordon's hats and that she, in turn, would try to provide him with what he might need. The common sense notion that the parties did not go to the trouble of negotiating and signing an agreement without some modest expectation of mutual performance was a sufficient basis for finding an agreement subject to enforcement by a court. The Court of Appeal did not define the scope of either party's obligation but did conclude that the reasonable expectations of each party were sufficient to form an agreement of mutual obligation. The same line of reasoning has been important in the consideration of requirements and outputs contracts.[3]

**2.4** From the simple case of Lady Duff-Gordon's hats developed the American notion of an implied obligation of good faith in all contracts.[4] The scope of that obligation and its application have been the subjects of countless cases in the many decades since the publication of Judge Cardozo's opinion. The strength

---

2 *Wood v Lucy, Lady Duff-Gordon*, 222 NY 88, 118 NE 214 (1917). Judge Cardozo was then a member of the New York Court of Appeal, the highest court of that state and a court that has been influential in the development of commercial law. He later served as a Justice of the United States Supreme Court.

3 See, generally, Hunter, *Modern Law of Contracts*, §10:13, Thomson Reuters (2019).

4 The implied obligation applies, if at all, only to performance and not to pre-contractual negotiations. See, e.g., *West Palm Beach Hotel, LLC v Atlanta Underground, LLC*, 2014 WL 4662318 (DNJ 2014). Deceit, fraud or misrepresentation during negotiations may give rise to a claim in tort but not to one in contract. Likewise, a party negotiating in reliance on the statements and representations of the other party may be able to set out a claim based on reliance expectations, but not one for breach of contract by reason of a breach of an implied obligation of good faith. See, e.g., *Columbia Park Golf Course, Inc v City of Kennewick*, 160 Wash App 66, 248 P3d 1067 (2011).

of the concept in the common law of the United States is clear. It is included in section 205 of the *Restatement (Second) of Contracts*[5] and in the Uniform Commercial Code.[6]

**2.5** The concept of good faith has had a mixed reception in other parts of the common law world. English courts have not adopted the concept and have been explicit in not doing so.[7] Singapore has followed the UK courts.[8] In Canada, there has been more sympathy to the concept than in the UK or Singapore although there has not been the level of full-blown discussion one finds in many cases from the United States.[9] Australia also occupies something of a middle ground in which the concept of good faith has developed as a factor in the construction of contracts.[10]

**2.6** The discussion in the following paragraphs of this chapter will be devoted to clarification of the concept as it is now understood in several of the leading common law countries together with thoughts about the likely directions of further development in the next generation.

---

5  Restatement of Contracts (2d), s 205 (1981) states: 'Every contract imposes upon each party a duty of good faith and fair dealing in its performance and enforcement'. The Restatement is not *law*. It is a collection of principles derived from thousands of common law decisions. The various sections represent the consensus views of the common law systems of the different states. Some state courts have not gone as far as s 205 with respect to good faith. See, e.g., *Merrett v Liberty Mutual Insurance Company*, 2012 WL 1481511 (MD Fla 2012); *Niedojadlo v Central Maine Moving & Storage Co*, 1998 ME 199, 715 A2d 934 (Maine 1998); *Stewart Title Guaranty Co v Aiello*, 941 SW 2d 68 (Texas 1997). In the states which have not been as comfortable with a general concept of good faith, the courts have used good faith principles in situations that involve a level of trust such as insurance contracts. See, e.g., *Perkins v Hermitage Insurance Co*, 2012 WL 899065 (Conn Super 2012); *Merrett v Liberty Mutual Insurance Co*, 2012 WL 1481511 (MD Fla 2012); *Marquis v Farm Family Mutual Insurance Co*, 628 A 2d 644 (Maine 1993); *FDIC v Coleman*, 795 SW 2d 706 (Tex 1990).

6  UCC s 1–203. The provisions of Article 1 of the UCC apply to all articles. Aspects of the good faith obligation can be found in other articles and sections of the UCC which clarify or amplify the application of the concept in specific contractual circumstances. Section 102 of Article 2, the article that governs sales of goods, applies a standard of 'honesty in fact and reasonable standards of fair dealing in the trade' to merchants, who are defined as commercial parties who regularly deal in the goods which are the subject of the transaction. The UCC, unlike the Restatement, is statutory law, and courts are expected to give effect to the legislative will as expressed through the statute even if the common law of the state has not adopted in full the concept of an implied obligation of good faith. Article 2 has not been adopted in Louisiana, but good faith is part of that state's law because it is a civil law jurisdiction which adheres closely to the French Civil Code. The private law of Louisiana is much the same as the private law of Quebec in Canada.

7  See, e.g., *Union Eagle Ltd v Golden Achievement Ltd* [1997] AC 514. See for general discussion Peden, *Good Faith in the Performance of Contracts* (LexisNexis Butterworths Australia 2003).

8  See, e.g., *The One Suites Ltd v Pacific Motor Credit (Pte) Ltd* [2015] 3 SLR 695. Good faith was not, in fact, a determining issue in that case, and the comments were *obiter*, but the comments reflected the sentiments of the Court. For more discussion, see Ter Kah Leng, 'Good Faith in the Performance of Contracts Revisited' [2014] 26 SAcLJ 111.

9  See, e.g., *Bhasin v Hrynew* [2014] SCC 71.

10  See, generally, Robertson, 'The International Harmonisation of Australian Contract Law' [2012] 29 JCL 1; Carter and Peden, 'Good Faith in Australian Contract Law' [2003] 19 JCL 155.

## The American experience

**2.7** The concept of an implied obligation of good faith in contracts[11] may be accepted by most courts in the United States, but the definition of 'good faith' varies.[12] At the very least, there is a consensus that 'good faith' means the absence of 'bad faith'. The late Supreme Court Justice Antonin Scalia wrote, while he was a federal appeals court judge, that good faith is no more than an 'implied obligation not to engage in the particular form of conduct which, in the case at hand, constitutes "bad faith"'.[13] Even that rather limited understanding of good faith suggests more than the absence of tortious behaviour. Fraud, deceit, misrepresentation and other sharp or devious practices can support claims for relief not for breach of the implied obligation of good faith but because such practices are tortious.[14] The subordinate clause 'in the case at hand' in then-Judge Scalia's opinion ties the behaviour to the specific agreement and implies that there is some level of reasonable expectation of performance. Showing that an action, or a failure to act, was the result of a dishonest purpose or some sinister motive even if not expressly prohibited by the contract might suffice to establish 'bad faith' according to a Connecticut court.[15] A bad motive may not be necessary if the action complained of is decidedly inconsistent with the reasonable overall expectations of the parties.[16]

**2.8** There have been hundreds of American cases. Many have related to the question whether strict adherence to the specific terms of an agreement can amount to a violation of the implied obligation of good faith. In principle, the exercise of a right under a contract cannot be a violation of good faith,[17] but

---

11 There must be a contract as a predicate for the implied obligation of good faith. It does not exist separate and apart from an actual contract. *Roman v Tyco Simplex Grinnell*, 723 Fed Appx 813 (11th Cir 2018).

12 For those unfamiliar with the federal system in the United States, it is important to remember that contract law is state law – not national law – and, as such, there are variations among the 50 states. Most of the variations are minor, but the understanding of good faith is one area in which the differences are sometimes more substantial. Also the state of Louisiana adheres to the civil law of France, the original European colonial power of Louisiana. Many other states that were previously part of Mexico or had strong French influences also adhere to some aspects of the civil law, mostly with respect to property and family law.

13 *Tymshare, Inc v Covell*, 727 F 2d 1145, 1152 (DC Cir 1984).

14 Good faith is not a requirement in the negotiations phase. But 'bad faith' in the negotiating process can lead to a claim for damages. *Siga Technologies, Inc v PharmAthene, Inc*, 132 A 3d 1108 (Del 2015). The 'bad faith' occurred during negotiations between the parties about the settlement of a disagreement with respect to the development and marketing of a pharmaceutical product.

15 *Perkins v Hermitage Insurance Co*, 2012 WL 899065 (Conn Super 2012). The court's approach seems to have been unnecessarily convoluted. A straightforward application of the good faith doctrine would have been enough. That is, a reasonable contracting party would have expected certain behaviour in the context of the transaction. The absence of that behaviour, or actions inconsistent with the expected behaviour, could be characterized as a form of 'bad faith', but that argument seems a rather roundabout way of getting to the point.

16 See, e.g., *Rekter v State Department of Social and Health Services*, 180 Wash 2d 102, 323 P 3d 1036 (Wash 2014); *Columbia Park Golf Course, Inc v City of Kennewick*, 160 Wash App 66, 248 P 3d 1067 (Wash App 2011).

17 See, e.g., *Bob Smith Automotive Group, Inc v Ally Financial, Inc* 2016 WL 3613402 (Md Ct Spec App 2016) (unambiguous right to demand payment).

sometimes there is uncertainty about the scope of the right and sometimes there is a question about the timing or method of the exercise. In any event, the action taken (or not taken) that is the cause for complaint must amount to a breach of the contract itself. There is no independent cause of action for breach of the implied covenant of good faith.[18]

**2.9** Some courts have looked no further than the language of the agreement. If the action taken is within the scope of the agreement, then there is no breach of good faith even if the action might seem to have been surprising in the context. One of the most stunning examples of strict adherence to the contractual language was a decision by the Supreme Court of Tennessee in a dispute between the owner of a shopping centre and one of the major tenants. A large supermarket chain occupied more than 70% of the retail space in a strip shopping mall and had a 20-year lease with an option to renew. Toward the end of the lease term, the tenant gave timely notice of its intention not to renew. The area around the strip mall had changed over the course of the lease term and business was insufficient to justify continuation of the lease. Evidence adduced during the proceedings indicated that merchants had expressed concerns about maintenance of the premises, including the parking area. The various lease agreements provided that the tenants would share in the overall costs of maintenance for common areas in accordance with their respective proportions of the total retail space. The owner estimated annual costs in advance and billed the tenants in 12 equal monthly instalments for their shares. There was an annual reconciliation with tenants being billed for shortfalls and with surpluses being credited against rents due. As the ending date for the supermarket lease approached the owner decided to re-pave the entire parking area, which was a large expense that had not been included in the estimated expenses for the year. The contract for re-paving was let six days prior to the end of the supermarket lease, and, after the re-paving was completed, the owner sent a bill for more than 70% of the total re-paving costs to the supermarket, which objected because it had had no benefit whatsoever from the re-paving. The supermarket also complained that the timing was specifically tied to its departure so that the owner could use the newly paved parking area as an enticement to prospective tenants for the vacated space. On appeal, the owner prevailed because the letter of the contract allocated maintenance costs proportionally to the leased space as of the time the costs were incurred. The date of letting was taken as the date of the costs.[19]

**2.10** Although the Tennessee decision may seem extreme in its deference to the letter of the contract, the parties involved were sophisticated and substantial business entities who were not without market power and knowledge.

---

18 See, e.g., *Aaron v State Farm Fire and Casualty Company*, 2017 WL 3484087 (ED Pa 2017).

19 *Cornerstone Square Associates, Ltd v Bi-Lo, LLC*, 2008 WL 2388124 (Tenn 2008). If the landlord had suggested a re-paving project earlier, then Bi-Lo could have negotiated about some reduction in the allocable costs due to its impending departure or have decided to remain somewhat longer. As it was, Bi-Lo wound up liable for the lion's share of the costs of a re-paving job from which it derived no benefit whatsoever, after having suffered from the marketing disadvantages of a poorly maintained parking area.

A financing case from a federal court in Illinois is a more typical example of strict adherence to the terms of the agreement. The borrowing business operated a small chain of four retail shoe stores. It began a banking relationship with First Bank of Whiting in 1981 which continued, successfully for both borrower and lender, for several years until the shoe stores began to have cash flow problems. The bank refused to extend further credit unless the borrower were to obtain a government-backed small business loan or to do a corporate reorganization under applicable bankruptcy laws. The borrower opted for the latter, and the bank agreed to create a $300,000 line of credit against which the borrower drew down $75,000. Within a month the bank announced that it would not issue any more advances. The agreement for the line of credit reserved to the bank the discretion to terminate financing at any time, but the borrower argued that doing so was inconsistent with the spirit of the agreement taken as a whole and that it had made commitments in reliance on the line of credit. The Court of Appeals for the Seventh Circuit agreed with the bank and found that there had been no breach of an implied obligation of good faith which was tantamount to a breach of contract even though the termination came at a particularly inopportune moment for the borrower.[20]

**2.11** At the opposite end of the spectrum was another financing case, *KMC Co v Irving Trust Company*.[21] KMC had negotiated a line of credit for $3 million from Irving Trust which took a security interest in KMC's accounts receivable. KMC could request advances against the line of credit according to a formula, but Irving Trust retained the discretion to refuse were the bank to feel insecure. KMC began to experience business problems, and Irving Trust refused to advance funds as requested. KMC's situation went from bad to worse. It sued Irving Trust for breach of contract based on an alleged violation of the implied obligation of good faith and won a substantial judgment. Both the trial court and the appellate court viewed the entire agreement as something akin to a joint venture entered into for the purpose of stabilising the finances of KMC. The hypothetical joint venture then fell apart when the bank exercised its discretion to refuse advances. The decision was sharply criticized as being naïve about the realities of business financing and the risks associated with lending to enterprises that are having cash flow and related problems.[22]

---

20 *First National Bank of Whiting v Kham & Nate's Shoes*, No 2, Inc, 908 F 2d 1351 (7th Cir 1989). 'Firms that have negotiated contracts are entitled to enforce them to the letter, even to the great discomfort of their trading partners, without being mulcted for lack of 'good faith''. *Ibid.* at 1357. The Seventh Circuit decision was criticized sharply. See, e.g., Patterson, 'A Fable from the Seventh Circuit: Frank Easterbrook on Good Faith', 76 Iowa Law Review 503 (1990). It was, however, a not unreasonable result in the construction of a contract between two experienced business entities, one of which was experiencing financial difficulties that made lending to it a risky proposition.

21 *KMC Co, Inc v Irving Trust Company*, 757 F 2d 752 (6th Cir 1985).

22 See, e.g., Comment, 'Lender Liability for Breach of the Obligation of Good Faith Performance', 36 Emory Law Journal 917 (1987). See also *Albright v Burke & Herbert Bank & Trust Co*, 249 Va 463, 457 SE 2d 776 (1995).

**2.12** A more realistic appraisal of the relationship between borrower and creditor can be found in a Massachusetts decision. A steel fabricating company and its bank had a good relationship over a considerable period of time. The company had loans, a line of credit and other financial services from the bank. When the fabricating company began to experience difficulties, the bank cooperated with the fabricating company to help its customer work through various financial setbacks. The bank extended the payment terms for loans and agreed to various re-financing arrangements. Eventually, the bank decided to cut its losses and sold the loans to a third party factor at a discount. The third party enforced the default provisions of the loans which resulted in a sale of assets to satisfy the indebtedness. The refusal of the bank to extend the outstanding loans any further and then to sell them at a discount to a factor was not a breach of an implied obligation of good faith. It was simply a reasonable business decision that was not in violation of any of the terms of the loan agreements. The fabricating company may have hoped for a continuing relationship and assistance from the bank based upon prior history, but at some point the bank was entitled to minimize its own risks if it did not seem that the borrower would be able to repay the loans.[23]

**2.13** Most decisions of the past quarter-century fall somewhere between strict adherence to the letter of an agreement and attempts to discern the scope of overall intentions with respect to an agreement notwithstanding the precise language. The implied obligation of good faith, in the overwhelming majority of cases, is not a separate substantive provision but is a useful guide to the construction and interpretation of an agreement in the context of the parties' relationship. Not surprisingly, the balance tilts toward a literal reading of the terms of an agreement when the parties are both experienced commercial enterprises. When one party is clearly more sophisticated than the other or has a substantially stronger bargaining position, the balance may lean more toward a nuanced contextual understanding as opposed to a strict application of the literal terms. As the late Judge Richard Arnold stated, 'The implied covenant simply prohibits one party from depriving the other party of its expected benefits under the contract'.[24] The various cases are so fact-sensitive that some examples may assist in fleshing out an understanding of the implied obligation.

**2.14** A dispute about a Lamborghini dealership in New York closely resembled the much earlier dispute about the millinery of Lady Duff-Gordon. The dealer complained that Lamborghini violated the dealership agreement by

---

23 *Gavin v Sovereign Bank*, 2008 WL 2622839 (DMass 2008), aff'd 571 F 3d 93 (1st Cir 2009). The same bank was involved in another case that had a different result (one that was borrower-friendly) by reason of equitable estoppel even though there was no actual breach of the implied obligation of good faith. *Renovator's Supply, Inc v Sovereign Bank*, 72 Mass App Ct 419, 892 NE 2d 777 (Mass App 2008). For another banking case in which one of the key points was that the complainants were individuals with small personal accounts as opposed to experienced and sophisticated commercial banking customers, see *White v Wachovia Bank*, NA 563 F Supp 2d 1358 (ND Ga 2008). See, generally, Hughes, 'Duty Issues in the Ever-Changing World of Payments Processing: Is It Time for New Rules?' 83 Chicago-Kent Law Review 721 (2008).

24 *Comprehensive Care Corp. v RehabCare Corp*, 98 F 3d 1063, 1066 (8th Cir 1996).

authorizing another dealership in the middle of the market area of the existing dealer. Although the dealership contract did not specify exclusivity, the court reasoned that granting another dealership in such close proximity was contrary to the expectations of the parties in the first agreement even if doing so was not, in the strictest sense, a technical violation of the letter of the original dealership agreement.[25] If the dealership had been for a common automobile such as an ordinary Ford or Toyota, the analysis may have been different. Lamborghinis, by comparison, are produced in small numbers and each one is expensive. The market for such cars, even in a densely populated city such as New York, is small, and the costs of maintaining a dealership in Manhattan are high. The first dealer undoubtedly did not expect the car company to set up a competitor almost next door after the first dealer had invested large sums in establishing the dealership.

**2.15** As one court has noted, the implied obligation of good faith can be seen as nothing more than a method for reinforcing the purposes and expectations of the parties. For example, a contract may include a term that allows one party to terminate the agreement for reasons of convenience, but that term should not be used as a screen to allow termination for some other reason nor should the terminating party be able to create the 'inconvenience' used as an excuse.[26] A manufacturer's representative was required to get clearance from the manufacturer before submitting price quotes to customers. The manufacturer repeatedly was slow to respond to requests for clearance with the result that the representative missed some sales opportunities on which it could have earned commissions of 5%. Even though the slow response time was not a violation of an explicit term of the agreement, it was found to be a breach of the implied obligation of good faith in that the parties clearly expected regular and timely communications with each other.[27]

**2.16** Most American courts seem to be in agreement toward the end of the second decade of the twenty-first century that the implied obligation of good faith does not create any new rights for the parties but simply protects the reasonable expectations that each party has about the benefits to be derived from the agreement.[28] An exercise of discretion, for example, should be consistent with the overall purpose of the agreement and not arbitrary, capricious or unduly surprising.[29] As one court noted,

> This implied covenant is a judicial convention designed to protect the spirit of an agreement when, without violating an express term of the agreement, one side uses oppressive or underhanded tactics to deny the other side the fruits of the parties' bargain.[30]

---

25 *Manhattan Motorcars, Inc v Automobili Lamborghini*, S.p.A. 244 FRD 204 (SDNY 2007).

26 *WSC/2005 LLC v Trio Ventures Associates* 460 Md 244, 190 A 3d 255 (Md App 2018).

27 *Winter-Wolff International, Inc v Alcan Packaging Food and Tobacco*, Inc 872 F Supp 2d 215 (EDNY 2012).

28 See, e.g., *Whited v WestRock Services, Inc* 2018 WL 3416704 (MD Tenn 2018)

29 See, e.g., *Lath v BMS Cat* 2018 WL 1835966 (DNH 2018).

30 *Keating v Applus±Technologies, Inc*, 2009 WL 261091, p 3 (ED Pa 2009).

## Canada

**2.17** Canada has two distinct private law jurisdictions. Quebec follows the civil law and good faith has been a part of the contract law of Quebec for generations.[31] The other provinces are part of the common law family, and the consideration of good faith generally followed the lead of the UK courts until 2014 when the Supreme Court of Canada, in a unanimous judgment, clearly indicated that a concept of good faith does, indeed, play a role in the law of contracts. The particular case was *Bhasin v Hrynew*,[32] a dispute among commercial parties in the sale of educational savings plans. The complainant was a retail dealer with an exclusive dealing arrangement on a three-year, renewable contract. Either party could decide not to renew by giving appropriate notice to the other party. A director of the company that ran the plans also held a controlling interest in a competing company, and he intended to take over the company and, in due course, merge it with the competing enterprise. He asked each of the retail dealers to provide detailed information about customers and other confidential business items. One of the retailers refused to do so, and its contract was not renewed. In the subsequent dispute, the retailer that was not renewed argued that the demand for detailed confidential business information and the subsequent non-renewal were intended to benefit the particular director and not to advance the general business interests of the company and its retail dealers. The court determined that the retailer had a reasonable cause for complaint in that the actions, although not tortious or, strictly speaking, bad faith, were not consistent with the overall purpose of the agreement. In the words of the Court,

> parties must be able to rely on a minimum standard of honesty from their contracting partners in relation to performing the contract as a reassurance that if the contract does not work out, they will have a fair opportunity to protect their interests.[33]

**2.18** The *Bhasin* judgment suggests that good faith, or more specifically 'honesty in performance', is a standalone principle and not just a modifier of the negotiated terms of the contract. It is something less than a fiduciary duty, and compliance with the expectation of honesty in performance does not necessarily require full disclosure of all matters by one party to the other. The scope of the duty is to be determined by a contextual analysis of the relationship between the parties to the contract at issue. An entire agreement clause does not preclude a review to determine whether the parties have complied with the expectation of honesty in performance.[34]

---

31 Civil Code of Quebec, Article 7.

32 [2014] SCC 71. There had been earlier hints of an interest in the doctrine of good faith expressed by some provincial courts, but until 2014 the Supreme Court had not taken a clear position. See, O'Byrne, 'The Implied Terms of Good Faith and Fair Dealing: Recent Developments', 86 Canadian Bar Review 193 (2007).

33 *Bhasin v Hrynew* [2014] SCC 71 at 86.

34 See, generally, Young, 'Justice Beneath the Palms: *Bhasin v Hrynew* and the Role of Good Faith in Canadian Contract Law', 9 Saskatchewan Law Review 79 (2016); Scott, '*Bhasin v Hrynew* – The New Duty of Good Faith in Contract', 10th I&Q Conference Proceedings Session II: Ethical Societies I (2016).

**2.19** If a party exercises a right which clearly is allowed by the contract, it is unlikely that such an exercise will violate the *Bhasin* holding even if the other party is disappointed. An employment case from Alberta helped to clarify the boundaries of the *Bhasin* rule of good faith. An investment manager was employed for three years on an at-will basis. The company had a long-service incentive bonus scheme for employees who remained for at least four years. To be eligible for the bonus, an employee had to be 'active' as of his fourth anniversary. Then the employee's rights in the bonus programme were vested. The particular investment manager was terminated after three years of employment. The termination was 'without cause' which was permissible under the terms of the employment and which, of course, did not prejudice the employee's standing in the marketplace as a 'for cause' termination might have done. The employee argued, however, that the termination was in violation of the *Bhasin* standard of good faith because it was intended to deprive him of the opportunity to have vested rights in the bonus programme. The Alberta Court of Appeal disagreed. The employment arrangement was clear. Both parties, employer and employee, had the right of termination at any time for any reason, and the exercise of that right by the employer was not, by definition, a violation of good faith or honesty in performance.[35]

**2.20** The decision in the employment case was sensible. A different result might have led to many more disputes between employers and employees about terminations or resignations or to more detailed limitations on schemes such as the long-service bonus programme at issue in the case. The power of termination was bilateral, but, of course, the relative position of most employers is superior to that of most employees even if the employee has a discretionary right to resign. One could imagine some fact situations in which the *Bhasin* good faith notion might have a role to play. What if the discharged employee had received consistently good reviews and then was discharged just a day or so before his rights in the bonus programme were to vest? What if a complainant could show that the employer consistently terminated employees, despite good reviews, after 3.5 years of service so that none, or hardly any, ever qualified for the bonus scheme? A change in the facts could support an argument that the employer did not meet the standard of honesty in performance even without showing a specific breach of contract.[36]

---

35 *Styles v Alberta Investment Management Corp* [2017] ABCA 1. The Supreme Court refused to allow an appeal.

36 A long-term bonus scheme is intended to encourage employees to remain loyal, and long-term relationships can be especially important for investment managers. It may be unlikely that an employer would adopt such a bonus plan and then undercut the basic purpose of the plan by dismissing productive, loyal employees, but, in theory, doing so might raise questions under the *Bhasin* doctrine even if the employer complies with the letter of the contractual relationship. The American rule is not all that different. A party may have a discretionary right to take or refrain from certain actions, but, in general, the exercise of discretion should be consistent with the overall purpose of the agreement and not contrary to that purpose. See, e.g., *Lath v BMS Cat*, 2018 WL 1835966 (DNH 2018).

## Australia

**2.21** Australia, another major common law jurisdiction, is also another federal union, and sometimes the details of principles followed by the courts of one state, such as New South Wales, may be slightly different from those followed in another state, such as Western Australia. There also is a federal overlay and some of the more interesting contract judgments have come from the federal courts. The approach to the concept of good faith is unclear and in flux. There has been some reluctance to accept the notion,[37] but the concept has been considered in numerous situations. Two respected legal scholars, Professor Elisabeth Peden and Emeritus Professor John Carter, both of Sydney Law School, have reviewed many of the cases and have presented what may be the clearest and most cogent statements about the implied obligation of good faith in Australia. Their view is that the doctrine is most useful as an aid to construction. It is a tool that can be used by a court in construing and applying contractual provisions in ways that are consistent with the overall purposes of the agreement and that are sympathetic to the contextual relationship of the parties.[38]

**2.22** The greatest development of the good faith concept has come in a series of cases dating from 1993 in New South Wales.[39] The cases, taken together, provide a good example of how doctrines emerge within the common law. In the first of the series, the *Renard* case from 1993, the dispute centred on a termination clause in a standard building contract. Among the judgments published in the proceedings, that of Priestley, JA, became the one most often cited in subsequent cases in which one party or the other raised a question about good faith. Priestley concluded that in a standard form termination clause there was an implied term of 'reasonableness', and, in the remainder of his judgment he discussed the concept of good faith although it was not, as such, necessary to the case. The most far-reaching application of the discussion in the *Renard* judgment of Priestley, JA, came in what might be called the 'dueling hamburgers' dispute between Burger King and Hungry Jack's.[40] The Court reasoned that the agreement in dispute included implied obligations of cooperation, good faith and

---

37 See, e.g., *Service Station Association Ltd v Berg Bennett & Associates Pty Ltd* [1993] ALR 393.

38 See, generally, Carter and Peden, 'Good Faith in Australian Contract Law', 19 Journal of Contract Law 155 (2003). See also Carlin, 'The Rise (and Fall?) of Implied duties of Good Faith in Contractual Performance in Australia', 25 University of New South Wales Law Journal 99 (2002); Peden, 'Incorporating Terms of Good Faith in Contract Law in Australia', 23 Sydney Law Review 221 (2001).

39 In chronological order: *Renard Construction (ME) Pty Ltd v Minister for Public Works* [1993] 26 NSWLR 234; *Hughes Bros Pty Ltd v Trustees of the Roman Catholic Church Archdiocese of Sydney* [1993] 31 NSWLR 91; *Burger King v Hungry Jack's Pty Ltd* [2001] NSWCA 187; *Overlook Management BV v Foxtel Management Pty Ltd* [2002] NSWSC 16; *Adventure World Travel Pty Limited v Newsom* [2014] NSWCA 174; *Bartlett v ANZ Banking Group Limited* [2016] NSWCA 30.

40 *Burger King v Hungry Jack's Pty Ltd* [2001] NWSCA 187. That dispute arose from a complex franchising transaction between two large, well-established commercial entities. The relationships in franchise agreements are not fiduciary but the parties are considered to be somewhat closer to one another than in a purely arm's length one-off commercial transaction.

reasonableness. That judgment took the idea of 'reasonableness' in a termination clause a step further by implying, without reference to a specific contract clause, independent mutual obligations. On its face, the 'hamburger' judgment suggests the implication of a substantive standard of expected behaviour, which is a step beyond the implication of good faith reasonableness in a specific contractual clause. The decision raises the question whether an alleged violation of the implied obligation would support an independent claim. If so, that would be a step beyond the American rule which considers 'good faith' to be included within the existing terms and not to create an implied obligation that provides an independent basis for a claim separate from straightforward breach of contract. Indeed, a subsequent case stated that the rule in New South Wales is that an 'additional term' of good faith in performance is implied in all commercial contracts.[41]

**2.23** The courts of Victoria have accepted the concept of good faith but in not exactly the same way as in New South Wales. In one of the leading cases, *Esso Australia Resources Pty Ltd v Southern Pacific Petroleum NL*,[42] the Court agreed that there is a concept of good faith in Australian commercial contracts but that it derives from a reading and application of the terms of the contract. It is not, so the Court suggested, an independent implied obligation. The Victorian approach is close to that proposed by Professors Carter and Peden, who see the good faith concept as an important aid to construction and not as a separate independent obligation.[43]

**2.24** The High Court of Australia has not spoken definitively on the subject of good faith, and until such time as that Court does so, lawyers will have to navigate the subtle, nuanced differences among the various state decisions. The High Court suggested, however, an approach not too different from that of Professors Carter and Peden in an employment case, *Commonwealth Bank of Australia v Barker*.[44] The Court found that in an employment context there is implied a duty of mutual trust and confidence. The implied duty did not go so far as to create an implied duty of good faith, although mutual trust and confidence seems quite close to a reasonable understanding of good faith. Importantly, the implied duty was grounded in the actual contractual arrangement between employer and employee. That relationship created a connection between the two in which trust and confidence were understood to be part of the agreement. Thus the implied duty arose from the agreement, and not from a more generalized external concept of good faith.[45]

---

41 *Overlook Management BV v Foxtel Management Pty Ltd* [2002] NSWSC 16 [62], Barrett, J. Note that the implication applies to 'commercial contracts'. Consumer transactions are subject to other policy rules, some by statute and some by administrative regulation. In addition, a common law court usually will take into account disparities in bargaining power and sophistication when called upon to construe the terms of an agreement.

42 [2005] VSCA 228.

43 See n 36 and McDougall, 'The Implied Duty of Good Faith in Australian Contract Law', NSWJSchol 2 [2006].

44 [2014] HCA 32.

45 A helpful discussion of this and other cases may be found in a background paper prepared by the Hon Justice Susan Kiefel of the Australian High Court for the Judicial Colloquium in Hong Kong, September 2015.

**2.25** One of the strongest statements about good faith in Australia came from a practising lawyer, Donald Robertson, who has been a long-time adjunct professor of law and who has written extensively on commercial law issues.

> The adoption of good faith does not mean that all statements of contract law principle are reduced to a single set of words. Nor is good faith an alien concept that resides outside the logic of the contractual instrument. Good faith is a principle that provides integrity to the contractual bargain, recognizing at the same time that contracts are a social institution that are subject to overriding obligations to the public good in certain circumstances. Thus, good faith works itself out across the full spectrum of contract law in subtle and sophisticated ways and plays a central role in the autonomous interpretative and gap-filling process.[46]

**2.26** The content of the quoted paragraph is consistent with the notion of good faith as a tool to be used in the construction of contract terms and in the enforcement of agreements. Commercial parties, for the most part, are able to look after their own interests and usually have the support of professional advisers. Actions by one party or another that violate norms of behaviour in ways that are anti-social (fraud, deceit, misrepresentation) are governed by tort law and need no assistance from the law of contracts. Other protections or defenses that may be available to less sophisticated parties, such as unconscionability, duress or undue influence, are not so easily used by commercial entities except in the most egregious circumstances. The implied duty of good faith provides commercial parties with support for reasonable expectations in the performance of an agreement and with some measure of protection from surprise or caprice. If, however, Australian courts take the additional step of creating an independent implied obligation of good faith, as some language in judgments from New South Wales suggests, then lawyers and their clients will have to pay more careful attention to the drafting of agreements.

### Singapore

**2.27** Singapore is a jurisdiction of interest to many commercial parties. Not only is it a wealthy common law country, but it also is the locus for a great deal of dispute resolution in cases that arise in Asia. The court system is efficient and reliable. There is a major arbitration centre in Singapore, and, in recent years, the City State has created a new international commercial law court. Until 1993 Singapore courts were bound by decisions of the highest court in the United Kingdom, but since then Singapore courts have been independent and are no longer bound by English precedents. Even so, the Singapore courts regularly look to English courts for guidance and, for the most part, continue to adhere to English precedents on matters of contract law. More than two centuries of a close relationship, first as a colony and in more recent decades as an independent

---

46 Robertson, 'The International Harmonisation of Australian Contract Law' 29 Journal of Contract Law 1, 21 (2012).

nation and an active member of the Commonwealth, have created strong bonds among lawyers and judges in the two countries. On the question of good faith, the Singapore courts have, in principle, followed the UK lead and have refrained from adopting a general rule of implied good faith.[47] That being said, the Singapore Court of Appeal (the highest court) has come very close to doing so in ways that relate to implications of fact from the details and nature of the contract in question and the relationship of the parties.

**2.28** An interesting Singapore judgment involved a dispute between a remisier and a stockbroking firm about commissions. The remisier claimed that he was due commissions for finding two new customers for the firm. The firm dealt directly with the customers and refused to pay commissions to the remisier. Although not directly relevant to the ultimate decision in the case, Andrew Phang, JA, discussed at length the possibility that a duty of good faith could be implied as a matter of fact from the relationship of the parties in the performance of the particular contract.[48] An employment contract, for example, may require a more delicate consideration of the details of the actions by the employer (almost always the party with superior power) as against those of the employee (who may be in a position of trust and confidence by reason of access to confidential proprietary information).[49]

**2.29** A case more directly connected with much of the discussion about good faith in commercial contracts was *AREIF (Singapore I) Pte Ltd v NTUC Fairprice Co-operative Ltd.*[50] Both parties were large, experienced businesses and each was advised throughout by respected legal, financial and realty professionals. AREIF was the landlord for a commercial property along Somerset Road in the centre of Singapore's shopping and commercial district. NTUC Fairprice (a major supermarket chain) was the lessee of a portion of the property which it used for one of its smaller, specialty food markets. The lease was for a stated term and the agreement included a renewal clause which provided the parties with the opportunity to renew the lease if they were able to negotiate a mutually agreeable rate within a stated period prior to expiration of the lease. NTUC expressed interest in a renewal and there were negotiations but they came to naught. After the lease expired, NTUC was surprised to find that AREIF had

---

47 *The One Suites Pte Ltd v Pacific Motor Credit (Pte) Ltd* [2015] 3 SLR 695. The discussion of good faith, a doctrine that the Court noted was 'in flux', was not directly relevant to the particular case being decided and the comments were *obiter*, but the Court of Appeal clearly indicated that it was not yet ready to adopt an implied obligation of good faith along the lines of Australia or the United States. For more discussion, see Ter Kah Leng, 'Good Faith in the Performance of Contracts Revisited' 26 SAcLJ 111 (2014). See also *Max-Sun Trading Ltd v Tang Mun Kit* [2016] 5 SLR 815; [2016] SGHC 203 [55].

48 *Ng Giap Hon v Westcomb Securities Pte Ltd* [2009] 3 SLR(R) 518. In order to reach a fact based implication, Phang, JA said that a claimant first must satisfy the 'business efficacy' and 'officious bystander' tests, two tests which are beyond the scope of this chapter but which are relevant to identifying the exact basis of a contractual claim. For more on the subject, see Phang (ed.), *The Law of Contract in Singapore*, 06.058–06.064, Academy Publishing (2012).

49 See, e.g., *Tempcool Engineering (S) Pte Ltd v Chong Vincent* [2015] SGHC 100.

50 [2015] SGHC 28.

leased the premises to Cold Storage, its arch-rival in the supermarket business. NTUC claimed that the landlord had breached the agreement by not negotiating in good faith because it was carrying on separate negotiations with a competing retail food market chain. When the case reached the Court of Appeal, that Court noted that both parties were knowledgeable, sophisticated enterprises with good lawyers and other advisers, and that each was capable of looking after its own interests. There was no showing of actual deceit or misrepresentation by the landlord, and failure to reach an agreement on an extension of the lease was not evidence of anything except that the parties were unable to agree. Although not stated, one could read between the lines a suggestion that NTUC would not have been nearly so upset had the new tenant been some other kind of enterprise such as a clothing or shoe store. It was the lease to a rival in a desirable commercial location that was especially upsetting.

**2.30** The Court of Appeal did not accept the argument about a breach of implied good faith in the *ARIEF* case, but, if one reads the judgment carefully, the door was left open for consideration of good faith in a proper case on much the same basis as in the remisier case. Neither party in the *ARIEF* case was required to renew the lease. If NTUC had decided that the location was not a good one and that it should either close its small market or move it somewhere else, the landlord would have had no basis for complaining about a failure to renew. Likewise, if NTUC wanted to renew, but the landlord insisted on a rental rate that was higher than NTUC wanted to pay, it would be difficult to make out a complaint. A landlord in a commercial district is entitled to seek prevailing market rates and owes no special duty to an existing tenant to offer anything other than those rates even if they are high.[51] The relationship of the parties, however, and their course of dealing over a period of time, may be relevant in determining whether there are any understood limitations on the actions of either party or reasonable expectations about the nature of the negotiations. From the language of the agreement and the course of dealing between the parties, a court may be able to discern, through the implication of facts, that one side or the other has failed to meet reasonable expectations. Doing so is difficult in a purely commercial setting when the parties operate at arm's length and with considerable business power. In Singapore, the willingness of courts to undertake contextual analyses of contract terms and the parties' performances, provides some basis for a possible fact-based good faith concept as suggested in the remisier case. Judge of Appeal Phang noted in a 2016 judgment that construction of contract terms is 'anchored in the express contractual language, the internal and external contexts of the contract, and, more broadly speaking, the contractual purpose'.[52]

---

51 That assumes the absence of a rate formula or some other negotiated mechanism in the existing agreement that sets boundaries on what may be demanded.

52 *Hewlett-Packard Singapore (Sales) Pte Ltd v Chin Shu Hwa Corinna* [2016] 2 SLR 1083 [53]. For an application by the Singapore International Commercial Court of a contextual analysis in seeking to identify mutual expectations, see *BCBC Singapore Pte Limited v PT Bagan Resources BK* [2016] 4 SLR 1; 2016 SGHC(I) 1.

## United Kingdom

**2.31** Where is the mother country of the common law in the discussion of good faith? The received wisdom is that the English courts have refused to accept the notion and have left developments to former colonies. Closer examination suggests that the situation is not so clear cut and that much of the difference between the English approach and, for example, Australia or Canada, lies in terminology or nuances of methodology.[53] A hint of something less than rejection of the good faith concept can be found in a judgment of High Court Judge Leggatt, who stated, 'I respectfully suggest that the traditional English hostility towards a doctrine of good faith in the performance of contracts, to the extent it still persists, is misplaced'.[54]

**2.32** The dispute which resulted in Judge Leggatt's comments was one that might well have been handled similarly in other common law jurisdictions. A trading company (ITC) granted defined distribution rights to Yam Seng Pte Limited to market toiletries branded by the Manchester United football club in 42 duty-free sales centres across Asia. Yam Seng argued that ITC breached the agreement in two ways: (i) by providing false information to Yam Seng on which it knew Yam Seng would rely for its marketing efforts and (ii) by selling the same products to third parties in the distribution areas at prices lower than the agreed upon duty-free retail prices.[55] After a detailed analysis of the distribution agreement and the performance of the parties, the Court concluded that the agreement gave rise to an implied duty of honesty and that such an implied duty is necessary to support business efficacy. Although the judgment used the term 'good faith', what the court did was construe the contract based on its specific terms, the overall purpose of the agreement and the actual performances of the parties. Deriving an implied duty of honesty in the relationship is not substantially different from what Phang, JA, of Singapore suggested when he discussed the importance of considering the contractual purpose as well as the details of the contractual language in a 2016 judgment.[56]

**2.33** In some situations the parties may include a good faith clause in the contract. If they do so, then each will be expected to act consistently with reasonable commercial standards of fair dealing and to act in accordance with the spirit and mutual expectations of the contract.[57]

---

53 One commentator has argued that there is no need for a separate doctrine of good faith because the reasonable expectations of the parties can be met through a pragmatic exercise in the use of existing approaches to construction. Steyn, 'Contract Law: Fulfilling the Reasonable Expectations of Honest Men', 113 Law Quarterly Review 433 (1997).

54 *Yam Seng Pte Limited v International Trade Corporation Limited* [2013] EWHC 111 (QB).

55 Competition law is beyond the scope of this chapter, but lawyers should advise their clients that vertical price restrictions (e.g., a requirement that a downstream seller not sell a product above or below a price established by the manufacturer or original distributor) may run afoul of competition laws in numerous jurisdictions. Likewise, when an upstream seller enters a downstream market and undercuts its own distributor's prices or agrees with its distributor on retail pricing, other competition law issues may be triggered.

56 *Hewlett-Packard Singapore (Sales) Pte Ltd v Chin Shu Hwa Corinna* [2016] 2 SLR 1083 [53].

57 See, e.g., *CPC Group Ltd v Qatari Diar Real Estate Investment Co* [2010] EWHC 1535 (Ch) [246]; *Berkeley Community Villages Ltd v Pullen* [2007] EWHC 1330 (Ch) [97]. See, for a general and helpful discussion, Braithwaite, Brown, Coffey, Little and Robertson, 'Towards an Implied Duty of Good Faith Under English Law', JonesDay Commentary (London) (May 2013).

**2.34** The English courts do not appear likely to adopt a generalized doctrine of implied good faith, but the concept will continue to be developed in the context of specific agreements and relationships beyond those governed by fiduciary or similar obligations. The most likely direction will be one similar to that suggested by Professors Carter and Peden in the Australian context in which the notion of good faith is intertwined with the construction of terms and a court's attempt to ascertain the expectations of the parties.

### Internationalization

**2.35** In deciding the *Bhasin* case, the Canadian Supreme Court was sensitive to the role of good faith in Quebec and to the general adoption of the concept in the United States, which is by far Canada's largest trading partner.[58] Decisions from foreign jurisdictions are not binding, but the Court's recognition of them, whether from Quebec or from south of the border, was not unrealistic. Many contracts of Canadian businesses were already subject to the implied obligation of good faith if the governing law of the contract was that of Quebec or one of the jurisdictions of the United States. Extending the doctrine to cover the common law provinces of Canada did not amount to a radical change in the contractual relationships of Canadian businesses. Indeed, one could argue that by adopting something similar to the American concept in which the focus is on performance, the Court avoided the possibility of a wholesale adoption of the civil law concept which, in general, includes good faith in the negotiations phase as well as in performance.

**2.36** The withdrawal of the United Kingdom from the European Union may remove immediate pressures on the British to join in the general project to promote contractual uniformity in the EU. However the exit unfolds, British businesses will continue to have many contractual relationships with businesses throughout Europe. The civil law approach to good faith will be a regular aspect of cross-Channel transactions unless care is taken to negotiate a term that makes English law applicable to the agreement. Absent a choice of law provision specifying English law, the private international law of conflicts may result in the application of the law of one of the civil law jurisdictions. Of course, a contracting party on the Continent will try to negotiate a choice of law clause that specifies the law of that party's home jurisdiction.

**2.37** Other common law countries face the same issue. Australia, New Zealand, Singapore and Malaysia have substantial trading activities with many Asian civil law countries such as China, Japan, Korea and Vietnam. There has been a nascent effort to systematize pan-Asian contract law that is somewhat similar to the effort in Europe. Doing so makes a great deal of sense for the major East Asian economies of China, Japan and Korea.

---

58 Mexico, the third member of the North American Free Trade Agreement, is also a civil law jurisdiction with contract law similar to that of Quebec.

Extending the effort to include Hong Kong, Malaysia, Singapore, Brunei, Australia and New Zealand presents more difficulty. The focus of this chapter is on the one issue of good faith and not on the entirety of contract law. There are a number of more fundamental differences which would have to be addressed before the creation of a systematized body of contract law across multiple jurisdictions.

**2.38** A living experiment in the attempt to harmonize contract law across jurisdictions is the United Nations Convention on the International Sale of Goods (CISG). The CISG has been around for about four decades but has become much more commonly used in the past two decades or so. Some 92 countries have joined the CISG and, collectively, they account for about 75% of total world trade.[59] There are limitations on the scope of the CISG. It only applies to commercial transactions. Consumer transactions are excluded. A contract must be across borders.[60] Consignment contracts are not covered even if the contracts involve goods because a 'consignment' is not a 'sale'.[61] A sales transaction that is wholly within a single jurisdiction is not covered even if the parent company of one of the contracting parties is from a different jurisdiction. The place of business is the critical factor, not the place of incorporation.[62] Several countries have adopted a reservation that both contracting parties must be from member states of the CISG.[63] Absent such a reservation, the CISG may apply if the choice of law clause in a contract or the private international law rules of conflicts require application of the law of a party that is within a member state.[64] Article 6 allows

---

59 An up-to-date list of countries that have joined the CISG is available at www.uncitral.un. org/en/texts/salegoods/conventions (accessed 15 April 2020). Common law (or predominantly common law) jurisdictions that have joined include Australia, Canada, New Zealand, Singapore and the United States. Among large economies the members include China, Japan, Korea, most member states of the European Union, Russia and most former republics of the USSR, and Brazil. The United Kingdom, India, other South Asian common law jurisdictions and Malaysia are notable non-members.

60 Article 2 of the CISG identifies excluded transactions. Some exclusions are not unexpected for an international 'sales' convention. These include sales by foreclosure or under authority of law, sales of intangible securities, sales by auction and sales of electricity. Perhaps more surprising, and probably the result of lobbying efforts during drafting, are sales of ships, vessels, hovercraft and aircraft. One case held that a sailing yacht was a 'ship' within the meaning of Article 2 and that the sales transaction was not covered by the CISG. *Rechtbank Middleburg* [57465/HAZA-07-210] (The Netherlands 2 April 2008).

61 See, e.g., *Martini E Ricci Iamino S.P.A. – Consortile Societa Agricola v Trinity Fruit Sales Co*, Inc 30 F Supp 3d 954 (EDCal 2014).

62 Compare, e.g., *Asante Technologies, Inc v PMC-Sierra, Inc*, 164 F Supp 2d 1142 (ND Cal 2001) with *McDowell Valley Vineyards, Inc v Sabate USA, Inc*, 2005 WL 2893848 (NDCal 2005).

63 China and the United States are the only truly large economies to have adopted the two-state reservation. Smaller countries that have the two state reservation are: Singapore, The Czech Republic, Slovakia, Saint Vincent and the Grenadines.

64 For a negative application, see, e.g., *Princesse D'Isenbourg Ltd v Kinder Caviar, Inc*, 2011 WL 221702 (EDKY 2011). The contract was between a US party and a UK party, and the applicable law was that of the US state of Kentucky. Under the Supremacy Clause of the US Constitution, the CISG, as a ratified treaty, is the law of Kentucky, but because of the two-state reservation, the CISG could not apply. The domestic law of Kentucky, which in this situation was Article 2 of the UCC, applied.

parties to an international sales agreement to opt out of CISG coverage, in whole or in part, but the parties must be explicit about 'opting out'.[65]

**2.39** The committee that worked for a number of years to draft the CISG included representatives from both common law and civil law jurisdictions, but, in the end, the United Kingdom decided not to join the CISG while the United States was one of the first to join. Two issues that caused some concern among common lawyers were the absence of a parol evidence rule,[66] and the possibility of the inclusion of a civil law concept of good faith.[67]

**2.40** There have been several thousand judicial decisions under the CISG which are publicly available. Many of these are from the United States, Canada and Australia with a particularly important one from New Zealand. These cases provide an opportunity to consider the relative effect of internationalization on the common law in these jurisdictions. The question of the role of 'good faith' has been raised most often in connection with Article 7 of the CISG.

**2.41** The first part of Article 7 seems quite straightforward.

> In the interpretation of this Convention, regard is to be had to its international character and to the need to promote uniformity in its application and the observance of good faith in international trade.

**2.42** The first half of the section quoted simply requires courts to seek to achieve one of the major goals of the CISG which is to establish a set of rules for international sales transactions that is as close to uniform around the world as possible. It is an affirmation of the customary law used for centuries by traders who move goods across political boundaries and who want predictability and certainty in their transactions regardless of the political differences among venues.[68] The second part is the source of some anxiety because of the reference to 'good

---

65 See Article 6, CISG, and, e.g., *Shantou Real Lingerie Manufacturing Co Ltd v Native Group International, Ltd*, 2016 WL 4532911 (SDNY 2016); *Roser Technologies, Inc v Carl Schreiber GmbH*, 81 UCC Rep Serv 2d 693 (WDPa 2013).

66 Not only is there no parol evidence rule, Article 8 of the CISG strongly encourages a reviewing court to consider the pre-contractual and post-contractual discussions as well as other extrinsic evidence to ascertain the true intent of the parties. In effect, a common law jurisdiction with a parol evidence rule may wind up allowing extrinsic evidence to be used in a CISG case even though the same evidence would be excluded in a standard domestic contract dispute. The leading US case on the topic is *MCC-Marble Ceramic Center, Inc v Ceramica Nuova d'Agostino, SpA*, 144 F3d 1384 (11th Cir 1998).

67 The key provision is Article 7 of the CISG. Different approaches to remedies are handled directly in the CISG. The default remedy under Article 46 is specific performance, but Article 28 allows a court in a common law jurisdiction to choose to employ remedies that are consistent with the domestic law.

68 Consider, for example, the disintegration of Yugoslavia. What was a purely domestic transaction between a buyer in Belgrade and a seller in Zagreb in 1990 is now an international sale between a buyer in Serbia and a seller in Croatia. The CISG, at its best, minimizes differences in the transaction between 1990 and the present notwithstanding the fundamental political changes. The clearest affirmation of the role of the CISG in the promotion of uniformity came from a common law jurisdiction in a decision from New Zealand which held that courts considering CISG disputes should look to other CISG decisions and eschew reliance upon local, domestic precedents. *RJ & AM Smallmon v Transport Sales Ltd* [2011] NZCA 340.

faith in international trade'.[69] Do those few words open the door to the application of a civil law concept of good faith which would include the negotiations phase as well as the performance phase? The short answer, so it seems, is 'no'.

**2.43** Taken together with the other words in the first section of Article 7, the entire article may be read as an admonition to judges and arbitrators.[70] The introductory clause, 'In the interpretation of this Convention', modifies the remainder of the section. A judge is, by this article, instructed to keep in mind that a goal of the CISG is to achieve a greater degree of uniformity in the treatment of cross-border sales agreements and to harmonize decisions with the reasonable expectations of international traders thereby helping to create a more modern version of the *lex mercatoria*.[71] 'Good faith' does not appear anywhere else in the CISG and certainly not in the way that it does in the American UCC where the doctrine is applied to all contracts subject to the UCC. The risk of a generalized concept of something akin to the civilian notion of good faith sneaking into the common law through cases governed by the CISG seems to be remote. What is more likely is that the specific law applicable to international sales agreements may develop slightly differently from purely domestic contract law, but the same is true for a variety of other areas of the law in which certain kinds of contracts (e.g., insurance, trusts, consumer sales) are subject to various public policy choices.

**2.44** Nevertheless, there is the possibility that case law developed in CISG cases may eventually find its way into the larger body of contract law. There may not be a wholesale adoption of 'good faith' but there could be subtle developments in a number of areas including the methods for construction and realization of the parties' mutual intentions. When a court decides a dispute under the CISG and the same court, or another one, later faces a dispute arising under domestic law that is similar to the CISG dispute, a common law court may well look to the CISG decision for guidance by way of analogy.[72]

## Concluding thoughts

**2.45** Who could possibly be against 'good faith'? The very term suggests behaviour that is desirable. Opposition to good faith is almost akin to approval of 'bad faith', at least in the use of bare language. In the common law the arguments

---

69 See Hofmann, 'Interpretation Rules and Good Faith as Obstacles to the UK's Ratification of the CISG and to the Harmonization of Contract Law in Europe', 22 Pace International Law Review 145 (2010).

70 See Farnsworth, 'A Common Lawyer's View of His Civilian Colleagues', 57 Louisiana Law Review 227 (1996); Hunter, *The Law of Sales in Singapore*, §s 10.16, 10–17, Academy Publishing (2017).

71 For competing views on the reality of an agreed upon concept of *lex mercatoria* or, more broadly speaking, a form of 'world law', compare, e.g., Berman, 'World Law', 18 Fordham International Law Journal 1617 (1995) with Kadens, 'The Myth of the Customary Law Merchant', 90 Texas Law Review 1153 (2012).

72 For an example see *C9 Ventures v SVC-West*, LP 202 Cal App 4th 1483; 136 Cal Rptr 3d 550 (Cal App 4th Dist 2012) citing with approval a CISG governed decision, *Chateau des Charmes Wines Ltd v Sabate USA, Inc* 328 F 3d 528 (9th Cir 2003). See, generally, Hunter, 'Is the CISG Slowly Becoming Part of the Common Law?' 35 Journal of Contract Law 1 (2018).

about obligations of good faith have been lengthy and sometimes have approached the surreal. The arguments, generally speaking, have to do with two quite different matters. First, is a concept of good faith something that exists all the time and in every contract as a matter of principle and as a separate substantive obligation of each party? Second, if the answer to the first question is negative, then what role does the notion of good faith play in the application of the terms of the contract in dispute? Underlying the debates about these two issues is the fundamental theoretical difference between the civil law and the common law about the nature of contract. In common law jurisdictions contracts are, for the most part, private bargains and the role of a court is to give effect to the terms of the bargain created by the parties. Each one is *sui generis*, and it is not the business of a court to add or delete terms but to give effect to the bargain as negotiated. In civilian jurisdictions contract is much more intimately connected with the overall social contract, and individual contracts are considered within the context of the larger society and societal norms as opposed to discrete bargains privately negotiated. The role of good faith in negotiations as well as in performance reflects the overall role of contract as a building block of the society while common law courts look at contracts as individual economic transactions.[73]

**2.46**  Common law jurisdictions that have, to one extent or another, embraced a notion of good faith as an implied obligation in contracts include Australia, Canada and the United States. Even among those jurisdictions there is considerable variation in the details. For an outsider, the differences from one state to another in the United States and to a lesser extent in Australia (not because the differences are fewer but because there are far fewer states) can be frustrating. Whatever the differences, there is a consensus in these countries that some form of good faith is inherent in all contractual undertakings. The Canadian courts have left open the possibility that good faith may be a substantive element separate from the underlying contract such that a breach of the implied obligation of good faith may be sufficient to support a claim on its own even absent a straightforward breach of contract. That approach is definitely not the consensus among all the common law cases, which, as a group, suggest that good faith is an element within the terms of the agreement. It is a measuring rod for performance and not a standalone requirement. The absence of good faith (e.g., arbitrary and capricious exercise of a power under the contract) may support a claim for breach but the claim is one for breach of the contract itself and not for breach of an obligation separate from the contract.

**2.47**  The most common use of good faith is as an aid in construction. What is meant by a particular clause? What are the mutual expectations? The simple old case of *Wood v Lucy, Lady Duff-Gordon* set the stage. The original agreement between Lady Duff-Gordon and Mr. Wood had no meaning if neither were expected to do anything. He might not be effective or the market may not be right,

---

73 For a good discussion of the theoretical differences from the perspective of remedies, see Rowan, *Remedies for Breach of Contract*, Cambridge University Press (2012).

but the contract, by its very existence, created an expectation that he would make a reasonable effort to market and sell Lady Duff-Gordon's millinery. Likewise, the contract created in an ordinary businessperson's mind the expectation that she would provide him with millinery as needed for the sales and that she would not set up a directly competing operation nor grant another firm the right to market her goods in direct and immediate competition with him. Nothing was complicated in the analysis employed by Judge Cardozo. He merely applied a common-sense rationale. Commercial parties do not go to the trouble of negotiating and executing agreements without having some minimal expectations of mutual performance.

**2.48** A straightforward example of common-sense reasoning and a result that is consistent with both a general concept of good faith and the goal of creating harmony in international transactions was a 2009 judgment from Germany about the inclusion of standard terms in an agreement. The domestic German rule is that standard non-negotiated terms automatically become part of an agreement if the parties have reasonable opportunities to gain access to the standard terms. These might, for example, be terms that by practice or suggestion of a trade association are expected terms within a building contract, or an architect's contract, or a sales agreement having to do with a regularly traded commodity.[74] The particular agreement in dispute was subject to the CISG and one party was from a foreign jurisdiction. The court reasoned that the foreign party might not be aware of the German domestic rule and, therefore, evidence could be taken on the issue of whether the foreign party was aware of the standard terms and had, directly or implicitly, agreed to them. It was a sensitive approach that was consistent with the Article 7 direction to construe and apply terms in ways that are consistent with international standards of good faith, and, at the same time, the court did not introduce any new obligations or concepts. It simply construed the German rule in context – a context that recognized the possibility that a foreign party would not be aware of the specific domestic rule and might not have access as easily as a domestic party to the relevant sources for the standard terms.[75]

**2.49** The most likely direction of common law courts in connection with the doctrine of good faith is toward a pragmatic path. Contracting parties, especially commercial ones, presumably go to the trouble of negotiating contracts to achieve a reasonable expectation. A concept of good faith can assist the finder of fact in determining the scope of the mutual expectations and the reasonableness of actions taken under the agreement. Even if courts in the United Kingdom and other common law jurisdictions continue to avoid explicit adoption of a notion of good faith, they are likely to achieve much the same results by the use of existing rules of construction and other factors having to do with the understood limits of mutual behaviour.

---

74 For a common law example, see *RI International Pte Ltd v Lonstroff* [2015] 1 SLR 521 (Singapore and standard terms in the rubber trading industry).

75 13 W 48/09 (24 July 2009) (Oberlandesgericht Celle, Germany). For a similarly thoughtful consideration of international traders in cocoa, see *Transmar Commodity Group Ltd v Cooperativa Agaria Industrial Naranjillo Ltda* 721 Fed Appx 88 (Mem) (2d Cir 2018).

## CHAPTER 3

# Good faith in the Supreme Court of Canada

## *Stephen Waddams*

### Introduction

**3.1** In *Bhasin v Hrynew*[1] the Supreme Court of Canada asserted 'a general organizing principle' of good faith contractual performance. The purpose of this chapter is to explore the meaning and implications of this assertion, and to assess the probability and desirability of its being adopted in other common law jurisdictions.

### *Bhasin v Hrynew*

**3.2** The facts in *Bhasin v Hrynew* were that Bhasin had an agreement with Canadian American Financial Corporation (Can-Am) to market educational savings plans. This was (perhaps a little surprisingly, considering the nature and purpose of educational saving) a highly profitable enterprise, described by the court as 'a lucrative niche market'.[2] The agreement was for three years, to be automatically renewed unless one party gave six months' notice to the contrary. Hrynew was a competitor of Bhasin who wanted to take over Bhasin's business, and Can-Am was considering a restructuring that would have had this consequence. Can-Am did not inform Bhasin of its intentions, and 'responded equivocally' when Bhasin asked whether the restructuring was a 'done deal'.[3] Can-Am appointed Hrynew as Provincial Trading officer to represent Can-Am's interests with the Securities Commission, and misled Bhasin by telling him that the Commission had rejected Can-Am's attempt to appoint a neutral person, and that Bhasin was required to give confidential information to Hrynew. When Bhasin refused, Can-Am gave the six months' notice to terminate the contract, and Bhasin commenced litigation against Can-Am and Hrynew. The trial judge held against Can-Am on the ground (among others) of breach of an implied term of good faith. The Alberta Court of Appeal reversed the decision on the grounds that there was no implied term of good faith, and, in any event such a term would be excluded by an entire agreement clause in the contract. The Supreme Court allowed Bhasin's appeal as against Can-Am. Cromwell J, giving the unanimous

---

1 [2014] SCC 71, [2014] 3 SCR 494.
2 Ibid, [9].
3 Ibid, [12].

judgment of the court, said that there was a general organizing principle of good faith, which included a non-excludable duty of honesty in the performance of contractual obligations. Can-Am was found to have broken this duty, and was accordingly liable for damages.

**3.3** This reasoning was sufficient to determine the result of the case, but the judgment potentially has important implications for many other aspects of contract law, including the power of the court to grant relief against unfair contracts. The significance of the case in the latter context is that relief for unfairness was included by the court as an established instance of the general organizing principle of good faith:

> Thus we see, for example, that good faith notions have been applied to particular types of contracts, particular types of contractual provisions and particular contractual relationships. It also underlies doctrines that explicitly deal with fairness in contracts, such as unconscionability ... Considerations of good faith are apparent in doctrines that expressly consider the fairness of contractual bargains, such as unconscionability. This doctrine is based on considerations of fairness and preventing one contracting party from taking undue advantage of the other.[4]

**3.4** In dealing with the power to exclude the obligation of honesty the court said:

> I am at this point concerned only with a new duty of honest performance and, as I see it, this should not be thought of as an implied term, but a general doctrine of contract law that imposes as a contractual duty a minimum standard of honest contractual performance. It operates irrespective of the intentions of the parties, and is to this extent analogous to equitable doctrines which impose limits on freedom of contract, such as the doctrine of unconscionability ... Because the duty of honesty in contractual performance is a general doctrine of contract law that applies to all contracts, like unconscionability, the parties are not free to exclude it.[5]

**3.5** It is understandable that, in promoting its thesis of a general organizing principle of good faith, the court should look for established instances, and should include in them the cases on unfairness. But there is a danger in this approach, namely that to subordinate the cases on unfairness to a concept of good faith might, unless 'good faith' is clearly given an objective meaning, actually have the perverse effect of restricting the existing powers of the court to give relief against unfair contracts. Well-established instances of relief, such as relief against forfeitures and penalties, have never required proof of absence of good faith, or of conscious wrongdoing. It is fairly clear that Cromwell J, giving the judgment of the court, did not intend to restrict existing instances of relief against unfair contracts, but, as we shall see, the judgment contains several passages restricting the meaning of 'good faith' which, if applied to the question of contractual unfairness, might have the effect of restricting relief to instances of conscious wrongdoing.

---

4 Ibid, [42] and [43].
5 Ibid, [74] and [75].

**3.6** The court relied also on the cases of implied terms as showing the operation of a principle of good faith. It is true that many of the implied term cases are concerned with the concept of good faith, but it would be another thing altogether to suggest that *all* cases of implied terms must be cases of absence of good faith, or of bad faith. In an important case on implied terms decided in 1999, the Supreme Court of Canada had held that there was an implied term in a contract for tenders that the owner would not accept a non-conforming bid.[6] It had been argued that the owner had acted in good faith in accepting a non-conforming bid, and there was no reason to doubt that, in the light of the law as previously understood, the owner honestly believed that it was entitled to do so. But the court rejected this defence, saying that 'acting in good faith or thinking that one has interpreted the contract correctly are not valid defences to an action for breach of contract'.[7] A search for a single explanation of the implied term cases seems attractive, but to *subordinate* implied term cases to the concept of good faith would have an unduly restrictive effect if proof of improper motive were to be required.

**3.7** One of the difficulties here is that the judgment in *Bhasin v Hrynew* touches on several different issues, and it is doubtful whether a single 'general organizing principle' can be successfully employed in respect of all of them. The concept of good faith has frequently been used as a guide to interpretation (or construction) and this accounts for many of the cases in which the phrase 'good faith' has been used in the past. In this sense, good faith remains subordinate to the intention of the parties. But the court also said that 'considerations of good faith are apparent in doctrines that expressly consider the fairness of contractual bargains, such as unconscionability'.[8] This addresses a very different question, namely, whether good faith might explain and justify the power of the court to set aside or to modify agreements in order to avoid unfairness and disproportionate enrichment. An added problem is that the concept of good faith has also been deployed to resolve questions concerning the duty of disclosure of relevant facts, and to the again quite separate question of when a party can break off pre-contractual negotiations without liability. To add to the difficulties, the concept has also been used in Canadian cases to determine when punitive damages are available for breach of contract. The actual decision in *Bhasin* was on yet another question, whether there was a duty of honesty. It is hardly surprising that a 'general organizing principle' cannot readily be discovered that will deal satisfactorily with all these separate issues, either as a description of past law, or as a guide to the future.

**3.8** A related problem, not resolved in *Bhasin v Hrynew*, is whether the test for absence of good faith is subjective (requiring bad motive) or objective (unreasonableness). The judgment includes conflicting statements on this important point, and since the actual decision was merely to impose a duty of

---

6 *MJB Enterprises Ltd v Defence Construction (1951) Ltd* [1999] 1 SCR 619.
7 Ibid, [54].
8 n 4.

honesty, the matter remains unsettled. A number of subsequent cases have given the decision a rather cautious reception, and the opinion of many Canadian observers has been that it has had less impact than initially anticipated. The last word, however, has not necessarily been spoken, and a more expansive interpretation remains possible.

## Good faith and equity

**3.9** Professor Martijn Hesselink of Amsterdam University has made a comparison between good faith and equity:

> The concept of good faith in itself should not keep common law and civil law divided ... Good faith does not differ much from what the English lawyers have experienced with equity ... It does not make any more sense for a common lawyer to fight the concept of good faith than it would have been to fight the whole of equity.[9]

**3.10** A similar comparison has been made by Mindy Chen-Wishart of Oxford University.[10] These comparisons invite the question whether, and to what extent, the concept of good faith might do the work of equity in English law, and in systems closely related to it.

**3.11** In *Çukurova Finance Int. Ltd v Alfa Telecom Turkey Ltd.*[11] (simplifying the facts) a loan was made of $1.352 billion at a high interest rate, the loan being secured by shares that represented a controlling interest in a very profitable Turkish cell phone company. On the occurrence of certain events of default the lender was entitled to immediate repayment of the loan, and, on default of immediate repayment, entitled to appropriate the shares. An event occurred that was found to be an 'event of default', and the lender demanded repayment, which was tendered, but rejected on the ground that it was too late, the lender's real motive being not to recover the loan but to take control of the cell phone company. The borrower then paid the amount into an interest-bearing escrow account, but the lender persisted in its refusal to accept the payment.

**3.12** This might seem to be a promising case for the application of a concept of good faith, the lender's motive being not to secure repayment of the loan, but to profit by the excess value of the security. This argument was made, but was rejected in short order by the unanimous Privy Council:

> Bad faith and improper purpose
> ÇH and ÇFI [the borrowers] contend that ATT's [the lender's] decision to appropriate the charged shares was void, even if there was an event of default, because it

9 Martijn W Hesselink, 'The Concept of Good Faith', in Arthur S Hartkamp and others (eds), *Towards a European Civil Code*, 4th edn (Kluwer Law International BV, 2010) 619, 648.

10 Mindy Chen-Wishart, 'The Nature of Vitiating Factors in Contract Law', in G Klass, G Letsas and P Saprai (eds), *Philosophical Foundations of Contract Law* (Oxford University Press, 2014) 296, 313.

11 *Çukurova Finance Int. Ltd v Alfa Telecom Turkey Ltd (Nos 3 to 5)* [2013] UKPC 2, 20 and 25, [2016] AC 923 (PC: British Virgin Islands).

was vitiated by its improper and collateral reasons ... In equity, a mortgagee has a limited title which is available only to secure satisfaction of the debt. The security is enforceable for that purpose and no other ... It follows that any act by way of enforcement of the security (at least if it is purely) for a collateral purpose will be ineffective, at any rate as between mortgagor and mortgagee. The reason is that such conduct frustrates the equity of redemption which ... a court of equity 'is bound to regard with great jealousy.'

In principle, this is straightforward enough, but the facts are rarely simple. The acceleration of the loan on 16 April 2007 in this case was not part of the process of realising the security. It merely brought forward the date of repayment of the loan and ascertained the amount. Given that there was an event of default, there was a contractual right to do this. It follows that the debt of $1·352 billion (plus interest) was repayable in full at the time when ATT satisfied it by appropriating the charged shares.

Under clause 9.3 of the charges, ATT was entitled to 'appropriate any charged asset ... in or towards satisfaction of the liabilities in accordance with the Regulations', at its 'fair price' (as defined). This means that, by virtue of regulation 18 of the Financial Collateral Arrangements (No 2) Regulations 2003 ('the Regulations'), the lender was entitled to appropriate the security at that price, any difference between the valuation and the liabilities being settled separately.

It necessarily follows from an arrangement on these terms that the lender may satisfy the debt by crediting the borrower with the Fair Value of the security and retaining the charged assets as their own property: see the advice of the Privy Council delivered by Lord Walker of Gestingthorpe: see *Çukurova Finance International Ltd v Alfa Telecom Turkey Ltd* [2009] Bus LR 1613, paras 12–13. As Lord Walker also observed at para 27, this is a remedy new to English law which allowed what was 'in effect a sale by the collateral-taker to himself, at a price determined by an agreed valuation process'.

ÇH and ÇFI do not dispute that ATT appropriated the charged shares in order to satisfy the debt. They hardly could do so, since appropriation is a mode of satisfying the debt. Their real complaint is that ATT only wanted to do so because that would enable it to obtain control over ÇFI and ÇTH and indirectly of Turkcell, instead of (say) selling the shares onto the market. Since this was the very thing that the contract and the Regulations permitted, it is impossible for them to contend that ATT was exercising its power of enforcement for a collateral purpose. The acquisition of control was a necessary incident of a permitted mode of satisfying the debt. The fact that it was an incident which was highly attractive to ATT does not mean that the right of appropriation was exercised in bad faith.

That is enough to decide this particular issue in the present case. More generally, however, the Board considers that if a chargee enforces his security for the proper purpose of satisfying the debt, the mere fact that he may have additional purposes, however significant, which are collateral to that object, cannot vitiate his enforcement of the security. If the law were otherwise, the result would be that the exercise of the right to enforce the charge for its proper purpose would be indefinitely impeded because of other aspects of the chargee's state of mind which were by definition irrelevant.

Of course, there may be other ways of satisfying the debt which involve less drastic consequences for the Çukurova Group. But since no alternative mode of satisfaction was available at the time when ATT were entitled to, and did, appropriate the security, that consideration is relevant only to the question of relief from forfeiture. To that question, therefore, the Board now turns.[12]

---

12 *Çukurova (No 3)* (n 11), [69–79].

**3.13** This rejection of the borrower's argument shows the limitations of the concept of good faith as at present understood in English law. Three inter-related assumptions limit the concept: first, that the obligation of good faith is conceived of as an implied term, and so it can always be displaced by explicit language, second, that it cannot be bad faith for a party to exercise what has been determined to be a contractual right, and, third, that the absence of good faith means the same as bad faith.[13] These assumptions are wholly different from the equitable perspective, whereby enforcement of an undoubted contractual provision could be judged to be inequitable, substance prevailed over form, equity could never be defeated by careful or ingenious drafting, and no misconduct (at the time of the transaction) was required to be proved. What was against conscience was to seek to enforce, or to retain, the benefit of a transaction now adjudged to be inequitable. The contract was assumed to be valid at law, and it was just because it *was* valid at law that intervention of equity was both justified and required. The tendency of modern courts to marginalize the powers of equity is demonstrated by the treatment of the argument, in the passage just quoted, concerning frustration of the equity of redemption. The Privy Council answered this argument by saying that

> the acceleration of the loan … in this case was not part of the process of realising the security. It merely brought forward the date of repayment of the loan and ascertained the amount. Given that there was an event of default, there was a contractual right to do this.

This might be said, from an equitable perspective, to allow form to prevail over substance.

**3.14** But, having taken a narrow view of good faith, the Privy Council went on to take an expansive view of the power to relieve against forfeiture. The court held unanimously that relief from forfeiture was available, that such relief was not confined to mortgages of land,[14] that it was available in commercial cases, and that the court had power to set 'appropriate conditions'[15] in determining the precise terms of relief. The Board cited with approval a case affirming 'the breadth of the court's discretion both in granting relief and as to the terms on which to grant it'.[16] On the subsequent hearing to settle the terms of relief the court held, by a majority, that, though normally a party seeking relief from forfeiture would have to comply with all the terms of the original contract, this was not an inflexible rule, and in this case, where the lender had rejected the tender of repayment, and the borrower had paid the money into an escrow account, it

---

13 In *Times Travel (UK) Ltd v Pakistan International Airlines Corp* 2019 EWCA Civ 828, at [111], David Richards LJ said, in the context of duress, 'The judge accepted that [the claimant] had not established bad faith. That should have been the end of the discussion of good or bad faith. It was not for [the defendant] to establish its good faith'.

14 Cited with approval on this point in *Cavendish Square Holding BV v Makdessi* [2015] UKSC 67, [2016] AC 1172.

15 *Çukurova (No 3)* (n 11) [126].

16 Ibid, [123].

was appropriate to grant relief from the high interest required under the contract during the period when the escrow account had existed. An order was made permitting redemption of the shares on payment of the appropriate sum by a certain date. The lender then took steps, including obtaining an injunction in New York, designed to prevent the borrower from raising the necessary sum, the motive again being to obtain control of the cell phone company. On a further hearing, the Judicial Committee held, unanimously, that a further extension of time for repayment would be allowed. The reasons for taking this comparatively expansive view of the equitable power are significant in the present context, for they are, in substance, the very reasons that were rejected when advanced under the rubric of good faith. It could be suggested, with some justification, that the argument on good faith, though ostensibly rejected, seems to have influenced the Privy Council to take a comparatively generous view of the power to relieve against forfeiture. This supports Professor Hesselink's suggestion of a close relationship between equity and good faith, but, at the same time, it shows the difficulty that English courts would have in accepting the concept of good faith as equivalent to equity.

**3.15** This complex case manifests a dynamic and flexible approach to the court's equitable jurisdiction. The unanimous holding that the jurisdiction to grant relief extends beyond mortgages of land is significant,[17] as is the reaffirmation that 'the mere fact that the transaction is commercial in nature does not preclude the jurisdiction to grant relief from forfeiture, provided that the forfeiture is of possessory or proprietary rights'.[18] In the second of the three cases reported in the Law Reports, *Çukorova (No 4)*, the majority of the Board adopted a flexible approach to setting the terms of relief, with frequent references to equity and unconscionability.[19] On the question of the need for certainty (an understandable reason for restraint in modifying contractual obligations, and a central concern of the minority in this case), the majority quoted Holmes, with approval:

> The language of judicial decision is mainly the language of logic. And the logical method and form flatter that longing for certainty and for repose which is in every human mind. But certainty generally is an illusion and repose is not the destiny of man.[20]

**3.16** On the relation of equity to the powers of the modern court, the majority quoted, with approval, Lord Simon's view that 'equity has an unlimited and unfettered jurisdiction to relieve against contractual forfeitures and penalties'.[21] They approved also of what they called the 'approbatory' comment in the fourth edition of the treatise *Equity: Doctrines and Remedies* by Meagher Gummow

---

17 Ibid, [92].
18 Ibid, [95].
19 *Çukurova (No 4)* (n 11), [13], [17], [26], [44], [45].
20 Ibid, [43], quoting OW Holmes, 'The Path of the Law' (1897) 10 Harv LR 457.
21 *Shiloh Spinners Ltd v Harding* [1973] AC 691, 723 (HL).

and Lehane 'that what was really involved was "a return to the more remote past when equity jurisprudence had [a] dynamism lost with the attainment of the rigidity for which Lord Eldon was so praised by nineteenth century positivists"'.[22] The approving reference to 'dynamism' is significant. This might sound like signal proof of the continuing vitality of equity, and a vindication of the thesis to this effect for which Meagher Gummow and Lehane's treatise is well known, though it is less clear that the editors of the current edition take the same view.[23]

**3.17** The majority in *Çukurova (No 4)* were themselves conscious of the need not to open too wide a door to judicial relief from disadvantageous contracts. They added that

> nevertheless, the Board emphasises that it is in no way suggesting that equity recognizes any general or open-ended discretion. The Board's reasoning and decision in this case are based on and confined to what it sees as an exceptional situation, in which it would, in the Board's view, be both inequitable and unconscionable to ignore the background and circumstances of the tender ... the unusual facts of this case are in this respect probably unlikely to be repeated.[24]

**3.18** These words indicate an understandable concern to preserve a measure of certainty and predictability. But it might be observed that these words are unlikely, in practice, to restrict greatly the future powers of the court, for in any case in which the court will be inclined to grant relief it will not be difficult to describe the circumstances as 'inequitable', 'unconscionable' or 'exceptional'. This observation might be thought to lend support to criticism of the majority view. On the other hand it might be argued that the approval of a general power of relief, to be used in extreme cases but that cannot be precisely defined, recognizes the force of what the majority had implied in the previous paragraph, that certainty, though important, cannot be a consideration that overrides every other value in legal decision-making. Lord Neuberger of Abbotsbury PSC, one of the two minority judges in *Çukorova (No 4),* has spoken more recently of 'the familiar tension between the need for principle, clarity and certainty in the law with the *equally important* desire to achieve a fair and appropriate result in each case'.[25]

**3.19** Another significant feature of the majority judgment in *Çukorova (No 4)* is the recognition of the link between the forfeiture and the penalty cases:

> Likewise, Nicholls LJ ... treated forfeiture of a lease on non-payment of rent and forfeiture of a mortgage together and both as stemming from the same underlying

22 *Çukurova (No 4)* (n 11) [43].
23 The passage quoted seems to be absent from the Fifth Edition (JD Heydon, MJ Leeming and PG Turner, 2015) which contains some adverse comments on *Çukorova* at 18–295 and 18–305. See also PG Turner, "Mending Men's Bargains' in Equity: Mortgage Redemption and Relief against Forfeiture' (2014) 130 LQR 188, 190, criticizing *Çukorova.*
24 *Çukurova (No 4)* (n 11) [44].
25 *Jetivia SA v Bilta (UK) Ltd* [2015] UKSC 23, [2016] AC 1, [13] (emphasis added).

principle as that governing penalty clauses. For centuries, he said, 'equity has given relief against such provisions by not permitting the innocent party to recover ... more than his loss'.[26]

**3.20** This comment recognizes the force of the unjust enrichment perspective. The fundamental objection to strict enforcement of the contractual provisions is, both in forfeiture and in penalty cases, the undue or disproportionate enrichment of the claimant, who may recover far more by strict enforcement than could reasonably have been expected from the ostensible purpose of the forfeiture or penalty clauses (that is, to give security for performance of the other party's principal obligation). It is true that judgment is required to determine the 'ostensible purpose' of the transaction, and in some cases this might present difficulties, but often it does not: the substance of an ordinary mortgage, for example, is readily perceived as a way of giving security for repayment of a loan, not as a kind of wager entitling the lender to derive random and disproportionate profits from trivial defaults.

**3.21** The Supreme Court of Canada, in *Bhasin v Hrynew*, has accepted the idea of a non-excludable duty of good faith in contract law, but without making it clear whether the test is subjective (dishonesty) or objective (reasonableness). In referring to Quebec law the court said that the concept of good faith includes the concept of abuse of rights, and that it has an objective meaning:

> The *Civil Code of Quebec* recognizes a broad duty of good faith which extends to the formation, performance and termination of a contract and includes the notion of abuse of contractual rights ... While this is not the place to expound in detail on good faith in the Quebec civil law, it is worth noting that good faith is seen as having two main aspects. The first is the subjective aspect, which is concerned with the state of mind of the actor, and addresses conduct that is, for example, malicious or intentional. The second is the objective aspect which is concerned with whether conduct is unacceptable according to the standards of reasonable people. As J-L Baudoin and P-G Jobin explain ... 'a person can be in good faith (in the subjective sense), that is, act without malicious intent or without knowledge of certain facts, yet his or her conduct may nevertheless be contrary to the requirements of good faith in that it violates objective standards of conduct that are generally accepted in society'.[27]

**3.22** If the civilian concept of good faith is to be embraced as equivalent to equity it is essential to note, as Hesselink also explained,[28] that the concept is widely understood in civilian systems in an objective sense. The *Draft Common Frame of Reference*, which incorporates many references to 'good faith and fair

---

26 *Çukurova (No 4)* (n 11) [19]. In *Cavendish Square Holding BV v Makdessi* (n 14), however, distinctions were drawn between penalty clauses and relief against forfeiture. In Ontario and most other Canadian jurisdictions there is a statutory provision to the effect that 'a court may grant relief against penalties and forfeitures on such terms as ... are just', Courts of Justice Act (Ont) s. 98.

27 *Bhasin v Hrynew* (n 1), [83].

28 Hesselink (n 9).

dealing', while ambiguous in some places, also appears to give an objective meaning to the phrase ('community standards of decency and fairness').[29]

**3.23** The Supreme Court of Canada referred at several points in *Bhasin v Hrynew* to good faith in American law, with the implication that a duty of good faith could safely be adopted without endangering security of contracts. However, the court did not point out that the duty of good faith has been very narrowly construed by many American courts, so as to require actual misconduct, or conduct close to fraud, in order to establish a breach of the duty.[30] Probably the Supreme Court of Canada did not intend to import such a narrow interpretation into Canadian law, but the matter is not entirely free from doubt. Though the overall tone is expansive in the direction of granting relief for unfairness, the court says that 'experience in Quebec and the United States shows that even very broad conceptions of good faith have not impeded contractual activity or contractual stability',[31] and a US decision refusing to find a breach of the duty of good faith was cited with approval.[32] This appears to suggest approval of the American experience. On the other hand, the amalgamation of Quebec and United States experience, and the immediate reference to a Quebec author, point towards an objective standard of good faith. In one passage[33] the Court says that appropriate regard for the other party's legitimate contractual interests 'merely requires that a party not seek to undermine those interests in bad faith'. This comment was made in the context of distinguishing good faith from the exceptional obligations associated with fiduciary duty, and, it could be argued, was presumably not intended to require proof of (subjective) bad faith in determining relief for unfairness, or in implying terms. But there will be uncertainty on the point until the Supreme Court of Canada revisits the question. As indicated above (s. 3.7), the concept of good faith has been deployed in many different contexts. Good faith might be welcomed, not as supplying a single simple solution to all these problems (this is not attainable), but as recognizing a residual power in the court to do practical justice where doctrines of contract law of general application would otherwise lead to a highly unreasonable result.

## Security of contracts

**3.24** Due weight must, as the Supreme Court of Canada recognized, be given to security of contracts. Inequality of values exchanged cannot in itself be sufficient to set aside an otherwise valid contract, or the courts would 'throw every

---

29 Christian von Bar, Eric Clive and Hans Schulte-Nölke, *Principles, Definitions and Model Rules of European Private Law: Draft Common Frame of Reference* (Sellier, 2009) i, 677.

30 Paul McMahon, 'Good Faith and Fair Dealing as an Underenforced Legal Norm' (2015) 99 Minnesota LR 2051; Jay M Feinman, 'The Duty of Good Faith: A Perspective on Contemporary Contract Law' (2015) 66 Hastings LJ 937; Peter Goodrich, 'The Wrecking Ball: Good Faith, Preemption and U.S. Exceptionalism', in Pier Giuseppe Monateri (ed.), *Comparative Contract Law* (Edward Elgar, 2017) 385.

31 *Bhasin* (n 1), [85].

32 Ibid, [87].

33 Ibid, [65].

thing into confusion and set afloat all the contracts of mankind'.[34] A contract may allocate the risk of loss to one party and gain to the other, and the contract may be perfectly fair at the time when it is made and yet turn out to be highly advantageous to one of the parties, as where property sold at a fair price subsequently increases in value. The test of fairness must be applied to the time when the contract is made, but this does not mean that subsequent events are irrelevant. A contractual clause that, as later construed and applied, has very unfair consequences may properly be described as, from its inception, an unfair clause, even though the unfair consequences have only become apparent at a later date, for the contract is the juridical source of the result. A penalty clause may seem reasonable at the time of the contract, but subsequent events may show it to be extravagant, as in a case where a penalty is agreed to be paid for late completion of a bridge, but it turns out that late completion causes no loss because the connecting road to the bridge is also incomplete.[35] The fairness of the clause may be judged as at the time of the contract, but the subsequent events will be relevant in determining (as a matter of interpretation) whether the clause applies in the unforeseen circumstances, and (if it does) whether, as interpreted, it is so unreasonable as to warrant relief.

**3.25** It is possible that control over highly unreasonable contracts might be conceptualized in terms of good faith, or of avoidance of abuse of rights, as suggested in *Bhasin v Hrynew*,[36] but these concepts have their own difficulties. It is very likely that a doctrine of good faith, even if generally accepted in common law jurisdictions, would be interpreted, in the context of unreasonable agreements, as has occurred in American jurisdictions, to require proof of some sort of bad motive as a prerequisite to the granting of relief, as has occurred also in respect of unconscionability. Although it would be possible, as the Supreme Court of Canada said was true of Quebec law, to interpret the phrase 'good faith' in a purely objective sense, so as to make it the equivalent of reasonableness, the ordinary meaning of the phrase 'good faith' would constantly give support to those arguing for a narrow view of the court's power. Although the general tenor of the judgment in *Bhasin v Hrynew* is in the direction of approval of the existing powers of the court to relieve against unfair contracts, there are internal tensions.

**3.26** In a codified system, without a tradition of separate equity but containing a provision requiring 'good faith', it is understandable, and in many respects admirable, that the phrase 'good faith' should be interpreted so as to give to the court the kind of powers that were exercised in English law by courts of equity. But, ironically, it has proved more difficult to achieve this object by this route in a system that already includes the powers derived from equity, and that ostensibly gives them priority where they differ from the common law.[37]

**3.27** There is much to be said in favour of some kind of reformulation of the equitable powers of the modern court: knowledge of historical equity is fading,

---

34 *Griffith v Sprately* (1787) 1 Cox 383, 388, 29 ER 1213 (Eyre LCB).
35 *Massman Construction Co v City Council of Greenville* 147 F 2d 925 (5th Cir, 1945).
36 *Bhasin* (n 1).
37 Judicature Act, 1875, s. 25 (11) and modern counterparts.

especially in North America; there is a danger that equitable powers will be marginalized, or fossilized by being confined to precise categories where equity had intervened before 1875; borderline anomalies arise with 'near forfeiture' and 'near penalty' clauses, or instances that fall just outside areas of statutory protection; recognition of a general power in the modern court is needed for the sake of transparency and for the sake of consistency and harmony with powers derived by the modern court from sources other than historical equity.[38]

**3.28** Good faith could possibly meet these objectives, but only if the implied term approach were abandoned, if express recognition were given that the concept of good faith could contradict or modify the parties' agreement, and if good faith were authoritatively defined by an objective test (such as 'highly unreasonable') so as not to depend on proof of any kind of misconduct on the part of the advantaged party. No doubt it would be possible for supreme courts in Commonwealth jurisdictions to establish such a meaning of good faith, but, as the *Çukorova* case demonstrates, this would be a difficult task strenuously resisted by powerful interests and by conceptual inertia, and would probably involve a long and inconclusive struggle, with little uniformity across jurisdictions. Any supreme court inclined to accept and adopt such a meaning of 'good faith' would probably be open to a simpler, clearer, more transparent and more direct recognition of a power in the modern court, based on general principles of justice, to modify contracts where modification was necessary in order to avoid highly unreasonable consequences.

**3.29** In *Bhasin v Hrynew* the Supreme Court of Canada said at one point that the duty of good faith could not be excluded by the parties' agreement. This enabled the court to avoid the effect of an entire agreement clause, which had been held by the Alberta Court of Appeal to exclude any implied term of good faith. The Supreme Court said

> Viewed in this way, the entire agreement clause in cl 11.2 of the Agreement is not an impediment to the duty arising in this case. Because the duty of honesty in contractual performance is a general doctrine of contract law that applies to all contracts, like unconscionability, the parties are not free to exclude it...[39]

**3.30** The reference to the equitable concept of unconscionability in this contest is significant, and would indicate a recognition that the court has power not only to interpret agreements but, like the old court of equity, in appropriate circumstances, to set them aside or to modify them. On the question of the power to exclude the duty, however, the court added that the parties were free to 'determine the standards by which performance of those obligations is to be measured, if those standards are not manifestly unreasonable',[40] and then added

---

38 For example, admiralty law, duress, control of exemption clauses, limitations on remedies for breach of contract, frustration, control of domestic contracts, control of contracts through public policy.

39 *Bhasin* (n 1), [75].

40 Ibid, [77] quoting UCC 1–302(b).

further, 'certainly any modification of the duty of honest performance would need to be in express terms',[41] which would seem to imply that the duty of good faith *can* be excluded by clear language.

**3.31** One of the difficulties of unanimous judgments in appellate courts is that the single judgment sometimes contains conflicting lines of thought. On some kinds of question unanimity is highly desirable, but it has the drawback that the unanimity achieved is more apparent than real, as conflicting ideas are incorporated into a single narrative. This conceals from the reader the extent to which there was a consensus among the judges, or a majority view, on particular points. This phenomenon is apparent in the *Bhasin* case. Some passages in the judgment, apparently drafted in order to allay fears that a test of good faith will introduce uncertainty into the law, seem designed to persuade the reader that sanctity of contracts remains paramount. The judgment includes assurances that there is no duty of loyalty or of disclosure nor any requirement that a party 'forego advantages flowing from the contract',[42] that in commerce, a party may sometimes cause loss to another – even intentionally – in the legitimate pursuit of economic self-interest,[43] that 'this court has been reluctant to extend the requirements of good faith beyond honesty for fear of causing undue judicial interference in contracts',[44] that 'the duty of honest performance interferes very little with freedom of contract',[45] that the organizing principle of good faith 'merely requires that a party not seek to undermine [the other party's legitimate interests] in bad faith'[46] and that the decision is 'a modest, incremental step'.[47] There is a warning that

> the principle of good faith must be clear not to veer into a form of ad hoc judicial moralism or 'palm tree' justice. In particular, the organizing principle of good faith should not be used as a pretext for scrutinizing the motives of contracting parties.[48]

**3.32** The suggestion that a duty of good faith requires only the avoidance of bad faith is not compatible with an objective interpretation of the duty of good faith: 'good faith' might be given a wholly objective meaning, but 'bad faith' usually implies some sort of misconduct. The court cited, with apparent approval, an article by Robert Summers:

> The notion of 'good faith' in the *Restatement* [Second Restatement of Contracts, s. 205] substantially followed the definition proposed by Robert Summers in an influential article, where he proposed that 'good faith' is best understood as an 'excluder' of various categories of bad faith conduct.[49]

---

41  Ibid, [78].
42  Ibid, [73].
43  Ibid, [70].
44  Ibid, [89].
45  Ibid, [76].
46  Ibid, [65].
47  Ibid, [73].
48  Ibid, [70].
49  Ibid, [84], citing Robert S Summers, "Good faith' in General Contract Law and the Sales Provisions of the Uniform Commercial Code' (1968) 54 Va LR 195 (1968). See also n 13.

**3.33** Several approving references in *Bhasin v Hrynew* to American law, where, as mentioned, good faith has been very narrowly interpreted, also tend in the same direction, though they are counterbalanced by the equally approving references to Quebec law and an objective test. Since the actual decision in the case was merely to establish a duty of honesty, the passages mentioned will supply ammunition for those seeking to support the argument either that no change has been made in the power of the court to grant relief against unfair contracts, or that proof of some kind of misconduct or subjective dishonesty is necessary for the court to grant such relief. The general tenor of the judgment, including its many references to reasonableness and fairness,[50] strongly suggests that this was not the intention of the court, but uncertainty on this important question is likely to give rise to argument for some time to come.

**3.34** The insistence that 'in particular, the organizing principle of good faith should not be used as a pretext for scrutinizing the motives of contracting parties'[51] is puzzling. The term 'good faith' itself suggests that motive may be relevant, and many of the cases on implied terms, and on the power to terminate contracts, do take account of motives. It is a little surprising that the court should go to such lengths to establish a principle of good faith only to declare that the motives of the parties are irrelevant. Another puzzling statement, as pointed out by Professors Carter and Furmston,[52] is that

> contracting parties must be able to rely on a minimum standard of honesty from their contracting partner in relation to performing the contract as a reassurance that if the contract does not work out, they will have a fair opportunity to protect their interests.[53]

**3.35** The context indicates that the court was seeking here to distinguish the new duty of honesty from a fiduciary duty, in order to alleviate fears that there was anything in the current decision that was alarmingly new, or radical. The line of thought appears to be that a party disappointed in an attempt to enforce a contract should nevertheless have a remedy for loss caused by a dishonest false statement. This would be a reasonable argument, but its natural conclusion would seem to be that the remedy should be for the tort of deceit, or civil fraud.

### Subsequent decisions

**3.36** Later decisions of Canadian courts have varied very substantially in the scope they have given to the *Bhasin* case. In *Energy Fundamentals Group*

---

50 Ibid, [41], [42], [43], [54], [56], [63], [66], [89]. See Waddams, 'Unfairness and Good Faith in Contract Law: A New Approach' (2017) 80 Supreme Court L. Rev., 309.

51 *Bhasin* (n 1), [70].

52 Michael Furmston and JW Carter, 'Good Faith in Contract Law: A Commonwealth Survey', in *Eppur si muove: The Age of Uniform Law. Essays in Honour of Michael Joachim Bonnell to Celebrate his 70th Birthday* (UNIDROIT, 2016) 988, 1016, note ('With respect, we find this a somewhat obscure statement').

53 *Bhasin* (n 1), [86].

*Inc v Veresen Inc*[54] the Ontario Court of Appeal accepted the close relation between good faith and implied terms, quoting with approval the following passage from *Bhasin*:

> The implication of terms plays a functionally similar role in common law contract law to the doctrine of good faith in civil law jurisdictions *by filling in gaps in the written agreement of the parties.*[55]

**3.37** This association of concepts is significant, and allows considerable scope for the doctrine of good faith, but subordinates it to express provisions of the parties' agreement. It will be recalled that in *Bhasin* the Supreme Court of Canada appeared to accept the proposition that a standard boilerplate entire agreement clause would have the effect of excluding any implied term. A subsequent decision of the Ontario Court of Appeal gives *Bhasin* a wider interpretation. In *Mohamed v Information Systems Architects Inc.*[56] a consulting agreement permitted termination if 'ISA [the defendant] determines it is in ISA's best interest to replace the consultant for any reason'. The trial judge found that there was a breach of the duty of good faith, but, on appeal, it was objected that the trial judge had based his conclusion on interpretation of the clause, and that this was an error because the clause was not ambiguous. The Court of Appeal agreed that the clause could not be interpreted to require good faith, but it upheld the judge's conclusion on the basis that the judge's conclusion had been based on the propositions that good faith was 'an operative principle in the performance of contracts' and 'not a principle applicable to the interpretation of contracts', and that 'the principle qualifies ISA's rights to terminate without cause'.[57] The reasoning of the Court of Appeal indicates that *Bhasin v Hrynew* can be interpreted to support a power not only to interpret, but to modify contractual agreements even where they are unambiguous. Another significant aspect of the case is that it tends to support an objective test of good faith. The defendant's decision to terminate the contract was made at the request of the client on whose project the plaintiff was working. The client's request was made pursuant to a provision in the contract between the client and the defendant to the effect that the defendant would not engage, for the client's project, anyone with a criminal record. The plaintiff had a dated criminal record which he had disclosed in good time to the defendant. The termination of the contract was therefore unreasonable (as between plaintiff and defendant), but there was no finding that the defendant had acted dishonestly, or with any bad motive. The defendant may well have believed that it was fully entitled to terminate the contract in the circumstances, and its predominant motive may well have been simply to retain the good will of the client. The case thus suggests that the concept of good faith can be used to modify contractual provisions that are

---

54 2015 ONCA 514.
55 Ibid, [48] from *Bhasin* (n 1), [44] (emphasis in *Energy Fundamentals*).
56 2018 ONCA 428.
57 Ibid, [12].

applied in ways that are highly unreasonable, and in this respect it could indeed be said that the power is analogous to the power of the old court of equity to modify highly unreasonable contracts.

**3.38** On the other hand, many other cases have given a very narrow interpretation to *Bhasin*. A recent instance is *CM Callow Inc v Zollinger*,[58] where the plaintiff had two separate contracts with the defendant, one to do maintenance work in the summer, and the other for snow clearance in the winter. The winter contract contained a right to terminate on ten days' notice, and the defendants decided in March or April to terminate that contract, but did not give the notice until September in order to induce the plaintiff to do extra work, free of charge, under the summer contract in the expectation that the winter contract would not be terminated. The trial judge found that the defendants had acted in bad faith by withholding the fact that they intended to terminate and by falsely representing to the plaintiff that the winter contract was not in danger of non-renewal. The facts were thus quite close to those in *Bhasin* where the Supreme Court of Canada had held that Can-Am had acted dishonestly in giving an equivocal answer to a question as to whether they intended to terminate the contract. But in the *Callow* case the Ontario Court of Appeal reversed the trial judgment, putting a very narrow interpretation on *Bhasin*. The court said that 'the Court [in *Bhasin*] was at pains to emphasize that the concept of good faith was not to be applied so as to undermine longstanding contract law principles, thereby creating uncertainty'.[59] The Ontario court cited passages in *Bhasin*, some of which have been already mentioned, stating that 'a party may sometimes cause loss to another – even intentionally – in the legitimate pursuit of economic self-interest', that 'the organizing principle of good faith should not be used as a pretext for scrutinizing the motives of contracting parties', and that

> [the] duty means that parties must not lie or otherwise knowingly mislead each other about matters directly linked to the performance of the contract. This does not impose a duty of loyalty or of disclosure … it is a simple requirement not to lie or mislead the other party about one's contractual performance

and that *Bhasin* was 'a modest, incremental step'.[60] The court accepted that the defendants had 'actively deceived Callow as to their intentions and accepted the "freebie" work he performed in the knowledge that the extra work was performed with the intention/hope of persuading them to award the respondent additional contracts',[61] but this was not enough to amount to failure of good faith: *Bhasin* was distinguished on the basis that 'this was not a case in which the contract would renew automatically, nor were the parties required to maintain

---

58  2018 ONCA 896 (leave to appeal to Supreme Court of Canada granted, 27 June 2019, case number 38463).

59  Ibid, [11].

60  *Bhasin* (n 1), [70], [73].

61  *Callow* (n 58), [15].

an ongoing relationship',[62] and that the dishonesty was not directly linked to the winter contract.[63]

**3.39** The decision of the trial judge was held to have substantially modified a 'key term of the contract' and to have gone 'beyond what the duty of honest performance requires or permits'.[64] This case shows how the restrictive passages in the *Bhasin* case can readily be seized upon in order to limit the operation of the 'organizing principle of good faith', even in a case where actual dishonesty was found to have occurred. Where there is proof of a deliberate false statement causing loss, an action in tort for deceit, or civil fraud, may still be the more reliable route to compensation.

**3.40** Other recent cases tend in the same direction. In *Styles v Alberta Investment Management Corp*[65] an employee was entitled to earned commissions if he remained in employment at a certain date. He was dismissed before the named date, and the question was whether he was entitled to relief from what was, in effect (as was argued), forfeiture of the commissions. The trial judge held that there had been a breach of the obligation of good faith, but the majority of the Alberta court of Appeal reversed the decision, saying that there was no general principle of 'reasonable exercise of discretion', adding that 'this radical extension of the law is unsupported by authority, and contrary to the principles of the law of contract'.[66] Another example is the decision of the British Columbia Court of Appeal in *Greater Vancouver Sewerage and Drainage District v Wastech Services Ltd.*[67] This case involved a complex and long-term agreement between sophisticated parties for the disposal of urban waste. The City (the Drainage district) had the right under the contract to allocate waste disposal to various sites, and disposal was remunerated at different rates for different sites. A dispute arose when the city reduced the amount of waste allocated for disposal to a site that was more remunerative to Wastech than the other sites. The contract contained an arbitration clause, and the arbitrator found that the reallocation was in breach of the obligation of good faith established in *Bhasin v Hrynew*. The award was reversed by the British Columbia Supreme Court, and the reversal was upheld by the Court of Appeal. The Court of Appeal said

> Again with due respect to the contrary view, I read *Bhasin* as concerned substantially with conduct that has at least a subjective element of improper motive or dishonesty ... In *Bhasin* itself, the Court described the 'organizing principle' of good faith as meaning 'simply that parties generally must perform their contractual duties honestly and

---

62 Ibid, [17].

63 Ibid, [18].

64 Ibid, [19].

65 2017 ABCA 1.

66 Ibid, [49]. *Styles* was followed by the Nova Scotia Court of Appeal in *Matthews v Ocean Nutrition Canada Ltd* 2018 NSCA 44, where a similar issue arose in calculating damages; leave to appeal in that case to the Supreme Court of Canada has been granted (31 January 2019, case number 38252).

67 2019 BCCA 66 (leave to appeal to Supreme Court of Canada granted, 18 July 2019, case number 38601).

reasonably and not capriciously or arbitrarily (at para 63) and again, as 'merely' requiring that a party not 'seek to undermine' the other's contractual interests 'in bad faith.'...
As a matter of law, I doubt the Court in *Bhasin* intended that the principle of good faith would be extended so far as to attribute 'dishonesty' (which, it will be remembered, carries a 'stench') to a party in the Circumstances of Metro [Vancouver] in this case.[68]

**3.41** The case also involved the question of the degree of respect due by the courts to arbitrators, an aspect of the matter that is not addressed here. The result may well be correct in the particular case, but the reasoning demonstrates how the restrictive phrases in *Bhasin v Hrynew* can readily be used to support a very narrow reading of the decision.

**3.42** The search for a single principle to explain apparently disparate cases has a natural attraction. As Lord Hoffmann said, in a different context,[69] 'the example of what Lord Atkin achieved for negligence in *Donoghue v Stevenson* always beckons'.[70] Cromwell J, in *Bhasin v Hrynew*, referred to another area of law in which a general principle had successfully superseded a collection of apparently disparate cases, namely the law of unjust enrichment, or restitution:

> This approach is consistent with that taken in the case of unjust enrichment. McLachlin J (as she then was) outlined the approach in *Peel (Regional Municipality) v Canada* ... 'This case presents the Court with the difficult task of mediating between, if not resolving, the conflicting views of the proper scope of the doctrine of unjust enrichment. It is my conclusion that we must choose a middle path, one which acknowledges the importance of proceeding on general principles but seeks to reconcile the principles with the established categories of recovery....the tri-partite principle of general application which this Court has recognized as the basis of the cause of action in unjust enrichment is this seen to have grown out of the traditional categories of recovery. It is informed by them. It is capable, however, of going beyond them, allowing the law to develop in a flexible way as required to meet the changing perceptions of justice'.[71]

**3.43** One can see the attraction of this line of thinking, but Lord Hoffmann, immediately after his comment that the example of what Lord Atkin achieved for negligence always beckons, added 'But this too is a form of seduction which may lure writers onto the rocks'.[72] Lord Hoffmann's reason for rejecting a single explanation of the economic torts was that he thought that a single explanation elided an important distinction, namely that between inducing breach of contract, and the other economic torts. Whether Lord Hoffmann was right about the economic torts need not be determined for present purposes, but I would suggest that he was right in saying that single explanations of disparate cases may sometimes do more harm than good. The search for elegance and simplicity

---

68  Ibid, [71] and [73].
69  The search for a single principle to explain the economic torts.
70  *OBG Ltd v Allan* [2008] AC 1, [31].
71  *Bhasin* (n 1), [67].
72  n 70.

is, in itself, admirable, but not where it leads to the obscuring of real differences and to the elimination of important distinctions.

**3.44** *Bhasin v Hrynew* has been cited in a number of Commonwealth jurisdictions on particular aspects of good faith. Some cases indicate apparent approval;[73] others indicate some doubt: in a case in the Federal Court of Australia, Edelman J said that there was 'no universal implication of any particular duty to be discerned from the principle of good faith',[74] and the Singapore Court of Appeal has said that 'whether or not the formulation in [*Bhasin v Hrynew*] is too vague and general is a question which is (fortunately) outside the province of the present appeal'.[75]

**3.45** The probable reaction of the higher English courts to *Bhasin v Hrynew* is indicated by the decision of the Court of Appeal in *MSC Mediterranean Shipping Co SA v Cottonex Anstalt*,[76] where the trial judge, Leggatt J,[77] had relied on *Bhasin v Hrynew*. In allowing the appeal Moore-Bick LJ said

> The judge drew support for his conclusion from what he described as an increasing recognition in the common law world of the need for good faith in contractual dealings. The recognition of a general duty of good faith would be a significant step in the development of our law of contract with potentially far-reaching consequences and I do not think it is necessary or desirable to resort to it in order to decide the outcome of the present case. It is interesting to note that in the case to which the judge referred as providing support for his view, *Bhasin v Hrynew*, 2014 SCC 71, [2014] 3 S.C.R.494, the Supreme Court of Canada recognised that in *Mid Essex Hospital Services NHS Trust v Compass Group UK and Ireland* [2013] EWCA Civ 200 this court had recently reiterated that English law does not recognise any general duty of good faith in matters of contract. It has, in the words of Bingham L.J. in *Interfoto Picture Library Ltd v Stiletto Visual Programmes Ltd* [1989] QB 433, 439, preferred to develop 'piecemeal solutions in response to demonstrated problems of unfairness', although it is well-recognised that broad concepts of fair dealing may be reflected in the court's response to questions of construction and the implication of terms. In my view the better course is for the law to develop along established lines rather than to encourage judges to look for what the judge in this case called some 'general organising principle' drawn from cases of disparate kinds. For example, I do not think that decisions on the exercise of options under contracts of different kinds, on which he also relied, shed any real light on the kind of problem that arises in this case. There is in my view a real danger that if a general principle of good faith were established it would be invoked as often to undermine as to support the terms in which the parties have reached agreement. The danger is not dissimilar to that posed by too liberal an approach to construction, against which the Supreme Court warned in *Arnold v Britton* [2015] UKSC 36, [2015] AC 1619.

---

73 *Heli Holdings Ltd v The Helicopter Line Ltd* [2016] NZHC 976, [114] (express good faith provision), *Sino Iron Pty Ltd v Mineralogy Pty Ltd (No 2)* [2014] WASC 444 (implied term), *SCC (NZ) Ltd v Samsung Electronic New Zealand Ltd* [2018] NZHC 2780 (obligation to deal honestly and reasonably).

74 *Mineralogy Pty Ltd v Sino Iron Pty Ltd (No 6)* [2015] FCA 855, [1007].

75 *The One Suites Pte Ltd v Pacific Motor Credit (Pte) Ltd* [2015] SGCA 21, [44].

76 [2016] EWCA Civ 789, [45].

77 The earlier decision of Leggatt J in *Yam Seng Pte Ltd v Int Trade Corp Ltd* [2013] 1 All ER (Comm) 1321 had been relied on in *Bhasin* (n 1), [57] for the proposition that 'good faith has received increasing prominence in English law despite its 'traditional hostility' to the concept'.

## Conclusion

**3.46** The passage just quoted from *MSC* suggests that the 'general organizing principle' proposed in *Bhasin v Hrynew* is likely to have only limited influence in English law, partly because of uncertainty as to its meaning and scope, and partly because of fear that an unrestricted doctrine of good faith would endanger the security of contracts. Good faith will, however, as Moore-Bick LJ indicated, continue to be relevant to questions of interpretation and implied terms.[78] This is an important feature of the law, and has often been successfully employed to avoid injustice, but it has a serious limitation: it cannot prevail over an explicit contractual right.[79] The reference in *MSC* to *Arnold v Britton* is significant. This was a case in which the UK Supreme Court, giving a strict literal interpretation to a clause in a lease governing maintenance expenses, enforced an agreement that had very harsh consequences, leading to a result that the dissenting judge described as 'grotesque', and as 'commercial nonsense'.[80] It can certainly be argued that *Arnold v Britton* and cases like it manifest an unduly formalistic approach to enforcement of contracts, but, if such cases are to be successfully challenged, it must be by recognition of a power to modify highly unreasonable contracts, even where, as a matter of interpretation, or construction, they are clear and unambiguous. There is an argument to be made in favour of recognizing such a power,[81] for the avoidance of severe injustice and of extravagant enrichment. In a codified system it is readily understandable that an express code provision on good faith could lend itself to various uses, including control of highly unreasonable contracts, but in uncodified systems derived from English law the argument for control of unreasonable contracts is unlikely to succeed if conceptualized only in terms of good faith.

---

78 In *Braganza v BP Shipping Ltd* [2015] UKSC 17, [2015] 1 WLR 1661, the UK Supreme Court held that there was normally an implied term that a contractual discretion would be exercised in good faith and rationally, in the sense used in administrative law. See [18], [28] and [53].

79 See discussion of the *Çukurova* case (text at nn 10–12).

80 *Arnold v Britton* [2015] UKSC 36, [2015] AC 1619, [104], 138], [115], [158] (Lord Carnwath). Professor Furmston describes the dissent as 'impressive': Michael Furmston, *Cheshire, Fifoot & Furmston's Law of Contract*, 17th edn (Oxford University Press, 2019) 174. One of the majority judges, Lord Sumption, while commending the court's approach to interpretation, also described the result, extrajudicially, as 'grotesque ', Lord Sumption, 'A Question of Taste: The Supreme Court and the Interpretation of Contracts' (2017) 17 Oxford University Commonwealth LJ 301, 312; another of the majority judges, Lord Neuberger, said he had reached his conclusion 'reluctantly', but nevertheless defended it: Lord Neuberger, Lecture, 'Express and Implied Terms in Contracts' (School of Law, Singapore Management University, 19 August 2016), available at www.supremecourt.uk/docs/speech-160819.02.pdf (accessed 14 April 2020), para 13.

81 The argument is developed in Stephen Waddams, *Sanctity of Contracts in a Secular Age: Equity, Fairness and Enrichment* (Cambridge University Press, 2019).

## CHAPTER 4

# The quagmire of utmost good faith in insurance law

## A comparative study of Malaysian, Australian and English laws in consumer insurance contracts

*Cheah You Sum*

### Introduction

**4.1** For more than 250 years since the principle of utmost good faith was enunciated by Lord Mansfield in *Carter v Boehm*, the principle has been regarded as being the keynote principle in governing all insurance pre-contractual negotiations and transactions. Most courts in the Commonwealth have adopted the principle dutifully in their judgments. Nevertheless, the introduction of the Insurance Act 2005 (UK) and the Financial Services Act 2013 (Malaysia) has resulted in the death of the principle![1]

**4.2** The implied obligation of good faith is not required in most commercial contracts in the United Kingdom (UK,)[2] Australia[3] and Malaysia.[4] Where the implied obligation of good faith differs in the application in English law is with the application of good faith in insurance contracts. The principle of utmost good faith requires any proposal of risk to be insured that is not made based on utmost good faith by either party to the insurance contract to be rendered void. Utmost good faith breaches have always been based on the premise of misrepresentation of facts or non-disclosure from the party that possesses all the relevant knowledge as compared to the other party who underwrites the risk, but there is reciprocity in the duty as the insurer must also exercise utmost good faith in offering insurance coverage and advice.

**4.3** A breach of utmost good faith in an insurance contract is based on the fact of whether a reasonable underwriter had been affected by the misrepresentation and this had led the underwriter into accepting the contract. The basis of the test was objective which is commonly found in the torts; known to many as the reasonable man test. A material fact is one that affects the judgment of a prudent underwriter in his assessment of the risk, in the pricing of the risk and whether

---

1 Atillio M Costabel, 'Utmost Good Faith' in Marine Insurance: A Message on the State of the Dis-Union', 2017, Journal of Maritime Law & Commerce, Vol 48, No 1, 1.

2 Howard Hunter, Chapter 2 in this volume.

3 Ibid, paras 24 and 25.

4 *Aseambankers Malaysia Berhad & Ors v Shencourt Sdn Bhd & Anor, [2013] (Civil Appeal No. W-02-808-2009, 27.*

or not to accept the risk in question. If the fact is material and this had been with-held or misrepresented, then the proposer will be in breach of this duty.

**4.4** The decision of the court in *Container Transport International Inc. (CTI) v Oceanus Mutual Underwriting Association (Bermuda) Ltd 1984,*[5] shifted the reasonable underwriter duty to the duty of 'a typical, reasonable underwriter...'. This means, that the opinion of the particular individual who is making the decision on the acceptance of the risk to be insured is tested. This is significant in law as the test is now subjective rather than objective. The finding of this court was later reaffirmed in the case of *Pan Atlantic Insurance Co v Pine Top Insurance Co*[6] (*Pine Top*) where the House of Lords affirmed the decision in *CTI* and added a second element to the test, that is, the actual inducement test. The 'actual inducement' test is similar to misrepresentation in the law of contract applied to all commercial contracts. Lord Mustill expressed the view in *Pine Top* that once the court had decided that a fact was material, the insured would 'have an uphill task' in persuading the court that the non-disclosure made no difference, that is, a *presumption of inducement* element was introduced. The case of *St. Paul Fire v McConnell Dowell Construction*[7] confirmed that induce-ment will usually be presumed about facts which 'the market' generally regards as material. This placed the consumer in a contractual tight spot, as no insurance underwriter then would claim that the facts would not have induced them when their case appears before the courts.

**4.5** These cases led to an outcry by consumer bodies who were concerned about how the decisions in these cases were affecting the rights of the consumers unfairly, as the weight of disclosure requirements as evidenced by these cases seems to have grown heavier on the shoulders of the consumers.

**4.6** The initial section of this chapter focuses on how the legal principles of utmost good faith in insurance contracts have evolved and what causes its demise. The chapter will analyzes how the historical developments of case law, such as CTI, Pan Atlantic and subsequent similar case, led to a heavy burden on the shoulders of consumers; how Parliament and consumer bodies reacted to the legal principles established in the *CTI* and *Pan Atlantic* cases; how the law on misrepresentation was reintroduced into utmost good faith in insurance law and as such bringing consistency into contract law; whether the objectives of introducing a fairer set of laws has been met. The chapter will also analyze the details found in the statutory provisions and bring these discussions into con-text with what is happening to the general development in the law of contract, with a focus on assessing whether will there be a legal flavour for extending the scope to insurance contract when the development of general contract law is favouring consumerism. The chapter will turn to a discussion on the proposers' bearing of responsibilities for contractual negligent misrepresentation. What has happened to the sanctity of the principle of utmost good faith in insurance?

---

5 (1984) 1 Lloyd's Rep 476 (CA).
6 (1993) 1 Lloyd's Rep 496.
7 (1996) 1 All ER 96, 74 BLR 112 (1995) 2 Lloyd's Rep 116, 45 ConLR 89 (CA).

How are underwriters equipped with detailed knowledge of risks not revealed to them? Can the balance be tipped towards a fairer, more central position in the discharge of the legal burden of proof? The practical difficulty of sifting through hundreds or thousands of proposals for insuring risks each day! Finally, the chapter will end with the recommendation to adopt the sharing of responsibilities for negligent misrepresentation.

## The evolution of the legal principle of utmost good faith in the English insurance law

### Carter v Boehm

**4.7** The key legal principles for utmost good faith are derived from the judgment of Lord Mansfield in *Carter v Boehm*[8] where he states that:

> Insurance is a contract upon speculation. The special facts, upon which the contingent chance is to be computed lie most commonly in the knowledge of the insured only: the underwriter trusts to his representation, and proceeds upon the confidence that he does not keep back any circumstances in his knowledge, to mislead the underwriter into a belief that the circumstances do not exist, and to induce him to estimate the risk as if it did not exist.

**4.8** The facts of the case were that Roger Carter, who was appointed as the Deputy Governor of Fort Marlborough in Sumatra by the East India Company, was concerned that the fort may come under attack by French forces based in the far east of Sumatra. The fort was ill-prepared for war and had only operated as a trading post. Roger Carter had instructed his brother to arrange for insurance cover with Charles Boehm, a well-known merchant in London. The French forces sailed a warship into the bay outside the fort, attacked the fort and sent Roger Carter and his people into the interior of Sumatra and seized their properties. By this time, Roger Carter's brother had instructed an insurance broker who had then placed the risk with Charles Boehm for £10,000. Roger Carter had submitted a claim of £10,000 after the incident but this was rejected by Charles Boehm citing misrepresentation in terms of the weaknesses of the fort and the concealment of the fear of imminent attack by the French forces. The court held that the defence presented by the insurer failed, as the animosity between England and France was common knowledge to all and Charles Boehm would certainly have had knowledge of those facts.

**4.9** Time has certainly moved on since the decision in *Carter v Boehm* and facts such as those presented in the case would be commonly known and instantaneously communicated by many social media platforms of today. Furthermore, war insurance cover or war risks cover are commonly excluded from insurance contracts as the risk is deemed uninsurable and losses suffered from such hostile activities are within the purview of the government of nations at war.

---

8 (1766) 1 Blackstone W 593.

**4.10** The contemporary approach towards making law on utmost good faith takes an approach that is less dependent on case law decisions and focuses much more on introducing statutory provisions to ensure a better balance is achieved as compared to the present inequalities, which were a result of legal principles developed by common law cases. Consumers, private consumers, buying personal insurance covers do not have equal footing as evidenced by the fact in *Carter v Boehm*. In *Carter v Boehm*, these were contractual negotiations between equal tradesmen, on one hand of the East Indian Company and on the other of Charles Boehm. Private consumers do not have access to specialist staff who could advise them and seek legal advice when unsure of the purchase of a relatively low valued insurance policy. They are nevertheless required to follow legal principles established by law based on the trading of powerful merchants.

**4.11** It is due to this realization that lawmakers in Parliament in the United Kingdom, Malaysia and Australia have introduced statutory provisions to balance out the interest of the private consumers and that of the insurers. New statutes that were introduced[9] to protect consumers as the previous laws tended to favour insurers over the rights of the consumers.[10] The Law Commissions (or in the case of Malaysia, the Central Bank) specifically cited the protection of consumers and the need to amend the law to deal with the current reality of mass-market consumers as being the key reason in introducing changes to the law affecting the principle of utmost good faith.

## The evolution of the burdensome duty of utmost good faith – misrepresentation in insurance contracts under common law

**4.12** The clear legal principle established in *Carter v Boehm*[11] is that the insured must not conceal what they have known and they also should not misrepresent the risk in such a way as to induce the insurer into the contract.

**4.13** There are two duties that are imposed by the principle of utmost good faith on the parties to an insurance contract; the first part of the duty requires that when the proposer is making representations to the insurer there is a duty not to misrepresent any matter relating to the risk to be insured, i.e. a duty to inform the insurer of factually accurate facts pertaining to the risk. The second part of the duty requires the proposer not to conceal facts which are material to the risk to bring the insurer into the contract of insurance or to attract better terms from the insurer. This duty is imposed upon the proposer, primarily because one party, the proposer, knows everything about the facts surrounding

---

9 Financial Services Act 2013 (Malaysia), the Insurance Act 2015 (UK) and Insurance Contracts Act 1984 (Australia).

10 Australian Law Reform Committee Report number 20, citing comments of Mr. John Gayler MP, Member of Leichhardt, House of Representatives, June 4, 1984. Official Statement published by the House of Common Report of the 3rd Meeting, Fifth Term, 12th Parliamentary Sitting of Malaysia, para 1810, page 78. November 27, 2012, Law Commission and Scottish Law Commission.

11 *Carter*, 3 Burr 1906 at 1909–10; All ER Rep 183 at 184.

the risks, and the other party to the contract, the insurer, knows nothing and relies on the proposer/insured to make full disclosure. This in law applies to all contracts of *uberima fidei*.

**4.14** There are debates by academics[12] as to whether Lord Mansfield had intended such strict duty when he enunciated the principle. He started his judgment by explaining the limits that would be placed on insurers in the application of the principle of utmost good faith to deny the claim submitted by the insured. His seminary exposition is in three parts, of which one receives significant emphasis for later judgments from courts in preceding cases concerning utmost good faith, which is that for the insurer to apply the principle of utmost good faith in order to reject claims due to the breaches of that principle, they must show that they have been induced into the contract believing facts contrary to their beliefs because they had relied on representation made by the insured.

**4.15** However, the basis which Lord Mansfield had relied on for the first part of this exposition is not based on something new that he had developed. Indeed, his Lordship was merely restating what was a precedent in courts then and recorded in unreported cases. The second part of his exposition dealt with the fact that insurance contracts, in particular, had consisted of an element of hidden knowledge of the risk, one only known to the proposer himself, and as such the proposer is under a duty to reveal what he knows and ought to have known in the ordinary course of business. If the proposer had induced the insurer into entering into an insurance contract either through fraud or negligence, the insurer is then entitled to deny liability on claims made under the insurance contract.[13]

**4.16** Finally, Lord Mansfield's third exposition contains a limit to which an insurer could apply the principle of utmost good faith. His Lordship states that for the insurers to deny liability for a claim in an insurance contract, the misrepresentation or non-disclosure must have materially affected the judgment of a prudent underwriter. Based on this statement, it would appear that his Lordship has introduced an objective standard in testing materiality of facts not made known or misrepresented to the insurers.[14]

**4.17** The remaining part of his Lordship's judgment provided a list of circumstances for which insurers could not use the principle of utmost good faith to deny claims on an insurance contract and these are facts which concerns matters of law; matters which lessen the risk; facts already known to insurers; facts which the insurers ought to know; where the court takes the view that the insurer has 'constructive knowledge' of the circumstances, for example, facts which are notorious (that is, matters of common knowledge) and things in the public domain like a state of war – *Carter v Boehm*,;[15] facts about the trade that

---

12 Charles Mitchell and Paul Mitchell, Landmark Cases in Law of Contract, Hart Publishing, 2008, p 79; John Lowry, Paul Rawlings and Robert Merkin, Insurance Law Doctrines and Principles, 3rd edn, Hart Publishing, 2011, p 86.

13 Mitchell and Mitchell, n 12, p 81.

14 Ibid, p 82.

15 (1766) 3 Burr 1905.

the underwriters insure, i.e. normal trade practices and their usual risks. This, however, does not extend to include recent events affecting the particular trade, for example in the case of *Bates v Hewitt*[16] where a refitted commercial (previous Confederate naval ship) vessel was seized by an American warship due to her recent history as a fighting ship. The fact that it was previously a warship and that this fact was withheld leg to the court deciding that this was a non-disclosure of a fact material to the risk.[17]

**4.18** The materiality factor had not received much analysis in the early days of the development of the principle, not until later cases such as *Durrell v Bederly*,[18] *Ionides v Pender*[19] and *Rivaz v Gerussi*[20] did courts start developing the objective approach and tortuous-like requirements for the test of materiality. This approach has influenced a string of cases that had used the reasonable underwriter test to determine whether or not the underwriter had been influenced materially in accepting the risks. This approach was, of course, debunked in later cases where it was firmly established that the test should be a subjective test of whether the particular underwriter or insurer had been so influenced as to be induced to enter into the contract of insurance.

**4.19** Based on the analysis of the decision by Lord Mansfield, it is arguable that his Lordship has ever intended for the principle to be applied which such onerous duty on the part of the insured. Subsequent case laws as discussed further (see cases discussed in paragraphs 4.23 to 4.29) show how courts in the UK subsequently took the precedent developed in *Carter v Boehm* and turn it into such strict rules in insurance contracts to the extent of it being labelled as the insurers' friendly clause.

### Influencing the judgment of the prudent underwriter

**4.20** The requirements of the prevailing law, in attempting to determine whether a particular circumstance influences the judgment of a prudent underwriter, is akin to moving the boundaries of civil law uncomfortably close to the standard of proof required by criminal law.

**4.21** This puts an onerous burden on the shoulder of the proposer because the proposer will now need to understand what would influence the insurer in their proposal for the risk, although the fact lies within the knowledge of the proposer, nevertheless one would not be able to fathom fully what information would or would not influence the judgment of another individual because there is absolutely no benchmark or standard to follow.[21] In practice, most proposers will never meet the insurer as the bulk of transactions are made

---

16  [1867] LR 2 QB 595.
17  Mitchell and Mitchell, n 12, p 82.
18  (1815) Holt 283; 286.
19  (1874) LR 9 QB.
20  (1880) 6 QBD 222.
21  Lowry, Rawlings and Merkin, n 12, p 93.

either through intermediaries or electronic means and as such, it will be a very onerous duty for the proposer to know what will or will not influence an insurer.

**4.22** A 'prudent insurer' has been held by the courts to mean a 'reasonable' insurer.[22] Of course, this is derived from the earlier cases discussed where the term reasonable underwriter was used by the courts and the objective test similar to the objective test as applied to cases in tort and was used to determine whether the underwriter was influenced by non-disclosure or misrepresentation on the part of the proposer or insured. Another possible influence could have arisen from the wordings used in section 18(2) Marine Insurance Act 1906, where it is stated that 'every circumstance is material which would influence the judgment of a prudent insurer in fixing the premium, or determining whether he will take the risk'. This had led to attempts by the courts to substitute the test of influencing the judgment of the particular insured (subjective test) to test the 'prudent insurer' (objective test).[23]

**4.23** However, this approach has not been followed in recent cases. The term 'influence the judgment of' is found in the decision of *Container Transport International Inc v Oceanus Mutual Underwriting Association (Bermuda) Ltd*[24] to mean that the fact must be one which a typical, reasonable underwriter would have wanted to know about when forming his opinion of the risk. It need not necessarily be a decisive fact that would have caused such an underwriter to act differently had he known about it.

**4.24** The decision in *Container Transport International Inc v Oceanus Mutual Underwriting Association (Bermuda) Ltd* was affirmed in *Pan Atlantic Insurance Co v Pine Top Insurance Co*[25] but a second element was added in this case, i.e. the 'actual inducement test'. This 'actual inducement' test is similar to the law on misrepresentation for commercial contracts.

**4.25** The second element that was added to this case was the question by the House of Lords, on what if the fact in question was material, in that a typical, reasonable underwriter would have wanted to know about it, but it would have made no difference to the decision of the actual underwriter who took the risk? What if the particular underwriter in question has a greater risk appetite? This means that the courts must determine that the underwriter who wrote the risk must have been induced to take the risk. Lord Mustill stated that:

> I conclude that there is to be implied in the 1906 Act a qualification that a material misrepresentation will not entitle the underwriter to avoid the policy unless the misrepresentation induced the making of the contract, using 'induced' in the sense in which it is used in the general law of contract.

---

22 See *Joel v Law Union and Crown Insurance Co* (1908) 99 LT 712.
23 Lowry, Rawlings and Merkin, n 12, p 89.
24 (1984) 1 Lloyd's Rep 476 (CA).
25 [1993] 1 Lloyd's Rep 496.

**4.26** Lord Mustill went on to express the view in *Pine Top* that once the court had decided that a fact was material, the insured would 'have an uphill task' in persuading the court that the non-disclosure made no difference, i.e. a presumption of inducement element was introduced.

**4.27** In *St. Paul Fire v McConnell Dowell Construction*,[26] it was confirmed that inducement will usually be presumed in relation to facts which 'the market' generally regards as material.

**4.28** Later cases show that the courts were not in consensus among themselves about this legal issue.[27] In *Assicurazioni Generali SpA v Arab Insurance Group (BSC)*,[28] the Court of Appeal held that although misrepresentation or non-disclosure need not be the only inducement operating on the insurer, it must be effective in causing the actual insurer to enter into the contract. Most significant is the fact that courts of law followed earlier decisions that the insurer must give evidence to his state of mind. Clarke LJ summarized the position effectively as follows:

1. In order to be entitled to avoid a contract of insurance or reinsurance, an insurer ... must prove on the balance of probabilities that he was induced to enter into the contract by material non-disclosure or by material misrepresentation.
2. There is no presumption of law that an insurer ... is induced to enter into a contract by a material non-disclosure or misrepresentation.
3. The facts may, however, be such that it is to be inferred that the particular insurer ... was so induced even in the absence of evidence from him.
4. In order to prove inducement, the insurer must show that the non-disclosure or misrepresentation was an effective cause of his entering into the contract or on the terms which he did. He must, therefore, show at least that, but for the relevant non-disclosure or misrepresentation, he would not have entered into the contract on those terms. On the other hand, he does not have to show that it was the sole effective cause of his doing so.[29]

**4.29** In a more recent development, the judge in *Lewis v Norwich Union Healthcare Ltd*[30] stressed that inducement 'is not to do with what a hypothetical prudent underwriter would or would not have done'. It focuses on what the actual underwriter does.

---

26 [1996] 1 All ER 96, 74 BLR 112, [1995] 2 Lloyd's Rep 116, 45 Con LR 89 (CA).

27 See *Marc Rich & Co AG v Portman* [1996] 1 Lloyd's Rep 430 (where the Courts narrowed the scope of inducement) and in *Insurance Corporation of the Channel Islands v Royal Hotel Ltd* (1997) LRLR 20; [1998] Lloyd's Rep IR 151 (where the courts expanded the scope of inducement).

28 [2003] 1 WLR 577.

29 Ibid, p 64.

30 (2009) EW Misc (EWCC).

### Current regulation and legislation under English law

**4.30** The Consumer Insurance (Disclosure and Representations) Act 2012 (UK) received Royal Assent on March 8, 2012. It came into force on April 6, 2013. From the title of the statute, it is clear that it was intended for consumers' insurance contracts and the definition of a consumer insurance contract is found in section 1 of the Act.

**4.31** The relevant provisions of this statute which have a bearing on the duty of disclosure is found in section 2(2), which has usurped the common law and statutory duties laid down in the Marine Insurance Act 1906.

Sections 2(4) and 2(5) provides as follows:

> (4) The duty set out in subsection (2) replaces any duty relating to disclosure or representations by a consumer to an insurer which existed in the same circumstances before this Act applied.
> (5) Accordingly –
>   (a) Any rule of law to the effect that a consumer insurance contract is one of the utmost good faith is modified to the extent required by the provisions of this Act, and
>   (b) The application of section 17 of the Marine Insurance Act 1906, (contracts of marine insurance are of utmost good faith) in relation to a contract of marine insurance which is a consumer insurance contract, is subject to the provisions of this Act.

**4.32** Section 2(2) of the Act has replaced the consumer insured's duty of disclosure with that of 'taking reasonable care not to make a misrepresentation'. Misrepresentation is not defined in the Act but section 2(3) states that

> A failure by the consumer to comply with the insurer's request to confirm or amend particulars previously given is capable of being a misrepresentation for the purposes of this Act (whether or not it could be apart from this subsection).

As such, Parliament has made a significant change to the duty on the part of the consumer insured. The proposer now faces a less daunting task in discharging their duty of good faith in their contractual transactions with insurers.

**4.33** Furthermore, the Statement of Insurance Practice, which is an industry-owned self-imposed guideline, has now been replaced by the Insurance: Conduct of Business (ICOB) Rules introduced by the Financial Services Authority in 2005. In particular, ICOB rule 7.3.6 states:

An insurer must not:

> 1. Unreasonably reject a claim made by a customer;
> 2. Except where there is evidence of fraud, refuse to meet a claim made by a retail customer on the grounds:
>   a. of non-disclosure of a fact material to the risk that the retail customer could not reasonably be expected to have disclosed;
>   b. of misrepresentation of a fact material to the risk, unless the misrepresentation is negligent.

**4.34** Section 3 (3) provides that the standard of care that is required is that of a reasonable consumer which is then restricted by requirements in sections 3 (1), 3 (4) and 3 (5). This restricted form of standard of care places a heavier burden of duty on the part of the insurers and not just solely on the part of the assured. It examines the interactions between the insured and the insurers at the pre-contractual stage on how much information was exchanged between them. This modified standard of care would consist of a dualistic test of a reasonable consumer and the second part would be how the particular consumer insured would have reacted to the information contained in the literature produced by the insurers and the questions that they asked before concluding the insurance contract.

**4.35** One of the more significant development in the Consumer Insurance (Disclosure and Representations) Act 2012 (UK) is the provision for insurers' remedies arising from misrepresentation by the insured.

**4.36** Section 4 (1) of the Act provides remedies for the insurer in the event of misrepresentation or non-disclosure on the part of the insured. The section provides that

> ... an insurer has a remedy against a consumer for a misrepresentation made by the consumer before a consumer insurance contract was entered into or varied only if: -
>
> > (a) the consumer made the misrepresentation in breach of the duty set out in section 2(2), and
> > (b) the insurer shows that without the misrepresentation, that insurer would not have entered into the contract (or agreed to the variation) at all, or would have done so only on different terms.
>
> (2) A misrepresentation for which the insurer has a remedy against the consumer is referred to in this Act as a 'qualifying misrepresentation'.
> (3) The only such remedies available are set out in Schedule 1.

**4.37** The remedies contained in schedule 1 provide a novel but not useful solution to the UK insurance market place. If the insured commits what is termed to be a 'qualifying misrepresentation' and it is either deliberate or reckless, then paragraph (2) of Schedule 1 states that the insurer in subparagraph (a) may avoid the contract and refuse all claims, and subparagraph (b) need not return any of the premiums paid, except to the extent (if any) that it would be unfair to the consumer to retain them.

**4.38** There is a new provision for careless misrepresentations in Schedule 1, and when such careless misrepresentation results in claims, paragraph 3 of Schedule 1 provides that it is a qualifying misrepresentation and will be subjected to paragraphs 4 to 8.

**4.39** Paragraph 4 provides that the insurer's remedies are based on what it would have done if the consumer had complied with the duty set out in section 2(2). Whereas paragraphs 5 through to 8, provide for actions which the insurers are permitted to take in the event of a qualifying misrepresentation.

**4.40** Paragraph 5, provides that if the insurer would not have entered into the consumer insurance contract on any terms, the insurer may avoid the contract and refuse all claims, but must return the premiums paid. Paragraph 6 states that if the insurer would have entered into the consumer insurance contract, but on different terms (excluding terms relating to the premium), the contract is to be treated as if it had been entered into on those different terms if the insurer so requires.

**4.41** It is in paragraphs 7 and 8 of Schedule 1 of the Act that the novelty of proportionality is introduced into the UK insurance marketplace. Although pervasively used in European insurance markets, this is not practised in the UK. Paragraph 7 provides that if the insurer would have entered into the consumer insurance contract (whether the terms relating to matters other than the premium would have been the same or different), but would have charged a higher premium, the insurer may reduce proportionately the amount to be paid on a claim.

**4.42** Paragraph 8 defines what 'reduce proportionately' means, this is when the insurer need pay on the claim only X% (see Table 4.1) of what it would otherwise have been under an obligation to pay under the terms of the contract (or, if applicable, under the different terms provided for by virtue of paragraph 6), where:

$$X = \frac{\text{Premium actually charged}}{\text{Higher premium}} \times 100$$

**4.43** These two subparagraphs will cause most of the problems in practical applications of the law. In using the proportionality principle, the insurer may not entirely avoid the policy, unless there is a fraud. In the event of a breach of good faith, the insurer's liability for loss is reduced in line with the reduction in premium, which the proposer achieved through his misrepresentation or non-disclosure. This practice has been adopted in France and some other European countries. It has also been put forward in the proposed EC Directive on insurance contract law.[31]

*Table 4.1* An example of how the proportionality principle will be computed for an insurance claim

| | |
|---|---|
| Premium charged | £400 |
| Correct premium (if full disclosure) | £500 |
| Actual loss | £10,000 |
| | £8,000 |
| Reduce proportionately: $\dfrac{£400 \times £10,000}{£500}$ | Balance £2,000 borne by the insured |

---

31 Basedow et al (eds), Principles of European Insurance Contract Law (PEICL), Sellier, 2009, whose membership includes two English members who thus represent a common law tradition, including Professor John Birds, University of Manchester, co-editor of MacGillivray on Insurance Law, 12th edn, Sweet & Maxwell, 2012. See further Appendix C on the relationship between the PEICL and a possible proposal from the European Commission for an 'Opt-In' Regulation on Insurance Contract Law. Nevertheless, until the date of this research publication, it would appear that there are more issues that require resolutions due to differences in national law before a harmonized insurance contract law can be achieved.

**4.44** There will be practical constraints when applying this statutory provision in the United Kingdom, as there is no mechanism in place to ensure that the price of the premium is fairly computed. There are no official tariffs or scales of insurance rates in the UK insurance marketplace and this means that what is fair pricing will be then left to the subjective opinion of the particular insurer on trial. It will be difficult for the court to determine the 'correct premium' and this would be open to dispute.

**4.45** Compared with the conventional method that was practised in the United Kingdom previously, where non-disclosure or misrepresentation had resulted in a breach of utmost good faith, the entire £10,000 loss would not be payable. Furthermore, there could also be situations, where had the full facts been disclosed, the insurer would not have taken the risk at all. Proportionality cannot be applied to such cases then. The approach taken would mean that pricing of fair treatment would be left to the subjective assessment of the particular underwriter, and the court not being appraised in matters of pricing for insurance risks would find it very challenging to mete out a fair judgment when it comes to apportioning the correct amount of losses to be deducted from insurance claims.

## The Malaysian treatment of the principle of utmost good faith

**4.46** In Malaysia, the Civil Law Act 1956 (Revised 1972)[32] consolidated the earlier Ordinances and provided for a single source of authority for the application of English laws into Malaysian laws and thereby incorporating English laws where appropriate as a source of law in Malaysia. The application of English law is prescribed in sections 3, 5 and 6.

**4.47** Section 3 (1) provides for the general application of English law. It provides that in absence of written laws in Malaysia, the Court shall in as far as states in

(a) Peninsular Malaysia or any part thereof, apply the common law of England and the rules of equity as administered in England on the 7th day of April 1956; as for (b) Sabah, apply the common law of England and the rules of equity, together with statutes of general application, as administered or in force in England on the 1st day of December, 1951; and for (c) Sarawak, apply the common law of England and the rules of equity, together with statutes of general application, as administered or in force in England on the 12th day of December,1949.

The application of English laws is only possible when 'the circumstances of the States of Malaysia and their respective inhabitants permit and subject to such qualifications as local circumstances render necessary'. This would mean that either the Courts in Malaysia or Parliament has accepted and incorporated English laws into Malaysian laws.

## The reception of English law into Malaysia – cut-off dates

**4.48** What part of English laws are applied to Malaysia? In general, common law precedents, rules of equity and in some instances English statutes of general

---

32 Act 67.

application may be applied by virtue of the provision found in section 3(1) Civil Law Act 1956, with the exception of the expressed restrictions found in the Act, with the first being the absence of local legislation, and the second being the cut-off dates and finally the requirement of 'local circumstances'.

**4.49** In the event that local legislation is absent, there is statutory permission, found in section 3(1) of the Civil Law Act 1956, which empowers judges in Malaysian courts to follow precedents developed under English law to fill in the vacuum that exists in local laws. In the case of *Attorney-General, Malaysia v Manjeet Singh Dhillon*,[33] the Supreme Court held that the absence of specific local legislation concerning contempt of court will allow the common law of contempt as stated in *R v Gray*[34] to be applied under section 3 of the Civil Law Act 1956.

**4.50** The second qualification for application of English law is cut-off dates and as stated for Peninsular Malaysia the date is April 7, 1956, December 12, 1949 for Sarawak and December 1, 1951 for Sabah. In the Privy Council case of *Lee Kee Choong v Empat Nombor Ekor*,[35] their Lordships needed not to consider developments in English law after 1956 because under section 3(1) Civil Law Act 1956 which is *pari materia* to section 3(1)(a) Civil Law Act 1956, 'any subsequent march in English authority is not embodied'.

**4.51** However, despite the clear and categorical wording of section 3(1) to the effect that Malaysian courts shall apply English law existing on the specified dates, in practice, the courts may follow developments in English common law after such dates and our courts often do. English decisions made after such dates, though not binding, are persuasive. This was made clear by the Privy Council in *Jamil bin Harun v Yang Kamsiah* in 1984. This case concerns an appeal from Malaysia, where the counsel for the appellant argued that the Federal Court had erred following the English case of *Lim Poh Choo v Camden & Islington Area Health Authority [1980]*,[36] wherein the decision of the House of Lords, in this case, had allowed for the itemizing of damages in a personal injury case. The Privy Council rejected the argument of the counsel for the appellant, Lord Scarman stating that:

> Their Lordships do not doubt that it is for the courts of Malaysia to decide, subject always to the statute law of the Federation, whether to follow English case law Modern English authorities may be persuasive but are not binding.

**4.52** The Malaysian judiciary has the discretion as to whether they choose to adopt English precedents; but the decision, in this case, had the effect of not only endorsing the judicial practice before *Lee Kee Choong v Empat Nombor Ekor* but also leaving the door open to the continuing reception of principles of English common law and equity into Malaysian laws.

---

33 [1991] 1 MLJ 167.
34 [1900] 2 QB 36.
35 [1976] 2 MLJ 93, 95.
36 AC 174.

**4.53** The third qualification of the general application of English law into Malaysian laws is the 'local circumstances' restriction, that English law applies only to the extent permitted by local circumstances and its inhabitants. English law fits into English society more comfortably as compared to the acceptance of such laws into Malaysia where the local environment and inhabitants may deem it to be an alien system, as English law is premised upon a socially and culturally different society in the United Kingdom. This qualification is found in the concluding provision to section 3(1) and is commonly referred to as the 'local circumstances' proviso.

**4.54** The position adopted by the Malaysian courts has always been that they will adopt legal developments from English law where doing so will expedite the development of insurance law in Malaysia. The Civil Law Act 1956 (Malaysia) provides that where local laws are introduced this then takes priority over the application of English law. With the Financial Services Act 2013 (Malaysia) receiving the Royal Assent on March 18, 2013, the law on disclosure is now governed by section 129.

**4.55** Subsection (1) of section 129 provides that the pre-contractual duty of disclosure and representations for contracts of insurance, and the remedies for misrepresentations relating to contracts of insurance, are set out respectively in Parts 2 and 3 of Schedule 9. Subsection (2) provides that any person who contravenes the duty of disclosure under paragraph 11 of Schedule 9 commits an offense and shall, on conviction, be liable to imprisonment for a term not exceeding five years or to a fine not exceeding RM10 million or to both.

### Pre-contractual duty of disclosure for consumer insurance contracts

**4.56** Schedule 9, paragraph 5 of the Financial Services Act 2013 provides for the pre-contractual duty of disclosure for consumer insurance contracts.

> 5(1) Before a consumer insurance contract is entered into or varied, a licensed insurer may request a proposer who is a consumer to answer any specific questions that are relevant to the decision of the insurer whether to accept the risk or not and the rates and terms to be applied.
>
> (2) It is the duty of the consumer to take reasonable care not to make a misrepresentation to the licensed insurer when answering any questions under subparagraph (1).
>
> (3) Before a consumer insurance contract is renewed, a licensed insurer may either –
>
>   (a) request a consumer to answer one or more specific questions in accordance with subparagraph (1); or
>
>   (b) give the consumer a copy of any matter previously disclosed by the consumer in relation to the contract and request the consumer to confirm or amend any change to that matter.

(4) It is the duty of the consumer to take reasonable care not to make a misrepresentation to the licensed insurer when answering any questions under sub-subparagraph (3) *(a)*, or confirming or amending any matter under sub-subparagraph (3) *(b)*.

(5) If the licensed insurer does not make a request in accordance with subparagraph (1) or (3) as the case may be, compliance with the consumer's duty of disclosure in respect of those subparagraphs shall be deemed to have been waived by the insurer.

(6) Where the consumer fails to answer or gives an incomplete or irrelevant answer to any request by the licensed insurer under subparagraph (1) or sub-subparagraph (3)(a), or fails to confirm or amend any matter under sub-subparagraph (3)(b), or does so incompletely or provides irrelevant information, as the case may be, and the answer or matter was not pursued further by the insurer, compliance with the consumer's duty of disclosure in respect of the answer or matter shall be deemed to have been waived by the insurer.

(7) A licensed insurer shall, before a consumer insurance contract is entered into, varied or renewed, clearly inform the consumer in writing of the consumer's pre-contractual duty of disclosure under this paragraph, and that this duty of disclosure shall continue until the time the contract is entered into, varied or renewed.

(8) Subject to subparagraphs (1) and (3), a consumer shall take reasonable care to disclose to the licensed insurer any matter, other than that in relation to subparagraph (1) or (3), that he knows to be relevant to the decision of the insurer on whether to accept the risk or not and the rates and terms to be applied.

(9) Nothing in this Schedule shall affect the duty of utmost good faith to be exercised by a consumer and licensed insurer in their dealings with each other, including the making and paying off a claim, after a contract of insurance has been entered into, varied or renewed.

**4.57** As for consumer insurance contracts, the rules in the Financial Services Act 2013 mirror the approach taken by English law for the duty of good faith in the UK as contained in the Consumer Insurance (Disclosure and Representations) Act 2012 (UK). This means that for consumer insurance transactions, the common law position would not apply and the proposer is required to take reasonable care not to misrepresent the facts stated therein in the proposal forms or the broking slip or in whatever manner the information may be transmitted to the insurer.

**4.58** This lessens the burden of the consumer which was previously harsh under the older common law rules, where the insured is under a duty of utmost good faith to reveal all he knows or ought reasonably to know in the reasonable course of the business, and to also reveal what the proposer feels will influence the judgement of the prudent insurers as found in the cases that were developed in later parts of the 1990s in the UK.

**4.59** The duty to take reasonable care is further provided for in paragraph 6 of Schedule 9, where the test is that of a reasonable consumer. This means that the courts will take an objective test as far as the proposers are concerned but under prevailing laws in the UK, the insurers are subjected to the subjective test. Paragraph 6(3) and paragraph 7(7)[37] seem to suggest that this will be the measure for insurers where it is stated that:

> 6.(3) If the licensed insurer was, or ought to have been, aware of any particular characteristics or circumstances of the consumer, the insurer shall take into account such characteristics or circumstances.
>
> 7.(7) It is for the licensed insurer to show that a misrepresentation was deliberate or reckless on a balance of probability.

**4.60** The obvious issue arising from this is the equity of adopting two different tests for the same area of law in insurance contract disputes. The insurer now bears the burden of proving that misrepresentation was a deliberate or reckless act by the insured and adducing evidence to prove that such acts have taken place will be difficult for insurers. If, however, the insurers can provide such evidence then they may avoid the contract altogether and refuse all claims with the proviso for life assurance being that the contract of life assurance is effective for not more than two years.

**4.61** Section 16 (4) of the Financial Services Act 2013 (Malaysia) introduced the proportionality principle into the payment of claims and the courts in Malaysia will also be affected by the same issue that the courts in the UK will be confronted with. Furthermore, in 2018, the Malaysian insurance industry had embarked on a de-tarrification exercise, where the determination of risks pricing is left to insurers to create greater competitiveness in the insurance marketplace. This means that like the UK, we will not have an established pricing mechanism to ensure that proportionality is based on a fair and objective pricing mechanism but instead will be exposed to the vagaries of subjective pricing determination of individual underwriters and their experience which will result in more legal challenges.

### The Australian treatment on the duty of utmost good faith in insurance contracts

**4.62** Australia modelled their insurance law on that of English law until 1984 and this included the development of common law which except for minor variations is identical to the development of English law.

**4.63** Divergence between the two jurisdictions emerged in the 1970s as the UK was subjected to the changes as required by the EC Directives and released a report in 1980 to chart the course for the UK in the adoption of the EC Directive, which

---

37 See Schedule 9, paras 6 and 7 of the Financial Services Act 2013.

has a direct implication on English law in the areas of disclosure requirements for insurance contracts. Nevertheless, implementation of the report was shelved and recommendations not acted upon until it was revived much later in 2012.[38]

**4.64** The Australian attempt to review insurance law, on the other hand, proved to be more successful as the Australian Law Commission under the chairmanship of Justice Michael Kirby then went on to produce report No.20 Insurance Contracts in 1982, which was duly passed by the Australian Parliament, with some important amendments to the proposed Bill, and which became the Insurance Contracts Act 1984.[39] The Insurance Contracts Act, however, does not apply to marine insurance contracts which have to cater to a more international requirement, bearing in mind the Marine Insurance Act 1906 (UK) is often the basis of overwhelming numbers of reinsurance contracts.

**4.65** The substantive change made to the duty of utmost good faith was the virtual abolition of the duty of disclosure in certain forms of domestic policies.

**4.66** The Insurance Contracts Act 1984[40] did not remove the concept of good faith but retains it. Section 12 describes good faith to be a paramount requirement to which the remainder of the 1984 Act and other laws are subject. Nevertheless, the 1984 statute alters the nature of good faith fundamentally. The discussion in the following paragraphs explain the structure of the legislation and its operation is then examined in detail.

**4.67** What is abundantly clear is that there is now a separation of non-disclosure and misrepresentation from the duty of utmost good faith. The duty of utmost good faith is contained in section 13 of the 1984 Act and is defined as follows:

> A contract of insurance is based on the utmost good faith and there is implied in such a contract a provision requiring each party to it to act towards the other party, in respect of any matter arising under or in relation to it, with the utmost good faith.

**4.68** Based on section 13 of the Act, the duty of utmost good faith is now an implied term in contracts of insurance. This governs the relationship between the parties to the contract. The provision serves to regulate their dealings with each before entering the contract, as the term 'in relation to it' suggests, and during the currency of the contract. Furthermore, section 14 of the Act provides that parties to the contract cannot rely on any other terms other than good faith. The breach of the duty of good faith is a breach of contract, and this will give rise to a claim for damages or estoppel but will not allow the grieving party to avoid the contract *ab initio*.

**4.69** Although the duty of utmost good faith is bilateral, the provisions of the Insurance Act 1984 suggest that the burden has been shifted more to the insurers rather than as previously borne by the insured. Two observations can be made

---

38 Robert Merkin, A Report for the English and Scottish Law Commissions on the Australian Experience of Insurance Law Reform – Reforming Insurance Law: Is there a Case for Reverse Transportation?, 2015.
39 Act No 80 of 1984.
40 Ibid.

on the statute that affirms this phenomenon. First, section 14 (3) singles out insurers to not rely on policy provisions that may result in them breaching good faith. The fact that a statutory provision is created to identify the insurers as a party to the contract who may rely on unfair policy terms in the course of business would suggest that the insurers tend to rely on policy terms to deny claims. This is a negative perspective to paint insurers in, as the burden has shifted to them to demonstrate that they have not breached utmost good faith when using policy terms. Second, under section 12 the assured is not required to make any disclosure to the insurers unless it falls within the assured's entirely distinct pre-contractual obligation of disclosure, this means that the insurers' duty is more onerous than that of the assured.

**4.70** This clear shift from the insured's burden of the strict requirements to comply with the duty of utmost good faith as laid down in common law cases prior to 1984 indicates Australian's parliament intentions to strike a fairer and more balanced approach towards consumer insurance contracts.

**4.71** The Australian Insurance Contracts Act 1984, which are now amended by the Insurance Contract (Amendment) Act 2013,[41] contains a similar provision to the original Insurance Contracts Act 1984 in as far as the duty of utmost good faith is concerned. Nevertheless, there are some significant changes made to protect the insured even more and this is found in section 21 of the amended Act, but it is subjected to three significant limitations. The first is that the test of materiality is now based on the prudent assured and not the prudent underwriter.

**4.72** Section 21A of the amended Act provides that unless insurers have asked specific questions the duty of disclosure is waived for most forms of domestic policy; and under section 22 now requires the insurers to inform the assured of the existence of the duty of disclosure, and if they have failed to perform this duty the insurers cannot rely on it unless they can prove fraud on the part of the insured. Insurers are granted remedies for non-disclosure under section 28 of the Insurance Contracts Act 1984 and this has not changed. Section 28 affects general insurance contracts. Section 28 (2) provides that if the failure was fraudulent or the misrepresentation was made fraudulently, the insurer may avoid the contract and in (3) If the insurer is not entitled to avoid the contract or, be entitled to avoid the contract (whether under subsection (2) or otherwise), the liability of the insurer in respect of a claim is reduced to the amount that would place the insurer in a position in which the insurer would have been if the failure had not occurred or the misrepresentation had not been made.

**4.73** We observed again that for remedies the same approach is taken in the Australian statutory provision. Again, where the marketplace does not rely on a standard published set of pricing, reliance will be based on the subjective pricing opinion of the underwriter on trial and may not produce the intended fairness to the insured.

---

41 Act No 75, 2013.

## The future of utmost good faith in insurance contracts: is the application of utmost good faith in insurance contracts dead?

**4.74** In the development of English law of utmost good faith, Lord Mansfield had not used the term 'utmost good faith' in his seminal judgment in *Carter v Boehm*. The term he used was 'good faith'. In subsequent cases concerning insurance matters, Lord Mansfield had consistently used the term good faith and not 'utmost' good faith.[42] The term utmost good faith was added on in later cases and this contrasted Lord Mansfield's decisions in cases that appeared before his lordship. Lord President Inglis in *Life Association of Scotland v Foster* adopted the term *uberrima fides* or utmost good faith.[43] In the case *Rozanes v Bowen*,[44] Lord Justice Scrutton explicitly refers to the insurance contract being the contract of utmost good faith. In his judgment, Lord Justice Scrutton placed emphasis on the imbalance of information between parties to the contract and said:

> It has been for centuries in England the law in connection with insurance of all sorts, marine, fire, life, guarantee and every kind of policy that, as the underwriter knows nothing and the man who comes to him to ask him to insure knows everything, it is the duty of the assured, the man who desires to have a policy, to make full disclosure to the underwriters without being asked of all the material circumstances, because the underwriter knows *nothing and the assured knows everything. That is expressed by saying that it is a contract of the utmost good faith – 'uberrima fides'.*[45]

**4.75** The term utmost good faith was later incorporated into the Marine Insurance Act 1906. Section 17 of the Marine Insurance Act 1906 provides that: 'A contract of marine insurance is a contract based upon the utmost good faith and, if utmost good faith is not observed by either party, the contract may be avoided by the other party'.

## Resurrection of utmost good faith – striking a more balanced approach

**4.76** Section 17 of the Marine Insurance Act 1906 has now been modified by section 2(2) of The Consumer Insurance (Disclosure and Representations) Act 2012 (UK). The consumer insured's duty of disclosure now only requires the proposer or insured to take 'reasonable care not to make a misrepresentation'. Misrepresentation exists only when there is a 'failure by the consumer to comply with the insurer's request to confirm or amend particulars previously given is capable of being a misrepresentation for the purposes of this Act (whether or not it could be apart from this subsection)'.[46]

---

42 *Noble v Kennoway* (1780) 99 Eng Rep 326; *Mayne v Walter* (1782) 99 Eng Rep 548; *Frier v Woodhouse* (1817) 171 Eng Rep 345.
43 *Life Association of Scotland v Foster* (1873) 11 M. 351.
44 (1928) 32 L.I.L.R. 98.
45 Ibid, p 102 (emphasis added).
46 Section 2 (3) The Consumer Insurance (Disclosure and Representations) Act 2012.

**4.77** In Australian law, section 17 of the Marine Insurance Act 1906 is mirrored, word for word, in section 23 of the Marine Insurance Act 1909 (Australia). Nevertheless, this changed by virtue of the Insurance Contracts Act 1984 where section 13 provides a

> contract of insurance is based on the utmost good faith and there is implied in such a contract a provision requiring each party to it to act towards the other party, in respect of any matter arising under or in relation to it, with the utmost good faith.

**4.78** Analysis of the earlier part of this chapter indicates a shift of the burden to discharge the duty of good faith to the insurers rather than the insured. The move towards reinforcing the burden on the part of insurers is now encapsulated in section 21 of the Insurance Contracts (Amendment) Act 2013.

**4.79** While in Malaysia, the recently enacted Financial Services Act 2013, would be the first time Malaysia has codified the common law principle of utmost good faith into statute law. Schedule 9, paragraph 5 (2), (4) and (5) requires the insured or proposer to the insurance contract to take reasonable care not to make a misrepresentation. The onus to make enquiries for information or to follow-up on incomplete information is placed upon the shoulders of the insurers. Otherwise, the duty of disclosure is deemed waived by the insurers.

**4.80** Based on these observations made of the English, Australian and Malaysian laws, it is clear that the law on utmost good faith for insurance contracts is certainly not dead but indeed it has evolved. What is clear is the shift of the burden to discharge the duty of disclosure from being imposed heavily on the part of the insured to being shared by the insurers. Interestingly the term utmost good faith can only be seen in the Australian legislation and has disappeared from the English and Malaysian statutes. This may be alluded to as being the death knell of utmost good faith in its original form but this detracts the intentions of the new legislative provisions in the UK, Australia and Malaysia to enhance consumer protection and provide a more level playing field for the mass consumer. Perhaps this could also be seen as an attempt to place greater emphasis on the other part of the statement that Lord Mansfield has made in *Carter v Boehm* of ensuring the limited circumstances for which an underwriter can exercise their rights upon the breach of good faith. Indeed, the wheel of justice has come one round to ensure that this part of Lord Mansfield's judgment should be given the equivalent emphasis.

**4.81** Good faith as enunciated in *Carter v Boehm* was consistent with the legal principles laid out in the law of contracts, in that the test is whether the party who is the victim to misrepresentation has been induced by the terms of the misrepresentation and had then entered into the contract under terms they had not contracted for. The test of inducement is therefore subjective. Nevertheless, a 'prudent insurer' has been held by the courts to mean a 'reasonable' insurer. Primarily, the confusion could have arisen from the provisions contained in section 18(2),[47]

---

47  Marine Insurance Act 1906.

where it is stated that, 'every circumstance is material which would influence the judgment of a prudent insurer in fixing premium, or determining whether he will take the risk'. This had led to attempts by courts to substitute the test of influencing the judgement of the particular insured (subjective test) to test the 'prudent insurer' (objective test).[48]

**4.82** The earlier decisions such as *Bates v Hewitt* sees the court favouring the insurer in the exercise of the duty of good faith where it was evident that the court was easing the application of the weight of the duty even where the insurer had constructive knowledge of the material fact but they were not required by the court to probe further in exercising the duty of good faith. Shee J acknowledged that the insurer had constructive knowledge of the material facts relevant in the case but found that the insurer was under no onus to make enquiries.

**4.83** The more recent cases have seen courts moving away from the objective test to the subjective test, which brings consideration of the weight of the test to be aligned with the requirements of the law on misrepresentation, that the test is a subjective test, and this is consistent with precedents in the law of contracts.

**4.84** The contemporaneous law on utmost good faith for insurance contracts focuses on the insured's knowledge of the risks and how he or she has represented the facts of the risks as a prudent assured would in reaction to the information provided by the insurers and the questions asked by them. There is clearly a shift of burden of the disclosure requirements to the insurers in the pre-contractual role that they played and not just relying on the insured's representation alone. This approach is adopted by the Consumer Disclosure and Representation Act 2012 (UK), Insurance Contracts Amendment Act (2013) Australia and the Financial Services Act 2013 (Malaysia).

**4.85** The introduction of statutory protection created a more balanced and consumer friendly duty of disclosure, on the other hand treatment of negligent misrepresentation through the mechanism of proportionality may be seen as being unfair as insurers can reduce their loss proportionally based on the revised premium to be charged over the actual premium charged. As the test is subjective, the pricing mechanism resides only in the mind of the particular underwriter who is now representing the insurer in a court trial with the insured. In such an antagonistic environment of a court trial, the insured would surely feel disadvantaged by reference only to the underwriter's opinion on the determination of the actual rates and hence the pricing of the risk leading to a reduced claim payment.

**4.86** This point alone may defeat all the good work that lawmakers have made in these jurisdictions to afford better consumer protection for insurance contracts that they have entered into which in the past has seemed to lean in favour of insurers. The resolution towards this anomaly may be to step out of the box of legal precedents and develop an approach that is more transparent in the determination

---

48 Lowry, Rawlings and Merkin, n 12, p 89.

of the pricing mechanism. One approach may be to enable the court to seek expert help by way of reference to a professional institution where a national level database of risks pricing is established and such pricing is determined objectively by individuals who have no relation to the court trial underway and is not associated to the parties in dispute in any manner. The database for risk pricing should be verified and certified as accurate by an appointed independent actuary to ensure that the highest level of transparency is established.

## Conclusion

**4.87** The criticism on misrepresentation and non-disclosure is that it weighed unfairly against the insured, that is, although the insured may have acted honestly if a non-disclosure or a misrepresentation of the material fact had occurred, the insurers would normally proceed to 'avoid' the policy.

**4.88** The way in which 'material fact' is defined in law and that the 'prudent underwriter' views are not known by the insured as the issues surrounding the legal requirement of knowing what will or will not affect the judgment of a prudent underwriter is mired in complexities and requires the ability to burrow into the mind of the said underwriter.

**4.89** Proposals for reforms have come from many quarters including the Law Reform Committee in 1957, European Commission in 1979 and the Law Commission in 1980, and in 2006 the English and Scottish Law Commissions launched a second joint investigation into the law of insurance after the first yielded no legal consequences. Three issue papers were published in 2006 and 2007, and after consultation, a consolidated paper, Misrepresentation, Non-Disclosure, and Breach of Warranty by the Insured, appeared in July 2007. This resulted in the passing of the Consumer Insurance (Disclosure and Representations) Act 2012 (UK). In Australia, where the initiative first began with the introduction of the Insurance Contracts Act 1984 and the subsequent amendments made in 2013 through the Insurance Contracts (Amendment) Act 2013, we can see governments through the process of law makings adopting a fairer and softer approach in dealing with the mass consumer market. The same could be said of the efforts in Malaysia with the introduction of the Financial Services Act 2013.[49]

**4.90** Nevertheless, what could derail the exuberance of better consumer protection is perhaps the approach taken by these legislations in addressing the remedies to negligent misrepresentation where the proportionality principle is applied in all three jurisdictions examined in this chapter. The notion that claims settlement (computed based on proportionality) is dependent upon the correct risk premium pricing, which is based mostly on a mixture of the underwriter's own experience of their risk portfolios and reinsurance rates (mostly subjective

---

49  Act 758.

in nature) be used as the benchmark for fair valuation of claims payment is highly questionable.

**4.91** A fairer approach is to adopt a national pricing approach which is based on underwriting experience of all indemnity classes of insurance to be developed and actuary certified as the basis of determining the price to be introduced as a provision in future versions of the statutory laws. This idea may not, however, be popular as there are further cost implications and this may not be attractive viz-a-viz the number of cases brought to courts for negligent misrepresentation. However, if the issue is not addressed, this will be the proverbial sticking out like a sore thumb in the development of the law concerning the utmost good faith in insurance contracts.

CHAPTER 5

# Objectivity

## J. W. Carter and Michael Furmston*

## Introduction

**5.1** The common law of contract usually applies an objective approach when working out whether—and on what terms—a contract has been agreed. An objective process called 'construction' (or 'interpretation') is also used to generate conclusions about the intended meaning of a contract. This concern with objectivity at the level of process does not deny the importance of subjective ('actual') intention at the level of purpose or goal. To remain faithful to purpose, notice is sometimes taken of actual knowledge and beliefs. Indeed, the extent to which objectivity is (or should be) preferred over a subjective approach to intention is often debated.[1]

**5.2** Adoption of the objective approach by the common law is sometimes portrayed as a change of heart, a departure from eighteenth- and nineteenth-century cases preferring subjectivity.[2] Concrete support for this is actually quite difficult to find. Of course, in the past as much as today, different judges say different things. It is dangerous to generalise from particular instances, or to ignore historical context. For example, when attempting to explain how the order of contractual performance—'whose turn first?'—should be determined, in *Kingston v Preston*[3] Lord Mansfield said much depends on 'the intent of the transaction'. Any thought[4] that he saw the inquiry as subjective is betrayed by the fact that in

* Our thanks to Patrick Hall for research assistance.

1 See, e.g., William Howarth, 'The Meaning of Objectivity in Contract' (1984) 100 *LQR* 265; J P Vorster, 'A Comment on The Meaning of Objectivity in Contract' (1987) 103 *LQR* 274 (and reply by William Howarth (1987) 103 *LQR* 527); Anne De Moor, 'Intention in the Law of Contract: Elusive or Illusory' (1990) 106 *LQR* 632; David McLauchlan, 'A Contract Contradiction' (1999) 30 *VUWLR* 175; Brian Coote, 'Reflections on Intention in the Law of Contract' [2006] *NZ Law Review* 183 (*Contract as Assumption II: Formation, Performance and Enforcement*, J W Carter, ed., Hart Publishing, Oxford, 2016, Ch 2); David McLauchlan, 'Contract Formation and Subjective Intention' (2017) 34 *JCL* 41.

2 See *Taylor v Johnson* (1983) 151 CLR 422 at 428–30 per Mason ACJ, Murphy and Deane JJ.

3 (1773) 2 Doug 689 at 690; 99 ER 437.

4 Cf P S Atiyah, *The Rise and Fall of Freedom of Contract*, Clarendon Press, Oxford, 1979, pp 213, 424. Different views about subjectivity may reflect competing versions of the 'will theory'. Cf *Cundy v Lindsay* (1878) 3 App Cas 459; *Air Great Lakes Pty Ltd v K S Easter (Holdings) Pty Ltd* (1985) 2 NSWLR 309 at 335 per McHugh JA; Michael Furmston, *Cheshire, Fifoot & Furmston's Law of Contract*, 17th edn, Oxford University Press, Oxford, 2017, pp 15–18.

Lord Mansfield's time 'intent' could be used in the sense of 'intendment',[5] that is, the meaning attached by the common law. He was therefore searching for what are now termed 'default' rules to be applied in construction, not advocating a subjective approach.

**5.3** It is also common to say that civil law systems apply a subjective test for intention. Examination of this in detail is outside the scope of this chapter but it is, we think, clearly an oversimplification. There is an excellent discussion by Hugh Beale.[6] The laws of France and Germany are clearly not the same, and German law has flirted with objectivity. An instructive German hypothetical concerns the Trier Wine Auction. A comes from another part of Germany to visit Trier, the birthplace of Karl Marx and a centre for Moselle. Trier is a somewhat remote city, which A has not visited before. While there, A goes to look for a friend, who happens to be at a wine auction. The auction is in progress and the auctioneer is taking bids. A sees the friend and waves. By the custom of Trier, the wave is treated as a bid and the auctioneer knocks the wine down to A. We shall come back to this story.

## Purpose, rules and a presumption

**5.4** What seems to us of fundamental importance is that the purpose of the objective process—and therefore the objective theory of contract—is always to determine actual intention. *Consensus ad idem* (a 'meeting of minds') remains essential to the formation of any contract[7] and the goal of any construction exercise is to arrive at a reliable conclusion about actual intention.

**5.5** *Williston on Contracts* says:[8] 'Mutual assent is to be judged by overt acts and words rather than by the hidden, subjective or secret intention of the parties'. The statement runs together a number of ideas, some of which are more central to objectivity than others. It treats subjectivity and secrecy as necessarily connected. Certainly, there are restrictions on the ability of a party to assert a subjective view. So A cannot usually say that, to A, 'apples' means 'US Dollars'. But as we illustrate later, even when the overt act is signature on a document, the restrictions are by no means total.[9]

**5.6** In addition, saying that 'mutual assent' is 'judged by overt acts' merely calls up the objective process, and is not quite the same as saying that subjective intention plays no role and must be ignored. For example, assume B alleges a

---

5 The sense is now regarded as obsolete by the *Oxford English Dictionary*.

6 Hugh Beale, Bénédicte Fauvarque-Cosson, Jacobien Rutgers and Stefan Vogenauer, *Cases, Materials and Text on Contract Law*, Hart Publishing, Oxford, 2019, especially Chs 5, 8 and 14.

7 See, e.g., *R v Clarke* (1927) 40 CLR 227 at 239 per Higgins J; *Shogun Finance Ltd v Hudson* [2004] 1 AC 919 at 947; [2003] UKHL 62 at [55] per Lord Hobhouse (with whom Lord Walker agreed).

8 R A Lord, *Williston on Contracts*, 4th edn, Lawyers Cooperative Publishing, New York, Vol 1, §4.1. See also O W Holmes, *The Common Law*, M De W Howe, ed., Little Brown & Co, Boston, 1963, p 242 (the law 'must go by externals').

9 But cf Murray Gleeson, 'The Objectivity of Contractual Interpretation' in Hugh Dillon, ed., *Advocacy and Judging: Selected Papers of Murray Gleeson*, Federation Press, Sydney, 2017, p 283.

contract with A in circumstances where (1) A has no such intention, but (2) a reasonable person would infer an intention to contract from A's 'overt acts and words' and (3) B knows fact (1). In these circumstances, the common law would not usually allow B to deny knowledge of A's lack of intention, that is, allow B to use the objective process as a shield against reality.[10]

**5.7** Many contract rules emphasise the objective process, including to establish *consensus ad idem*. These rules serve important purposes. Take, for example, the humble rule that an offeree must communicate acceptance of the offer, unless dispensed with by the offeror. As a matter of fact a 'meeting of minds' will precede any overt act of acceptance. The rule requiring communication ensures that the offeree's cognitive assent is not sufficient in itself to create a contract.[11] A different rule would in practice be unworkable. Whether the postal acceptance 'exception' to the rule truly reflects the objective approach might be debated.

**5.8** The starting point under the objective approach—and very often the finishing point—is that the purport of an expression of intention depends on the conclusion of a reasonable person. Pivotal to this is a presumption that actual intention is the intention manifested by an utterance, as it would be understood by a reasonable person ('objective intention'). Contract lawyers therefore side with Alice at the tea party:[12] 'I mean what I say' and 'I say what I mean' are 'the same thing'. A written contract is similarly presumed to state the parties' actual intention. However, since the 'construction of the contract' is a conclusion about the intention shared by (common to) two or more people, 'intention' is necessarily a 'construct', based on the document and such other raw material as is admissible under substantive rules of the law of contract.

**5.9** Just about any presumption that operates under contract law can be displaced or rebutted. For various reasons, some are stronger than others. The presumption central to the objective approach—that objective intention and actual intention coincide—is difficult to shift because it is fortified by technical rules. These often prevent recourse to raw material that might otherwise be used to displace or rebut the presumption. Importantly, direct evidence of actual intention is inadmissible in construction.[13]

**5.10** Key aspects of the objective approach nevertheless remain unclear. Should the approach be applied on the basis that the reasonable person whose views determine intention stands in the position of one of the parties? Or is the reasonable person detached from both? If the former, is the position that of the speaker (or promisor) or the addressee (or promisee)? Or should 'stance' vary according to the circumstances? Support for all these views can be found in the cases and

---

10 See *Paal Wilson & Co A/S v Partenreederei Hannah Blumenthal* [1983] 1 AC 854 at 915–17 per Lord Diplock, 924 per Lord Brightman.

11 See *Brogden v Metropolitan Railway Co* (1877) 2 App Cas 666 at 688 per Lord Selborne, 691 per Lord Blackburn. The classic example is *Felthouse v Bindley* (1862) 11 CBns 869; 142 ER 1037.

12 Lewis Carroll, *Alice's Adventures in Wonderland*, 1865, Ch 7.

13 *Reardon Smith Line Ltd v Yngvar Hansen-Tangen* [1976] 1 WLR 989 at 996 per Lord Wilberforce (with whom Viscount Dilhorne and Lords Simon and Kilbrandon agreed).

literature. Further issues relate to what information the reasonable person should be taken to know, how the information can be used and its weight or significance. For example, can all the information be applied directly in the construction process, or must some be given a purely circumstantial role? A thorny issue relates to the use of commercial purpose to resolve construction questions.[14]

**5.11** Notwithstanding the importance of the proposition that actual intention must usually be deduced within the framework of an objective approach, it is no less important that situations will arise in which objectivity must yield to the circumstances. Actual beliefs and understandings may then be directly relevant. Since the presumption on which the law relies is by no means conclusive, objective intention is not the sole concern. As Lord Phillips said in *Shogun Finance Ltd v Hudson*:[15]

> … the task of ascertaining whether the parties have reached agreement as to the terms of a contract can involve quite a complex amalgam of the objective and the subjective and involve the application of a principle that bears close comparison with the doctrine of estoppel.

Diversity of view about matters such as what the objective approach entails likewise shows that the contrast between objectivity and subjectivity is by no means a crisp one. Indeed, although a court may say that it is solely concerned with objective intention, we doubt that this is always accurate.

### Focus of discussion

**5.12** This chapter focuses more on the means by which courts strive to give effect to actual intention than on how the technical rules associated with the objective theory are applied. However, technical rules provide some of the context.

**5.13** Discussion divides naturally between objectivity in contract formation (is there a contract?) and objectivity in construction (what does the contract mean?).[16] It is convenient to take construction first. Since the topic of implied terms to some extent straddles the divide, we also discuss the role of objectivity in the process of implying terms.

### What does the contract mean?

**5.14** Some contract disputes boil down to a very basic question: 'What does the contract mean?'. Under the objective approach, intended meaning is the meaning a reasonable person would attribute to the parties, taking factual context ('background' or 'surrounding circumstances') into account. The fact that many leading

---

14 Compare *Rainy Sky SA v Kookmin Bank* [2011] 1 WLR 2900; [2011] UKSC 50 and *Wood v Capita Insurance Services Ltd* [2017] AC 1173; [2017] UKSC 24.

15 [2004] 1 AC 919 at 964; [2003] UKHL 62 at [123].

16 It is unnecessary to deal with the use of construction to determine the legal effect of a contract.

cases have concerned meaning questions shows that 'basic' cannot be equated with 'easy to resolve'. But whether the question is easy or difficult, the answer is nearly always unique to the contract (or other utterance) at issue.[17] On that basis, recourse to precedent is pointless.[18] The fact that in some earlier case a court gave a particular meaning to a disputed word or expression has no bearing on the dispute.

**5.15** Three critical points are illustrated below:

(1) even when the contract is in documentary form, restrictions on the use of evidence to explain what the parties mean are not total;

(2) a real understanding of a contract (or other utterance) often has both subjective and objective elements the balance between which is infinitely variable; and

(3) what is depicted as the conclusion of a reasonable person is often the product of a concerted effort to get at the meaning actually intended.

**5.16** Assume the A Bank and the B Bank enter into a contractual relationship under which each working day they will trade between 11:45 and 12:15 in US Dollars, Euros, Pounds Sterling and Japanese Yen. The transactions are to be by email and the banks are worried about security. It is agreed that the emails will talk of apples, oranges, bananas and plums and that the written contract will not disclose the currencies delineated. The relationship between fruits (and therefore currencies) is to float daily on a carefully structured basis. Assume a dispute arises. It will surely be open to a party to give evidence that, in the circumstances, 'apples' means 'US Dollars'.[19] The rationale is that the parties' actual intention in relation to the words used must be established as a matter of fact before the objective approach can be applied, that is, to construe the contract. In short, the 'key' to the parties' code must be established by evidence.[20]

**5.17** A single word may of course have many different meanings. Sometimes the meanings may be close and the differences subtle. If A says 'I expect it will rain tomorrow', A is expressing an opinion or making a forecast and, even if a professional weather forecaster, A is not asserting any control over the weather, or assuming contractual responsibility for tomorrow being a rainy day.[21] On the other hand, if Albert says of his son, 'I expect Simon to do his homework before supper', there may be an element of direction or admonition in the statement. It is possible for the word 'expect' to have both meanings at the same time as in Nelson's famous signal on the morning of Trafalgar, 'England expects that every man will do his duty'.

---

17 An important exception is a conclusion about the meaning a third-party standard form, such as the Law Society's *Standard Conditions of Sale*.

18 See, e.g., *Deeny v Gooda Walker Ltd (in liq)* [1996] 1 WLR 426 at 435 per Lord Hoffmann. But some words and expressions are taken to have *prima facie* meanings even if in common use (e.g., 'month' means a calendar month).

19 See *Falck v Williams* [1900] AC 176.

20 Cf *Chartbrook Ltd v Persimmon Homes Ltd* [2009] 1 AC 1101 at 1122; [2009] UKHL 38 at [45] per Lord Hoffmann with whom the other members of the House of Lords agreed ('private dictionary' principle).

21 At least at common law, A could do so. See *Canham v Barry* (1855) 15 CB 597; 139 ER 558. But see Samuel Stoljar, 'Promise, Expectation and Agreement' [1988] *CLJ* 193 at 198.

**5.18** It is interesting that Nelson's original draft of the signal said 'confides', which would have been used in the now somewhat dated sense of 'entrusts'. But the Flag Lieutenant pointed out that 'confides' would have to be spelled letter by letter whereas 'expect' has a single flag. Nelson's signal can be said to have both an objective aspect (as a forecast) and a subjective aspect (as a requirement). The reference to 'England' puts Nelson's actual intention to include the latter aspect beyond doubt. Returning to the previous example, if Simon's sister made the same statement as his father, we should usually treat it as forecasting, but there are families where an older sister is as likely to give instructions as her parent— perhaps more likely. Should the issue arise, much will turn on the relationship in the particular family, a matter that might be proved by evidence.

**5.19** Whether an objective or a subjective approach is being applied, account may need to be taken of the fact that different people may use the same word to mean different things. This is not necessarily a matter of idiosyncrasy or even subjective preference. To take an apparently simple example, North Americans talk of 'pants' when the English will speak of 'trousers', using pants for the undergarments. However, research has shown that the use of pants to mean the outer garments is common in the north west of England.[22]

**5.20** When the lady at the beginning of Albee's *Who's Afraid of Virginia Woolf*, 1962, tells us that she wears the pants this is not a sartorial statement but tells us that in her relationship with the man in her life, she is the boss. Now that ladies wear pants (trousers) all the time, another metaphor may be needed to convey the same message.

**5.21** In the contract context, for example, if a seller in the north west of England sells 'pants' to a southern buyer, whose meaning prevails? It seems fair to say that English law does not deal very satisfactorily with this sort of issue. The subjective and objective approaches lead to different conclusions. Indeed, the objective approach may do the same. Meaning will differ according to whether the reasonable person who is taken to construe the contract stands in the position of the seller or the buyer. At another level, meaning may depend on what question must be asked as a matter of law. Is it whether the buyer is actually aware of the seller's usage, or is the question whether the technical rules on 'custom and usage' are satisfied?[23]

**5.22** In his judgment in *Mannai Investment Co Ltd v Eagle Star Life Assurance Co Ltd*[24] and in a recent article[25] Lord Hoffmann refers to Mrs Malaprop in an instructive way. In *Mannai* he says:[26]

> No one, for example, has any difficulty in understanding Mrs Malaprop. When she says 'She is as obstinate as an allegory on the banks of the Nile,' we reject the conventional or literal meaning of allegory as making nonsense of the sentence

---

22 *The Economist*, 8 July 2017, p 70.

23 See JW Carter, *The Construction of Commercial Contracts*, Hart Publishing, Oxford, 2013, Ch 12 (matter depends on applicable 'standard of interpretation').

24 [1997] AC 749.

25 Leonard Hoffmann, 'Language and Lawyers' (2018) 134 *LQR* 553.

26 [1997] AC 749 at 774. In fact, 'obstinate' should read 'headstrong'.

and substitute 'alligator' by using our background knowledge of the things likely to be found on the banks of the Nile and choosing one which sounds rather like 'allegory'.

This raises a number of interesting questions.

**5.23** It is clear that Mrs Malaprop gets words wrong. However, the error is of a special kind. Her usages are idiosyncratic, and therefore inherently subjective, but since they follow a pattern (and to that extent are systematic) her usages may also have objective significance. Today, the nature of Mrs Malaprop's mistake is widely known and discussion usually starts from that base, but Sheridan was not speaking to us but to the first night audience of *The Rivals* at Drury Lane in 1775. Mrs Malaprop makes so many mistakes that most of the audience would recognize that she gets words wrong and at some stage many will appreciate the nature of her idiosyncrasy. Sheridan helps the audience by giving them a big clue, Mrs Malaprop's name. The use of the word 'malapropism'[27] to describe this kind of mistake goes back to the beginning of the seventeenth century. The first example in the *Oxford English Dictionary* is from 1630. Surely, some of the first night audience would have been familiar with the word.

**5.24** How do we reach the conclusion that when Mrs Malaprop says 'allegory' she means 'alligator'? The objective test for intention would not allow her to say so, but in any case she could not say so because she does not know. Lord Hoffmann's solution is that there are many alligators on the banks of the Nile. Although Sheridan may have thought the same, in fact no alligators bask on the banks of Nile. The animals are crocodiles. Crocodiles have been known in Europe and the Near East for many centuries. The original name was Greek. There were very probably crocodiles on the Nile when Mark Anthony visited Cleopatra. Alligators come from China or what are now the southern states of the United States. When Spanish colonists met alligators for the first time in what is now Florida they could be forgiven for thinking they saw crocodiles and in fact the colonists used the same word for both animals (*largato*).

**5.25** To return to Mrs Malaprop, as we have said, the 'big clue' is the name given by Sheridan. The clue does not lie in Lord Hoffmann's 'background knowledge of the things likely to be found on the banks of the Nile'. On his approach we could make nothing of Mrs Malaprop's reference to Captain Absolute (another character in the play) as 'the very pine-apple of politeness'. The point is simply the nature of her usage errors. To her, 'pine-apple' means 'pinnacle'. Lord Hoffmann acknowledges this point when discussing different examples in his recent article. But however the passage in *Mannai* is examined, it seems to us clear that Lord Hoffmann's purpose was not to arrive at objective meaning. Mrs Malaprop does not always mean what she says and his concern was to reach a conclusion on what she actually means by 'allegory'. Although Lord Hoffmann's analysis is ostensibly objective, a reliable conclusion can

---

27 See Chris Baldick, *The Concise Oxford Dictionary of Literary Terms*, Oxford University Press, Oxford, 1990, p 128 ('after the French *mal à propos*, 'inappropriately").

only be arrived at by bringing Mrs Malaprop's language proclivity into account. Carrying over this analysis to a communication such as an alleged offer might perhaps be controversial.

## Is there a contract?

*Introduction*

**5.26** In relation to contract formation, if the objective approach applied under English law habitually led to results that conflict with what parties actually intend, it seems reasonable to say that the approach would by now have been forsaken. Longevity reflects success and the measure of that success can only be that the objective approach usually yields results that conform to actual intention or, as is sometimes said,[28] give effect to the 'reasonable expectations' of contracting parties.

**5.27** Choice between the two approaches by a legal system is unlikely to be based on a perception that one is right and the other wrong. Choice seems largely historical, and a reflection of contrasting views about how intention disputes *ought* to be resolved. Some guidance on the extent to which the common law prefers objectivity over subjectivity may be obtained by considering situations in which the two approaches are likely to agree or disagree.

*Agreement between the two approaches*

**5.28** When considering possible analyses of alleged contracts in the light of the objective-subjective contrast, both approaches will often say that there is a contract (and also agree on what it is). That the same result would be achieved by applying either approach is unsurprising, and the fact that on both approaches there is a binding agreement means that in many cases there is no room for discussion of the contrast. Assume that, when in London, Michael always dines at the Reform Club. Having taken a train from Bristol to Paddington, Michael opens the door of a taxi and spies that the driver has been reading Jules Verne's *Around the World in Eighty Days*, 1873 while waiting for a fare. If Michael says, 'I have a dinner engagement with Phileas Fogg', and the driver says, 'the Reform Club, Pall Mall it is', and sets off, it would be clear under both approaches that there is a contract on the usual terms.

**5.29** There are also millions of contracts made every day in supermarkets without any word being said. An English lawyer would naturally explain the phenomenon of agreement in objective terms, but all legal systems would think there is a contract. Differences might still be discerned, if only on matters of detail such as the moment of contract formation. Substantive rules may play a role in other contexts. For example, while English law generally adheres

---

28 Johan Steyn, 'Contract Law: Fulfilling the Reasonable Expectations of Honest Men' (1997) 113 *LQR* 433.

to a requirement of 'consideration', a civil system may apply a different, but similar, concept. The same conclusion may be reached even though there is disagreement about the concept applied to justify the conclusion as a matter of law.

**5.30** The two approaches may also agree that there is no contract. In particular cases the explanation will be that, even under the common law, evidence of actual intention is sometimes admissible. Consider this example. Over a cup of coffee with Fred, Mabel has been lamenting that her expensive sports car spends more time in the mechanic's workshop than on the road. Mabel says, 'I'm fed up. If anyone paid me £100 for the car, they could have it!'. If Fred says 'I'll have the car, here's £100', and goes to put the money in Mabel's hand, it could not realistically be contended that Mabel is bound by a contract. And it would make no difference if Fred hastily prepares, and Mabel signs, a document addressed by Mabel to Fred saying 'I agree to sell my sports car to Fred for £100'. Notwithstanding her signature, Mabel is entitled to deny that she intended to contract and to prove that Fred knew it was all a joke.[29]

### Disagreement between the two approaches

**5.31** Cases may nevertheless arise in which a subjective approach would say that there is no contract but an objective approach would hold that there is. The converse may of course also occur. There may be disagreement on the terms of the contract or the parties' rights, even in the supermarket example given above.[30] That all these results are possible is clear. What is meant by objectivity is less clear, as are the relevance of the parties' actual knowledge and the weight to be given to their knowledge.

**5.32** Although the purpose of the objective approach is to reach a conclusion on actual intention, situations can arise in which A and B are bound even though, as a matter of fact, only A intended to contract. B may be bound simply because—unlike the sports-car example—there is nothing to rebut or displace the objective interpretation of B's words or conduct, or because B is estopped. Much more difficult to find are categorical instances of cases holding that there is a contract on the basis that, objectively speaking, the parties have agreed even though, subjectively, *neither* intended to contract. But in at least one decision of the Court of Appeal 'objective intention' appears to have trumped the actual intention of both parties.

**5.33** This is the strange decision in *Upton-on-Severn RDC v Powell*.[31] A fire broke out at the defendant's farm. He wished to call the fire brigade. If he called the correct brigade (Pershore) the service would be free. In fact, he telephoned his

---

29 See *Air Great Lakes Pty Ltd v K S Easter (Holdings) Pty Ltd* (1985) 2 NSWLR 309 at 318 per Hope JA, 331, 333 per Mahoney JA, 336 per McHugh JA. More general analysis of this sort of issue relates to the much-debated 'sham principle'. See, e.g., *Snook v London and West Riding Investments Ltd* [1967] 2 QB 786 at 802 per Diplock LJ.

30 Indeed, variety in consumer protection regimes around the world may lead to different conclusions as between any two common law jurisdictions.

31 [1942] 1 All ER 220.

local police station at Upton. The police inspector called the Upton fire brigade who attended the fire. Neither the defendant nor the police nor the fire brigade realized that the boundaries of responsibility for the police and the fire brigade were different. The Upton fire brigade exceeded their statutory duty by attending the fire. Therefore, in principle, they would be entitled to charge.[32] But neither they nor the defendant realized this at the time. Actual intention to contract therefore seems implausible, if not impossible.

**5.34** In due course the fire brigade submitted an account, claiming that there was indeed a contract with the defendant. The Court of Appeal upheld the claim, saying[33] that it was 'sufficient' that a reasonable person in the position of the Upton police inspector would interpret the request for assistance as made to him, that is, to call the Upton brigade for the defendant. The court considered the position so clear that an unreserved judgment was given without calling on counsel for the brigade. Even allowing for the fact that the contract may have been seen as implied rather than express, it is conspicuous that at the time of the fire neither objectively nor subjectively did either party think it was making a contract, or intend to contract.

**5.35** The decision in *Upton-on-Severn RDC v Powell* has rightly been largely ignored by contract texts. Patrick Atiyah[34] gives the case as a leading example of 'a long series of low quality decisions' in the 1940s. An award of a reasonable sum by way of restitution could possibly be supported, but that was not the decision.[35]

### Two great nineteenth-century cases

**5.36** Two great nineteenth-century cases are still extensively discussed. The first is *Raffles v Wichelaus*,[36] which concerned an alleged contract, made in Liverpool, to sell cotton. It is sensible to put this case in its historic context. In 1860 the Lancashire cotton industry was of world class, employing nearly half a million workers. The cotton came very largely from the southern states of the United States. It was of high quality and relatively accessible. The outbreak of the American Civil War in 1861 had shattering effects. These are helpfully explained in *The Lancashire Cotton Famine 1861–1865*, by WO Henderson.[37]

**5.37** Cotton was searched for worldwide but during the war the pre-war level of supply was never achieved. The fluctuations in supply were accompanied by fluctuating prices and much speculation. In 1862 speculation made up over 46

---

32  See Paul Mitchell 'A Ratio Decidendi for Upton-on-Severn Rural District Council v Powell' (1997) 12 *JCL* 76.

33  [1942] 1 All ER 220 at 221 per Lord Greene MR (with whom Luxmore and Goddard LJJ agreed).

34  See Patrick S Atiyah, *The Rise and Fall of Freedom of Contract*, Clarendon Press, Oxford, 1979, pp 662–3.

35  For suggestions that it should have been, see AL Corbin, *Corbin on Contracts*, West Publishing Co, St Paul, Vol 3, 1960, §561; Edwin Peel, *Treitel's Law of Contract*, 14th edn, Sweet & Maxwell, London, 2015, §2-048.

36  (1864) 2 H & C 906; 159 ER 375.

37  Second edn, Manchester University Press, 1969.

per cent of the market. Henderson says:[38] 'It was stated at the end of 1863 that "transactions in cotton to arrive no longer imply any real foundation. Sales are made on a large scale for shipment months hence that are purely fictitious"'.

**5.38** In *Raffles v Wichelaus*, the plaintiff-seller's pleading alleged that the parties had agreed that the plaintiff should sell to the defendants '125 bales of Surat cotton ... to arrive ex *Peerless* from Bombay ... at 17¼d per pound', that he offered to deliver such cotton after arrival of the ship at Liverpool and that the defendants refused to accept the goods. The plaintiff used a form of procedure called 'demurrer' which is no longer employed, at least not under that name. This involves argument and decision based on the pleadings, and therefore assumed facts, without the calling of any evidence.

**5.39** The facts were that two ships called *Peerless* had come from Bombay with Surat cotton, that one had sailed in October, the other December and that the plaintiff offered to deliver goods off the latter.[39] Essentially, the seller was arguing he could perform the contract by tendering Surat cotton of the right amount and quality off any ship called *Peerless* which should come from Bombay. This argument was apparent from the seller's pleading, which did not refer to either of the two vessels. The Court of Exchequer rejected the argument, holding in favour of the buyers without giving reasons (other than judicial observation during the argument). The case has generated much debate.[40] Some writers have thought they know what the case decides. This seems to us uncertain. There are too many imponderable facts and the decision is consistent with more than one legal rationale.

**5.40** It is hard to know what is the effect of an ex-ship contract in this context. The contract in *Raffles v Wichelaus* fixed the price of the cotton on delivery but delivery was weeks, if not months ahead. The market was highly volatile and speculation rife. That the market price when the *Peerless* arrived would be different from the contract price was virtually certain. As always in a forward contract, if the market price had gone up the seller would be tempted to sell in the market. If it had gone down the buyers would be tempted to reject. The facts in the report are consistent with the seller having cotton on both ships, although that seems unlikely.

**5.41** Most discussions assume that the parties only knew of one *Peerless* (not necessarily the same one). This is actually counter-intuitive. For two ships with the same name to be sailing between the same ports with similar cargoes is unusual but must have been noted in Bombay. It also seems entirely possible that the seller had employees or agents in Bombay who would know this. By this time there was telegraphic communication between Liverpool and Bombay. The seller

---

38 Pages 15–16.

39 Apparently, the October ship arrived in February 1863 and the December ship in April 1863.

40 See Robert Birmingham, 'Holmes on Peerless: Raffles v Wichelaus and the Objective Theory of Contract' (1985) 47 *University of Connecticut Law Review* 183; Brian Simpson, *The Beauty of Obscurity: Raffles v Wichelaus and Busch (1864)* in *Leading Cases in the Common Law*, Oxford University Press, Oxford, 1995, Ch 6; Catharine MacMillan, *Mistakes in Contract Law*, Hart Publishing, Oxford, 2010, pp 186–90.

was likely to be aware that the contract was ambiguous, and was perhaps seeking to take advantage of the fact. As speculators, the buyers were less likely to know.

**5.42** As far as the relationship between objective and subjective approaches is concerned, the decision is not necessarily helpful. Since there was a literal 'match' between the words used in the contract and what the seller offered to deliver, an objective approach would favour the seller. In deciding for the buyers, the court may have applied a subjective approach. However, the court was not required to investigate what would have been crucial had the buyers brought an action. This is whether the buyers could establish, under the objective approach, a contract to sell goods ex the October *Peerless*. The case appears to be about ambiguity. The basis for the decision can perhaps be found by asking what sort of ambiguity was at issue.

**5.43** *Raffles v Wichelaus* was not about patent ambiguity, which must appear on the face of the document. Patent ambiguity would have arisen if the contract had said that the seller agreed to sell cotton to arrive ex the December *Peerless*, and that the buyers agreed to buy cotton to arrive ex the October *Peerless*. Such an ambiguity would be resolved by applying the objective approach, that is, by construction of the contract. The date of the contract—which does not appear from the report—might have been crucial. Since evidence of actual intention would be inadmissible, the buyers' 'plea', that they 'meant a ship called the "*Peerless*" which sailed from Bombay, in October', would have been quite worthless.

**5.44** The point of counsel for the buyers' argument in support of the plea is therefore that ambiguity would arise, not in construction, but when the contract was applied to the facts. Before he was stopped by the court, Mellish said:[41] 'parol evidence may be given for the purpose [of] shewing that the defendant[s] meant one "*Peerless*" and the plaintiff another'. In demurrer proceedings, the truth of the plea had to be accepted. It must also have been regarded as a sufficient answer to the claim. In that respect, as suggested above, a subjective approach was applied to decide in the buyers' favour. The case then illustrates an established rule,[42] namely, that direct evidence of intention can be given in a case of latent ambiguity in the description of the subject matter of a contract.

**5.45** The other case that has also generated extensive discussion[43] is *Smith v Hughes*,[44] which some regard as the starting point on the approach for objectivity in English contract law. Smith was a farmer and had oats for sale. The defendant-buyer was the owner of a number of racehorses and wanted to buy

---

41  (1864) 2 H & C 906 at 908; 159 ER 375 at 376.

42  See *Shore v Wilson* (1842) 9 Cl & F 355 at 556–7; 8 ER 450 at 529 per Parke B. See also *Sharp v Thomson* (1915) 20 CLR 137 at 142 per Isaacs J; *Life Insurance Co of Australia Ltd v Phillips* (1925) 36 CLR 60 at 79–80 per Isaacs J, 85–6 per Starke J.

43  See John Phillips, '*Smith v Hughes* (1871)' in Charles Mitchell and Paul Mitchell, eds, *Landmark Cases in the Law of Contract*, Hart Publishing, Oxford, 2008, Ch 7; Mindy Chen-Wishart, 'Objectivity and Mistake: The Oxymoron of *Smith v Hughes*' in JW Neyers, Richard Bronough and SGA Pitel, eds, *Exploring Contract Law*, Hart Publishing, Oxford, 2009, Ch 14; Catharine MacMillan, *Mistakes in Contract Law*, Hart Publishing, Oxford, 2010, pp 207ff.

44  (1871) LR 6 QB 597.

oats to feed them. An important fact is that it is unwise to feed new oats to horses, especially racehorses. Smith said he had oats for sale at 35s a quarter and provided a sample. The defendant's manager later sent an order, but the first delivery (16 quarters) was refused on the ground that the oats were new. Smith brought an action for breach of contract. Two questions were left to the jury, which found a verdict for the buyer. The trial judge dismissed the action and the seller appealed. A new trial was ordered by the Court of Queen's Bench. The judge did not ask for a specific answer to each question left to the jury and the court was dissatisfied with the judge's formulation of the second question.

**5.46** All three judges delivered judgments which were to the same legal and practical effect, but they are not identical in the reasoning. It is common to cite a passage in the judgment of Blackburn J:[45]

> I apprehend that if one of the parties intends to make a contract on one set of terms, and the other intends to make a contract on another set of terms, or, as it is sometimes expressed, if the parties are not *ad idem*, there is no contract, unless the circumstances are such as to preclude one of the parties from denying that he has agreed to the terms of the other ... If, whatever a man's real intention may be, he so conducts himself that a reasonable man would believe that he was assenting to the terms proposed by the other party, and that other party upon that belief enters into the contract with him, the man thus conducting himself would be equally bound as if he had intended to agree to the other party's terms.

There seems no better evidence of the diversity of view on what the objective approach entails than that no less an authority than the High Court of Australia regards[46] Blackburn J's statement as embodying the subjective theory, qualified only by the question of estoppel incorporated by the final sentence. This seems to us to ignore the court's reasoning and what it regarded as the vital issue.

**5.47** In a case of this kind there are a wide range of possibilities. The seller may explicitly say that old oats are on offer, or the buyer may give no clue that old oats are needed. The case was not either of these alternatives. It appears that old oats were more expensive and that, oats being in short supply, the seller was asking for what was, in substance, an old oat's price. It was surely relevant if it could be established that the seller knew that new oats should not be fed to horses, and to know what each party said.[47] The court must have thought that either party might win in the retrial.[48] Although the case is cited as a leading authority on objectivity, the state of mind of each of the parties seems highly relevant. In fact, the case is a good illustration of the 'complex amalgam of the

---

45  (1871) LR 6 QB 597 at 607.

46  *Taylor v Johnson* (1983) 151 CLR 422 at 428 per Mason ACJ, Murphy and Deane JJ. They expressed the same view about Hannen J's judgment ((1871) LR 6 QB 597 at 609).

47  The seller gave evidence that 'I do not know that trainers never use new oats', and the buyer said 'I never buy new oats if I can get old. Trainers, as a rule, use old oats'. See (1871) LR 6 QB 597 at 598.

48  John Phillips, n 43, p 215 records that the claim failed in the retrial because the jury were unable to agree.

objective and the subjective' referred to by Lord Phillips in the passage quoted at the beginning of the chapter from *Shogun Finance Ltd v Hudson*.

**5.48** The judgments in *Smith v Hughes* emphasise that the objective theory would apply if the facts involved no more than the subjective belief on the part of the defendant-buyer that he was buying old oats. There would then be a contract, as the seller argued. Even if the seller knew of the buyer's self-deception, the result would be the same. The problem that arose went beyond these situations. The buyer's contention was a belief on his part, known to the seller, that the seller had, in effect, warranted that the oats were old. It appears to have been common ground in the case that no such warranty was given. If the buyer could make good his contention, there was no contract unless (as Blackburn J explained) he was precluded from asserting his actual belief.

**5.49** *Smith v Hughes* is typically analysed in textbook discussions of 'unilateral mistake' (as is *Shogun Finance*). *Raffles v Wichelaus* is typically discussed as a 'mutual mistake' case. Now is not the occasion to consider how subjectivity and objectivity interact from the perspective of doctrines of mistake. But it is worth mentioning that because the objective theory is concerned to establish (and give effect to) actual intention, a mere appearance of concordance between offer and acceptance is not always sufficient. There is no contract if the 'offeree' knows that the 'offeror' does not intend to contract on the terms stated. A striking example is the decision of the Singapore Court of Appeal in *Chwee Kin Keong v Digilandmall.Com Pte Ltd*.[49]

**5.50** In this case, Digilandmall, a Singapore IT firm, had Hewlett Packard laser printers for sale. Digilandmall marketed them on its website. The normal price was nearly S$4000. One afternoon, the price shown was a mere S$66. During the following evening Digilandmall's automated contracting process accommodated the purchase between the six appellants of a very large number of printers. Digilandmall denied that any contracts had been agreed and refused to fill the orders. The Singapore Court of Appeal affirmed the holding of the trial judge[50] that no contracts arose. It is clear that in general it is bad luck on the shop if it puts too low a price on goods it is offering for sale, but in this case the discrepancy was enormous and ought to have been obvious to those who sought to become buyers, all of whom were graduates. The facts were so far over the line that it was not necessary to decide where the line would be drawn. This case would surely be followed in any other common law country.[51]

---

49 [2005] 1 SLR 502; [2005] SGCA 2.

50 [2004] 2 SLR 594; [2004] SCHC 71. See Andrew Phang, 'Contract Formation and Mistake in Cyberspace' (2005) 21 *JCL* 197.

51 Cf *Hartog v Colin & Shields* [1939] 3 All ER 566. At the moment when we were correcting the proofs, on 24 February 2020, the Singapore International Court of Appeal delivered a very important judgement in *Quoine Pte v B2C2 Ltd* [2020] SGCA (I) 2. In this case contracts for the sale and purchase of cryptocurrencies were made in the middle of the night by two computers without human intervention (other than the programming of the computer). In the morning it was clear that the transactions were approximately 250 times the going rate. The court was divided as to the result. The majority held that there was a binding contract; Lord Mance IJ dissented. Both judgments contain much of interest for the present discussion.

## Implied terms

### *Introduction*

**5.51** Many contracts include implied terms. This is self-evident for the informal contracts that pervade daily life. We would also venture the guess that, even for the most detailed contract, if all the issues that could arise were litigated, some would be resolved by implying terms. Implied terms are therefore very important. Legal analysis of the topic relies on a taxonomy under which the rules vary according to the category at issue. We focus on the two main categories: terms implied 'in law' and terms implied 'in fact' (further categories include 'custom' and 'course of dealing').

**5.52** Terms implied in law state recognised 'incidents' for particular classes of contract. An example of a term implied at common law is the duty of care owed by a solicitor. A familiar statutory context is the sale of goods legislation. For example, a term requiring goods to be fit for the buyer's purpose may be implied. Terms implied in fact are different. These are implied on an *ad hoc* basis, but only when 'necessary'. The 'in fact' description signifies that implications are specific to particular fact situations. Of course, the facts are infinitely variable.

**5.53** Three questions about the objective-subjective contrast and implied terms are discussed below:

(1) Does the role of objectivity vary as between the two main categories?
(2) To what extent does the process of implying a term on an *ad hoc* basis differ from 'construction'?
(3) What does it mean to say that a term can be implied in fact only when the term is 'necessary'?

**5.54** The important points for the objective-subjective contrast are that the process (implying a term) is objective, the purpose is to give effect to actual intention, that the contrast is an oversimplification and that objectivity does not always carry the day.

### *Does the role of objectivity vary?*

**5.55** Whether the role of objectivity varies as between terms implied in fact and those implied in law is not altogether clear. Various views can be found in the cases, and the courts' terminology is rather confusing. A useful starting point is *Greaves & Co (Contractors) Ltd v Baynham*,[52] where Lord Denning MR suggested that a 'term implied by law' rests 'on the presumed intention of both parties; whereas, a term implied in fact rests on their actual intention'. Another view is that both categories give effect to 'presumed intention'.[53] Yet

---

52 [1975] 1 WLR 1095 at 1099. Browne and Geoffrey Lane LJJ agreed.
53 See, e.g., *Khoury v Government Insurance Office of New South Wales* (1984) 165 CLR 622 at 636 per Mason, Brennan, Deane and Dawson JJ.

another is that terms implied in law are different because they are implied independently of the parties' intention.[54]

**5.56** It is first necessary to explain the two ingredients of the elliptical expression 'presumed intention'. If an implied term is based on presumed intention (1) it states the conclusion which a reasonable person would reach in relation to the implied term and (2) the parties are 'presumed' to have that intention. The approach is therefore objective. The sense in which the term states the parties' actual intention is the same as that explained earlier, namely, application of a presumption that subjective intention and objective intention coincide. In other words, subjective intention is not a direct concern. This seems the orthodox analysis in the case of a term implied in fact. For example, when in *Attorney General of Belize v Belize Telecom Ltd*[55] Lord Hoffmann said (for the Privy Council) that the implied term states what the 'contract actually means', he was not suggesting that the parties can give evidence of their actual intention. Such evidence is inadmissible. Lord Denning's view in *Greaves & Co (Contractors) Ltd v Baynham*, that terms implied in fact are derived directly from actual intention, therefore seems doubtful.

**5.57** Suggestions that the parties' intention is irrelevant for terms implied in law rest on the rather shaky proposition that people cannot have an intention on any matter governed by a rule of the common law or statute. Given that it is generally open to the parties to agree that a term which would otherwise be implied in law should not be implied, it cannot be right to say that implication is independent of intention.[56] There is an exception. Where the implied term is mandated by statute, the implication is independent of intention in the sense that it is imposed on the parties.

**5.58** A broader perspective on the point that terms implied in law can usually be excluded is that *all* implied terms must be consistent with the actual intention of the parties. Although this seems fundamental, it can pose problems for the objective approach. For expressly agreed terms, actual intention is determined by construction, and is represented by the conclusion a reasonable person would reach. Prior negotiations cannot be relied upon, at least not directly.[57] But what if the parties' actual intention on the subject matter of the implied term can be found in their negotiations? The evidence might be that during negotiations B rejected a proposal by A to include as an express term the term later sought to be implied. There is support for the view that the evidence must be taken into account.[58] This tends to show that the approach to implication is not always wholly objective.

---

54 Cf *Commonwealth Bank of Australia v Barker* (2014) 253 CLR 169; [2014] HCA 32. See generally Elisabeth Peden, *Good Faith in the Performance of Contracts*, Butterworths, Sydney, 2003, Ch 3.

55 [2009] 1 WLR 1988 at 1995; [2009] UKPC 10 at [27].

56 However, an express statement may be necessary. See *Geys v Société Générale London Branch* [2013] 1 AC 523 at 547; [2012] UKSC 63 at [55] per Baroness Hale.

57 *Chartbrook Ltd v Persimmon Homes Ltd* [2009] 1 AC 1101; [2009] UKHL 38.

58 See *Codelfa Construction Pty Ltd v State Rail Authority of New South Wales* (1982) 149 CLR 337 at 352–3 per Mason J; Donald Nicholls, 'My Kingdom for a Horse: The Meaning of Words' (2005) 121 *LQR* 577. See also AL Corbin, *Corbin on Contracts*, West Publishing Co, St Paul, Vol 3, 1960, §564.

## Are implication and construction different?

**5.59** The role of construction in the implication process is a much-debated issue. Most of the debate has centred on terms implied in fact.[59] Two rationalisations for such terms can be found in the cases. The term may be so obvious that 'it goes without saying'.[60] Had they been asked the question by an officious bystander, the parties would have replied 'of course', and done so in unison. Alternatively, the term may be implied to give 'business efficacy' to the contract. The same specific legal requirements apply in both cases.[61] For example, as mentioned above, the term must be necessary and also consistent with the express terms. This all suggests that implication in fact is governed by dedicated legal requirements. The conventional view is therefore that the law dictates a rule-based analysis. The role of construction is to *apply* the rules.

**5.60** In *Attorney General of Belize v Belize Telecom Ltd* the Privy Council favoured a different analysis. Lord Hoffmann suggested:[62] 'the question for the court is whether such a provision would spell out in express words what the instrument, read against the relevant background, would reasonably be understood to mean'.

**5.61** The viability of Lord Hoffmann's construction approach was hotly contested in the literature[63] from two related perspectives. One is his apparent rejection of what is referred to above as the conventional view, in favour of an analysis under which the 'rules' merely state relevant factors to be considered when construing the contract. The other perspective is that Lord Hoffmann's criterion—'what the instrument ... would reasonably be understood to mean'—appears to contradict the rule that only a 'necessary' term can be implied. Focusing mainly on this perspective, to which we return below, in *Marks and Spencer Plc v BNP Paribas Securities Services Trust Co (Jersey) Ltd*[64] the Supreme Court of the United Kingdom declined to adopt Lord Hoffmann's suggestion.

**5.62** There is no difficulty in saying that construction and implication are sometimes alternative processes leading to the same conclusion. For example, if A contracts to provide IT services to B, and the written contract does not indicate expressly its intended duration, the parties are unlikely to intend the contract to last forever. 'Construction' and 'implied term' may be alternative justifications for concluding that either party can bring the contract to an end by

---

59 For a term implied in law the role of construction is to classify the contract and decide whether the parties agreed that the term should not be implied.

60 *Shirlaw v Southern Foundries (1926) Ltd* [1939] 2 KB 206 at 227 per Mackinnon LJ (affirmed *sub nom Southern Foundries (1926) Ltd v Shirlaw* [1940] AC 701).

61 Cf *BP Refinery (Westernport) Pty Ltd v Shire of Hastings* (1977) 180 CLR 266 at 282–3 per the Privy Council.

62 [2009] 1 WLR 1988 at 1994; [2009] UKPC 10 at [21].

63 Most of the literature is noted in JW Carter and Wayne Courtney, 'Unexpressed Intention and Contract Construction' (2016) 37 *Oxford Journal of Legal Studies* 326.

64 [2016] AC 742; [2015] UKSC 72. See also *Foo Jong Peng v Phua Kiah Mai* [2012] 4 SLR 1267; [2012] SGCA 55.

giving reasonable notice.[65] A recent illustration of the phenomenon is *Devani v Wells*,[66] where an (alleged) oral contract was at issue. The case is not nearly so straightforward as our IT example.

**5.63** Mr Wells was having difficulty in selling some of the flats in a block that he had built in Hackney. A friend introduced him to Mr Devani, an estate agent. There was a telephone conversation between Wells and Devani during which, so Devani alleged, the terms of a contract were agreed. They were to the effect that if Devani found a purchaser for the flats Wells would pay a commission equal to two per cent of the price. Wells refused to pay even though the flats were sold to a purchaser introduced by Devani, and notwithstanding that the purchaser paid Wells the purchase price. Wells's case was that there was no contract because no agreement was reached on the 'trigger' event for payment of the commission. The trial judge held in favour of Devani, deciding that the event was completion of the sale contract. His decision was reversed by the Court of Appeal[67] but restored in the Supreme Court.

**5.64** Commission agency contracts vary considerably. However, it is reasonable to suppose that Devani and Wells would have debated two trigger events:[68] (1) entry into a sale contract with a ready and willing purchaser introduced by Devani, and (2) completion of the sale contract, that is, payment of the purchase price to Wells. While Devani would have wanted (1), Wells would have wanted (2). The trial judge found that both parties intended to contract. Given that the purchaser introduced by Devani paid the price, one might be forgiven for thinking that the parties' failure to choose between the two events would be irrelevant: both had occurred. However, it was assumed at each level of the case that agreement on the trigger event was essential to the formation of a binding contract. That the parties intended to contract was therefore regarded as insufficient.

**5.65** The disagreement between the Court of Appeal and the Supreme Court in *Devani v Wells* suggests that the case raised a difficult problem. But the Supreme Court thought the case relatively straightforward. The parties' agreement on (2) as the trigger event could be established by construction or by way of a term implied in fact. In relation to construction, the court said[69] 'it would naturally be understood that payment would become due on completion', and that this was 'the only sensible interpretation of what [the parties] said to each other in the course of their telephone conversation'. The court also thought its conclusion supported by authority. Several problems arise.

**5.66** The objective approach applies whether the alleged contract is oral or in writing. If the contract is oral, the content of the contract is a question of fact. The express terms of the contract must therefore be found in the parties'

65 Compare *Winter Garden Theatre (London) Ltd v Millennium Productions Ltd* [1948] AC 173 and *New South Wales Cancer Council v Sarfaty* (1992) 28 NSWLR 68.

66 [2020] AC 109; [2019] UKSC 4.

67 [2017] QB 959; [2016] EWCA Civ 1106.

68 They might have discussed a third: introduction of a ready and willing purchaser.

69 [2020] AC 129 at 141; [2019] UKSC 4 at [19] per Lord Kitchin (with whom the other members of the court agreed).

words and conduct. An obvious problem on the facts in *Devani v Wells* is that the trigger event was never discussed. There were no words to construe. Nor did parties' conduct suggest a common intention about the event. A second problem is the court's view that its conclusion supported by authority. As we mentioned earlier, the meaning of a contract does not depend on prior authority. A third problem is the objective-subjective contrast. There is no doubt that the Supreme Court thought it was applying the objective approach. However, a view about Wells's actual intention when he spoke to Devani may underlie the decision. In effect, the court held that, had he been asked, Wells would have agreed to trigger event (2). A fourth problem is therefore that 'construction' looks to be implied term in disguise.[70]

**5.67** Turning then to the implied term basis for *Devani v Wells*, Wells argued that it was impermissible—as a matter of law—to complete the contract by implying a term. He relied on *Scancarriers A/S v Aotearoa International Ltd (The Barranduna and The Tarago)*.[71] Speaking for the Privy Council, Lord Roskill said:[72]

> the first question must always be whether any legally binding contract has been made, for until that issue is decided a court cannot properly decide what extra terms, if any, must be implied into what is *ex hypothesi* a legally binding bargain, as being both necessary and reasonable to make that bargain work. It is not correct in principle, in order to determine whether there is a legally binding bargain, to add to those terms which alone the parties have expressed further implied terms upon which they have not expressly agreed and then by adding the express terms and the implied terms together thereby create what would not otherwise be a legally binding bargain.

The Supreme Court rejected the argument and distanced itself from Lord Roskill's statement.

**5.68** There is certainly a conceptual difficulty in saying that a court can imply a term to complete an incomplete contract. A clear case is where S and B reach stalemate in their negotiation of the price for the sale of certain goods. The fact that they agreed all the other terms does not entitle a court to step in and imply a promise to pay a reasonable price. That would be making a contract which the parties refused to make. The position is generally the same if the parties intend to contract but fail to agree a term that is essential as a matter of law.[73] In these respects, Lord Roskill was clearly correct.

**5.69** It is equally true both that a term may be implied into an offer—which is of course not in itself a contract—and that courts regularly imply terms which can reasonably be described as 'essential'. For example, if a contract for the sale of land is silent on the date for completion, an obligation to complete within

---

70 Given that authority supported the construction conclusion, it might be possible to justify the result on the basis of a term implied in law. But that was not considered.

71 [1985] 2 Lloyd's Rep 419; [1985] 1 NZLR 513.

72 [1985] 2 Lloyd's Rep 419 at 422; [1985] 1 NZLR 513 at 556.

73 See, e.g., *Whitlock v Brew* (1968) 118 CLR 445; *Walford v Miles* [1992] 2 AC 128.

a reasonable time is implied. Lord Roskill would not have overlooked either type of case. The dividing line between these cases and those referred to in the previous paragraph is a conclusion that the term in question was not one that the parties would have wished to negotiate and the availability of a standard of reasonableness. By contrast, in *Devani v Wells* there was no 'reasonable' trigger event and it seems clear that the parties would have wanted to negotiate the event. To say that the parties' silence on the trigger event gave the court jurisdiction to complete the contract by implying a term would be simplistic, and the court implied a term that favoured Wells.

**5.70** In applying the implied terms rules, it may be necessary to distinguish between an executory contract and a partly performed contract. Assume that in the sale of goods example S gives up hope of reaching agreement on price and in desperation tenders the goods to B. If B chooses to accept the goods, there is no doubt that B must pay a reasonable sum. Whether B's obligation is contractual or restitutionary might be debated. From an implied term perspective, it may be obvious that the parties have resolved their disagreement by impliedly agreeing on a reasonable sum as the price. By contrast, in *Devani v Wells* the fact that the purchaser introduced by Devani completed the sale contract could not resolve the trigger-event issue and Devani did not claim a reasonable sum by way of restitution.

**5.71** As between obviousness and business efficacy, the Supreme Court concentrated on the latter.[74] It also agreed with the trial judge, who seems to have thought that the term could be justified under both rationalisations. Assuming it was permissible to imply a term to complete the contract, the same logical problem arises whichever rationalisation is preferred. Why did the rules dictate trigger event (2) at the expense of (1)? The term implied would not have been obvious to Devani, and since a term to either effect would have given business efficacy to the contract, the latter rationalisation left the matter in the air. In choosing (2) over (1), the court may—as suggested above—have acted on a view about Wells's subjective intention. However, the ambivalence of the business efficacy criterion confirms that the trigger event remained open for negotiation. It was therefore appropriate to apply Lord Roskill's statement, as the Court of Appeal decided.

*What does 'necessary' signify?*

**5.72** A term can be implied in fact only if it is a 'necessary' implication. While different judges undoubtedly take different views on what must be shown in order to reach the standard of necessity, it is not easily reached. The point on which everyone agrees is that 'necessary' does not mean 'reasonable'. The second perspective for debate about Lord Hoffmann's suggestion in *Attorney General of Belize v Belize Telecom Ltd* is whether it embodies a reasonableness standard.

---

74 See [2020] AC 129 at 148; [2019] UKSC 4 at [35] per Lord Kitchin (with whom the other members of the court agreed).

**5.73** As noted above, his suggestion is that the question is whether the term 'would spell out in express words what the instrument, read against the relevant background, would reasonably be understood to mean'. This certainly sounds like a standard of reasonableness. No standard of necessity is incorporated, for example, Lord Hoffmann does not say 'would *necessarily* be understood to mean by a reasonable person'. A perceived risk that it might lead to implication under a standard of reasonableness is the main basis on which the suggestion was disowned in *Marks and Spencer Plc v BNP Paribas Securities Services Trust Co (Jersey) Ltd*. In the article referred to earlier, Lord Hoffmann responded with a strong denial, saying:[75]

> On the contrary, *Belize Telecom* emphasises the reluctance of courts to accept that something significant has been left out of a legal document and I have tried in this article to explain why, consistently with ordinary techniques of interpretation and common sense, this should be so.

Lord Hoffmann's explanation includes the following illustration:[76]

> David and Hugh are Welsh rugby fans living in London. They are both going to Cardiff to see Wales play South Africa at the Principality Stadium. David tells Hugh that he proposes to go by train. Hugh replies: 'I am going by car. Would you like a lift?'
> Has Hugh promised that after the game, he will bring David back again? He has not expressly said so. But David would be entitled to understand the offer to mean that he would also be taken home after the game, and to feel aggrieved if, after the game, Hugh revealed that he was not going back but proposed to go on to Swansea and spend a few days with his aunt. In the absence of express disclaimer, he has made an implied promise to bring David back.

With the greatest respect, the example lets the cat out of the bag. It confirms that *Belize Telecom* does not address the more stringent requirement of necessity. There are at least two relevant points.

**5.74** First, under the suggestion in *Belize Telecom*, the express terms must be 'read against the relevant background'. In the illustration, the express term is the promise by Hugh to drive David to Cardiff. The relevant 'background' comprises the fact that both David and Hugh want to see the match, where the match is to be played and David's intention to go by train (a fact not mentioned is that the train station is a short walk from the ground). Lord Hoffmann notes Hugh's failure to disclose his actual intention and 'the absence of express disclaimer'. It is difficult to see either as a background fact. The promise implied by Lord Hoffmann—'to bring David back'—does not seem a 'necessary' implication. To reach that standard under a construction approach, the facts

---

75 Leonard Hoffmann, 'Language and Lawyers' (2018) 134 *LQR* 553 at 572. See also (2018) 134 *LQR* 553 at 563. Lord Hoffmann also disagreed with the criticism by Lord Sumption, 'A Question of Taste: The UK Supreme Court and the Interpretation of Contracts' (2017) 8 *The UK Supreme Court Yearbook* 74. Lord Sumption was a member of the court in *Marks and Spencer*.

76 Leonard Hoffmann, 'Language and Lawyers' (2018) 134 *LQR* 553 at 557.

would need to include some feature showing to a reasonable person that David would be stranded in Cardiff if Hugh did not drive him home. An example might be knowledge that the railway company would only accommodate passengers holding a return ticket to London.

**5.75** Second, we doubt that even a reasonableness standard is reached for the 'implied promise to bring David back'. Certainly, in any contest between necessity and reasonableness, the point seems unarguable. The only intention communicated by David is 'that he proposes to go by train'. Those of a literal persuasion might say, simply, that David has not communicated an intention to return to London immediately after the match. No doubt he intends to return home, but when? In effect, Lord Hoffmann intrudes an inference about David's actual—but uncommunicated—intention. Even if David stated expressly an intention to purchase a return ticket, that would not evidence the intention to return to London immediately that Lord Hoffmann infers. The result is therefore the same. David has communicated to Hugh a willingness to buy a ticket to and from Cardiff, and his wherewithal to do so. Why would David, as a reasonable person, 'feel aggrieved' about having to travel home by train when his friend has saved him money?

**5.76** Returning to *Devani v Wells*, the Supreme Court said it was acting consistently with *Marks and Spencer* in deciding that a term should be implied to state the trigger event. However, the decision is not easily reconciled with 'necessity'. The court was confronted by competing terms. Both were 'reasonable'— either might reasonably have been agreed on by the parties. The sense in which either term was a 'necessary' implication seems unclear.

### Conclusions

**5.77** Our argument is not that the objective approach should be abandoned, far from it. The objective theory is clearly fundamental to the common law of contract. It has also been a successful approach. Equally, to say that the common law is concerned exclusively with 'objective intention' is clearly wrong. An ingredient of success is that objectivity is tempered by subjective elements.

**5.78** That the approach is not always purely objective can be traced to the fact that the objective theory operates at the level of process. The purpose or object is to arrive at reliable conclusions about actual intention. While the approach relies heavily on a presumption that people mean what they say, it is clear not only that courts are guided by subjective indicia of intention but also that contract law includes mechanisms which ensure that decisions remain faithful to the purpose of the process. Of course, the fact that in the construction of written contracts the search is for a common intention means that there is rarely room for consideration of individual beliefs and intention. A contract in writing is not the sum of two unilateral intentions.

**5.79** In most cases where the objective and subjective analysis seem to produce different results it is because one seems clearly to point to a contract and the other to leave the situation in the air. However, in the Trier Wine Auction with which we introduced the chapter the situation is more difficult if we ask what the answer would be if English law applied. The facts are clearly designed to present a problem that is not easy. The objective and subjective approaches seem to lead in opposite directions.

**5.80** Of course, all legal systems recognise particular ceremonies as indicative of a mutual intention to contract, the classic example being a clasping of hands. There is a well-recognised ceremony for auction contracts. It must be common knowledge that anyone who waves their hand at an auction without intending to bid does so at their peril. At Trier, there may be something about the visitor who shouts that he or she is a visitor. The visitor may not be so lucky if wearing a Bayern Munich t-shirt. If so the court will have to decide whether there is a contract when it is completely clear that subjectively the parties have not agreed.

## CHAPTER 6

# Automated transactions and the law of contract

## When codes are not congruent

### Roger Brownsword

### Introduction

**6.1** According to some commentators, contract lawyers should start to imagine a world of automated transactions, where commerce is, so to speak, a 'conversation conducted entirely among machines'.[1] In line with this vision, Michal Gal and Niva Elkin-Koren foresee a world in which

> [y]our automated car makes independent decisions on where to purchase fuel, when to drive itself to a service station, from which garage to order a spare part, or whether to rent itself out to other passengers, all without even once consulting with you.[2]

**6.2** In that world, humans have been taken out of the transactional loop leaving it to the technology to make decisions that humans would otherwise be responsible for making. Precisely how the law in general, and the law of contract in particular will engage with that future, is difficult to know. While some legal rules might be revised and refocused, others might be redirected (from users of transactional technologies to designers and controllers of the same), and yet others might be simply redundant.[3] As ever, the future is uncertain.

**6.3** In this context, how should we begin to think about the relationship between the automated enforcement of contracts, such as that promised by blockchain, and the law?[4] Karen Yeung, in an insightful discussion of blockchain and

1 Per W. Brian Arthur, 'The Second Economy' (October 2011) *McKinsey Quarterly,* quoted in Nicholas Carr, *The Glass Cage* (London: Vintage, 2015) 197.

2 Michal S. Gal and Niva Elkin-Koren, 'Algorithmic Contracts' (2017) 30 *Harvard Journal of Law and Technology* 309, at 309–310.

3 For discussion, see Roger Brownsword, 'The E-Commerce Directive, Consumer Transactions, and the Digital Single Market: Questions of Regulatory Fitness, Regulatory Disconnection and Rule Redirection' in Stefan Grundmann (ed.), *European Contract Law in the Digital Age* (Antwerp: Intersentia, 2018) 165; and *Law, Technology and Society—Re-imagining the Regulatory Environment* (Abingdon: Routledge, 2019) Ch 11.

4 For discussion, see Roger Brownsword, 'Smart Contracts: Coding the Transaction, Decoding the Legal Debates' in Philipp Hacker, Ioannis Lianos, Georgios Dimitropoulos and Stefan Eich (eds), *Regulating Blockchain: Techno-Social and Legal Challenges* (Oxford: Oxford University Press, 2019) 311; and 'Regulatory Fitness: Fintech, Funny Money, and Smart Contracts' (2019) 20 *European Business Organization Law Review* 5.

its many applications, highlights three ways in which the law community (and the rule of law) might relate to the blockchain community (and the rule of code).[5] First, where the blockchain community challenges the authority of the law community, we can expect the relationship to be adversarial as the latter strives to assert its sovereignty; the pressure will be for technological code to yield to legal code. Second, where the technology seeks to complement or supplement the law, the relationship should be positive and supportive. Third, where the technology represents an alternative to the law (being, as it were, 'competitive' but not conflictual as such) the relationship is more complex and less predictable. In cases of this third kind, Yeung suggests that the relationship is likely to be one of 'uneasy co-existence' characterised by an attitude of 'mutual suspicion'.[6]

**6.4** Taking up this idea of a relationship of uneasy co-existence between the legal community and the blockchain community, this chapter is concerned with the relationship between the law of contract and automated transactional technologies (including so-called 'smart' contract applications that run on blockchain). On the face of it, where such transactional technologies are employed, the relationship with the law will be of the third kind; it will be one of uneasy co-existence. For, these are not technologies that are designed directly to challenge the authority of the law or simply to complement existing laws but rather to give transacting parties an enforcement option that is an alternative to taking court action. Where technologies offer options that are also 'work-rounds' relative to the limits of legal assistance, they might or might not be viewed as corrosive or unhelpfully disruptive relative to the law.

**6.5** To the extent that the legal community (guided by the law of contract) and the blockchain community (guided by smart contract coding) operate with their own logics, there is the possibility that there might be a lack of congruence between the legal and the technological view of the transaction. In other words, in the blockchain universe we might find some transactional features and effects that would not be supported in the legal universe (by a court applying the law of contract). For example, where the law of contract has restrictive rules in relation to the enforcement of claims by third-party beneficiaries, a smart contract (or some other automated process) might achieve a transfer of value to a third-party with which the law of contract (and the courts) would not assist. Or, again, the performance of transactions that would not be recognised as legally enforceable because, say, the law treats the parties as lacking the necessary intention, might be technologically guaranteed when the agreed payment obligations are committed to a smart contract. Similarly, a smart contract might be coded for particular remedial payments in ways that are out of line with the law of contract's position on fair and appropriate compensatory awards of damages. What should we make of such a lack of congruence?

---

5 Karen Yeung, 'Regulation by Blockchain: The Emerging Battle for Supremacy between the Code of Law and Code as Law' (2019) 82 *Modern Law Review* 207.

6 Ibid, at 210.

**6.6** At one level, we can certainly regard cases of a lack of congruence as exemplifying a state of uneasy co-existence between the technology community and the law community, between a community that relies on blockchain enforcement and a community that relies on court-authorised enforcement in accordance with the law of contract. However, in this chapter, I want to focus on an uneasy co-existence that is *internal* to, and that goes right to the heart of, the law community itself. This state of affairs arises from the tension between the paradigmatic 'coherentist' thinking of lawyers and judges (where the logic is one of applying general principles) and the 'regulatory' thinking that is sometimes reflected in the courts but which is more characteristic of legislative and executive reasoning (where the logic is instrumentalist and policy-driven). In other words, what I want to highlight in relation to the question of congruence is not so much a new story about the relationship between the technology community and the law community but a much older story about the relationship between legal thinking that is guided by general principles and that which is guided by particular policies.

**6.7** Three key points emerge from my discussion. First, where courts are guided by coherentist thinking, they will default to a principle of 'detachment' and a principle of 'equivalent treatment'. The former principle holds that, where a smart contract or some other technologically supported transaction fails to correspond with the specification of a fiat contract, then it should be treated as a non-qualifying transaction (i.e., as a transaction that does not qualify as a 'contract' as judged by the criteria of the law of contract). It follows that, whatever the position in the blockchain transactional universe, the courts have no reason to become involved—either as enforcers of transactions or as protectors of contracting parties—with issues arising from such transactions. However, if smart contracts are treated as qualifying transactions, then the latter principle applies. So, for example, applying the principle of equivalent treatment, the technological displacement of an optional rule of contract law should be treated by the courts in just the way that it would be treated had it been displaced by human contractors; and, if the technological displacement relates to a rule that, for either reasons of regulatory policy or principle, is regarded as mandatory, then the courts should disallow that displacement in just the way that they would if the displacement had been by human contractors. The second key point is that these two default principles are always subject to regulatory override. Accordingly, if there are policy reasons for treating smart contracts as qualifying transactions, then the courts might find that detachment is no longer acceptable; and, if there are policy reasons for treating smart contract provisions differently to the provisions in fiat contracts, equivalent treatment might also be unacceptable. Finally, even if there is no regulatory override in play, there might be some tension in the application of the default principles, not because we are engaging smart technologies or facing a question of non-congruence, but simply because the reference rules of the law of contract are themselves unclear or contested—in other words, because the law of contract itself suffers from a lack of coherence.

**6.8** The chapter is in two principal parts. In the first part, I suggest that we should differentiate between two classes of reasons that might underlie a court's refusal to enforce a transaction or to assist one of the transacting parties. We can express this distinction as one between principle and policy. While reasons of the former class focus on the coherence or integrity of the law and its concepts, reasons of the latter kind focus on whether non-enforcement and non-assistance will assist regulatory purposes. Then, in the second part of the chapter, a number of illustrative cases of non-congruence are discussed, taking into account both coherentist and regulatory perspectives. While some of these cases of non-congruence arise by virtue of technological enablement of a payment, others arise by virtue of technological disablement (of recovery of a payment or enjoyment of goods or services that are the subject of the transaction).

## Two classes of reasons for non-enforcement: principle and policy

**6.9** In a masterly historical survey, Stephen Waddams argues that neither 'principle' nor 'policy' holds the key to explaining the development of the common law of contract.[7] Quite simply, the leading doctrines of contract law reflect the complementary influence of both principle and policy. First, putting aside any attempt to fix a correct usage for the terms 'principle' and 'policy', the history of contract law shows that the formulation of the leading 'principles' has very commonly been influenced by considerations of 'policy' in the shape of 'convenience, common sense, a general sense of what is just in the particular case and a judgment of what is desirable for the future'.[8] Second, in particular cases, judicial decision-making is 'constrained by the need to formulate generalized justifying propositions, capable of sufficient precision to be appropriate for judicial application, and likely to ensure a measure of regularity, predictability and stability'.[9] Third, where judges act on countervailing 'policy' considerations, they will often cast these reasons 'in the form of a proposition that itself has been called a principle'.[10] So, where we are dealing with judge-made contract law, we find an array of 'principles' which reflect (at their origin) various 'policy' considerations; and, as it evolves dynamically, the law continues to reflect a tension between established principles and current policy considerations which, in turn, generates the articulation of further policy-guided principles.

**6.10** Nevertheless, I want to say that, in the present century, there is a difference between (i) judicial reasoning and decision-making that is guided by the general principles of the law of contract, (ii) judicial reasoning and decision-making that is guided by regulatory policies that have been initiated and adopted by judicial decision-makers, and (iii) judicial reasoning and decision-making that is

---

7 Stephen Waddams, *Principle and Policy in Contract Law—Competing or Complementary Concepts?* (Cambridge: Cambridge University Press, 2011).
8 Ibid, at 21.
9 Ibid.
10 Ibid.

guided by and reflects regulatory policies that have been initiated, adopted and authorised by a legislative enactment. Consider, for example, the modern development of the law in response to concerns about unfair terms in standard form contracts, especially in the emerging mass consumer marketplace. When these concerns were litigated—as they frequently were in the middle decades of the last century—some judges were guided by traditional principles of freedom and sanctity of contract.[11] Others, however, were guided by both openly declared (as with the deployment of the doctrines of fundamental breach and fundamental terms)[12] and covert policy reasoning (as when the principles of incorporation of terms and interpretation of terms were manipulated for protective purposes).[13] This phase of the jurisprudence was closed when the Unfair Contract Terms Act 1977 (UCTA) was enacted. Certainly, so far as consumer contracts were concerned, UCTA articulated a very clear policy agenda; and, from that point on, judicial reasoning could continue to be policy-orientated but now in a way that reflected *legislatively* authorised consumer protection rather than judicially adopted policies.

**6.11** When judges are guided by the general principles of contract law (or, indeed, the general principles of tort law or property law, or criminal law, or public law) they reason like pure 'coherentists'. When they are guided by particular policy purposes that have been initiated and adopted by themselves or by fellow judges, then they reason in a 'regulatory-instrumentalist' way—which invites the criticism that it is not for judges to act like 'legislators'.[14] And, when they reason in a way that tracks and reflects the policies mandated by the legislature, then this is generally seen as a progressive approach (for example, where statutes are interpreted purposively, in line with legislative objectives, rather than literally).

**6.12** In this part of the chapter, we can elaborate the two principal modalities: reasoning that is coherentist and based on principle; and reasoning that is regulatory-instrumental and based on policy.

### *Coherentism and reasons of principle*

**6.13** Coherentism is defined by four characteristics.[15] First, for coherentists, what matters above all is the integrity and internal consistency of legal doctrine. This is viewed as desirable in and of itself. Second, coherentists are not

---

11 See, e.g., the notorious decision in *L'Estrange v F. Graucob Ltd.* [1934] 2 KB 394, and *Suisse Atlantique Societe d'Armement SA v NV Rotterdamsche Kolen Centrale* [1967] 1 AC 361. On the latter, see Roger Brownsword, 'Fundamental Questions: *Suisse Atlantique* Revisited' in Paul Mitchell and Charles Mitchell (eds), *Landmark Cases in the Law of Contract* (Oxford: Hart, 2008) 299.

12 See, e.g., *Karsales (Harrow) v Wallis* [1956] 1 WLR 936.

13 For discussion, see Roger Brownsword, 'Remedy-Stipulation in the English Law of Contract: Freedom or Paternalism?' (1977) 9 *Ottawa Law Review* 95; and, John N. Adams and Roger Brownsword, *Understanding Contract Law*, 5th edn (London: Sweet & Maxwell, 2007) 144–145.

14 Seminally, see Ronald Dworkin, *Taking Rights Seriously* (rev edn) (London: Duckworth, 1978).

15 See Roger Brownsword, 'After Brexit: Regulatory-Instrumentalism, Coherentism, and the English Law of Contract' (2018) 35 *Journal of Contract Law* 139.

concerned with the fitness of the law for its regulatory purpose. Third, coherentists approach new technologies by asking how they fit within existing legal categories (and then try hard to fit them in). Fourth, coherentist reasoning is anchored to a number of general foundational principles. In the case of questions about the enforcement or non-enforcement of transactions, the foundational principles are that parties should be free to make their own deals and that it is the fact that parties have freely agreed to a deal that justifies holding them to the bargain. Coherentism is, thus, the natural language of litigators and judges, who seek to apply the law in a principled way.[16]

**6.14** However, according to Edward Rubin, the days of coherentism are numbered. Nowadays, Rubin claims, we live in the age of modern administrative states where the law is used 'as a means of implementing the policies that [each particular state] adopts. The rules that are declared, and the statutes that enact them, have no necessary relationship with one another; they are all individual and separate acts of will'.[17] In the modern administrative state, the 'standard for judging the value of law is not whether it is coherent but rather whether it is effective, that is, effective in establishing and implementing the policy goals of the modern state'.[18]

**6.15** In contrast to such modern regulatory thinking, coherentism presupposes a world of, at most, leisurely change. It is not geared for making agile responses to rapidly emerging and highly disruptive technologies. When they are called on to respond to new technological developments, coherentists tend to try to classify the new phenomena within existing legal categories. For example, while the initial response to embryonic e-commerce was clearly driven by a regulatory concern that e-transactions should be legally recognised and supported, there was, and still is, a distinctly coherentist response that tries to apply the legal template for offline contracts and the principles of contract law to the emerging world of online transactions.[19]

**6.16** In the case of blockchain, one of the principal topics of coherentist conversation is likely to be whether a smart contract is to be regarded as, in principle, a legally enforceable contract (as per the law of contract).[20] While some of the examples that might be given to illustrate the nature of smart contracts do not sit easily with the template for fiat contracts, this is simply a problem with

---

16 For a somewhat similar view, presented as a 'legalistic approach' to emerging technologies, see N. Petit, 'Law and Regulation of Artificial Intelligence and Robots: Conceptual Framework and Normative Implications', available at https://papers.ssrn.com/sol3/papers.cfm?abstract_id=2931339 (accessed 17 February 2018).

17 Edward Rubin, 'From Coherence to Effectiveness' in R. van Gestel, H.-W. Micklitz and E.L Rubin (eds), *Rethinking Legal Scholarship* (New York: Cambridge University Press, 2017) 311.

18 Ibid, at 328.

19 For discussion, see Roger Brownsword, 'The E-Commerce Directive, Consumer Transactions, and the Digital Single Market: Questions of Regulatory Fitness, Regulatory Disconnection and Rule Redirection' in S. Grundmann (ed.) (n 3) 165.

20 See Roger Brownsword, 'Regulatory Fitness: Fintech, Funny Money, and Smart Contracts' (n 4); and, generally, see Primavera De Filippi and Aaron Wright, *Blockchain and the Law* (Cambridge, MA: Harvard University Press, 2018) 74 et seq.

the particular examples rather than with smart contracts. Nevertheless, even with unhelpful examples out of the way, there will still be some puzzlement. In particular, coherentists will wonder where we find the offer, the acceptance and the consideration when all that we have is a coded instruction to transfer a specified value from A's wallet to B's wallet on the occurrence of some specified event. Moreover, the technology is designed to guarantee that, on the occurrence of the specified event, the value is duly transferred from A to B. So, how is it possible to apply doctrines that allow for the avoidance of a transaction—for example, doctrines such as duress and undue influence, or misrepresentation—to a smart contract; or, in the event that the technology fails to perform, how should we determine whether there has been a breach (and, if so, how are we to decide upon the nature of the breach and the appropriate remedy)?[21] Furthermore, how can this possibly be viewed as a contract when the terms and conditions are not written in natural language and when there are no humans in the blockchain loop? To the coherentist, the idea that a smart contract can be likened to an agreement for the supply of goods or services (the staple of the law of contract) will be perplexing indeed.[22]

### Regulatory-instrumentalism and reasons of policy

**6.17** In contrast with coherentism, regulatory-instrumentalism is defined by the following four features.[23] First, as Rubin explains, regulatory-instrumentalism is not concerned with the internal consistency of legal doctrine. Second, it is entirely focused on whether the law is instrumentally effective in serving specified regulatory purposes. Regulatory-instrumentalists do not ask whether the law is 'coherent'—other than in the sense of asking whether a group of related interventions pushes in the required regulatory direction—but whether it works. Third, regulatory instrumentalism has no reservation about enacting new bespoke laws if this is an effective and efficient response to a question raised by new transactional technologies. Fourth, the anchoring points for regulatory-instrumentalists are not the general principles that are established in the jurisprudence but current policy purposes and objectives. It follows that, for regulatory-instrumentalists, the enforcement or non-enforcement of transactions should turn on how the options stand relative to relevant regulatory purposes; and the justification for taking one option rather than the other is that this is

---

21 Compare the UK Jurisdiction Taskforce of the LawTech Delivery Panel's consultation paper on 'The status of cryptoassets, distributed ledger technology and smart contracts under English private law' (May 2019) at para 3.2:

> [I]f smart contracts are capable of giving rise to binding legal obligations, it will be important for parties to be aware of the circumstances in which this will be the case (notably if the parties' intention is not to create legal relations). It will also be important for parties to know if and how their rights might be enforced in the event that technology does not work as expected.

22 For example, see the discussion in K. Werbach and N. Cornell, 'Contracts *Ex Machina*' (2017) 67 *Duke Law Journal* 313, 338 et seq.

23 See Brownsword (n 15).

judged to be in line with regulatory policy. Regulatory-instrumentalism is, thus, the (democratically) mandated language of legislators, policy-makers and regulatory agencies.[24]

**6.18** From the industrial revolution onwards—at any rate, in the common law world—the direction of travel in criminal law, torts and contracts has been away from coherentism and towards regulatory-instrumentalism. While intentionality and fault were set aside in the regulatory parts of criminal law and torts, classical transactionalist ('meeting of the minds') ideas of consent and agreement were marginalised, being replaced in the *mainstream* of contract law by 'objective' tests and standards set by reasonable business practice. As Morton Horwitz puts it, there was a dawning sense that 'all law was a reflection of collective determination, and thus inherently regulatory and coercive'.[25]

**6.19** What we see across these developments is a pattern of disruption to legal doctrines that were organically expressed in smaller-scale non-industrialised communities. Here, the legal rules presuppose very straightforward ideas about holding to account those who engage intentionally in injurious or dishonest acts, about expecting others to act with reasonable care and about holding others to their word. Once new technologies disrupt these ideas, we see the move to strict or absolute criminal liability without proof of intent, to tortious liability without proof of fault and to contractual liability (or limitation of liability) without proof of actual intent, agreement or consent. Even if the development in contract is less clear at this stage, in both criminal law and torts we can see the early signs of a risk management approach to liability. Moreover, we also see the early signs of doctrinal bifurcation, with some parts of criminal law, tort law and contract law resting on traditional principles (and representing, so to speak, 'real' crime, tort and contract) while others deviate from these principles—often holding enterprises to account more readily but also sometimes easing the burden on business for the sake of beneficial innovation[26]—in order to strike a more acceptable balance of the benefits and risks that technological development brings with it.

**6.20** Unlike a coherentist conversation about blockchain, a regulatory-instrumentalist conversation will not focus on the application of the general principles of the law of contract to smart contracts. Rather, against the backcloth of relevant economic and social policies, the conversation will seek to identify the potential benefits and risks of committing transactions (or parts of transactions) to a blockchain and it will then strive to find an acceptable balance between

---

24 For example, the UK Financial Conduct Authority is conspicuously sensitised to 'reg tech' (in the sense of utilising information technologies to enhance regulatory processes with a particular emphasis on monitoring, reporting and compliance): see FCA Press Release, 20 February 2018, available at www.fca.org.uk/news/press-releases/fca-launches-call-input-use-technology-achieve-smarter-regulatory-reporting (accessed 26 May 2018).

25 Morton Horwitz, *The Transformation of American Law 1870–1960* (Oxford: Oxford University Press, 1992) 50.

26 For example, in the United States, the interests of the farming community were subordinated to the greater good promised by the development of the railroad network: see Morton Horwitz, *The Transformation of American Law 1780–1860* (Cambridge, MA: Harvard University Press, 1977).

management of the risks and not stifling enterprise. The challenge is to find the regulatory sweet spot, neither over-regulating (and stifling innovation) nor under-regulating and exposing parties to unacceptable risks.[27]

## The question of non-congruence: doctrinal principles, regulatory policies and automated transactional technologies

**6.21** In principle, there are many instances in which an automated transactional technology might generate outcomes that would not be supported by a judge applying the law of contract. It might be, for example, that a payment is made pursuant to a smart contract instruction despite a lack of an intention to create legal relations, or a lack of consideration, or even though there has been a fundamental mistake or improper pressure or duress; and it might be that the technology delivers benefits to third-parties where those third-parties would not be assisted by the law of contract. Or, again, it might be that the 'terms' and 'remedies' that are encoded in the smart contract are inconsistent with the terms that the courts would recognise and the remedies that they would order. In all these cases, there is a lack of congruence between the code of contract law and the code of the smart contract. How might this be viewed by the legal community?

**6.22** In principle, an automated transactional technology might (i) enable a payment or a (non-payment) performance or (ii) disable a payment or a (non-payment) performance. If such technological enablement or disablement is at variance with what a court applying the law of contract would order, then we have a question of non-congruence.

**6.23** In this part of the chapter, we can assess how the logic of coherentist and regulatory-instrumentalist reasoning might apply in such non-congruent states of co-existence by focusing on some test cases. We start with cases of technological enablement and then discuss cases of technological disablement.

### Technological enablement

**6.24** Here, we can consider four cases of non-congruence by virtue of technological enablement. These are: (i) a payment made to a third-party within a business network, (ii) a 'remedial' payment that a court would regard as either 'over-compensatory' or 'under-compensatory' to the extent that it deviates from the prevailing interpretation of the standard expectation measure, (iii) an 'agreed damages' payment that a court would disallow as being 'penal', and (iv) a payment for services that a court would not enforce as being part of an illegal transaction.

---

27 Compare the excellent discussion of the regulation of 'TechFins' in D.A. Zetzsche, R.P. Buckley, D.W. Arner and J.N. Barberis, 'From FinTech to TechFin: The Regulatory Challenges of Data-Driven Finance' European Banking Institute, EBI Working Paper Series 2017, no. 6, 31 et seq.

Networks

**6.25** Elsewhere,[28] I have asked how the law community might respond if smart contracts are utilised in business 'networks' (such as franchising or carriage or construction). With regard to such business arrangements, the law as formally articulated (if not always as practically applied by policy-sensitive courts) has been slow to recognise both third-party claims (even though the parties are 'economically connected') and the parties' expectations of heightened cooperative rights and responsibilities.[29] Might a transactional technology comprising networked machines or nodes be viewed as the answer to a set of questions presented by networked business relationships and in relation to which the law of contract is arguably unsatisfactory?[30]

**6.26** Stated shortly, my view is that the response of the law community will depend upon whether such technologically enabled networks raise questions of coherentist principle or also questions of regulatory policy. If the only reservation about such networks is that the technology has practical effects that are not congruent with what a court (applying the law of contract) would order, there is really no problem. The technological coding differs from the legal coding but, without more, we have no reason to think that such technologies and their transactional effects should be either actively discouraged or encouraged.

**6.27** This reflects what I am calling the principle of 'detachment'. On this analysis, contract law is simply an optional governance regime for transacting; and, if the parties choose to deal on some other basis then, *other things being equal*, they are permitted (but not encouraged) to do so. Smart contracts in networks simply operate in a separate transactional universe. That said, if there are policy reasons for taking a different view (whether for discouragement or

---

28 Roger Brownsword, 'Smart Transactional Technologies, Legal Disruption, and the Case of Network Contracts' in Larry di Matteo, Michel Cannarsa and Cristina Poncibò (eds), *The Cambridge Handbook of Smart Contracts, Blockchain Technology and Digital Platforms* (New York: Cambridge University Press, 2019) 313.

29 See, e.g., Marc Amstutz and Gunther Teubner (eds), *Networks: Legal Issues of Multilateral Cooperation* (Oxford: Hart, 2009); Gunther Teubner, *Networks as Connected Contracts* (Oxford: Hart, 2011); Roger Brownsword, 'Contracts in a Networked World', in Larry DiMatteo, Qi Zhou, Severine Saintier and Keith Rowley (eds), *Commercial Contract Law: Transatlantic Perspectives* (Cambridge: Cambridge University Press, 2012) 116; Roger Brownsword, 'Contracts with Network Effects: Is the Time Now Right?' in Stefan Grundmann, Fabrizio Cafaggi and Giuseppe Vettori (eds), *The Organizational Contract: From Exchange to Long-Term Network Cooperation in European Contract Law* (Aldershot: Ashgate, 2013) 137; and the chapters on networks in Part Two of Roger Brownsword, Rob van Gestel and Hans-W. Micklitz (eds), *Contract and Regulation: A Handbook on New Methods of Law Making in Private* Law (Cheltenham: Edward Elgar, 2017).

30 Specifically, on smart contracts and networks, see Florian Idelberger, 'Connected Contracts Reloaded—Smart Contracts as Contractual Networks' in Stefan Grundmann (ed.) (n 3) 205. But, nb, Stefan Grundmann and Philipp Hacker, 'The Digital Dimension as a Challenge to European Contract Law—The Architecture' in Stefan Grundmann (ed.) (n 3) 3, at 38 cautioning that we should take care in deriving 'lessons from arrangements in digital networks (typically highly formalised) for those in the analogue world'. For the question of whether the networked nodes might themselves form a contractual relationship (potentially leading to joint liability to third parties), see the excellent discussion in Dirk A. Zetzsche, Ross P. Buckley and Douglas W. Arner, 'The Distributed Liability of Distributed Ledgers: Legal Risks of Blockchain' European Banking Institute, EBI Working Paper Series 2017, no. 14, 26–27.

encouragement), that is another matter. On the face of it, though, there are no such reasons for interfering with transactors who operate in networks and who employ smart technologies to achieve the desired network effects.

**6.28** Suppose, though, a party to a network seeks the court's assistance, their complaint being that the smart technologies give effect to payments that have not been freely agreed because the weaker members of the network are subject to economic duress. Although a court might judge that it has no brief to apply the law of contract in such circumstances, it might judge that it has a role to play in discouraging unfair transactional practices and be willing to assist the claimant by making an appropriate restitutionary order.[31] Or, the court might judge that, as a matter of policy, it should act against duress in commercial dealing and make whatever ruling is required. Or, then again, it might judge that such a policy matter is better addressed by a regulatory body. If the matter is then remitted to a regulatory body, while such a body might wish to support business networks (or, networks of the kind that we find forming around a multitude of 'platforms'),[32] it might depart from a 'light touch' approach if the duress within networks is problematic relative to the guiding regulatory objectives.

Deviation from the expectation measure

**6.29** In the event that smart transactions are regarded as qualifying contracts (to which the law of contract applies), then I suggest that a second guiding principle comes into play. This is the principle of equivalent treatment. Just as it is said that 'online contracts' should be treated no differently to 'offline contracts', or that the rules that apply offline should also apply online, the idea is that smart contracts should be treated no differently to 'non-smart contracts'. Crucially, if it is open to parties to fiat contracts to switch rules that the law of contract regards as default options, then the same should hold where the switch is effectuated by a transactional technology.

**6.30** For example, let us suppose that a smart contract is coded for 'remedial' payments in a way that deviates from the standard expectation measure of damages for breach of contract (which measure is designed to put the innocent party in the 'same position' as if the contract had been performed).[33] This might be because, by the standards of contract law, the coded payments are over-compensatory (for instance, covering the cost of cure rather than diminution of value,[34] or sticking to assessment of loss at the date of breach rather than the

---

31 Even if the transactional record is immutable, an off-chain restitutionary payment could be ordered.

32 See, e.g., Vanessa Mak, 'Regulating Contract Platforms, the Case of Airbnb' in Stefan Grundmann (ed.) (n 3) 87; and Larry A. DiMatteo, 'Regulation of Share Economy: A Consistently Changing Environment' in R. Schulze and D. Staudenmayer (eds), *Digital Revolution: Challenges for Contract Law in Practice* (Baden-Baden: Nomos, 2016).

33 As classically expressed in *Robinson v Harman* (1848) 1 Exch 850.

34 Famously, as was the central issue in *Ruxley Electronics and Construction Ltd v Forsyth* [1996] AC 344.

date of the court hearing);[35] or, it might be because, relative to these standards, the coded payments are under-compensatory (for instance, because they provide only for the cost of replacement of defective goods and not for any consequential loss).[36] Either way, if it is open to human contractors to change the default measure in this way, coherentists will reason that it should also be open to a smart transactional technology to do so.

**6.31** That said, the expectation measure, while relatively easy to state, is notoriously difficult to apply and, in any particular case of alleged non-congruence, there might well be divergent judicial views as to the application of the standard rule. However, should this be the case, it is not a problem with smart contracts or non-congruence as such; it is a disagreement about the interpretation and application of the legal code.

## Penalties

**6.32** Some rules of the law of contract are mandatory. For example, one of the red lines for courts is that they will not enforce a provision that is judged to be 'penal'. Applying the principle of equivalent treatment, it should make no difference whether the provision is part of a smart or a non-smart contract. Quite simply, the provision will not be enforced. So far so good. However, for some time, the courts have been signalling that they are reluctant to treat 'agreed damages' provisions in commercial contracts as penalty clauses and, in the *Cavendish Square Holding*[37] case, the Supreme Court held that traditional indicators of a penalty (such as a 'deterrent' purpose behind the provision, or whether the sum represented 'a genuine pre-estimate' of the innocent party's loss) were unhelpful. Instead, the question is whether the innocent party is protecting a legitimate interest and whether the provision is proportionate relative to that interest. With this doctrinal shift, it is hard to know quite where the red line is drawn. Moreover, if the damages that are agreed in a smart contract are expressed in a cryptocurrency, and if that currency is subject to extraordinary fluctuations (as has been the case with Bitcoin), it is anybody's guess how a court will react if the provision is challenged as being 'penal'.

**6.33** Again, though, it is worth labouring the point that, in this particular instance, the problem that we now have in anticipating how the uneasy coexistence of smart contracts and contract law will unfold is primarily caused by the uncertain doctrinal landscape of some parts of the latter and not by the non-congruence of the former.

---

35 As was the central issue in *Golden Strait Corporation v Nippon Yusen Kubishka Kaisha (The Golden Victory)* [2007] UKHL 12.

36 Compare the competing measures in *Transfield Shipping Inc v Mercator Shipping Inc (The Achilleas)* [2008] UKHL 48, where the choice was between the standard rule with regard to recovery for consequential losses and the more restrictive local market rule.

37 *Cavendish Square Holding BV v Talal El Makdessi; Parking Eye Limited v Beavis* [2015] UKSC 67.

Payments associated with an illegal contract[38]

**6.34** What are the implications of a lack of congruence where illegal contracts are at issue? What does the coherentist principle of equivalent treatment indicate here?[39]

**6.35** Famously, Lord Mansfield—writing long before transactional technologies had presented questions of non-congruence—remarked that 'No court will lend its aid to a man who founds his cause of action upon an immoral or an illegal act'.[40] Taking this principle at face value, we would expect a court, at the very least, to decline to assist a litigant who is party to a transaction that is a means to an immoral or illegal end; and we would expect this to be the case whether the transaction is a fiat contract or a smart contract.

**6.36** For example, suppose that A employs B, a contract killer, to kill C for an agreed fee. The contract is committed to a technology that not only hides the identities of A and B but also automatically transfers the agreed fee to B once C has been killed. I take it that such an outcome would not be sanctioned by the law of contract. As Lord Neuberger said in *Patel v Mirza*,[41] where the whole purpose of a contract is 'the commission of a crime (eg a contract killing)' then 'the illegality would result in the court (if it could otherwise do so) not being able to order specific performance of the contract or damages for its breach'.[42] It seems to follow that the courts should (at minimum) do nothing to encourage such an illegal activity.

**6.37** However, what if the technology ensures that B is paid before B kills C but then B fails to kill C? Should a court assist A to recover the payment made to B? Recalling Lord Mansfield's seminal remarks, coherentists might think that, as a matter of principle, the courts should do nothing to assist either A or B. In other words, this variation on the facts makes no difference. However, in the recent case-law—notably in *Patel v Mirza* itself and in *DC Merwestone*[43]—we find the Supreme Court taking a somewhat nuanced approach. According to the Court, there are seriously (and intrinsically) illegal acts/transactions and there are merely illegal acts/transactions; and there are some lies that are more material than others. Instead of a general rule, we have a shift to a case-by-case examination which is sensitive to principles of fairness and proportionality—but an approach, nevertheless, that is still essentially coherentist in nature. Moreover, coherentists might also argue that where a court assists A by appealing to

---

38 For an interesting commentary on the jurisprudence relating to illegal transactions and trusts, see Remigius Nwabueze, 'Illegality and Trusts: Trusts-Creating Primary Transactions and Unlawful Ulterior Purposes' (2019)(2) *The Conveyancer and Property Lawyer* 1.

39 For a perceptive critique of coherentist thinking (*qua* simple doctrinal consistency) in this particular context, see Irit Samet, *Equity: Conscience Goes to Market* (Oxford: Oxford University Press, 2018).

40 *Holman v Johnson* (1775) 1 Cowp 341, 343.

41 [2016] UKSC 42.

42 [2016] UKSC 42, para 159.

43 *Versloot Dredging BV and anr v HDI Gerling Industrie Versicherung AG and ors* [2016] UKSC 45.

restitutionary principles (as was the case with four of the Supreme Court Justices in *Patel v Mirza*), then this can be squared with Lord Mansfield's general principle. That said, murder is the most serious of crimes, A is complicit, and it is hard to imagine that even a more nuanced application of general principles would help A's cause.

**6.38** Arguably, though, reliance on coherentist principles is not the right way to tackle the questions to which illegal contract cases can give rise. Rather, our approach should be more regulatory. For example, imagine that a legislative provision that is designed to protect tenants against rapacious landlords, makes it a criminal offence for a landlord to exact certain 'ancillary' charges on tenants. The legislation, however, is silent on the question of whether agreements between landlords and tenants concerning the now prohibited charges are legally enforceable. Clearly, the statutory silence notwithstanding, no court would contemplate ordering a tenant to make a prohibited payment to the landlord; and, it would be equally out of line with the regulatory policy if a court declined to assist a tenant to recover a prohibited payment to a landlord for the reason that this would be to aid a party to an illegal contract.[44]

In *Patel v Mirza*, Lord Neuberger—whose judgment we can treat as being 'representative' of the sweep of judicial views in this case[45]—hints at a more regulatory approach by noting on several occasions that the relevant law is 'based on policy'.[46] Moreover, in Lord Neuberger's rendition of the majority approach, we read that the courts (in illegal contract cases) should 'bear in mind the need for integrity and consistency in the justice system, and in particular (a) the policy behind the illegality, (b) any other public policy issues, and (c) the need for proportionality'.[47] It is not entirely clear, however, whose policy it is—judicial or legislative—or which policy it is that is being relied on. In particular, it seems to be assumed that, in general, it is good policy to return the parties to an illegal transaction to the position that they were in *ex ante*. In favour of such a policy, it can be said that there is no reason why one party to such a transaction should gain at the expense of the other. Yet, if these parties are complicit in a prohibited transaction, why should the law take an interest in correcting any inter-party unfairness? Why not simply treat the parties as acting entirely at their own risk if they engage in such dealings?

**6.39** In an ideal world, the legislature (or other regulatory body) should explicitly provide for any remedies that might be available in relation to illegal transactions. For example, if the legislation provides that the courts should, in all circumstances, act to discourage and disincentivise the relevant illegal activity,

---

44 Compare Lord Neuberger's general remarks in *Patel v Mirza* at para 162; and specifically, see *Kiriri Cotton Co. Ltd. v Ranchhoddas Keshavji Dewani* [1960] AC 192. More recently, the approach in *Hounga v Allen and Another* [2014] UKSC 47, might be thought to be analogous.

45 While Lord Neuberger's judgment starts with a restitutionary approach of the kind favoured by the concurring judges, it also adopts the essence of Lord Toulson's majority approach.

46 See *Patel v Mirza* at para 161.

47 At para 174.

then that is clear enough; and, even in a 'hard case' such as *Patel v Mirza*, no relief should be given to A. On the other hand, where the regulatory view is itself unclear, the courts might view themselves as having a discretion (i) to assist with such hard cases, or (ii) neither to assist nor to discourage in such cases, or (iii) actively to discourage the illegal acts in question; and, whatever discretions, uncertainties and tensions that we find in the law will be reflected in doubts about the equivalent treatment of illegal smart contracts.

**6.40** Taking stock, in some cases of technological enablement, the courts might simply keep the transactions in question at arm's length, taking the view that contract law has its limits but that the particular limits do not call for any response other than detachment. In other cases, however, where the courts eschew detachment and try to apply a principle of equivalent treatment, the most serious challenge might be, not that it is difficult to compare technologically mediated transactions with traditional face-to-face dealing, but that the reference points in the law of contract are not themselves entirely clear or coherent.

*Technological disablement*

**6.41** Here, we can consider two cases of non-congruence by virtue of technological disablement. These are: (i) a technological barrier to a creditor recovering the full amount of the debt that is owed, and (ii) the use of a technology that automatically disables one party from enjoying access to and use of goods or services in the event of a breach (such as a consumer purchaser or hirer failing to make the scheduled payments).

A creditor's promise to settle for less (with any attempt to recover the balance of the debt being disabled)

**6.42** A familiar puzzle arises in the English law of contract where creditor A agrees to accept a lesser sum from debtor B in full and final settlement of the debt. In such a case, the much-criticised rule is that A's 'agreement' notwithstanding, A may recover the balance of the debt from B.[48] Recently, it was thought that the Supreme Court in the *Rock Advertising* case[49] might change the rule; however, the Court avoided the issue and simply said that this area of the law is probably ripe for re-examination. Given that the rule is criticised both as a matter of principle (based on A's promise, B's reliance and B's reasonable expectation) and of policy (that utility is served by encouraging distressed debtors to clear their debts in this way) it might be that a legislative re-examination would be more appropriate than the courts (even an enlarged panel of the Supreme Court)[50] taking it on themselves to change the law. At all events, the law is settled but not in a way that invites confidence in its stability or persistence.

---

48 See Foakes v Beer (1883–84) LR 9 App Cas 605 HL.
49 *Rock Advertising Limited v MWB Business Exchange Centres Limited* [2018] UKSC 24.
50 As mooted in *Rock Advertising* by Lord Sumption at para 18.

**6.43** Suppose, then, that the agreement between A and B was in the form of a smart contract, the technology guaranteeing not only that the agreed 'lesser sum' would be paid to A but also that there would be no further payment to A (or that there would be a counter-payment to B should A succeed in a court action for the balance of the debt). Suppose, further, that the lesser sum having been duly paid, A now tried to by-pass the technological disablement by suing for the outstanding sum. What would the principle of equivalent treatment indicate in such circumstances? As in *Rock Advertising*, critics of the rule might hope that the courts would grasp the opportunity to correct the law, or that the legislature would intervene to rewrite the rules.

**6.44** If the courts were to rule in favour of the creditor A, this would suggest that a certain strand of coherentist thinking has persisted and prevailed. However, a ruling in favour of B could mean several things. It might mean that the court has taken advantage of a doctrinal opening to distinguish the case in question from the general line of cases (but not because a smart contract has been employed); or, that having revisited the jurisprudence, the court has taken a fresh view on the guiding principles for such cases; or that the court has abandoned coherentism to form a regulatory view of the matter; or, most radically, perhaps, that the court has regarded the use of a smart contract as material and has departed from the principle of equivalent treatment. In most (but not all) conceivable outcomes, therefore, it would be judicial business as usual, with the fact that a smart contract was used being irrelevant.

An unfair term in a consumer transaction

**6.45** According to section 61(1) of the Consumer Rights Act (CRA) 2015, that Part of the Act which relates to the regulation of unfair terms in consumer contracts 'applies to a contract between a trader and a consumer'. Suppose, then, that the technology that supports a transaction between a supplier and a consumer is such that it automatically disables the use of the goods or services in the event of the consumer failing to comply with the payment provisions of the contract. Admittedly, this scenario is unlikely to arise because, if smart contracts are being used, they will surely be set up by suppliers to guarantee that the agreed payments are made. Perhaps, then, a more realistic scenario is one in which the triggering event is the consumer failing to comply with a non-payment obligation (for example, an obligation to use the goods or services only for certain specified purposes). In such circumstances, would the application of the disabling technology be amenable to challenge under the unfair terms provisions of the CRA?

**6.46** If an individual consumer or a representative body brought this question to a court, there might be an initial argument about whether the smart contract should be treated as a 'contract' within the meaning of the CRA. While coherentists (applying the principle of detachment) might dismiss the case on this ground,[51] courts that take a more regulatory approach will be guided by

---

51 If this seems improbable, we should recall that, in *Fisher v Bell* [1961] 1 QB 394, the court held that the phrase 'offer for sale' in a criminal law statute should be interpreted as in the law of contract.

consumer protection policy considerations. Essentially, the question will be whether it is policy to protect consumers who participate in all permitted transactions with traders regardless of whether the transaction is offline, online, smart or otherwise. If so, the protections in the CRA will be applied. Moreover, even if there is no example of an unfair term in the statutory Schedule that squarely fits the case, the asymmetric nature of the technological effect, coupled with its potential unfairness and its lack of proportionality, will probably persuade a regulatory-minded court that it needs to take protective action.

## Conclusion

**6.47** With the prospect of increasing technological mediation and management of transactions and, concomitantly, with the prospect of different types of non-congruence catching our eye, how might we expect the courts, applying the law of contract, to respond? In this chapter, I have suggested that, while there might be a background tension between the technological-instrumental view of the blockchain community and the view of the law community, there is also a foreground tension *within* the law community between a regulatory-instrumentalist logic and a traditional coherentist logic. Moreover, the logic of coherentism is challenged, not only by a more regulatory approach, but by divisions and instability within the doctrinal body of the law of contract. Accordingly, there are three important spaces to watch.

**6.48** First, we should watch how traditional coherentist reasoning gives shape to judicial thinking. I have suggested that, other things being equal, coherentists will default to two general principles: a principle of 'detachment' and a principle of 'equivalent treatment'. According to the former principle, so long as coherentists understand the law of contract as an optional regime of governance for transactions, *and so long as they interpret smart contracts as non-qualifying transactions*, then they have no reason to become involved—either as enforcers of deals or as protectors of parties—with issues arising from such transactions. Alongside this first principle, the principle of equivalent treatment specifies that, *if smart transactions are recognised as qualifying contracts*, then coherentists should treat a technological choice in just the way that they would treat a transactional choice made by human contractors.

**6.49** Second, we should keep an eye on policy-guided interventions made with a regulatory intent. Generally, it will be the legislature rather than the courts who initiate these interventions but, once the policies are part of the jurisprudence, the courts will be expected to act on them. Most importantly, even if the logic of contractual coherentism points to a position of non-involvement (and non-encouragement), there might be reasons of regulatory policy (or of a broader coherentist kind) that indicate a more active role for the courts, whether as enforcers of agreements (e.g., between creditors and debtors) or as protectors of parties (such as consumers or small businesses) to smart transactions.

**6.50** Third, although there has been a bifurcation in contract law, so that we have the general principles of contract law applying to commercial contracts and a bespoke regulatory regime applying to consumer contracts, the general principles themselves are often unsettled (whether because they do not seem appropriate as a matter of principle or because they do not clearly serve favoured policies). So long as there is such turbulence within the doctrine, it is hard to predict how the principle of equivalent treatment will be applied in particular cases because the doctrinal reference points within the law of contract are themselves unclear. To this extent, if there is a problem, it is in relation to the law of contract rather than the automation of transactions.

## CHAPTER 7

# The resilience of contract law in light of technological change

## *Eliza Mik*

## Introduction

**7.1** The principles of contract law have shown continued resilience in light of constant technological advancements, including the mainstream adoption of the Internet. The ability to absorb technological change may be attributable to the broad manner in which such principles are formulated. Contract law centers on the 'intention' of the parties. Intention must be 'manifested' or 'communicated'. All of these terms can be easily re-interpreted to allow for the idiosyncrasies of email, instant messengers, tweets, etc. Similarly, the foundational proposition that 'intention can be expressed in any manner' has enabled a nearly seamless integration of online contracting. If intention can be manifested by a nod or a handshake, it can also take the form of a click or a swipe. The second prerequisite of an enforceable contract, consideration, can be met not only by peppercorns or money, but also by one's permission to share personal information in return for the provision of online content or by the transfer of cryptocurrencies, such as Bitcoin. In other words, the concept of 'consideration', is sufficiently plastic to accommodate new types of benefits and detriments. The behavior of the contracting parties is evaluated through the lens of 'reasonableness' – another term that changes its shape depending on the technology used. What constitutes 'reasonable notice' of terms on a website laden with interactive elements differs from what is reasonable in a plain email. 'Reasonableness' is always tailored to the situation of the parties.[1] It can thus be said that contract law has 'self-updating properties', or, that it is 'forward compatible'. Those claiming otherwise fail to appreciate the power of analogy and the flexibility of the *ratio decidendi*. Contract law, as it turns out, is not only form agnostic but also technology neutral.[2] Consequently,

---

1 *Hood v Anchor Line* [1918] AC 837, 844.
2 Chris Reed, 'Online and Offline Equivalence: Aspiration and Achievement' (2010) 18 (3) IJ L & IT 249; for a detailed discussion of its many potential meanings and legal implications see Bert-Jaap Koops, 'Should Regulation be Technology Neutral?' in *Starting Points for ICT Regulation, Deconstructing Prevalent Policy One-Liners* (ITeR 2006).

it is generally capable of addressing most problems pertaining to technological change.[3] It must be acknowledged, however, that an increasing number of commercial interactions is mediated by computers and the introduction of such technologies as machine learning or distributed computing (mainly under the guise of so-called blockchains) has lead to an *unprecedented* automation of the contracting process. Consequently, we cannot simply *assume* that contractual principles remain unaffected. Abstracting from sensationalistic statements containing the words 'revolution' or 'disruption', this chapter inquires whether the mainstream adoption of the aforementioned technologies challenges or changes legal principles in the area of contract law. It can be regarded as a common-sensical exploration of their impact (if any) and a slightly cynical confrontation of some 'legal theories' that traditionally accompany cyclical developments in such areas as Artificial Intelligence (or 'AI') or Human-Computer-Interaction ('HCI'). This chapter opposes all theories seeking to modify the principles of contract law due to the fact that a given transaction is mediated by technology.

**7.2** To set the stage for subsequent discussions, two broader points are required.

**7.3** *First*, technological change has always been accompanied by a drive to 'update', i.e. regulate, contract law. The regulation of contractual relationships is, however, an exception and has been historically confined to rectifying systemic deficiencies or codifying existing practices.[4] Contractual relationships have never been regulated on the basis of the technology used to facilitate the process of contract formation and/or performance. There is, after all, no concept of 'vending machine contracts' – although vending machines have been slowly transforming from simple analog automata to digital, interconnected vending computers enhanced with AI. New methods of communicating at a distance triggered the birth of telecommunication regulation. No regulations or 'updates' to contract law were, however, needed to accommodate 'telephone contracting'. The latter was integrated into the law of contract by means of judicial decisions.[5] Unless human life or public safety are at stake, the introduction of sophisticated technologies into the transacting process does not automatically warrant any changes to contract law.[6]

---

3 Lyria Bennet Moses, 'Recurring Dilemmas: The Law's Race To Keep Up With Technological Change' (2007) U Ill J L Tech & Pol'y 239, 244; Victor Mayer-Schönberger, 'The Shape Of Governance: Analyzing The World Of Internet Regulation' (2003) 43 Va J Int'l L 605, 609.

4 e.g., Contracts (Rights of Third Parties) Act 1999; Sale of Goods Act 1979, Misrepresentation Act 1967.

5 *Entores Ltd v Miles Far East Corporation* [1955] 2 QB 327; *Brinkibon v Stahag und Stahlwarenhandelsgesellschaft mbH* [1983] 2 AC 34; see also Juliet M Morignello, William R Reynolds, 'From Lord Coke to Internet Privacy: The Past, Present, and the Future of the Law of Electronic Contracting' (2013) 72 Maryland L Rev 452.

6 Chris Reed, *Making Laws for Cyberspace* (Oxford University Press, Oxford 2012) 106.

**7.4** *Second*, the reader's views on any technology-related legal topic can be framed[7] by carefully selecting the terminology. Paragraphs filled with arcane acronyms and incomprehensible technical terms can lead us to believe that everything has changed and that the law *in its present state* cannot address the (purported) problems resulting from the deployment of [insert: popular technical term].[8] We are also inclined to believe that authors building legal theories around complex concepts like 'self-learning algorithm' or 'neuromorphic computing' are not only familiar with their technical meaning but also with the basic legal principles that are, purportedly, challenged by their commercial application. Often, the opposite is true. Many papers evince a superficial grasp of technology and, quite often, a less-than-satisfactory understanding of the law. It is, after all, more interesting to read sensationalistic stories about the impact of emergent technologies in the popular press than to study the actual textbook on, say, artificial intelligence or on the theoretical underpinnings of contract law. Of course, once terms like 'artificial intelligence', 'algorithm' or 'robot' are replaced with the mundane 'software' or 'computer', the narrative loses its veneer of novelty – and probably the reader's attention. In the context of contract law, technical details are rarely (if ever!) relevant. Readers of this chapter will hence be spared technical descriptions of 'neural networks' or 'tensor processors'. The point of departure is always the legal principle – not some technological detail of questionable importance.

### Roadmap

**7.5** This chapter confronts a number of popular arguments relating to the theory that novel technologies challenge the principles of contract law. It contains three parts, each of which examines the potential legal implications, if any, of three groups of technological phenomena. The first part discusses automation or, to use a more exciting term, the introduction of artificial intelligence into the transacting process. Purportedly, advancements in AI challenge the core assumption in contract law: that of *human* parties intending to enter into legal relations. The problems created by the advancements in AI force us to inquire whether algorithmic trading, machine learning or autonomous agents affect the existence of intention and, on a broader level, raise problems concerning the validity and enforceability of any resulting contract. The second part continues the theme of automation with so-called 'smart contracts', which are often defined as the encoding of legal terms in self-executing computer code. Purportedly, as 'smart contracts' enable not only the automation of performance but also the delegation of enforcement to immutable code, traditional legal institutions become obsolete. The theory is that if both performance and enforcement are entrusted

---

7 I am referring to a term popularized by the Nobel-prize winner, Daniel Kahneman, which refers to the exploitation of a cognitive bias created by the manner certain problems are presented.

8 For a broader discussion see Ute Kohl, 'Legal Reasoning and Legal Change in the Age of the Internet – Why the Ground Rules are Still Valid' (1999) 7 IJ L & IT 123.

to impartial machines, breach becomes impossible. The successful commercial deployment of 'smart contracts' is premised, as it is argued, on their legal enforceability. Consequently, it becomes necessary to examine them through a lens of intention and consideration. The commercial success of 'smart contracts' is also premised on the ability to translate contractual obligations into algorithms, a process aimed at the elimination of ambiguity and enhancement of legal certainty, as well as on the ability to produce error-free, reliable computer code. The third part addresses the potential problems created by so-called ubiquitous computing, the user-facing end of the Internet-of-Things. Unlike the first two parts, which focused on transaction automation, this part addresses problems of manifesting intention by means of or *through* novel computer interfaces. Unlike the first two parts, this part concedes that *there are actual difficulties* in applying legal principles in novel transacting environments. Ubiquitous computing is probably the only technology that warrants serious academic attention. When the Internet spills over our computer screens and when we encounter unexpected requests for consent and contractual terms in contexts that have traditionally been non-commercial, it becomes difficult to rely on the objective theory of contract, which is based on shared communication conventions, and on the presumption that in a commercial context the parties intend to be legally bound. The latter is premised on a clear division between commercial and social settings. Each part explores the potential legal implications of the said technologies and, while abstaining from unnecessary futurism and technophilia, confronts the popular theories that have accrued around them. Particular attention is devoted to the overreaching question whether the principles of contract law, in their *traditional* formulation, are capable of accommodating (or *withstanding*?) technological change. Space constraints prevent a more in-depth evaluation of each of the said technological phenomena. Nonetheless, the arguments made in each part provide a sufficient albeit abbreviated exploration of the relevant legal principles.

## Contract automation and artificial intelligence

**7.6** A suite of technologies, commonly discussed under the labels of AI or Machine Learning ('ML'), are being integrated into the operation of many transacting systems. From vending machines and e-commerce websites to high frequency trading and financial services – the formation and performance of contracts is increasingly automated.[9] Computers are programmed to trade without human oversight, to respond to market information in real-time and to enter into transactions when certain pre-set conditions are met. In parallel with the advancements in AI and ML, it has become fashionable to doubt the validity of contracts formed by means of automated processes ('automated contracts'). The following paragraphs address these recurring doubts. Before proceeding it must be acknowledged that the automation of the transacting process does

---

9 Tom C W Lin, 'The New Financial Industry' (2014) 65 Ala L Rev 567.

raise significant concerns,[10] such as price discrimination or the distortion of financial markets. These concerns, however, fall outside of the ambit of 'pure' contract law. In the context of the latter, the concerns are that once output (e.g., a statement presented on a website) is not merely transmitted but also generated by computers, it becomes problematic to attribute such output to the person deploying the computer, the operator.[11] Given the absence of direct human participation in automated transactions, there is no 'meeting of minds' and no intention.[12] Most doctrinal discomfort is caused by the concept of 'autonomy', which is directly associated with both AI and ML. Existing theories present a melange of ill-understood technical terms and inconsistent claims. They deny the validity of automated contracts *or* attribute them to the computer. For this to work, however, the computer must be granted legal personhood.

### *Some terminology*

**7.7** Before addressing the theories that question the validity of automated contracts, we must clarify certain key terms. In particular, we must understand that many such terms have been imbued with normative connotations which are absent in their original, *technical* context.

### Agents

**7.8** The term 'agent', often accompanied by the adjectives 'electronic' or 'artificial', refers to a wide array of technologies, ranging from word processors, browsers, chat bots and mail servers to high-frequency trading systems.[13] In e-commerce, agents are used to calculate prices and to dynamically generate the contents of websites in response to user requests. As discussed in section 7.13, the technical meaning of 'agent', however, diverges from the legal meaning of the term. Technically, 'agents' are types of computer programs. Legally, 'agents' are persons acting on behalf of others.

### Autonomy

**7.9** Doctrinal problems concerning automated contracts arise only in the case of 'autonomous' systems,[14] i.e. those operating on the basis of built-in knowledge *and* their 'own experiences'.[15] Autonomy is an elusive concept. In a

---

10 Yesha Yadav, 'The Failure of Liability in Modern Markets' (2016) 102 Va L Rev 1031.

11 Leon E Wein, 'The Responsibility of Intelligent Artifacts: Towards and Automation Jurisprudence' (1992) 6 Harv J Law & Tech 103.

12 Tim Allen and Robert Widdison, 'Can Computers Make Contracts?' (1996) 9 Harv J Law & Tech 25.

13 For an attempted taxonomy of 'artificial agents' see Samir Chopra and Laurence F. White, *A Legal Theory for Autonomous Artificial Agents* (The University of Michigan Press, Ann Arbor 2011) 6.

14 Emily Weitzenboeck, *Electronic Agents and the Formation of Contracts* (2001) 9 Int JLIT 204.

15 For the classic definition see Stuart J Russell and Peter Norvig, *Artificial Intelligence: A Modern Approach*, 3rd edn (Pearson, Upper Saddler River 2016) 34.

legal context, the normative aspects of autonomy are instrumental in justifying moral and causal responsibility. In a technical context, however, autonomy is related to automation, the *mechanization* of tasks, and concerns the level of control that machines have over the execution of processes. On the extreme side of automation, machines complete tasks without direct and continuous human control.[16] In this context, autonomy has *no* normative connotations. Humans delegate control to autonomous systems to optimize the performance of pre-defined tasks if such tasks are too complex, dangerous or time-critical for direct human execution.[17] Alternatively, the task itself may be simple but the environment in which it is performed is dangerous or difficult to access.[18] More importantly, control over a system is premised on the ability to continuously communicate with the system. If, as is the case of space missions, communications are limited and the passing of ongoing instructions is technically infeasible, the system must be capable of operating 'by itself'. Autonomy is thus strictly tied to the ability to remotely control a system. Unfortunately, forgetting its close association with automation, legal scholarship has taken autonomy out of its technical context and imbued it with normative undertones. It has also ignored the fact that the concept of 'autonomous agents' concerns the manner in which one component of a software program relates to other components.[19] Oblivious to the original context of such terms, legal scholarship fixated on the agents' ability to pursue *their own* goals and started advocating legal personhood for autonomous agents.

Operators and users

**7.10** Throughout the discussion, we must separate the operator of a system from its user. The term 'operator' concerns persons controlling and/or deploying a particular system to derive economic benefits from its operations. Operators are generally Internet businesses, such as Amazon or Google, who maintain websites with transactional capabilities. They may not have designed or programmed the system but operate the system based on ownership or licensing arrangements.[20] The term 'users' concerns persons interacting with the system, who have no ability to control or influence its operation. The best example are consumers shopping on Amazon. Although *prima facie* the Amazon website (or, to be more precise, the suite of technologies operating in the background) assists them in achieving their objectives, the website operates for the benefit of its operator.

---

16 Thomas B. Sheridan, *Telerobotics, Automation and Human Supervisory Control* (MIT Press, Cambridge 1992).

17 Merel Noorman, *Mind the Gap* (Univeristaire Pers, Maastricht 2008).

18 David Mindell, *Our Robots, Ourselves* (Viking, New York 2015).

19 Michael Luck, Mark D'Inverno and Steve Munroe, 'Autonomy: Variable and Generative' in Henry Hexmoor et al (eds), *Agent Autonomy* (Kluwer, Alphen an den Rijn 2003) 9.

20 Wein (n 11) 105, 106.

## Confronting the theories

**7.11** Theories questioning the validity of automated contracts are character-ized by a misapprehension of technical terms and a lack of understanding of legal principles. They form three overlapping streams. The first separates the computer from its operator and endows it with legal personhood ('separation theories'); the second relies on agency law ('agency theories'), the third denies the existence of intention in automated transactions 'absence of intention'). All three streams aim to validate automated contracts and, in parallel, to develop mechanisms of protecting operators from the unplanned or unintended opera-tions of autonomous computers.

Separation theories

**7.12** Purportedly, once computers become autonomous, they must be sep-arated from their operators and granted legal personhood.[21] In other words, automated contracts are 'validated' by attributing them to computers. Two points arise. First, discussions as to when computers should be recognized as persons are outside of the scope of contract law. Although contractual ca-pacity is premised on legal personhood, contract law does not decide which entities 'deserve' such personhood. Second, recognizing an entity as a legal person is a normative choice dictated by commercial expediency, not the re-sult of fulfilling any technical or psychological criteria.[22] There is no tech-nological threshold beyond which computers require separation from their operators.[23] Moreover, as computers do not 'have' assets, their separation would be pointless because contractual liability requires that both parties be capable of paying damages. Somewhat humorously, the prominent AI re-searcher Daniel Dennett observed that having a robot sign a binding contract on its own, is not a question of getting the robot to understand the clause or to manipulate a pen. It is a question of the robot *deserving* legal status as a morally responsible agent.[24] The problem is that such robot would-be 'too invulnerable to make a credible promise'[25] and disregard the threat of legal enforceability. Abstracting from the fact that neither intelligence nor auton-omy render any computer 'deserving' of personhood, it can be anticipated that truly intelligent systems would indeed be too powerful to worry about the threat of judicial sanctions ...

---

21 Lawrence B Solum, 'Legal Personhood for Artificial Intelligences' (1992) 70 NCL Rev 1231.

22 Bartosz Brozek and Marek Jakubiec, 'On the legal responsibility of autonomous machines' (2017) 25 Art Int Law 293; Celia Wells, *Corporations and Criminal Responsibility* (Oxford University Press, Oxford 2001).

23 One notable exception is the granting of citizenship to Sofia, a social humanoid robot, by the Kingdom of Saudi Arabia.

24 Daniel C Dennet, 'What Can We Do?' in John Brockman (ed.), *Possible Minds: 25 Ways of Looking at AI* (Penguin Press, London 2019) 53.

25 *Ibid.*

Agency theories

**7.13** It is also claimed that, given the purported absence of human intention in automated contracts, a theoretical framework to 'validate' such contracts can be found in agency principles.[26] As agents are instruments of the principal, it is the intention of the principal, not of the agent that is legally relevant.[27] Moreover, as agency relationships may arise by operation of law, the agent's consent or the principal's willingness to have his or her position changed by the agent's actions are not absolute prerequisites. Somewhat illogically, it is also claimed that if computers 'can establish rights and duties on behalf of humans'[28] they should be treated as agents in the legal sense.[29] In such instance, the lack of intention on the side of the 'electronic agent' is conveniently overlooked.[30] Agency theories are, however, incorrect on a broader level. They misinterpret the technical term 'agent' and ignore the fact that computers act 'on behalf' of humans only in the figurative sense. More importantly, they ignore the fact that agency law requires that an agent be a person in the legal sense.[31] If there are no two separate *persons*, there can be no agency relationship. Interestingly, the North American Restatement (Third) of Agency expressly dismisses the idea of treating computer programs as agents and regards them as instruments of those who use them.[32] Despite their prevalence, agency theories must thus be discarded.

Absence of intention

**7.14** Multiple theories deny the existence of human intention in automated transactions. The first, less popular theory derives 'intentionality' from the technological sophistication of the system.[33] Such 'algorithmic intention' is, in turn, equated with 'contractual intention'.[34] Theories ascribing mental states to non-human entities are, however, of limited relevance as they ignore the fact that contract law focuses on outward actions – not on the mental states leading to such actions. The second line of theories emphasizes the absence of human intention in automated transactions and hence the inadequacy of all rules relying on psychological concepts. Three counter-arguments can be suggested.

**7.15** *First*, claims that there is no human intention whenever the computer is autonomous blatantly ignore the fact that autonomy derives from the computer's original programming. Computers do not 'program themselves' or 'make

---

26 Chopra and White (n 13) 32, 33.

27 Francis M B Reynolds, *Bowstead & Reynolds on Agency*, 16th edn (Thomson Professional, London 1968) 3, 4.

28 Chopra and White (n 13) 23.

29 Ugo Pagallo, *The Laws of Robots* (Springer, Dordrecht 2013) 82, 95; Chopra and White (n 13) 56.

30 Lauren Scholz, 'Algorithmic Contracts' (2017) 20 Stan Tech Rev 101, 135.

31 G H L Fridman, *Fridman's Law of Agency*, 6th edn (Butterworths, London 1990) 50–1, 80; in American law, this principle is stated in the Restatement (Third) of Agency, Restatement (Third) of Agency, para 1.04.

32 Restatement (Third) of Agency, para 1.04.

33 Chopra & White (n 13) 11, 17.

34 Pagallo (n 29) 3.

themselves' autonomous. Human intention is *embodied in* and *manifested by means* of computer instructions. The programming of the computer can be equated with *intending* all transactions enabled by such programming.[35] After all, intention can be manifested in any manner – even in computer code. The instructions contained in such code will only be executed in the future when the pre-programmed conditions are met. The very essence of programming is, after all, telling a computer what to do when the program is run.[36] There is always a time lag between programming and execution. The operator's intention persists from the moment of programming to the moment the program executes, i.e. enters into a transaction. According to Bostrom, 'software simply does what it is programmed to do. Its behaviour is mathematically specified by the code'.[37] Despite the lack of direct human involvement at the time of contract formation, the operator's intention derives from the original programming and persists as long as the computer is held out. Contract law does not require the minds of the parties to meet in perfect simultaneity.[38] Moreover, while it is true that in high-volume mass market transactions, operators may not know and specifically intend every transaction generated by their computers, it can be reasonably assumed that they *do not want to know* about each and every transaction. The purpose of automating the contracting process is commercial expediency and the elimination of the necessity to oversee each and every operation of the system.[39] We must also discard theories claiming that automated contracts are invalid because operators cannot anticipate all future transactions 'produced' by the computer. Leaving aside that such 'anticipation' is not legally required, such claims seem to derive from a misinterpretation of the requirement that every contract be certain and complete. 'Certainty and completeness' evince the parties' intention to be legally bound. It is true that a concluded contract must 'settle everything that is necessary to be settled'.[40] It is not true, however, that its contents must be determined or determinable *before* the time of formation. Even in a concluded contract, some obligations can be specified at a later stage by, for example, including price formulae[41] or mechanisms enabling the future determination of the parties' respective obligations.[42] Some 'uncertainty' is tolerated if it is clear that the parties intend to be bound. In automated contracts, the original programming contains the parameters which determine the contents

---

35 Raymond Nimmer, 'Electronic Contracting: Legal Issues' (1996) 14 J Marshall J Comp & Info L 211, 212.

36 Mindell (n 18) 220.

37 Nick Bostrom, *Superintelligence* (Oxford University Press, Oxford 2014) 184.

38 *Kennedy v Lee* 36 Eng Rep 170 (Ch 1817); J M Perillo, 'The Origins of the Objective Theory of Contract Formation and Interpretation' (2000) 69 Fordham L Rev 427, 439, 440.

39 See generally Parasuraman Raja, Thomas B Sheridan and Christopher D Wickens, 'A Model for Types and Levels of Human Interaction with Automation' (2000) 30(3) IEEE Transactions on Systems, Man, and Cybernetics – Part A: Systems and Humans 286, 292.

40 *May and Butcher Ltd v R* [1934] 2 KB 17n, HL per Viscount Dunedin at 21.

41 *Sudbrook Trading Estate v Eggleton* [1983] 1 AC 444.

42 *Queensland Electricity Generating Board v New Hope Collieries Pty Ltd* [1989] 1 Lloyd's Report 205 at 210; *Hillas & Co v Arcos Ltd* [1932] All ER Rep 494.

of all future transactions. In the case of vending machines, such parameters are simple and few, limited to the price and the goods. While the exact moment of contract formation as well as the identity of the counterparty are unknown when the machine is put on display, its operator can anticipate that the goods will be sold at specific price in the future. Other systems, such as websites, contain complex transaction parameters (e.g., customer-specific price variations, seasonal promotions, etc.). A larger set of parameters can create different configurations and operators, such as Amazon, may be unable to anticipate the exact price the goods will be sold for and to whom. Such inability is, however, incidental to the very decision to automate the transacting process[43] and unrelated to their intention to be bound. What is left uncertain – and sometimes unpredictable – is how the program will combine the transaction parameters in light of subsequent input. At the time the contract is formed, however, its contents are certain and complete. Theories questioning the validity of automated contracts on the basis that they 'cannot be anticipated' conveniently overlook the fact that principals cannot anticipate all the transactions of their human agents. In sum, the operator's intention is manifested in the program that determines the contents of all future contracts.[44]

**7.16** *Second*, it is often forgotten that contract law is oblivious to the 'meeting of minds'[45] and disregards actual, subjective intention.[46] Agreement is not 'an issue of fact, to be found by psychological investigation of the parties at the time of alleged origin'.[47] According to the objective theory of contract, which forms a cornerstone of commercial certainty, legal consequences derive from *outward manifestations* of intention. What matters is observable behavior, not the cognitive states underlying such behavior.[48] The subjective intention of the maker of a statement is not apparent from its contents thus legally irrelevant.[49] From a contract law perspective, the question is not how a statement came into being but whether a reasonable addressee would think the other party intends to contract on the terms provided. AI scholarship often emphasizes that it may be impossible to retrospectively explain the decision-making process underlying a particular transaction.[50] In contract law, however, such decision-making process is unimportant. So is the fact that the 'reasoning' underlying a decision made

---

43 Giovanni Sartor, 'Cognitive Automata and the Law' (2009) 17 Artificial Intel L 253.

44 This approach is also reflected in the UETA: 'When machines are involved, the requisite intention flows from the programming and the use of the machine'. UETA section 14 and comment 1.

45 *Byrne v Van Tienhoven* (1880) 5 C.P.D. 344.

46 Clare Dalton, 'An Essay in the Deconstruction of Contract Doctrine' (1985) 94 Yale L J 997, 1042.

47 Edwin Peel, *Chitty on Contract*, 31st edn (Sweet Maxwell, London 2012) 1–019.

48 Michael Furmston, *Cheshire, Fifoot & Furmston's Law of Contract*, 16th edn (Oxford University Press, Oxford 2012) 41, 42.

49 They acquire some relevance in the context of vitiating factors, see generally Rick Bigwood, *Exploitative Contracts* (Oxford University Press, Oxford 2003).

50 Noorman (n 17) 116.

'by' a computer cannot be understood or replicated.[51] The objective theory of contract examines the output of the decision-making process and disregards the decision-making process itself. The computer's programming or the complexity of its algorithm are equally unimportant as the operator's subjective state of mind. Moreover, the user, the reasonable addressee of the statement, cannot distinguish between offers generated by humans and offers generated by computers. Operators remain liable for the transactions concluded by their computers – unless the user, being a reasonable addressee, could not have assumed that the statement represented their true intention, e.g., it was obvious that it contained an error.[52] Most errors will look identical irrespective of their source.[53] In this sense, operators are protected from incorrect computer output by the doctrine of unilateral mistake.[54] Users cannot rely on the objective theory of contract when the 'actual reality of the situation is starkly obvious'[55] or 'snap up' offers which cannot reasonably represent the intention of their makers.[56] Everything turns on the question: *was the mistake apparent to a reasonable man?*[57] A balance must be struck between the objective theory of contract and some inquisitiveness on the side of the reasonable addressee when the price is 'too good to be true'.

**7.17** *Third*, irrespective of their technological sophistication, computers are tools. This approach relies on the objective theory of contract and preserves technological neutrality. The computer's autonomy, including its propensity to display emergent behaviour, does not change the fact that it is programmed and/ or controlled by the operator.[58] This reasoning underlies the scarce case law on the subject.[59] Most decisions derive from the US and involve ATMs, coin operated lockers and ticketing machines.[60] In *State Farm Mutual Insurance Co v Bockhorst*, the court regarded computer errors as errors of its human controllers.[61] In *Thornton Shoe Lane Parking*[62] the court stated that the machine was

---

51  Amitai Etzioni and Oren Etzioni, 'Keeping AI Legal' (2016) 19(1) Vanderbilt J of Ent Tech L 133, 137.

52  Chopra and White (n 18) 46–47.

53  In the famous case of *Chwee Kin Keong v Digilandmall.com Pte Ltd* [2004] SGHC 71 the erroneous price of the printers (S$67 instead of S$2,500) resulted from an accidental uploading of training data by an employee not from an erroneous computation.

54  *Hartog v Colin Shields* [1939] 3 All ER 566; *Smith v Hughes* (1871) LR 6 QB 597.

55  *Chwee Kin Keong v Digilandmall.com Pte Ltd* [2004] SGHC 71 at 105.

56  *Tamplin v James* (1880) 15 Ch D 215.

57  *Taylor v Johnson* (1983) 151 CLR 422; see generally A Phang, *Contract Formation and Mistake in Cyberspace* (2005) 21 JCL 1, 202.

58  Allen and Widdison (n 12) 46.

59  *Child's Dinning Hall Co v Swingler* 197 A 105 (Md 1938).

60  See *Bernstein v Northwestern National Bank in Philadelphia* 41 A2d at 442; *American Meter Co v McCaughn* 1 F Supp 753 (E D Pa 1932); *Marsh v American Locker Co* 72 A 2d 343 (NJ Super Ct 1950); *Ellish v Airport Parking Co of America* 345 NYS 2d 650 (NYAD 1973); *Lachs v Fidelity & Casualty Co of NY* 118 NE 2d 555 (NY 1954).

61  *State Farm Mutual Automobile Insurance Co v Bockhorst* 453 F 2d 533 (USCA 10th Circuit 1972).

62  *Thornton v Shoe Lane Parking Ltd* [1971] 2 QB 163.

a presenter of the defendant's offer, a 'booking clerk in disguise'.[63] Treating the computer as a tool places the risk of unpredicted transactions on 'those who program and control the computer'.[64] This approach encourages diligent programming and supervision.[65] It is also reflected in most e-commerce regulations,[66] none of which create a discrete liability regime for automated transactions. Arguably, this approach can be criticized as equating hammers with artificial neural networks. Nonetheless, only this approach ensures legal certainty, doctrinal integrity and the avoidance of creating technology-specific regimes. Seemingly, such regimes would be based on gradations of autonomy (or automation) and require a clear technology-specific line beyond which the computer is no longer a tool but a discrete legal entity. The progression in the sophistication in the tool must not lead to legal differentiations. Contract law focuses on the output of the tool's operations, not on the complexity of the tool. It also seems illogical to differentiate between tools augmenting our physical strength and those augmenting our cognitive strengths.

## Smart contracts

**7.18** 'Smart contracts' continue the theme of automation, albeit from a slightly different perspective. The said term has many inconsistent definitions.[67] It is commonly associated with the embedding of legal terms in hardware and software to prevent breach or to digitally control assets[68] as well as with 'code and data (sometimes referred to as functions and state) that is deployed using cryptographically signed transactions on the blockchain network'.[69] The concept has entered the mainstream narrative with the introduction of blockchains, i.e. cryptographically authenticated, programmable databases that are maintained by a distributed network of computer nodes and that serve as secure execution environments for 'smart contracts'. We must not, however, be seduced by the *quasi* legal terminology surrounding the concept or by the uninformed use of the term

---

63 *Thornton v Shoe Lane Parking Ltd* [1971] 2 QB 163 at 169; see also *R (Software Solutions Partners Ltd) v HM Customs & Excise* [2007] EWHC 971, para 67.

64 Margaret Jane Radin, 'Humans, Computers and Binding Commitment' (2000) 75 Ind L J 1125, 1128.

65 *eBay Inc v Bidder's Edge Inc* 100 F Supp 2d 1058 (ND Cal 2000).

66 See UNCITRAL Model Law on Electronic Commerce UNCITRAL Model Law on Electronic Commerce with Guide to Enactment (1996) with additional article 5 *bis* Art 13, this approach is also implicit in the Convention on the Use of Electronic Communications in International Contracting, Nov. 23, 2005, U.N. Doc. A/60/21, as adopted on 23 November 2005 and in the Uniform Electronic Transactions Act 1999.

67 For a general review see E Mik, 'Smart Contracts: Terminology, Technical Limitations and Real-World Complexity' (2017) 9 LIT 269; A. Walch, 'The Path of the Blockchain Lexicon (and the Law)' (2016) 36 Rev Banking & Fin L 713.

68 Nick Szabo, 'Smart Contracts: Formalizing and Securing Relationships on Public Networks' (1997) 2 (9) First Monday.

69 D J Yaga et al, *Blockchain Technology Overview*, National Institute of Standards and Technology Internal/Interagency Report 8202, 2018 at 54; J Sklaroff, 'Smart Contracts and the Cost of Inflexibility' (2017) 166 U Penn L Rev 263 at 263.

'contract'. In law, a 'contract' refers to an agreement between two or more parties and to the embodiment of such agreement, usually taking the form of a written document. In technical writings, however, 'smart contracts' are computational entities or a type of technology. Technical writings abound in sentences where 'smart contracts' *do, receive* or *communicate with* something. They also execute themselves and create other contracts. Moreover, 'smart contracts' are not formed or performed but *created, invoked* and *called.* Statements like these reveal that the technical meaning of the term radically diverges from its legal meaning – and that the entire debate around the legal validity of 'smart contracts' might derive from a terminological misunderstanding. Unfortunately, it has become common-place, in both legal and technical literature, to debate the legal implications and enforceability of 'smart contracts'. Of course, such debates can only be enter-tained in those instances where *a specific* 'smart contract' creates, embodies or executes contractual rights and obligations. Two questions arise. Terminological misunderstandings aside, can 'smart contracts' be contracts in the legal sense? What are the practical difficulties of expressing contracts in code?

**7.19** Before proceeding it is necessary to briefly clarify the source of the al-leged superiority of 'smart contracts' – the construct of 'self-enforcement'. It is claimed that contracts should be enforced (or performed?) by objective, infallible algorithms.[70] As blockchain-based 'smart contracts' preclude the possibility of modifying their code and interfering with their operation, they provide 'execution guarantees' by irretrievably binding both parties to their agreement as written.[71] 'Self-enforcement' is thus synonymous with guaranteed performance. The code, i.e. the *agreement embodied in such code,* becomes tamperproof: it cannot be amended or stopped.[72] It is claimed that if performance is guaranteed, there will be no disputes – and hence no need for judicial assistance or any other traditional forms of enforcement. In effect, although the concept of a 'smart contract' seems detached from the original, legal meaning of the term 'contract', the technology itself is supposed to ensure contractual performance and thus increase commer-cial certainty. The preceding claims must, however, be rejected as resulting from a misapprehension of legal concepts. Technical writings generally conflate 'enforce-ment' with 'performance',[73] collapsing two distinct stages in the life of a contract. 'Enforcement' is the *protection,* not a *guarantee* of performance. In common law systems, orders for specific performance, the only legal mechanism designed to compel the actual performance of an obligation, are granted in very limited cir-cumstances.[74] Moreover, as enforcement implies a recourse to an external system, to an entity that exists outside of the contract, the very idea of a contract *enforcing*

---

70 Kevin Werbach and Nicholas Cornell, 'Contracts Ex Machina' (2017) 67 Duke L J 313 at 365.

71 Raymond Cheng et al, 'Ekiden: A Platform for Confidentiality-Preserving, Trustworthy, and Performant Smart Contracts' (2019) IEEE European Symposium on Security and Privacy (EuroS&P).

72 Christopher D Clack et al, 'Smart Contract Templates: Foundations, Design Landscape and Research Directions' (2016) ArXiv e-prints 4.

73 Werbach and Cornell (n 70) 332.

74 John W Carter, *Carter on Contract* (LexisNexis, Sydney 2001) para 01–140.

*itself* is absurd. The idea of a contract *performing itself* is equally non-sensical. Contracts – or contractual obligations – can only be performed by the parties. Moreover, technical writings extol the benefits of the inability to change the code of the 'smart contract' and falsely suggest that the inability to change a contractual document somehow improves the chances of performance.

### The legal enforceability of 'smart contracts'

**7.20** Debates concerning the enforceability[75] of 'smart contracts' traditionally concern the question whether contracts can be expressed in code and whether the processes of formation and performance can be automated. The latter question has already been answered affirmatively.

Expressing intention

**7.21** There are no doctrinal obstacles to expressing contracts in code. Subject to some statutory exceptions, which dictate that some agreements be made or evidenced in writing, contract law is form free.[76] Assumedly, doubts concerning the enforceability of 'smart contracts' (which are, by definition, expressed in code) stem from a failure to distinguish between the *substance* of the contract, i.e. the rights and obligations agreed by the parties, and its *expression*, i.e. the words describing such. The term 'contract' refers both to the agreement and to its embodiment, the document (if any) evincing the existence of such rights and obligations. The source of the parties' rights and obligations is the agreement – not words or documents. Even if the document is destroyed, the rights and obligations persist – they only become more difficult to prove. The physical representation of the agreement, be it words printed on paper or code displayed on a screen, is not the agreement.[77] The latter can be said to have an abstract, independent existence as the writing only constitutes evidence of its contents. Moreover, although we commonly say that 'courts enforce contracts', it is more correct to say that 'courts enforce *obligations*'. As obligations are expressed in words, inquiring whether code is enforceable is tantamount to asking whether words are enforceable. As contract law is agnostic about the manner of expressing agreement, the parties can use any symbol to memorialize their obligations. Contracts can be expressed in code – even if neither party can understand such code or predict how it will execute. If the parties *agree* to express their agreement in code, they are deemed to have assumed the accompanying risks. In sum, both code and natural language are equally valid forms of expression, the difference being that code can be directly 'read' and executed by computers.

---

75 The difference between enforceability and validity is not always clear. A seemingly valid contract may be unenforceable due to the presence of vitiating factors, lack of contractual capacity as well as on grounds of illegality or public policy.

76 UK Law Commission Consultation Paper No 237, *Electronic Execution of Documents* (21 August 2018) 20.

77 Adam J Kolber, 'Not-So-Smart Blochchain Contracts and Artificial Responsibility' (2018) Stan Tech L Rev 198, 219.

Consideration

**7.22** Two questions arise with regards to consideration: 'can crypto-assets, such as bitcoin or tokens, constitute consideration?' and does the 'smart contract involve an exchange?' Regarding the first, it is trite law that consideration need not be adequate but 'only' sufficient in the eyes of the law.[78] The parties can exchange goats for gold and bitcoins for bubblegum. Courts do not measure or examine the value of the contractual subject matter. Any act or promise satisfies the definition of consideration, subject to certain exceptions dictated by morality or public policy. Despite their controversial legal status in some jurisdictions,[79] crypto-assets can constitute valid consideration. It is for the parties to decide what type or amount of consideration they are willing to accept. Challenges concern the second question: while contract law is principally indifferent to the object of the exchange, it is premised on the existence of an exchange. Contract law *assumes* reciprocity: one party does something for or promises something to the other party and *in return* obtains a promise or an act from that party.[80] Conceptually, contracts are bilateral[81] and enforceability concerns bargains.[82] The plaintiff must prove that his or her promise or act, together with the defendant's promise, 'constitutes one single transaction and are closely related to each other'.[83] If there is no exchange, there can be no contract and questions of enforceability become pointless. Present commercial practice demonstrates that most 'smart contracts' constitute *unilateral* transfer mechanisms: software programs enabling the automated generation or transfer of crypto-assets upon the occurrence of pre-defined conditions.[84] They operate (or *execute?*) *as a result* and *in performance of* an agreement.

**7.23** In light of the existing implementations of 'smart contracts' we can tentatively assume that most of them are not contracts in the legal sense. This is not to say that they cannot produce legal effects.

*Encoding contracts*

**7.24** While 'traditional' contracts *create* rights and obligations, 'smart contracts' can – at least theoretically – automate the performance of certain obligations. 'Smart contracts' are always confined to obligations that can be executed by a machine, i.e. automated. In practice and given the current state of the art,

---

78 *Currie v Misa* (1875) LR 10 Ex 153; *Chappell & Co Ltd v Nestle Co Ltd* [1960] A C 87 (H L).

79 Kelvin F K Low and Ernie G S Teo, 'Bitcoins and Other Cryptocurrencies as Property?' (2017) 9 LIT 235.

80 Ian Macneil, 'Relational Contract Theory as Sociology' (1987) 143 JITE 272, 274.

81 Furmston (n 48) 15.

82 See generally Brian Coote, *Contract as Assumption: Essays on a Theme* (Hart Publishing, Oxford 2010).

83 Furmston (n 48) 102.

84 Jenny Cieplak and Stephen Leefatt, 'Smart Contracts: A Smart Way To Automate Performance' (2017) 1 Georgia L & Tech Rev 417.

only obligations that can be expressed in numbers and formulae, such as interest rate swaps or other derivatives,[85] can be rendered 'smart'. As blockchain-based 'smart contracts' cannot (yet) control objects in the physical world, their current capabilities appear to be confined to the transfer of crypto-assets, such as bitcoin or Ether, under pre-defined conditions.[86] The preceding statement must be qualified with the observation that in many instances, a broader definition of the term creates the impression that 'smart contracts' can in fact control physical objects, such as cars or doors. In such instance, the term refers to the software restricting access to the object.

**7.25** We must acknowledge that although it is legally unobjectionable to express contracts in code, there are multiple technical challenges accompanying such expression. Fascinated by clear rules that cannot be broken, programmers often have an 'algorithmic view' of contracts, perceiving them as sets of executable, binary instructions. What programmers, or technical writings in general, fail to recognize is that code faces inherent limitations in light of the natural ambiguity of natural language and the complexity of contractual relationships. After all, contracts are relationships, not instruction sets. Even a purely commercial relationship may be difficult to express as an algorithm – and computer programs, including 'smart contracts', are formal representations of algorithms. To be able to express a contract in code, we must first be able to express it as an algorithm. Legal scholarship must hence approach the claims made in technical writings with caution as many of them derive from a misunderstanding of what contracts are and how they work. Surprisingly, technical writings also overlook the fact that the ability of 'smart contracts' to guarantee performance (i.e. the achievement of a specific, computable result or an objectively verifiable state) exactly *as agreed* depends on: (a) the absence of coding errors, (b) the ability to predict how the contractual relationship will be affected by external circumstances, and (c) the ability of code to express obligations exactly as agreed.

Coding errors

**7.26** The difficulties of coding 'smart contracts' are generally underestimated, especially given the fact that they control crypto-assets which often have a high market price.[87] We must think of 'smart contracts' as software that carries or controls value – not as software that edits documents or spreadsheets. Coding error may result in economic losses. Coding 'smart contracts' requires knowledge of specialized programming languages as well as knowledge concerning the idiosyncrasies of the execution environment, the blockchain itself. To date,

---

85  id 420.

86  See generally Kelvin F K Low and Eliza Mik, 'Pause the Blockchain Legal Revolution' (2020) 69 International & Comparative Law Quarterly 135.

87  See generally Firas Al Khalil, Tom Butler, Leona O'Brien and Marcello Ceci, 'Trust in Smart Contracts is a Process, As Well' in M Brenner et al (eds), *Financial Cryptography and Data Security*, Lecture Notes in Computer Science, Vol 10323 (Springer, New York 2017).

'smart contracts' have been notorious for their lack of security,[88] particularly on the Ethereum network where they have been proven to contain more errors than any other software.[89] The Ethereum ecosystem also suffers from a considerable lack of diversity: 'smart contract' code is extensively re-used, so that existing bugs and vulnerabilities are repeatedly copied.[90] It is a popular misunderstanding that the transparency of 'smart contracts' (i.e. the visibility of their code) contributes to their security and reliability. Nothing can be further from the truth. The inspection of the code cannot reveal how it will execute in practice.[91] Moreover, the visibility of the code enables more skilled programmers to discover and to exploit coding errors made by their less skilled 'colleagues'. We also must not forget that, once activated on the blockchain, the code of the 'smart contract' cannot be modified. Unlike most computer programs, which can be amended or upgraded when coding errors are discovered or when circumstances so demand, 'smart contracts' are immutable. Consequently, their creation should be more costly as they require extensive testing, including formal verification, and advanced programming skills.

Predictability

**7.27** Given their immutability, 'smart contracts' require that *all* details of the transaction be agreed at the time of their creation. Once expressed, the substance of the contract is set in stone. To ensure the commercial viability of the transaction the parties must contractually provide for all future circumstances, that is, predict how the contractual relationship will evolve and how their respective performances may be affected by external events. Arguably, subject to the comments in this section and 7.32, the perfect performance ('happy path') can be described with precision. While it appears easier to 'predict' what both parties have expressly agreed to (i.e. their respective performances), it appears difficult, if not impossible, to predict exceptional situations and deviations from the agreed performance, the 'unhappy path'. The latter is unpredictable and idiosyncratic.[92] Unforeseen circumstances are, after all, unforeseeable at the time of formation and are traditionally addressed by *force majeure* clauses that provide for the fate of the contractual relationship in the event something distorts the original risk allocation. 'Smart contracts' cannot, however, contain *force majeure* clauses as they are very limited in their ability to accept external input (i.e. information about external circumstances that are not natively visible

---

88 Nicola Atzei, Massimo Bartoletti and Tiziana Cimoli, 'A Survey of Attacks on Ethereum Smart Contracts (SoK)' in M Maffei and M Ryan (eds), *Proceedings of the 6th International Conference on Principles of Security and Trust* (Springer, New York 2017) 10.

89 Steve McConnell, *Code Complete*, 2nd edn (Microsoft Press, Washington 2004) 521.

90 Lucianna Kiffer et al, Analyzing Ethereum's Contract Topology IMC '18, 31 October–2 November 2018, Boston.

91 See generally K Bhargavan et al, 'Formal Verification of Smart Contracts: Short Paper' in T Murray and D Stefan (eds), *PLAS* (ACM New York, New York, 2016) 91.

92 Mark D Flood and Oliver R Goodenough, 'Contract as Automaton: the Computational Representation of Financial Agreements' (2015) Office of Financial Research Working Paper 8.

on the blockchain) and in their ability to react to such circumstances.[93] We can thus assume that 'smart contracts' are inherently unsuitable for long-term contractual relationships and for commercial transactions that may be detrimentally affected by a wide range of external circumstances, such as trade wars, natural disasters or political turmoil. The execution environment of the blockchain is not only secure but also isolated from the real world.

Encoding contracts – or obligations?

**7.28** A 'traditional' contract written in natural language cannot be executed by computers. Computers cannot extract instructions from natural language, including its more formalized version of legal prose, as such 'extraction' would require the ability to interpret and *understand* natural language. Understanding requires artificial general intelligence, which is currently beyond the state of the art. Contracts are directed at people. Computers need code. Unfortunately, 'traditional' contract contracts written in natural language cannot be directly *translated* into code or, even if written in precise language, serve as a 'technical specification' for a 'smart contract'. Programmers are unable to interpret legal prose, especially if the meaning of individual words depends on the context. After all, the formalistic, literal approach – one most likely to be adopted by a programmer – has been rejected.[94] As neither computers nor programmers can interpret contracts written in natural language – and most lawyers have no coding skills – a number of approaches have been developed to express agreements (or individual obligations) in a computer-readable manner. The overarching question being 'how do we express contracts in code?' one stream of technical scholarship has focused on the creation of domain-specific programming languages that could convey the semantic richness of legal prose and/or the complexity of commercial transactions,[95] while another stream has focused on the creation of an intermediary language to bridge the gap between legal prose and computer instructions.[96] The first approach assumes that the 'smart contract' constitutes a translation of an existing contract and encounters difficulties in mapping the contract's denotational semantics, which capture its legal meaning,

---

93 This is largely the result of the so-called 'oracle problem', i.e. the closed nature of permissionless blockchains, which need to rely on external data sources that do not share their attributes of security and trustlessness.

94 Gerard McMeel, *The Construction of Contracts* (Oxford University Press, Oxford 2010) 26.

95 F Al Khalil et al, 'A Solution for the Problems of Translation and Transparency in Smart Contracts', Government Risk and Compliance Technology Centre, Report, 2017.

96 Another debate concerns the selection of the most suitable type of programming language for 'smart contracts', the main options being imperative and declarative languages. The imperative approach requires that 'smart contracts' state the computational operations required to implement the agreement, while the declarative approach states the agreed legal arrangements but disregards the computations needed to implement them; see generally Guido Governatori et al, 'On Legal Contracts, Imperative and Declarative Smart Contracts, and Blockchain Systems' (2018) 26 Artif Intell L 377 at 378; Florian Idelberger et al, 'Evaluation of Logic-Based Smart Contracts for Blockchain Systems', in J Alferes et al (eds), *Rule Technologies. Research, Tools, and Applications. RuleML* 2016 (Springer, Cham 2016).

onto its operational semantics, which concern the execution of the respective obligations.[97] Such mapping requires the conversion of abstract legal concepts into specific computer instructions or, to be more precise, matching legal and computational ontologies. Arguably, 'smart contracts' can only gain popularity if legal language can be faithfully expressed in code. Ideally, the code should be *equivalent* to the legal prose, i.e. the conversion of contractual provisions into computer instructions should not modify or simplify the substance of the agreed obligations. While the creation of a domain-specific programming language for 'smart contracts' appears reasonable, two observations come to mind.

**7.29** *First*, attempts to achieve equivalence between denotational and operational semantics expose numerous misconceptions concerning the drafting of contracts. Natural language is naturally ambiguous and contractual relationships are not reducible to binary decision trees. Logically, if a programming language is to ensure equivalence with legal prose, it must be as complex and 'rich' as legal prose. As natural language is inherently imprecise, the idea of creating a domain-specific language that is not ambiguous *but* capable of expressing the semantics of legal prose appears questionable. If computers require precise instructions, the problem might be one of finding obligations that *can* be expressed unambiguously – not of creating a programming language that can replicate legal prose. In addition, technical scholarship fails to appreciate that the complexity of legal prose usually reflects the complexity of the underlying transaction. In a seminal paper on the computational representation of financial agreements, a basic loan had to be stripped of all the commercially relevant intricacies so that its structure could be mapped onto a deterministic finite automaton.[98] In other words: to be expressed in code, the transaction had to be simplified to a degree that made it commercially unrealistic. The search for programming approaches that achieve equivalence between legal and technical language might be futile.

**7.30** *Second*, the focus on *translating* legal prose into code seems ill-advised. As performance and enforcement concern *obligations*, not words, the focus should be on expressing obligations in code – not on translating contractual provisions. This necessitates a shift from developing programming languages that represent legal prose to developing programming languages that facilitate specific transactions.[99] The computational representation of legal prose can be regarded as a redundant intermediary step. It seems pointless to translate into code provisions describing obligations that cannot be automated or containing recitals, indemnities or clauses limiting the liability of the parties. 'Smart contracts' need not represent entire agreements because they are confined to those obligations that can be executed by a machine.

---

97 Al Khalil et al (n 95) 5.
98 Flood & Goodenough (n 92).
99 An example is the Digital Asset Modelling Language, DAML, which aims to model financial agreements.

**7.31** Another approach suggests the development of an intermediate pro-gramming language, which would facilitate the co-operation between lawyers and programmers.[100] Contracts written in such language could, in theory, serve as a specification for the final, 'smart' version and reduce the likelihood of in-terpretation errors. Such intermediary language would approximate legal prose, be transparent and rooted in formal logic. It would also achieve a high degree of equivalence between legal prose and code. While commendable, this approach underestimates the difficulties of developing a programming language bridging legal and computational expression as well as the required educational invest-ment for both lawyers and programmers.

Reducing ambiguity?

**7.32** With these observations in mind, we can conclude with a critique of the popular claim that 'smart contracts' will 'ensure legal certainty by removing the ambiguity inherent to natural language'.[101] The assumption that ambigu-ity is always undesirable is, however, incorrect. Broadly drafted, open-ended provisions often provide flexibility in dealing with uncertain future events and a continually evolving relationship. Legal and commercial certainty need not derive from precise contractual drafting but from a stable system of consistently enforced laws. Of course, a precise contract is better than an imprecise contract. Problems concern the fact that for any obligation to be encoded, or rendered 'smart', it must be drafted with extreme precision – a precision that may not be attainable in natural language as a matter of principle. Few obligations can be reduced to a decision tree or described as mathematical formulae. Many obliga-tions require broad terms, such as 'reasonableness' or 'good faith'.[102] While such terms could simply be eliminated, such elimination would deprive the contract of any flexibility and, effectively, limit the number of obligations that can be automated by means of 'smart contracts'. Arguably, instead of using open-ended concepts, the specific actions describing the agreed behavior or result could be described. This approach would, however, increase transactions costs given that more time will be spent negotiating every detail *as well as* the number of lines of code and hence the probability of coding errors.

## Ubiquitous computing

**7.33** To date, we have associated online transactions with computer screens and e-commerce with websites. As indicated, the ability to creatively re-interpret the principle 'intention can be manifested in any manner' permitted a

---

100 See generally Al Khalil et al (n 87) 2.

101 Michelle Finck, *Blockchain Regulation and Governance in Europe* (Cambridge University Press, Cambridge 2019) 26, 27.

102 M P Gergen, 'The Use of Open Terms in Contract' (1992) 92 Col L Rev 997; K E C Levy, 'Book-Smart, Not Street-Smart: Blockchain-Based Smart Contracts and The Social Workings of Law' (2017) 3 Engaging Science, Technology, and Society 10, 11.

nearly seamless integration of online contracting into mainstream contract law. Some seams start to show, however, when everyday things become computers and when the internet spills out from our screens. The present part demonstrates the difficulties of applying basic concepts of contract law to transactions occurring in the context of ubiquitous computing (or 'ubicomp'),[103] a term commonly associated with Internet-enabled objects ('smart objects') and the convergence of consumer electronics, telecommunications and computing.[104] Smart objects, like the proverbial smart fridge or the popular Amazon Echo, are often equipped with transacting capabilities, enabling the provision of goods and services *by means of* or *through* them.[105] Consequently, many interactions with smart objects can be regarded as transactions – exchanges between the user of the object and the business owning or operating the object (operator). Operators can provide services by means of smart objects or permit their use in return for monetary or non-monetary consideration ('ubicomp transactions').[106] In the home, ubicomp manifests itself through smart thermostats, speakers, fridges, etc. Such objects not only adjust their functionality to user preferences but also enable users to enter into contracts for the provision of goods or services. For example, Amazon's Dash Buttons enables purchases of via buttons placed throughout the home. Orders are placed from the object itself. In the retail context, stores are often enhanced by touch screens to facilitate a seamless movement between in-store and online shopping. Shop assistants are replaced with smart shopping baskets, cashiers with automated check-out terminals or smart mirrors with payment functionality. In public spaces, such as museums or train stations, we encounter self-service kiosks, humanoid robots or interactive walls and vending machines. In home environments, we are generally more familiar with 'our' smart objects and, at least theoretically, we know how to use them. Moreover, the placing of orders 'through' smart objects requires prior enrolment, which usually occurs during the purchase of the smart object or later, at the website of the seller or provider. In retail environments and public spaces, the presence of smart objects is not expected or even immediately apparent. There is also no *prior* enrolment process explaining how the object functions and how to interact with it. Enrolment, if any, may occur 'on' the object itself during the first interaction. Most challenges concern those initial interactions. Two problem areas arise.

---

103 The phenomenon is also discussed under the terms pervasive computing, everyware or autonomous computing environments; see Mohammad Obaidat (ed.), *Pervasive Computing and Networking* (Wiley-Blackwell, Chichester 2011); Adam Greenfield, *Everyware: The Dawning Age of Ubiquitous Computing* (New Riders, Berkeley 2006) (*'Everyware'*); Mireille Hildebrandt, *Smart Technologies and the End(s) of Law* (Edward Elgar, Cheltenham 2015).

104 The Internet-of-Things ('IoT') provides the technical infrastructure for ubicomp; see Rolf H Weber and Romana Weber, *Internet of Things: Legal Perspectives* (Springer, Cham 2010) 1.

105 Kayleen Manwaring, 'Emerging Information Technologies: Challenges for Consumers' (2017) 17 OUCLJ 265, 289.

106 Whether such 'transactions' should be governed by contractual principles is a separate issue for further research.

**7.34** *First*, to date, legal scholarship has discussed the difficulties surrounding the fact that smart objects combine hardware, software and, frequently, a service element.[107] Consequently, the use of the smart objects does in fact involve the creation of multiple contractual relationships. These problems, however, resemble those encountered when purchasing *all* computing devices. Scholarship has also addressed the difficulties of delivering terms or obtaining consent during the purchase and use of such objects,[108] focusing on the spatial and temporal disassociation of the *terms of use* of the smart object from the *contract of sale*.[109] The purchase occurs in a physical environment, but the terms are only available online. Again, while undesirable, this practice is not specific to smart objects. It is also sanctioned by contract law: cases on the incorporation by reference allow terms to be made available in a location which is different from that where the contract is formed.[110] Courts have 'tolerated' references to terms available in remote locations, recognizing the difficulties of providing terms at the point of sale. The present discussion focuses on problems of delivering information and obtaining consent *through* or *by means* of such objects.[111]

**7.35** *Second*, each ubicomp environment is different, equipped with smart objects from different manufacturers, with different interfaces, ranging from voice commands and gesture control, to touch screens and interactive display surfaces. We must not only learn new communication conventions but learn *many* new communication conventions. Each new interface requires adaptation, time to master new input methods. Gradual habituation is hampered by the inconsistent user experiences deriving from the differences between the respective interfaces. At the same time, ubicomp prevents users from relying on our prior experiences. We have grown up in analogue environments, gradually acquiring the governing communication rules and behavioural conventions.[112] We were not given instruction booklets on 'how to purchase groceries'. The assumption that 'consumers operate in the marketplace based on their prior experience'[113] underlies the operation of many legal principles, including the objective theory of contract as well as the evaluation of a party's 'reasonableness'. In ubicomp environments, 'traditional' actions acquire an additional layer of complexity due to the intermediation of a computer.[114] Ubicomp interfaces abound in *symbolic*

---

107 Manwaring (n 105) 283.

108 Scott R Peppet, 'Regulating the Internet of Things: First Steps Toward Managing Discrimination, Privacy, Security & Consent' (2014) 93 Texas L Rev 85.

109 Stacy-Ann Elvy, 'Contracting in the Age of the Internet of Things: Article 2 of the UCC and Beyond' (2016) 44 Hofstra L Rev 839; Elvy introduces the concept of 'contract distancing', and emphasizes that limited access to terms reduces the consumer's ability to understand the bargain.

110 *Hollingworth v Southern Ferries Ltd ('The Eagle')* [1977] 2 Lloyd's Rep 70; *Balmain New Ferry Co Ltd v Robertson* (1906) 4 CLR 379; *Parker v South Eastern Railway Co* (1877) 2 CPD 416.

111 One of the few authors who recognized this problem is Manwaring (n 105) 286.

112 Andrew Hinton, *Understanding Context* (O'Reilly, Sevastopol 2015) 20.

113 Aaron Perzanowski and Chris J. Hoofnagle 'What We Buy When We Buy Now' (2017) 165 U Pa L Rev 315, 322.

114 Golden Krishna, *The Best Interface is No Interface* (New Riders, San Francisco 2015).

*representations* of familiar actions or objects, replacing traditional acts with their digital substitutes. We are forced to respond with symbolic representations of certain communicative signs – instead of nodding in agreement, we press a 'yes' icon on a touch pad or nod towards a sensor. Problems arise when the translation of the traditional into the digital is imperfect or non-intuitive, when consent has too many digital equivalents to remember. After all, the objective theory of contract assumes that both parties attribute a common meaning to certain acts or utterances and share similar, if not identical, communication conventions.

### A brief reminder of the 'past' – the click-wrap debate

**7.36** To better explain the practical challenges accompanying the introduction of novel transacting interfaces, as implicit in the mainstream introduction of smart objects, it is worth recalling the hundreds of US cases concerning so-called click- and browse-wrap agreements, i.e. agreements formed 'on' websites. In comparison to traditional face-to-face interactions or contracts formed in writing, contracts formed on – or *by means* – of websites constitute a dramatic shift from the traditional forms of communication. The relevant cases revolve around the question whether the formation of a contract on a website requires users to click an 'I agree' button after being presented with the terms or whether consent can be expressed by the continued use of the website.[115] The cases also address the question whether the terms must self-display, i.e. be actively brought to the user's attention, or whether it suffices that they are made available through a hyperlink.[116] Click-wrap cases, which represent the mainstream approach, require that terms be displayed or *pushed* to the user, usually by means of pop-up windows.[117] Users are also obliged to deliberately click a graphical element labelled 'I agree', or similar. In contrast, browse-wrap cases suggest that it suffices that users be made aware of the terms and that such terms remain available by means of hyperlinks. Consent can be implied from proceeding within the website (or continuing to use the online service). Absent evidence of actual knowledge of the terms, the enforceability of browse-wraps usually depends on whether users had 'constructive notice' of their existence.[118] The adequacy of such notice depends on the prominence of the hyperlink, evaluated against the website's general design.[119] In recent cases, courts have required increasingly

---

115 *Specht v Netscape Communications Corporation* 306 F.3d 17 (2d Cir., 2002); *Nguyen v Barnes & Noble* 763 F.3d 1171 at 1179 (9th Cir., August 2014); the 'wrap' terminology has expanded to include hybrid forms, such as 'sign-in wraps' or 'scroll-wraps', see *Berkson v Gogo LLC, and Gogo Inc.* Memorandum and Order 14-CV-1199 (E.D.N.Y., 2015).

116 *Fteja v Facebook, Inc.* 841 F.Supp.2d 829 at 837 (S.D.N.Y., 2012); Register.com, *Inc. v Verio, Inc.* 356 F.3d 393 (2d Cir., 2004).

117 *Specht v Netscape Communications Corporation (Specht)* 306 F.3d 17 (2d Cir., 2002).

118 Register.com, *Inc. v Verio, Inc.* 356 F.3d 393 at 401–04 (2d Cir., 2004).

119 *In re Zappos.com, Inc. Customer Data Security Breach Litigation* 893 F.Supp.2d 1058 at 1064 (D. Nev 2012); *Hines v* Overstock.com 668 F.Supp.2d 362 at 367 (E.D.N.Y., 2009).

conspicuous and repetitive notices accompanied by an *affirmative acknowl-edgment* of terms and prescribed that websites display notices that a specified action would be regarded as consent.[120] Two observations are apposite. First, if we transposed the requirements imposed by click-wrap cases onto ubicomp environments, we would create environments saturated with notices, alerts and pop-ups. Each act of consent would have to be express and discrete. All notices would have to be conspicuous. What would, however, constitute a 'conspicuous notice' in an environment filled with visual and auditory alerts simultaneously coming from multiple sources? If every interaction with a smart object required express consent and the actual provision of terms by a ubicomp equivalent of a pop-up window, the nuisance would be unmanageable.[121] Second, if click- and browse-wrap agreements, which concern the relatively simple graphical user interfaces of websites, have generated nearly 20 years of legal controversies concerning the best position of a hyperlink (if any!), we must envisage a deluge of cases surrounding more complex interfaces. Debates regarding the enforceability of terms made available through hyperlinks placed in the lower portions of websites will be replaced with debates over terms projected on walls or made available through hyperlinks displayed on fridges. We must not forget that in click- and browse-wrap cases, courts have analyzed every website in minuscule detail.[122] As existing web-design conventions took years to develop and have been influenced by judicial decisions favouring certain layouts,[123] we must anticipate years of litigation before ubicomp 'crystallizes' its own display and consent conventions.

*Transactions in ubicomp*

**7.37** Many interactions 'with' smart objects are or purport to be commercial exchanges. The resulting problems concern the principles governing contract formation. As indicated, their broad formulation has enabled contract law to adapt to online transactions with relative ease. Problems arise when online interactions move from screens and keyboards to a multitude of voice, touch and gestural interfaces.[124] Consequently, users may deny the existence of a contract when their (purported) consent took the form of conduct that is not universally regarded as denoting 'consent' or when the interaction occurred in a context that was not clearly commercial.

---

120 See, e.g., *Cairo, Inc. v Crossmedia Services., Inc.* No. 04–04825, 2005 WL 756610 (N.D. Cal., Apr. 1, 2005).

121 Batya Fridman et al, 'Informed consent by design', in S. Garfinkel and L. F. Cranor (eds) *Security and Usability: Designing Secure Systems that People Can Use* (O'Reilly, Sevastopol 2005) 518.

122 See, e.g., *Nicosia v Amazon.com, Inc.* No. 15–423 (2d Cir. 2016).

123 Brett Frischmann and Evan Selinger, 'Engineering Humans with Contracts', Cardozo Legal Research Paper No 493 (2016) 27, available at https://papers.ssrn.com/sol3/Papers.cfm?abstract_id=2834011 (accessed 31 January 2020).

124 Adrian McEwen and Hakim Cassimally, *Designing the Internet of Things* (Wiley, Chichester 2014) 25.

A question of consent

**7.38** It is trite law that consent may be express, taking the form of an affirmative statement denoting agreement, or can be implied from conduct.[125] As consent must be manifested by an act,[126] silence and inactivity are generally insufficient. The complexity of the act expressing intention is generally irrelevant: a nod can denote consent to a multi-million-dollar transaction in the same manner as a handwritten signature. Before proceeding, it is necessary to emphasize that we must not idealize consent. In the context of contract law, consent has been gradually becoming a fiction, not only online but also in traditional transactions. We habitually 'consent' to various terms displayed during our online activities – even if such purported consent has substantial economic or legal consequences.[127] Consent has also become less expressive, often taking the form of continued browsing.[128] This 'erosion of consent' is not, however, attributable to technological progress but to generations of commercially oriented judges who recognized (or *tolerated*?) progressively inconspicuous manifestations of agreement. Contrary to popular assumptions, the analytical baseline for our discussion is not the 'informed, express and deliberate' consent encountered in face-to-face negotiations between peers, but the implied and often cursory consent encountered in mass-market transactions based on standardized terms.[129] Ubicomp transactions cannot be criticized on the ground that they involve unilaterally imposed terms and/or consent implied from conduct. They can be criticized, however, for attempting to 'derive' consent from conduct that is not *generally associated* with or *universally understood* as denoting such. Although consent can be manifested in any manner, we must balk at the possibility of imposing communicative signs or assigning legal consequences to acts that are not *universally* perceived as denoting consent.

**7.39** In ubicomp, users may argue 'I had no idea that "x" signifies consent to a contract governing my use of [smart object]'. Such claims seem easy to discard with the argument that subjective beliefs are irrelevant. After all, contract law identifies circumstances in which the parties are *regarded* as having reached agreement.[130] In theory, as commercial certainty trumps subjective intention, contracts can be formed against the wishes of one of the parties.[131] At the same

---

125 *Mott v Jackson* 172 Ala 448, 55 So 528 (1911) (offer accepted by piling the staves on the wharf); *Taylor v Allon* [1966] 1 QB 304 (taking a vehicle on the road is an acceptance of the insurance policy).

126 *Browne v Hare*, 157 Eng. Rep. 561, 565–66 (Ex. 1858).

127 R. Böhme and S. Köpsell, 'Trained to Accept? A Field Experiment on Consent Dialogs' CHI'10 Proceedings of the SIGCHI Conference on Human Factors in Computing Systems, 2403–2406.

128 *Century 21 Canada Limited Partnership v Rogers Communications Inc.*, 2011 BCSC 1196 (CanLII); *Ryanair Ltd v Billigfluege De GmbH/Ticket Point Reiseburo GmbH [2015] IESC 11*.

129 Margaret J Radin, 'Boilerplate Today: The Rise of Modularity and the Waning of Consent' (2006) 104 Mich L Rev 1223.

130 Richard Craswell, 'Offer, Acceptance, and Efficient Reliance' (1996) 48 Stan L Rev 481, 482.

131 William Howarth, 'A Note on the Objective of Objectivity in Contract' (1987) 103 LQR 527, 531.

time, the objective theory of contract assumes that 'x' can be interpreted in a single manner based on a common understanding. This is not to say that each act or utterance always has one meaning but that *in the context of a particular interaction* such meaning can be determined and that every *reasonable* addressee would understand certain words or acts in a similar if not identical manner. Radin observes:

> The applicability of the objective theory depends upon prevalent linguistic understandings, in the context of individual behaviors with the known implied meanings, such as tone of voice, facial movements and other physical behavior, in a context of cultural characteristics and expectations.[132]

If, however, we cannot determine the *prevalent* and *known* meaning of an act or utterance, we cannot determine the standard of a reasonable addressee[133] or establish what communication convention should be known to persons acting within a specific context. The objective theory of contract assumes the existence of reference points common to both parties[134] – reference points that presuppose a high degree of standardization of communicative signs. Words are interpreted in light of the prevailing language conventions.[135] Commercial dealings would become impossible if each transacting environment had different communication rules or ascribed idiosyncratic meanings to the same act. The very problem in ubicomp is, however, that it lacks standardized communication conventions. Each space or object comes with its own proprietary interface. Consequently, the same gesture or sign may constitute a different command or carry a different meaning depending on the space or object.

Who deserves protection?

**7.40** All of the above problems involve broader policy considerations. After all, stating that a practice is 'reasonable' constitutes an implicit approval of such practice.[136] Reasonableness assumes that both parties rely on a common meaning in the contracting process, on unspoken assumptions and general communication conventions.[137] As the objective theory involves a process of 'switching' between the perspectives of the addressee and the maker of a statement,[138] it assumes that *both* parties are reasonable in understanding the actions of the other and in anticipating how their actions will be understood. Operators must not take advantage of the users' misapprehension of the meaning of an act,[139]

---

132  Margaret Jane Radin, 'The Deformation of Contract' (2017) 37 OJLS 505–533, 519.

133  *Bowerman v Association of British Travel Agents Ltd* [1996] C.L.C. 451.

134  Coote (fn 82) 16.

135  Anne De Moor, 'Intention in the Law of Contract: Elusive or Illusory?' (1990) 106 LQR 639, 640.

136  Larry A DiMatteo, *The Evolution of Contractual Intent* (Michigan State University Press, East Lansing 1998) 62.

137  Jurgen Habermas, *The Theory of Communicative Action* (Beacon Press, Boston 1984) 34.

138  See generally Chapter 5 of this volume.

139  *Hartog v Colin & Shields* [1939] 3 All ER 566; *Smith v Hughes* (1871) LR 6 QB 597.

especially if, in a given context, such meaning is not obvious. Users must not, however, be allowed to neglect to inform themselves due to their own haste and inattentiveness. The reasonable person is 'constructed' in light of the available information and the practices of a specific marketplace.[140] Unfortunately, this argument is more complex. The objective theory protects the addressee's reliance on a statement but does not assist an addressee who knows that a statement does not represent the maker's true intention.[141] In ubicomp transactions, the addressee of the user's statement is the operator – the person who designed and imposed the communicative signs.[142] On one hand, operators should not enjoy the protection of the objective theory of contract if they have created the appearances they seek to rely on. On the other, the inattentiveness displayed by many users may be regarded as *un*reasonable. The solution to this conundrum depends on whether we accept that the mere availability of information explaining the meaning of an act suffices to burden the user with the consequences of such act. If we approach this situation exclusively on the basis of contractual principles, everything seems to depend whether the manner such information was provided was reasonable. Arguably, the more unusual the act expressing consent and/or the more novel a particular interface, the more conspicuous such information should be or the more notice about the meaning of an act should be provided.

A question of context

7.41 In ubicomp transactions, users could also deny the existence of an intention to be legally bound ('legal intention') and argue 'I had no intention to contract when I used the [smart object] etc'. In such instance, we do not focus on the meaning of a specific act but on the broader context in which it occurs. Courts establish an 'intention to create legal relations' by examining the circumstances of a particular interaction and that agreements made in a family or social context are presumed not to be intended to be legally binding[143] whereas agreements made in a business or commercial context are presumed to be intended to be legally binding.[144] These presumptions are dictated by public policy considerations[145] and, to date, have remained generally uncontroversial. They become difficult to apply, however, when the context is ambiguous. By extending the point-of-sale into public and private spaces and by equipping objects with transactional capacities, ubicomp obfuscates the distinction between commercial and social environments.[146] Commercial exchanges may occur in places that have

---

140  DiMatteo (n 136) 52.

141  J P Vorster, 'A Comment on the Meaning of Objectivity in Contract' (1987) 103 LQR 274 at 287; see also Lord Phillips in *Shogun Finance Ltd v Hudson* [2003] 3 WLR 1371 (HL) at 123.

142  See generally Eliza Mik, 'Contracts Governing the Use of Websites' (2016) SJLS 70.

143  *Balfour v Balfour* [1919] 2 KB 571 (CA); *Jones v Padavatton* [1969] 2 All ER 616 (CA).

144  *Kleinwort Benson Ltd v Malaysian Mining Corporation Bhd* [1989] 1 All ER 785 (CA).

145  Gerard McMeel, 'Contractual Intention: the Smoke Ball Strikes Back' (1997) 113 LQR 47–49.

146  Jerry Kang and Dana Cuff, 'Pervasive Computing: Embedding the Public Sphere' (2005) 62 Washington & Lee L Rev 93.

traditionally been regarded as non-commercial – a problem that is aggravated by business models that rely on 'trading' the right to use a particular smart object (which often acts as a 'gateway' for other services) for the right to collect personal information. The result is a contextual confusion and the destruction of the familiar cues which create meaning.[147] The validity of all arguments that question the presence of legal intention on the basis of an ambiguous context will depend on the prevalent market practice and/or the conventions governing specific spaces. As both take a significant time to develop, we can anticipate a long period of uncertainty. We can also anticipate that the said presumptions may become impossible to rely on and that the presence of legal intention will be decided on a case-by-case basis.

## Conclusions

**7.42** The revolution in how people conduct business need not result in a revolution in contract law. Contract law can absorb technological change. The question is not: *do traditional principles apply?* But *how do they apply?*[148] The *correct* application of the relevant principle requires a thorough understanding of the principle itself and of the technology that, purportedly, affects such application. Legal arguments must be based on correct technical assumptions. It is true that some 'doctrinal bottlenecks' may be created by technological advancements. Such 'bottlenecks' can, however, be addressed by revisiting such core concepts as the objective theory of contract or the prerequisites of enforceability.

**7.43** It has been demonstrated that automation comports with the objective evaluation of contractual intention and with the possibility to express such intention in any manner. Legal distinctions cannot be based on different levels of technological sophistication. The validity of a contract cannot depend on the speed of computer clock rates, the number of cores in a processor or the complexity of the algorithm used in its formation. Computers, irrespective of their sophistication, are 'only' tools and the output of their operations must be attributed to those who operate them. The introduction of AI (and related technologies) into transacting process is commercially exciting but contractually irrelevant. Moreover, it has been established that 'smart contracts' are not contracts but technologies automating the performance of obligations deriving from traditional contracts or, more specifically, as technologies enabling the generation and transfer of crypto-assets.[149] Their ultimate practical relevance remains questionable given that they can only be used to express simple contracts of short duration. Their subject matter must be capable of formulaic expression and the agreed result that triggering the transfer of crypto-assets must be objectively ascertainable. 'Smart

---

147 Andrew Hinton (n 112) 4; see also Manuel Castells, *The Rise of the Network Society*, 2nd edn (Wiley-Blackwell, Chichester 2000) 424.

148 *Chwee Kin Keong v Digilandmall.com Pte Ltd* [2004] SGHC 71 at 91 per V K Rajah JC.

149 Jean Bacon et al, 'Blockchain Demystified: A Technical and Legal Introduction to Distributed and Centralized Ledgers' (2018) 25 Rich J Law & Tech 2, 46.

contracts' leave no room for idiosyncratic, transaction-specific deviations, human discretion or dependence on external events that are not expressly provided for in the code. The question is not whether it is legally permissible to express contracts in code but whether a specific *obligation* can be automated and/or adequately expressed in a particular programming language. It is impossible to encode all types of contractual obligations and to predict all future events that might affect their performance. After all, the world outside of the blockchain is not computable. Those are, however, not problems of contract law. Problems of applying contractual principles become more apparent in the context of transactions created in ubiquitous computing environments. The latter create unfamiliar settings and abound in new communicative signs. Arguably, places permeated with 'smart objects' change the 'circumstances' which the law treats as giving rise to agreement and complicate the application of the objective theory of contract, putting strain on interpreting the concept of reasonableness and on applying the presumptions concerning the existence of legal intention. Once one of the parties acts in a self-designed transacting environment and prescribes the communication rules, while the other is limited in the range of responses and subjected to technical manipulations it becomes difficult to decide which of them deserves the protection of the objective theory of contract. The question is not whether contracts made with the assistance of 'smart objects' are valid or enforceable but whether, in the context of specific transactions, it is possible to speak of an intention to be contractually bound. We can anticipate that while judges will solve the 'problems' brought by automation with relative ease, their analytical skills will be challenged when confronted with ubiquitous computing and the multitude of novel, transactional interfaces.

## CHAPTER 8

# A collision of contract and privacy law in a digital environment—an accident waiting to happen!

## A comparative study

### *Cirami Mastura Drahaman*

## Introduction

**8.1** 'A' is a private individual who wishes to set up an account on a free social media platform. To sign up he has to reveal his name, date of birth, email address and consent to various conditions attached to his use of the social media platform, he does not read any of the added information on the general terms and conditions. The question here is, if his personal information is misused, or accessed by third parties due to a data breach, what redress would 'A' have? Furthermore, if he does not accept the terms of the agreement, he will not be able to use the social media platform.

**8.2** This is not a hypothetical situation as can be seen from Facebook's current Data Policy page.[1] The danger lies in the fact that the social media platform's terms and conditions can be widely interpreted, for example on the sign-up page for Facebook, it states in small letters that by signing up, you agree to Facebook's Data Policy and other terms and conditions. The Data Policy is available to read only on the click of another button.

---

1 **Information and content, you provide.** We collect the content, communications and other information you provide when you use our Products, including when you sign up for an account, create or share content, and message or communicate with others. This can include information in or about the content you provide (like metadata), such as the location of a photo or the date a file was created. It can also include what you see through features we provide, such as our camera, so we can do things like suggest masks and filters that you might like, or give you tips on using camera formats. Our systems automatically process content and communications you and others provide to analyze context and what's in them for the purposes described below. Learn more about how you can control who can see the things you share.

Data with special protections: You can choose to provide information in your Facebook profile fields or Life Events about your religious views, political views, who you are 'interested in,' or your health. This and other information (such as racial or ethnic origin, philosophical beliefs or trade union membership) could be subject to special protections under the laws of your country.

**Networks and connections.** We collect information about the people, pages, accounts, hashtags and groups you are connected to and how you interact with them across our Products, such as people you communicate with the most or groups you are part of. We also collect contact information if you choose to upload, sync or import it from a device **(such as an address book or call log or SMS log history), which we use for things like helping you and others find people you may know and for the other purposes listed** below.

**8.3** The Facebook Data Policy states in the first paragraph as follows: 'This Policy describes the information we process to support Facebook, Instagram, Messenger and other products and features offered by Facebook you can find additional information in the Facebook settings and Instagram settings'. In this paragraph alone we learn that our personal information would be shared amongst other Facebook products. Can this data be accessed by third parties?

**8.4** As can be seen in paragraph 8.3, these situations happen in real life more often than one thinks possible, which can be highlighted by the recent furore over the Facebook, Cambridge Analytica fiasco which saw the Personal Identification Information (PII)[2] of more than 50 million users of Facebook being unlawfully accessed.[3] A look at worldwide statistics on PII misuse or data

---

2 Personal Identification Information includes in the United States (42 USCS § 13925, Public Health and Welfare Act). Information relating to an identifiable person, personally identifying information or personal information means individually identifying information for or about an individual including information likely to disclose the location of a victim of domestic violence, dating violence, sexual assault, or stalking, including: (A) a first and last name; (B) a home or other physical address; (C) contact information (including a postal, e-mail or Internet protocol address, or telephone or facsimile number); (D) a social security number; and (E) any other information, including date of birth, racial or ethnic background, or religious affiliation, that, in combination with any of subparagraphs (A) through (D), would serve to identify any individual. In the UK the Data Protection Act 2018 (DPA 2018) defines personal data as an identifier such as your name, an identification number, such as your National Insurance or passport number, your location data, such as your home address or mobile phone GPS data, an online identifier, such as your IP or email address. Sensitive personal data is also covered in GDPR as special categories of personal data. The special categories specifically include: genetic data relating to the inherited or acquired genetic characteristics which give unique information about a person's physiology or the health of that natural person, biometric data for the purpose of uniquely identifying a natural person, including facial images and fingerprints, data concerning health which reveals information about your health status, including both physical and mental health and the provision of health care services, racial or ethnic origin, political opinions, religious or philosophical beliefs, trade union membership, sex life or sexual orientation. In Malaysia, personal data is defined in the Personal Data Protection Act 2010 (PDPA 2010) as that which relates to directly or indirectly to a data subject, who is identified or identifiable from that information or from that or other information in the possession of the data user, including any sensitive personal data and expression about the data subject. Sensitive personal data is further defined as any personal data consisting of information as to the physical or mental health of a data subject, his political opinions, his religious beliefs or other beliefs of a similar nature, the commission or alleged commission buy him of any offence or any other personal data as the Minister may determine by order published by Gazette.

3 Revealed: 50 million Facebook Profiles Harvested for Cambridge Analytica in Major Data Breach, *The Guardian* (International Edition, 17 March 2018), accessed 26 April 2019. The article described how personal information of millions of people were harvested purportedly for research purposes, people were paid to take a personality test, via an app called 'thisisyourdigitallife' built by academic Aleksandr Kogan, separately from his work at Cambridge University through his company Global Science Research (GSR). However, the app also collected the information of the test-takers' Facebook friends, leading to the accumulation of a data pool tens of millions-strong. Facebook's 'platform policy' allowed only collection of friends' data to improve user experience in the app and barred it being sold on or used for advertising. The discovery of the unprecedented data harvesting, and the use to which it was put, to influence, voter preferences during the US 2016 Presidential elections, raises urgent new questions about Facebook's role in targeting voters in the US presidential election. It comes only weeks after the indictments of 13 Russians by the special counsel Robert Mueller which stated they had used the platform to perpetrate 'information warfare' against the US.

breaches does not bode well for the future.[4] Although data protection laws are present in most jurisdictions, these may be insufficient to deal with the growing incidences of data breaches recorded. How will a Data Controller or Processor be held liable for a data breach?[5]

**8.5** The law many a time has to play catch-up to advances in technology and to provide swift closure to any lacunae that may exist in the current laws. This is true of any online transaction, dealing with data sharing or privacy issues bearing in mind that privacy and data protection require that information about individuals should not be automatically made available to other, third party individuals and organizations, without a data subject's express consent. Each person must be able to exercise a substantial degree of control over his personal data and its use.[6] It has been recognised that in return for the right to use online resources, website operators demand that users permit the harvesting of their personal information. Personal information have been regarded as the currency of the Internet economy, with a large number of online businesses built around its collection and commercial utilization.[7] Given this circumstance, how can a person gain redress for a data breach that renders his PII available to third parties.

**8.6** Are our civil laws sufficient to deal with the problem, specifically the law of contract? It has been argued that the position in relation to online contract formation should not differ from the formation requirements for an offline traditional contract.[8] However, in the context of personal data protection and contract law online, it may be best to make such differentiation, especially in the Asian region where data protection laws are in their infancy. For example, in Malaysia data protection laws do not provide compensation to those persons whose PII

---

4 In October 2017, Malaysia announced that 12 Malaysian telecommunication companies, a jobseeker website and databases belonging to three medical associations had been breached and some 46 million personal records dating to 2014 were offered for sale on the dark web. See article. Asia Moves to tougher data breach rules (18 April 2018), available at www.praktis.com.my (accessed 20 April 2019). As stated in the Breach Level Index website, overall, the total number of records compromised in the first half of 2018 was 3,353,172,708. That figure marks an increase of 72%. Not surprisingly, the amounts of records breached every day, hour, minute and second also surpassed the totals observed a year earlier. What is remarkable is that all of these figures almost doubled between 2017 and 2018. Surprisingly, there were just 944 security incidents reported in the first half of 2018: 18% fewer than the 1,162 breaches disclosed in H1 2017. Of those incidents, there were just 21 data breaches where encryption was reportedly used on the data in whole or in part, less than half the figure for the previous year. See https://breachlevelindex.com/ (accessed 26 April 2019).

5 A data breach is an incident that involves the unauthorized or illegal viewing, access or retrieval of data by an individual, application or service. It is a type of security breach specifically designed to steal and/or publish data to an unsecured or illegal location.

(Techopedia Online Dictionary, accessed 15 May 2019)

6 Parul Sinha, 'Electronic Contracts and Consumer Protection: Does Legislation Provide Adequate Consumer Protection' [2017] Bharati Law Review, 20.

7 Michael Furmston and Gregory Tolhurst *Contract Formation Law and Practice* (Oxford University Press 2016) para 6.04; see also Richard Warner and Robert H. Sloan, 'Behavioral Advertising: From One-Sided Chicken to Informational Norms' (2012) 15 Vand Jnl Ent L & Practice 49, 57–60.

8 Eliza Mik, 'Contracts Governing The Use of Websites' (2016) Singapore Journal of Legal Studies 74 (Research Collection School of Law).

may have been breached, a breach of personal data is seen as a statutory offence for which the perpetrator would be penalised, but no redress is given to the victims of a data breach. In contrast the European Unions, General Data Protection Regulation[9] and the English Data Protection Act provides for redress in the form of compensation and damages in cases where there have been breaches in data protection laws.

**8.7** Further it is questionable whether agreements relating to privacy on a social media website (service offered for free) would constitute data being shared on a commercial basis. The Malaysian Data Protection Act 2010 maintains that personal data protected via the Act must be the result of commercial transactions. There are two opposing views on this subject.[10] In this instance would contract law bridge the gap? The concept of online contracting and inherent problems thereto have not been considered in any court of law in Malaysia at time of writing. Thus it is necessary to consider, the law in other jurisdictions.[11]

### What maketh an online contract?

**8.8** The internet was born to the world at large in the late 1990s and since then there have been various attempts to apply offline laws to the online worldwide web and in most instances this has been successfully done. In the UK and the EU, the E-Commerce Regulations and in the US, the Uniform Computer

---

9 See Article 82 of the GDPR, Right to Compensation and Liability, which states as follows:
'Any person who has suffered material or non-material damage as a result of an infringement of this Regulation shall have the right to receive compensation from the controller or processor for the damage suffered.

Any controller involved in processing shall be liable for the damage caused by processing which infringes this Regulation. A processor shall be liable for the damage caused by processing only where it has not complied with obligations of this Regulation specifically directed to processors or where it has acted outside or contrary to lawful instructions of the controller'.

10 Section 2 (1) of the Personal Data Protection Act 2010, states that this Act applies to (a) any person who processes; and (b) any person who has control over or authorizes the processing of any personal data in respect of commercial transactions. See also N.A. Mohamed Yusof, N.A. Ahmad, Z. Mohamed 'A Study on Collection of Personal Data by Banking Industry in Malaysia' (2016) 2(1) Journal of Advanced Research in Business and Management Studies 43. However see Jason J. Turner and Puteri Sofia Amirnuddin 'Social Media Privacy and The Law: Perspectives from Malaysian and UK Consumers' (2018) (20(2) The Journal of the South East Asia Research Centre for Communication and Humanities 31–58, where they argue that Facebook is legally governed by the Personal Data Protection Act 2010 as Facebook has a local office in Kuala Lumpur and processes users' data thus it can be argued that there is a contract present between and its users as they are providing services in terms of accessibility to a social media website.

11 Malaysia as a former colony of the United Kingdom follows the common law system and legal authorities from United Kingdom and other common law jurisdictions have persuasive value in Malaysian Courts. Also refer to the Civil Law Act 1950, sections 5 and 7, whereby English common law up to, the date of Malaysian independence is binding precedent, 'provided always that the said common law, rules of equity and statutes of general application shall be applied so far only as the circumstances of the States of Malaysia and their respective inhabitants permit and subject to such qualifications as local circumstances render necessary'. Case law from the United States of America will also be looked at, in this chapter, as there are many decision in this jurisdiction on the validity of online contracts.

Information Transactions Act 2002 and the Uniform Electronic Transactions Act 1999, confirm that traditional contract law would apply equally in an online environment.

*International agreement on electronic contracts*

**8.9** Reference can also be made to the UNCITRAL Model Law on Electronic Commerce 1996 ('UNCITRAL Model Law'). However, this is a general convention that recognises online transactions as legitimate contracts and does not consider a detailed analysis on the formation of contracts online. The United Nations Convention on the use of Electronic Communications in International Contracts 2007 ('CUECIC'),[12] is more specific in trying to introduce offline contractual principles into the formation of online contracts.

**8.10** In the late 1990s and early 2000s countries passed legislation to accept electronic transactions as contracts following the UNCITRAL model law.[13]

**8.11** Malaysia has an Electronic Commerce Act 2006, but this also deals with electronically communicated contracts generally, and states that an e-commerce contract will not be denied, merely because it is in an electronic format. Section 7 of the Act states as follows:

(1) In the formation of a contract, the communication of proposals, acceptance of proposals, and revocation of proposals and acceptances or any related communication may be expressed by an electronic message.
(2) A contract shall not be denied legal effect, validity or enforceability on the ground that an electronic message is used in its formation.

**8.12** Thus, it would appear that a privacy policy entered into online would be binding on the parties as a contract. But having said this, it is still necessary to establish the formation of the contract.

## Formation-offer?

**8.13** In the Malaysian context, section 2 (a) of the Malaysian Contracts Act 1950 (CA 1950) defines a proposal (which is tantamount to an offer) as: when a person signifies to another his willingness to do or abstain from doing anything,

---

12 For example, Article 11 of the CUECIC states that a proposal to conclude a contract made through one or more electronic communications which is not addressed to one or more specific parties, but is generally accessible to parties making use of information systems, including proposals that make use of interactive applications for the placement of orders through such information systems, is to be considered as an invitation to make offers, unless it clearly indicates the intention of the party making the proposal to be bound in the case of acceptance.

13 In the USA, the Uniform Electronic Transaction Act 1999 allows for the recognition of e-contracts. In the EU Directive 2000/31/EC, regulates e-commerce transactions in the EU, and states inter alia that in every EU country, electronic contracts must be given equivalent legal status to paper contracts. But in these instances, it is important to note that the parties still have to show that a contract has been formed with reference to offline laws and more importantly these legislations deal with the provision of sale of goods and services online.

with a view to obtaining the assent of that other to the act or abstinence, he is said to make a proposal.

**8.14** For a contract to be formed there has to be a proposal (offer), acceptance and an intention to form legal relations. Are these present in a privacy agreement scenario considering the fact that an online privacy agreement is a standalone agreement, with no ancillary product or service being offered for sale? Is this a commercial transaction or a social one? This would depend on the parties' intention, at the time of the transaction.

*What does the social media platform offer, the use of the platform in exchange for PII?*

**8.15** In the case of online social media platform, the question would be when would the offer be made? Does Facebook, for example, make an offer open to a number of would-be offerees, and once accepted, this becomes a promise? Or is the social media platform an invitation to treat? If one takes into account Article 11 of CUECIC it would seem that all websites are invitations to treat.

**8.16** However, it may be best to treat a social media platform as an offer open to the public at large and only binding on those who accept the offer.[14] As long as it can be proved that the offer is clear and unambiguous, the offeree has to accept, the particular offer made, without adding any terms of his own.

**8.17** Having paragraphs 8.15 and 8.16 in mind, can it be said that an online privacy policy is an agreement? Who is the promisor in this case? Take the case of Facebook: it is offering a social media platform to people, once the person accepts the offer, but the offer also includes adherence to a privacy policy, then the transaction would become a promise. Is the privacy policy merely a policy document or an ancillary contract?

**8.18** It is argued for present purposes that the social media platform makes an offer to the world at large, which is unilaterally accepted by a person when he registers for the service.

### Acceptance – browse-wrap/click wrap agreements in the case of privacy agreements

*Acceptance general common law position, drawing on the experience in the United States*

**8.19** In general, contractual terms, therefore, acceptance must be absolute and unconditional, well informed and must mirror the offer made. It is also trite law that if a document is signed then the signing party cannot claim that he has not read the agreement, he has signed a binding agreement.[15] How do these pre-requisites to acceptance transfer to an online transaction?

---

14 *Carlill v Carbolic Smokeball Co* [1938] 1QB 256.
15 *L'estrange v F Graucob Limited* [1934] 2 KB 38, [1934] All ER Rep 16.

**8.20** In Malaysia, section 2 (b) of the Contract Act 1950 states when the person to whom the proposal is made signifies his assent thereto, the proposal is said to be accepted, and becomes a promise.

**8.21** When these principles are applied to the online environment, it may cause unfairness, especially in the case of privacy agreements or policies. The question here is whether the data user can claim that the data subject had ample knowledge of the provisions of the privacy agreement. The question becomes more controversial if the agreement is a browse-wrap agreement. A browse-wrap contract occurs when the terms to a contract appear in different parts of a website or in hyperlinks. Most websites have two documents that are related to each other, the terms and conditions of use and the privacy agreement or policy and the user of the website may actively have to search for these documents on the websites. In the case of a click-wrap agreement, however, the website user would not be able to proceed if they do not specifically accept the agreements.

**8.22** In the case of browse-wrap agreements therefore, could a valid acceptance be made, if the parties to the contract do not know of their existence? In the United States there is precedent to suggest that the courts would not generally hold browse-wrap agreements to be valid. Since browse-wrap agreements do not require affirmative action by the user to agree to the terms and conditions of an agreement, courts have held that the validity of such agreements turns on whether the user had actual or constructive knowledge of those terms and conditions.[16] In the case of *Re* Zappos.com *Inc Customer Data Breach Litigation*[17] the court held, in relation to a browse-wrap agreement, that the plaintiffs were not bound by an arbitration clause that was buried at the bottom of a page amid a variety of links. This was deemed too hard to find.

**8.23** Ultimately however, the Courts will consider whether a browse-wrap agreement is valid or not on a case by case basis by looking at the following factors: whether the terms of the agreement is sufficiently conspicuous; is easily accessible; and adequately notifies the consumer that continued use of the website or application will act as a manifestation of the consumer's intent to be bound by the terms and conditions of the agreement. Thus in Malaysian law, section 10 of the Contracts Act 1950 states that all agreements are contracts if they are made by the free consent of parties competent to contract, for a lawful consideration and with a lawful object, and are not hereby expressly declared to be void.

**8.24** Historically contract law dictates that if the parties show, by their conduct, that they have accepted the agreement, this acceptance is sufficient.[18] What is the position when it comes to data protection? Data protection laws require informed consent.

---

16 *Nguyen v Barnes & Noble Inc.*, 763 F.3d 1171, 1178 (9th Cir. 2014). *Rushing v Viacom, Inc.*, N.D. Cal., 17-cv-04492-JD (15 October 2018).

17 United States District Court District of Nevada 2012.

18 *Reveille Independent LLC v Anotech International (UK) Ltd* [2016 EWCA Civ 443], *Brogden v Metropolitan Railway Co* (1877),

*Informed consent in cases of personal data protection pursuant to the EU's general data protection regulation (GDPR), which came into force in the EU on 25 May 2018*

**8.25** Article 4(11) of the GDPR states that consent is '… any freely given, specific, informed and unambiguous indication of the data subject's wishes by which he or she, by a statement or by a clear affirmative action, signifies agreement to the processing of personal data relating to him or her'.

**8.26** Article 7 of the GDPR conditions for consent:

(1) Where processing is based on consent, the controller shall be able to demonstrate that the data subject has consented to processing of his or her personal data.

(2) If the data subject's consent is given in the context of a written declaration which also concerns other matters, the request for consent shall be presented in a manner which is clearly distinguishable from the other matters, in an intelligible and easily accessible form, using clear and plain language. Any part of such a declaration which constitutes an infringement of this Regulation shall not be binding.

(3) The data subject shall have the right to withdraw his or her consent at any time. The withdrawal of consent shall not affect the lawfulness of processing based on consent before its withdrawal. Prior to giving consent, the data subject shall be informed thereof. It shall be as easy to withdraw as to give consent.

(4) When assessing whether consent is freely given, utmost account shall be taken of whether, inter alia, the performance of a contract, including the provision of a service, is conditional on consent to the processing of personal data that is not necessary for the performance of that contract.

**8.27** It can be seen from the above that the issue of consent is taken very seriously in the data protection sense. Of particular interest is paragraph 2 the request for consent must be presented in a manner which is clearly distinguishable from other matters thus a privacy policy that is hidden away on a website or in a hyperlink, would not be considered as consented to by the data subject. Thus it is observed that a positive and unequivocal consent, based on the GDPR conditions, should be the norm in the case of an online privacy agreement.

**Protection of personal data**

**8.28** The GDPR provisions on consent have been included in the UK Data Protection Act 2018 as follows:

(1) The GDPR, the applied GDPR and this Act protect individuals with regard to the processing of personal data, in particular by –
   (a) requiring personal data to be processed lawfully and fairly, on the basis of the data subject's consent or another specified basis,

(b) conferring rights on the data subject to obtain information about the processing of personal data and to require inaccurate personal data to be rectified, and

(c) conferring functions on the Commissioner, giving the holder of that office responsibility for monitoring and enforcing their provisions.

**8.29** Following from the above it would appear that when considering consent in relation to data protection law that the data subject's consent has to be an informed one. The UK regulator for data protection, The Information Commissioners' Office, provided clarification as to what 'unambiguous consent' in terms of the GDPR would entail. These are as follows, namely: (a) unbundled – consent must be kept separate from other terms and conditions and should not be a pre-condition of signing up for a service; (b) active opt-in, pre-ticked opt-in boxes are invalid; (c) Granular – give options to consent to different types of processing where appropriate; (d) Named – the controller and any third party relying on the consent have to be named; (e) Documented – keep records of what data subjects have consented to, what they were told and when and how they consented; (f) Easy to withdraw – inform data subjects that their consent may be withdrawn at any time and give information on how to do this; and (g) there must be imbalance in the relationship between the data subject and the controller.[19]

**8.30** Should the future recognition of privacy agreements adopt these strict criteria *vis-à-vis* acceptance? It certainly looks as though this should be the case.

**8.31** How does this relate to contractual acceptance? One view is that contractual acceptance and consent to the use of personal data are two separate concerns, the function of consent in data protection is different from its function in contract, in the former instance it represents a permission for what would otherwise be a violation of a data subject's rights. In the contractual type of consent/acceptance by contrast the function of consent would not be to give one party a defence against the breach of the other party's rights, but rather it means to create new rights and duties in the relationship between the parties.[20] It is thus argued that in the case of a privacy agreement, that consent/acceptance should be only understood as such if the data subject is fully aware of what agreement he is entering into. The burden of proving consent/acceptance shall fall on the data user.

**8.32** But the question here is whether a contract, that is ancillary to the provision of services, for example in the case of a social media platform, an exception to the rules *vis-à-vis* consent. This cannot hold true, in fact consent is essential.

19 Consultation Draft GDPR Consent Guidance, 2 March 2017, available at https://ico.org.uk/media/about-the-ico/consultations/2013551/draft-gdpr-consent-guidance-for-consultation-201703.pdf (accessed 3 June 2019).

20 Maurizio Borghi and Federico Ferrretti, 'Online Data Processing Consent Under EU Law: A Theoretical Framework and Empirical Evidence from the UK' (2013) 21(2) Int J Law Info Tech 109.

**8.33** Another question that arises is, what happens if the terms and conditions of a privacy agreement are changed on the website and brought to the attention of the data subject by a notice in an obscure section of the website concerned? Are the data subjects bound by these amended terms and conditions?

**8.34** In contract law generally, unilateral variations to contract without the assent of the other party are not entertained.

**8.35** A case from the United States found that such a practice would not bind consumers who visited a website to purchase groceries online. In this case the plaintiff alleged that Safeway, the supermarket offering online grocery shopping facilities, charged higher prices for items ordered on its online store than purchased in-store. Naturally, the case then focused on whether or not Safeway's online terms of service promised the same prices online as in-store. Mid-case, Safeway unilaterally amended its terms of service to clarify that the prices in its online store were not necessarily the same prices as in-store. The Court had to decide whether this new term was sufficient to bind the user of the online website. The Court held that:

(1) the safeway.com agreement did not give Safeway the power to bind its customers to unknown future contract terms, because consumers cannot assent to terms that do not yet exist. A user confronting a contract in which she purports to agree to terms in whatever form they may appear in the future cannot know to what she is are agreeing.[21]

**8.36** If this holds true for general terms and conditions of use of websites, this would, it is argued, hold doubly true for any agreement dealing with the exchange or sharing of personal data. Thus, even if the social media platform sends an email to their subscribers notifying them that changes have been made to their privacy policy, the exact nature of the change will have to be spelled out to the data subjects so that they can make an informed decision whether to continue with the service or not.

*The right to withdraw consent (the right to be forgotten) and contract law*

**8.37** How would contract law deal with withdrawal of consent, in the case of a privacy agreement?

**8.38** There should not be a difference in approach to termination of a contractual relationship in the case of a privacy agreement. However, it is opined that there must be detailed provisions, within the privacy agreement, laying out the steps that need to be taken by the Data Controller/Processor to delete all PII shared by the user of the app or website from the commencement of the privacy agreement.

---

21 *Michael Rodman v Safeway Inc* No. 15–17, 390 (9th Circ. 2017).

**8.39** Therefore, given the foregoing, it is felt that it would be wise to re-look at the concept of consent/acceptance given the convergence of contract and data protection laws.

## Consideration

*What amounts to consideration in common law countries –*
*traditional views?*

**8.40** In the English case of *Curie & Ors v Misa*,[22] consideration was defined as 'A valuable consideration, in the sense of the law, may consist either in some, interest, profit or benefit accruing to the one party or some forbearance, detriment, loss or responsibility, given suffered or undertaken by the other'. This definition has been accepted in the Malaysian case of *Macon Works & Trading Sdn Bhd v Phang Hon Chin*.[23]

**8.41** The common law definition as given on this page lends interpretative value to the statutory definition as given in the Malaysian Contracts Act (CA) 1950.

**8.42** Section 2 (d) of the CA 1950 states that when, at the desire of the promisor, the promisee or any other person has done or abstained from doing or does or abstains from doing, or promises to do or to abstain from doing, something, such act or abstinence or promise is called a consideration.

**8.43** In fact, section 26 of the CA 1950 states that a contract without consideration is void.

*Information as a form of consideration*

**8.44** When a person signs up to use social media platforms, what consideration does the promisee give for the promise? It is a free social media platform.

**8.45** This brings us to an interesting proposition as to whether the exchange of PII in an online transaction amounts to sufficient consideration. There is a Canadian case on point, that appears to say just this, that information can amount to sufficient consideration.[24]

**8.46** The significance of sharing personal data cannot, in today's world, be underestimated, where personal data may be seen as a raw material, valuable and tradeable. In fact, personal data when shared provides information on potential customers, in terms of age group, income, social and financial background, which in turn helps businesses thrive.[25] Furthermore some scholars

---

22 (1875) LR10 Exch 153.

23 [1976] 2 MLJ 177.

24 *Century 21 Canada Limited Partnership v Rogers Communications Inc.* 2011 BCSC 1196 (CanLII).

25 N.A. Mohamed Yusof, N.A. Ahmad and Z. Mohamed, 'A Study of Personal Data by Banking Industry in Malaysia' (2016) 2(1) Journal of Advanced Research in Business and Management Studies 39.

have likened personal data to a kind of new currency for the digital world. There have in recent years been calls to render the exchange of personal data, in return for a service (free or otherwise), to be tantamount to consideration.[26] However even in Europe, the laws have not been amended to accept this view.

**8.47** It is paramount that these views are adopted into the contract law regime, to prevent abuse of personal data contracts/policies online. The law must not lend itself to a situation where data users can abuse or use data, without consent with impunity, or be excused for a data breach merely because of a lack of consideration, in the traditional sense.

**8.48** A case to look at on the sufficiency of consideration would be the English case of *De La Bere v Pearson*.[27] In this case the defendant newspaper offered that its editor would give financial advice to readers who cared to seek it. He answered one enquiry for the name of a good stockbroker, with a reference to a person who, had he made enquiries, he would have discovered to be an undischarged bankrupt, and the plaintiff sought damages having relied upon the advice. The Court held in this case that the publication of the letter in the newspapers had the tendency to increase the circulation of the newspapers and this benefitted the appellants. In the case of social media platforms too, could it not be similarly argued, that the sharing of personal data could benefit the social media operators?

**8.49** Further in *Tan Chiw Thoo v Tee Kim Kuay*[28] it was stated that

> It must be remembered that sufficiency of consideration is different in law from the adequacy of consideration, though any dictionary may show both words to bear the same meaning. In law the courts will often enquire into the "sufficiency" but not the 'adequacy' of consideration, 'sufficiency' in law is synonymous with 'validity' in regard to consideration.

**8.50** Thus, unless there is a contrary decision in court, it would be safe to say that the sharing of personal information is valid consideration in this instance.

## Other problems in taking civil action under the law of contract

### Class actions

**8.51** Perhaps the best way to bring an action for a major data breach would be to bring a class action.

**8.52** In the US, a class action is a form of representative litigation. A traditional lawsuit typically involves all plaintiffs and defendants in the case representing themselves and their own interests before a state or federal court.

---

26 Carmen Langhanke and Martin Schmidt-Kessel, 'Consumer Data as Consideration' (2015) 6 EuCML. See also World Economic Forum, *Personal Data: The Emergence of a New Asset Class* (Geneva 2011).
27 [1908] 1 KB 280.
28 [1997] 2MLJ 221 FC.

In contrast, a class action involves at least one of the parties, typically the plaintiff(s), representing a group of people who are similarly situated but absent from the proceedings to obtain class-wide relief for a civil wrong that the defendant(s) purportedly committed.[29]

**8.53** Although class actions are very common in the United States, they are not as common in the United Kingdom and Malaysia.[30] In the United Kingdom, the first ever data breach case to come to court via a class action was the case of *Various Claimants v Morrisons Supermarket Plc*.[31] In fact in the case of *Lloyd v Google*,[32] the High Court found that a class action (known as a representative action in UK) could not be entertained as representative claimant and the potential class of claimants were not deemed to have the same interest in the claim – many claimants would not have suffered any damage at all and those who had suffered damage would not be considered to have suffered the 'same' damage, given that each person's position is inherently fact-specific. A representative claim could not therefore be brought on this basis.

**8.54** It is opined that the procedural rules of court that set out the prerequisites for a class or representative action should be made clearer and should allow for redress via this route when the majority of the claimants have similar grievances against the defendants. This would make it easier to bring claims in data breach cases.

*Standing*

**8.55** In the United States a plaintiff would have to show standing in accordance with Article III of the Federal Constitution, not only that he has an interest in the case at hand but he has to also prove that he has suffered material damage. This in the case of data breaches has proved to be the death knell to would-be plaintiffs. In *re SuperValu, Inc.*[33] the Eighth Circuit held that 15 out of 16 plaintiffs failed to allege they had suffered identity theft and/or

---

29 Recent class actions for data breach in US, is Exactis, where 230 million individual records and 110 million business records were breached included phone numbers, home and email addresses, personal interests and preferences, and other sensitive information. Equifax case and Yahoo breaches also lead to class actions being filed in 2018. For further information see www.wired.com/story/exactis-database-leak-340-million-record (accessed 9 June 2019). These class action however, were brought in the tort of negligence.

30 In Malaysia class actions are known as representative actions and are brought pursuant to Rules of Court Order 15 r 12, Rules of Court 2012. The Rule states here numerous persons have the same interest in any proceedings, the proceedings may be begun and, unless the Court otherwise orders, continued by or against any one or more of them as representing all or as representing all except one or more of them.

31 [2017] EWHC 3113 (QB). A data breach case where Morrison's was held vicariously liable for a data breach orchestrated by one of its former employees. The case was brought to court pursuant to the Data Protection Act 1998.

32 *Lloyd v Google* [2018] EWHC.

33 870 F.3d 763 (8th Cir. 2017).

incurred fraudulent charges and, thus, they did not meet the constitutional requirements for standing. The Eighth Circuit concluded that the alleged risk of some future harm was not sufficient to satisfy the standing requirements to bring a lawsuit.

**8.56** Thus many cases that were brought to court for data breach and breach of contract fell at this hurdle.

### The use of disclaimers

**8.57** A case in point is the case of *Re Yahoo Inc. Data Security Breach Litigation US District Court for the Northern District of California*, 2016.

**8.58** In this case hackers accessed user accounts for Yahoo's free email and small business, email and website services, between 2013 and 2016. Yahoo notified users of the breach, several law suits were filed against Yahoo. The cases were based on breaches of the 'click-wrap agreement'.

**8.59** The Terms of Service of Yahoo made various promises about the security of users' personal information. In the same document Yahoo made certain blanket disclaimers. The court found that the disclaimers could not override affirmative security promises. Yahoo's statement that its security mechanisms had inherent limitations, itself implied that Yahoo had at least some reasonable security mechanisms in place. As a result Yahoo's caveat that the services were not 100 per cent secure could not defeat the plaintiff's breach of contract claim.

**8.60** The disclaimers were found to be procedurally unconscionable, under California law.

**8.61** The lesson to take away from this case is that boilerplate disclaimers that a service is not 100 per cent secure or is provided on an 'as is' basis are not likely to protect against data breach claims, when a company states that the system is secure.

### Breach of contract

**8.62** What would be considered a breach of contract in a privacy data agreement? Apart from a breach of the written terms and conditions themselves it is argued that there would be other implied contractual clauses (even if not included in writing) that would have to be taken into account.

**8.63** Implied terms may be derived from custom, or they may rest upon statute or may be inferred by the judges to reinforce the language of the parties and realise their manifest intention.[34]

---

34 Michael Furmston, *Cheshire, Fifoot, & Furmston's Law of Contract*, 17th edn (Oxford University Press 2017).

**8.64** It is argued here that certain terms may be implied by virtue of the provisions of data protection legislation. One would perhaps look at specifically the six universally applied principles *vis-à-vis* data protection.[35]

**8.65** These are namely as follows:

(1) **Lawfulness, fairness and transparency** – All personal data must be collected and processed lawfully, fairly and in a transparent manner in relation to the data subject.

(2) **Purpose limitation** – personal data must only be collected for a specific, explicit and legitimate purpose. The purpose must be clearly stated, and data should be collected only for as long as necessary to complete that purpose.

(3) **Data minimization** – The personal data you process must be adequate, relevant and limited to what is necessary in relation to the processing purpose.

(4) **Accuracy** – every reasonable step must be taken to update or remove data that is inaccurate or incomplete. Individuals have the right to request that their data is erased or rectified, erroneous data that relates to them must be rectified or removed within a month.

(5) **Storage limitation** – personal data must be deleted when no longer needed. The timescales in most cases are not set. They will depend on business' circumstances and the reasons why the data is collected.

(6) **Integrity and confidentiality** – personal data must be kept safe and protected against unauthorized or unlawful processing and against accidental loss, destruction or damage, using appropriate technical or organizational measures.

**8.66** If these principles are not adhered to in a privacy or data policy, the data controller would be in breach of contract and liable to the data subject. This could be likened to the implied terms in the context of sale of goods, should privacy or data policies not have similar implied terms, given the nature of the contract?

**8.67** In the event that it proves difficult to sustain the implied terms argument, would it be possible for the court to take into account the six data protection principles, when considering breach?

---

35 These principles or slight variations of the same are present in most legislation covered in this chapter including the Malaysian Personal Data Protection Act 2010. The General Principle of informed consent is the bedrock of the data protection regime, followed by the six principles:

*(b)* the Notice and Choice Principle;

*(c)* the Disclosure Principle;

*(d)* the Security Principle;

*(e)* the Retention Principle;

*(f)* the Data Integrity Principle; and

*(g)* the Access Principle.

The UK also included the six principles in the Data Protection Act 2018.

*Damages*

The position in the United States

**8.68** The United States case of *Kuhns v Scottrade*[36] illustrates the difficulties in proving damages in data breach cases.

**8.69** The case concerned a purported breach of privacy statement leading to loss. Unauthorized use by hackers of personal identification information (PII) of 4.6 million customers.

**8.70** The data was controlled by Scottrade, a security brokerage firm. Their privacy policy read as follows that they 'maintained physical, electronic and procedural safeguards that comply with federal regulations to your non-public personal information'.

**8.71** They further went on to claim that 'we comply with applicable laws and regulations regarding personal information...we use industry leading security technologies, including layered security and access controls over personal information'.

**8.72** A document on the firm's website also stated, 'we keep all customer information confidential and maintain strict physical, electronic and procedural safeguards to protect against unauthorised access to your information'.

**8.73** Class actions were brought for:

(1) Breach of contract
(2) Breach of implied contract
(3) Unjust enrichment
(4) Declaratory judgment
(5) And violation of state consumer protection regulations.

**8.74** At District court level the plaintiff's lost, the courts found no 'Article III standing'. On appeal to the Eighth Circuit. The plaintiffs again lost but for lack of sufficient detail.

**8.75** 'Bare allegations that Scottrade's efforts failed to protect customer PII' were not sufficiently specific. Kuhn's failed to identify the exact breach or any actual financial loss. The Eight Circuit stated that 'massive class action litigation should be based on more than allegations of worry and inconvenience'.

**8.76** Also breach of implied contract, unjust enrichment and declaratory judgment lacked sufficient detail failed to identify industry leading security measures and what specific portion of the brokerage fees went towards data protection. Or which of Scottrade's current security practices were allegedly illegal.

**8.77** Therefore, it can be concluded from this case that a plaintiff would have to allege that he relied on a specific statement made by the defendant in order to have standing and the plaintiffs would have to plead their breach of contract/ implied contract with much greater specificity to survive a motion to dismiss or failure to state a claim.

---

36 August 21, 2017 – Court of Appeals, Eight Circuit.

**8.78** The specific law breached would also have to be stated as well as the financial loss suffered as a result of the breach.

The position in Malaysia
**8.79** In Malaysia section 74 of the Contracts Act states that:

(1) When a contract has been broken, the party who suffers by the breach is entitled to receive, from the party who has broken the contract, compensation *for any loss or damage* caused to him thereby, which naturally arose in the usual course of things from the breach, or which the parties knew, when they made the contract, to be likely to result from the breach of it.

(2) Such compensation is not to be given for any remote and indirect loss or damage sustained by reason of the breach.

**8.80** The problem here is twofold: compensation has to be for loss or damage caused and the damages resulting from a data breach would not be considered too remote or an indirect loss. Can a victim of a data breach provide proof of loss or that the loss was a direct result of the data breach?

**8.81** In the case of *Lim Foo Yong & Sons Realty v Datuk Eric Taylor*,[37] for instance, it was held that loss or damage must be the actual amount of the damage suffered. In a data breach how can the damage suffered be quantified or proved? In this respect in the case of data breaches the loss or damage suffered may not be quantifiable, thus a data subject's claim may fail.

The position in the UK
**8.82** In the UK, the fact that monetary redress can be available under the Data Protection Act 1998 and now under the Data Protection Act 2018 for a data breach, breach of statutory duty, is a welcome development.[38] The courts do not now have to resort to mental acrobatics in order to assist a data subject in an action under contract law. However, despite the statutory provisions, the High Court has held in a recent decision[39] that the claimant would need to demonstrate material (i.e. pecuniary) loss, or emotional harm such as distress. However, the claimant sought to do neither – relying instead on the commission of the alleged tort (rather than its consequences) as the basis for seeking compensation. It is arguable, that if the case was brought in contract law, the decision would have been the same.

---

37 [1998]4 AMR 3354;[1998] 4 CLJ 440.
38 Section 168, Compensation for contravention of the GDPR states as follows:
 (1) In Article 82 of the GDPR (right to compensation for material or non-material damage), 'non-material damage' includes distress. (2) Subsection (3) applies where – (a) in accordance with rules of court, proceedings under Article 82 of the GDPR are brought by a representative body on behalf of a person, and (b) a court orders the payment of compensation. (3) The court may make an order providing for the compensation to be paid on behalf of the person to – (a) the representative body, or(b)such other person as the court thinks fit.
39 *Lloyd v Google* [2018] EWHC.

**8.83** In his judgment the High Court Judge stated as follows:

I do not believe that the authorities show that a person whose information has been acquired or used without consent invariably suffers compensable harm, either by virtue of the wrong itself, or the interference with autonomy that it involves... In short, the question of whether or not damage has been sustained by an individual as a result of the non-consensual use of personal data about them must depend on the facts of the case.[40]

**8.84** Damages were sought by the plaintiff by referring to the serious nature of the breach, taking into account the following:

(1) The lack of consent or knowledge of the representative claimant and each member of the claimant class to the defendant's collection and use of personal data;

(2) The fact that such collection and use was contrary to the defendant's public statements;

(3) The fact that such collection and use was greatly to the commercial benefit of the defendant

(4) The fact that the defendant ought to have known of the operation of the Safari Workaround from a very early stage during the Relevant Period. The representative claimant relies in support of this contention upon the fact that as a result of the operation of the Safari Workaround, the defendant tracked and collated information regarding the internet usage of many millions of Safari uses which could not have been tracked and collated but for this operation. In the circumstances it must have been apparent to the defendant that the volume of information it was collecting from Safari uses was substantially in excess of that which it would have expected to collect given the existence of the default security settings. It is to be inferred that the defendant was at all material times in fact aware of the Safari Workaround or became aware of it during the Relevant Period but chose to do nothing about it until the effect of the Safari Workaround came into the public domain as a result of the investigations of an independent third party.

**8.85** Despite the above, the Court found that there was no damage proved. In this sense, judicial precedent appears to have taken many steps backwards even though the Data Protection Act and the GDPR seems to encourage claims for material and non-material damages including those for distress and seems to be much broader in its interpretation of what damages could be claimed.

**8.86** In the interest of technological evolution in the area of contract law and particularly in relation to data or privacy agreements, could not the mere establishing of the causal link between the act of the defendant and the breach

---

40  Warby J, para 74.

be sufficient for damages to be awarded? It is believed that this should be so but having careful considerations of the facts of each individual case.

**8.87** This decision has been reversed by the Court of Appeal in October 2019 in *Lloyd v Google* LLC [2019]EWCA civ 1599. The Court of Appeal held that, pursuant to section 13 of the DPA 1998, that a claimant should be able to recover damages for loss of control of data, without having to prove pecuniary loss or distress. This is a welcome decision indeed. Although this case was decided on the DPA 1998, it would arguably be of invaluable assistance to the interpretation of the DPA 2018 and indeed when it comes to the determination of damages in contract cases.

### Conclusion: what is the difference between a normal contract and that relating to personal data?

**8.88** So, in the final analysis what is the difference between a normal contract and one that pertains to data privacy?

**8.89** Privacy, data policy or data agreements are very sensitive agreements and should not be treated in a complacent manner. As this chapter has proposed, stricter rules should be applied specifically when dealing with the issue of acceptance/consent, which is the overarching principle attached to all data protection laws.

**8.90** As can be seen from this discussion there are inherent problems when contract law is applied to an online privacy agreement dealing with personal data that has been exchanged or shared for access to a service online, the service offered free of charge. It is inevitable that these questions arise, as the law races to keep up with technological advances. The United States appears to have dealt with these grey areas better than others, adapting their laws to suit new circumstances, however as can be seen, there are still some issues that need to be ironed out. It is time for a re-thinking of contract law, to make this law a universally acceptable one, as a means to deal with data breaches.

## CHAPTER 9

# Setting out a comprehensive legal framework to govern exemption clauses in Malaysia

## Lessons from the United Kingdom and Australia

### *Loganathan Krishnan*

## Introduction

**9.1** This chapter will first examine the validity and legal effect of exclusion clauses under the Contracts Act (CA) 1950. Whilst doing so, reference will be made to cases decided by Malaysian courts. Observably, the courts relied on common law to determine the validity and effect of exclusion clauses. The cases were not consistent in deciding whether exclusion clauses are valid. Hence, in some cases, the courts held them to be valid which acts to the advantage of the businessmen but to the detriment of consumers. The chapter will show that clear principles of law were not laid down to test the validity of exclusion clauses. The chapter proceeds to examine other piece-meal legislations, namely, the Sale of Goods Act 1957, Hire Purchase Act 1967 and Consumer Protection Act 1999. Thus, this chapter will critically analyse the extent to which the above-mentioned legislations are effective in determining the validity of exclusion clauses. Then a comparative study with the legal position in the United Kingdom and Australia[1] will be carried out to understand the approaches taken. Finally, this chapter will discuss reforms that should be made to the Contracts Act 1950, Sale of Goods Act 1957, Hire-Purchase Act 1967 and Consumer Protection Act 1999 in order to set out a comprehensive legal framework to regulate exclusion clauses in view of the approaches taken in the UK and Australia.

## Background of study

**9.2** In many circumstances, exclusion clauses become the focus of unfairness to consumers.[2] Exclusion clauses are usually found in standard form contracts and they are non-negotiable leaving no options available to the consumer to reject the clause.[3] To that end standard form contracts are very

---

1 Hereinafter referred to as the UK.

2 Hugh Beale, 'Unfair Terms in Contracts: Proposals for Reform in the UK' (2004) 27 Journal of Consumer Policy 289.

3 Azimon Abdul Aziz and Sakina Shaik Ahmad Yusoff, 'Regulating Standard Form of Consumer Contracts: The Legal Treatment of Selected Asian Jurisdictions' (2010) 1 Asian Journal of Accounting and Governance 105.

common too.[4] Hence, this is oppressive.[5] They are prepared by one party and presented to the other party.[6] Though some consider a standard form contract to be transparent, what is important is that it should not contain terms which are unfair to any of the parties.[7] Standard form contract is a document prepared by a trader of goods and services and usually used by the trader in all transactions.[8] Hence it is a tool of convenience.[9] In fact, Lord Reid's judgment in *Suisse Atlantique Societe d' Armament Maritime SA v NV Rotterdamsche Kolen Centrale*[10] is noteworthy here;

> Exemption clauses differ greatly in many respects. Probably the most objectionable are found in the complex standard conditions which are now so common. In the ordinary way the customer has no time to reads them, and if he reads them he would probably not understand them. And if did understand or object to any of them, he would generally be told he could take it or leave it.

Donaldson J. in *Kenyon, Son and Craven Ltd v Baxter Hoare and Co*[11] stated that if the exemption clause occurred in a printed form of contract between parties of unequal bargaining power, it would be socially most undesirable. In any form of protection by the law, there must be an objective to achieve an equal bargaining position.[12] Hence, the legal regime governing exclusion clauses must be effective in ensuring business persons do not take advantage of customers/buyers/consumers. Most importantly, the legal framework governing exclusion clauses in Malaysia must be in tandem with the legal position in developed countries in ensuring equity and fairness between contracting parties. In England, the Parliament realised the ineffectiveness of common law in laying down sound principles of law to determine validity of exclusion clauses. There is no level playing field between business persons and consumers/customers/buyers.[13] Hence, the Parliament specifically enacted the Unfair Contract Terms Act 1977. In subsequent years, in order to further strengthen the legal framework to regulate exclusion clauses, the Parliament enacted the Consumer Rights Act 2015.

---

4 Saiful Azhar Abd Hamid, *The Exclusion Clause in Government Standard Form of Construction Contracts*, Master of Science in Construction Contract Management Dissertation, MARA University of Technology, 2013.

5 David Yates, *Exclusion Clauses in Contract* (Sweet & Maxwell 1982).

6 Guenter Heinz Treitel, *An Outline of the Law of Contract*, 4th edn (Butterworths 1989).

7 Chris Willett, 'The Functions of Transparency in Regulating Contract Terms: UK and Australian Approaches' (2011) 60(2) International and Comparative Law Quarterly 355.

8 Jeannie Paterson, *Unfair Terms in Australia* (Thomson Reuters 2012).

9 Mastura Mohd Zain, *Exclusion Clauses and Standard Form Contract, A Comparative Study of English and Malaysian Law*, Master of Comparative Law Dissertation, IIUM, 1993.

10 [1967] 1 AC 361.

11 [1971] 1 Lloyd's Rep. 232.

12 Sothi Rachagan, *Consumer Law Reform – A Report* (University of Malaya Press 1992).

13 Wendy K Mariner, 'Standards of Care and Standard Form Contracts' (1998) Journal of Contemporary Health Law and Policy 15.

## Legal framework governing exclusion clauses under common law

*Meaning and type of exclusion clauses*

**9.3** An exemption clause (also known as an 'exclusion clause' or 'exception clause') is a term of a contract that attempts either to modify the principal obligation(s) arising under the contract of a particular type, or limit or exclude liability of a party which will arise if that party breaches his primary obligations.[14] In certain circumstances, the rights of one party to the contract may in some way be limited under the contract without them even being aware of the exclusion clause or its possible effect. The House of Lords in *Ailsa Craig Fishing Co Ltd v Malvern Shipping Co Ltd*[15] has made a distinction between exclusion clauses and limitation clauses.[16] The House opined that the courts should be stricter in interpreting exclusion clauses compared to limitation clauses. It may take many forms, but they have one thing in common in that they exclude a person from liability.[17]

**9.4** Be that as it may, there are various types of exclusion clauses and it is impossible to categorise them.[18] In some cases they can exclude or modify contractual obligations.[19] Usually they are found in tickets, receipts, or invoices which are given after a contract has been concluded and the customer has no opportunity to read the terms.[20] In cases where exclusion clauses have been found to be valid, it is clearly one sided. In such a case it is substantively unfair.[21] The concern is the extent exclusion clauses are unfair. In most cases, an exclusion clause will exclude terms which are favourable to the buyer.[22]

**9.5** The courts have also used doctrines such as economic duress as in the case of *North Ocean Shipping Co Ltd v Hyundai Construction Co Ltd*[23] and inequality of bargaining power as in *Universe Tankships of Monrovia v International Transport Workers Federation*[24] to strike down exclusion clauses. The Law Commission (1975) describes these contractual issues in the following passage:

> The mischief is that they deprive or may deprive the person against whom they may be invoked either of certain specific rights which social policy requires that he should have (for example the right of a buyer in a consumer sale to be supplied with goods or merchantable quality or the right of a person to whom a service has been supplied to a reasonable standard care and skill on the part of the supplier) or the rights which the promise reasonably believed the promisor had conferred upon him ...

---

14 David Yates, *Exclusion Clauses in Contract* (Sweet & Maxwell 1982).

15 [1983] 1 All ER 101.

16 See also Ritchard Stone, *The Modern Law of Contract*, 7th edn (Routledge-Cavendish 2008) 288.

17 Patrick Atiyah, *Law and Modern Society* (Oxford University Press 1995).

18 Jill Poole, *Textbook on Contract Law* (Oxford University Press 2008).

19 Gerald H L Friedman, *The Law of Contract in Canada*, 3rd edn (Carswell Thomson 1999).

20 Syed Ahmad Al-Sagoff, *Principles of the Law of Contract in Malaysia* (Malayan Law Journal 2015).

21 Francis H Buckley, *Just Exchange: A Theory of Contracts* (Routledge 2005).

22 Patrick S Atiyah, *The Sale of Goods* (Pitman 1990).

23 [1978] 3 All ER 1170.

24 [1983] 1 AC 360.

**9.6** The Contracts Act 1950 does not address the validity of exclusion clauses. It is more concerned about the basic principles of contract law.[25] Thus, references were made to common law.[26] This is due to section 3 and section 5 Civil Law Act 1956[27] which permits the reception of common law if there is a lacunae in the domestic law. Thus, validity of exclusion clauses was dependent on case law. Consequently, results will depend on the ideologies and perspectives of the judges.[28] Cases such as *Sze Hai Tong Bank Ltd v Rambler Cycle Co. Ltd*[29] and *Sanggaralingam Arumugam v Wong Kook Wah & Anor*[30] held exclusion clauses to be void.

**9.7** Nevertheless, in *Malaysia Airlines System Bhd v Malini Nathan & Anor*,[31] a different approach was taken. The court took a very simplistic approach in determining the validity of exclusion clauses.[32] Similarly, an exclusion clause was held to be valid in *United Overseas Bank (Malaysia) Bhd v Lee Yaw Lin & Choo Yoke Peng.*[33] Observably, these cases create a concern on the proper legal framework to govern exclusion clauses.[34] For an exclusion clause to be valid, it must satisfy the Rules of Incorporation and Rules of Construction/Interpretation.

## Drawbacks of the rules of incorporation

**9.8** The purpose of the Rules of Incorporation is to determine whether an exclusion clause is incorporated in a contract. Although an exclusion clause is written in a contract or displayed, it does not automatically mean that it is valid. Once it is found that an exclusion clause is incorporated in a contract, the next step is to determine whether the exclusion clause covers the breach. This is where the Rules of Construction/Interpretation comes into picture.

**9.9** For an exclusion clause to be incorporated, the clause must be incorporated into the contract and not inserted after the contract is complete, i.e. after the acceptance of an offer – *Olley v Marlborough Court Ltd*,[35] *Thornton v Shoe Lane Parking Ltd*[36] and *Levison v Patent Steam Carpet Cleaning Co Ltd.*[37]

---

25  Nik Ramlah Mahmood, *Unfair Terms in Malaysian Consumer Contracts – The Need for Increased Judicial Creativity*, Asian Seminar on Consumer Law, 9–12 August 1993, Kuala Lumpur, Malaysia.

26  Visu Sinnadurai, *Law of Contract, Vol. 1*, 4th edn (Lexis Nexis 2011).

27  Hereinafter referred to as CLA 1956.

28  Sakina Shaik Ahmad Yusoff, *Regulating Exclusion Clauses in Consumer Contracts in Malaysia*, Research Development Fund, Law Faculty, National University of Malaysia, UU/001/2007, 2009.

29  [1959] MLJ 31.

30  [1987] 2 CLJ 255.

31  [1995] 2 MLJ 100.

32  Nik Ramlah Mahmood, *The Regulation of Unfair Contracts*, Asian Seminar on Consumer Law, 9–12 August 1993, Kuala Lumpur, Malaysia.

33  Civil Appeal No.: W-02(NCVC)(W)-2114-12/2014.

34  Elistina Abu Bakar and Naemah Amin, 'Consumers' Awareness and Practices Towards Exclusion Clause and Its Position Under Malaysian Law' (2016) 19 Malaysian Journal of Consumer and Family Economics 15.

35  [1949] 1 KB 532.

36  [1971] 2 QB 163.

37  [1978] 2 QB 69.

Second, the document containing the clause must be an integral part of the contract. Receipts, tickets and dockets are not integral to the contract – *Chapelton v Barry Urban District Council*,[38] *Parker v South Eastern Railway Co*[39] and *Interfoto Picture Library Ltd v Stiletto Visual Programs Ltd.*[40]

**9.10** However, this was not followed in the case of *Borhanuddin Bin Haji Jantara v American International Assurance Co Ltd*[41] whereby the court stated that some notices on receipts may be effective since each case depends on particular circumstances. Third, notice of the exemption clause must be reasonably sufficient which is based on the knowledge of a reasonable person – *Malaysian Airlines System v Malini Nathan & Anor.*[42] The appellant was sued for breach of contract for failing to fly the first respondent back to Kuala Lumpur. The appellant relied on the exclusion clause printed on the airline ticket. Hence, in *Ghee Seng Motor v Ling Sie Ting*,[43] the court stated that the onus is on the party who sought to rely on the clause to prove that adequate steps had been taken to inform the other party of the exemption clause.

**9.11** Nonetheless, the Rules of Incorporation are not free from difficulties. It is not fair in cases where customers/buyers/consumers did not read the document or if it is written in a small print or if it is a practice that certain industries usually have exclusion clauses to exclude or limit their liability. The fact that parties choose not to read the contract in its entirety does not mean that they are not bound by the terms of the contract as pointed by the courts in *Saunders v Anglia Building Society.*[44]

**9.12** There are two main methods to incorporate a term into a contract between the parties, namely by signature and by prior and sufficient information. Thus, the general rule is that a person who accepts an offer made in a written document by signing and delivering that document is bound by all the terms of that document, whether or not he has read them and this includes any terms incorporated from another document by reference. If the contract contains an exclusion clause, the party signing the contract is bound by the clause too – *L'Estrange v Graucob.*[45] Support can be found in cases such as *Wee Lian Construction Sdn Bhd v Ingersoll-Jati Malaysia Sdn Bhd*[46] and *Lee Teck Seng v Lasman Das Sundra Shah.*[47] One of the exceptions to the rule is if one party has been misled by the other – *Curtis v Chemical Cleaning and Dyeing Co Ltd.*[48]

---

38 [1940] 1 KB 532.
39 [1930] 1 KB 41.
40 [1989] QB 433.
41 [1986] 1 MLJ 246.
42 [1986] 1 MLJ 330.
43 [1993] MLJU 130.
44 [1970] 3 All ER 961.
45 [1934] 2 KB 394. See also *Polygram Records Sdn Bhd* v *The Search & Anor* [1994] 3 MLJ 127.
46 [2010] 3 MLJ 425.
47 [2000] 8 CLJ 317.
48 [1951] 1 KB 805.

The exception to prior and sufficient information would be if the parties had consistent previous dealings. Previous dealings are sufficient to show that the other party has constructive notice of the terms, provided that the dealings are regular and consistent – *Hollier v Rambler Motors (AMC) Ltd.*[49]

*Drawbacks of the rules of construction/interpretation*

**9.13** One of the rules is the doctrine of fundamental breach. An exclusion clause cannot be used to exclude liability for a fundamental breach of a contract – *Sze Hai Tong Bank Ltd v Rambler Cycle Co Ltd.*[50] The House of Lords in *Suisse Atlantique Societe d'Armenent Maritime SA v NV Rotterdamsche Kolen Centrale*[51] found that the rule is merely one of construction. However, the doctrine of fundamental breach of contract was rejected in *Photo Productions Ltd v Securicor Transport Co Ltd.*[52] Nonetheless, in the context of Malaysia, whether an exclusion clause applies is a matter of construction as was decided in *CIMB Bank Bhd v Maybank Trustees Bhd and other appeals.*[53]

**9.14** Another rule is the *contra proferentum* rule which provides that if the clause is ambiguous, the court will interpret it against the person asserting it – *Walis, Son & Wells v Pratt & Hynes,*[54] *Lee (John) & Son (Grantham) Ltd v Railways Executive*[55] and *Syarikat Lee Heng Sdn Bhd v Port Swettenham Authority.*[56] Support can also be found in *Malaysia National Insurance Sdn Bhd v Abdul Aziz bin Mohamed Daud.*[57] Thus, words such as 'park at your own risk' will unlikely be enforceable as it is unclear what type of risk the clause attempts to cover.

**9.15** The next rule is the 'Four Corners Rule'. This is where an exclusion clause will only be valid to a breach which occurs based on the text of the contract itself, without relying upon other resources or witnesses. Thus, a person should not be allowed to rely on the exclusion clause if it does not cover the breach in the contract – *The Council of the City of Sydney v West.*[58]

**9.16** Last but not least, one cannot exclude liability for negligence unless clear words have been used. Thus, the court in *Chin Hooi Nan v Comprehensive Auto Restoration Service Sdn Bhd & Anor*[59] held that the exclusion clause is not valid. However, other cases such as *Premier Hotel Sdn Bhd v Tang Ling Seng,*[60]

---

49 [1972] 2 QB 71.
50 [1959] 2 Lloyd's Rep. 114.
51 [1967] AC 361.
52 [1980] AC 827.
53 [2014] 3 MLJ 169.
54 [1911] AC 394.
55 [1949] 2 All ER 581.
56 [1971] 2 MLJ 27.
57 [1979] 2 MLJ 29.
58 (1965) 114 CLR 481.
59 [1995] 1 BLJ 25.
60 [1995] 4 MLJ 229.

*Syarikat, Cheap Hin Toy MFE Sdn Bhd v Syarikat Perkapalan Kris Sdn Bhd & Anor*[61] and *Chong Kok Weng & Anor v Wing Wah Travel Agency Sdn Bhd & Anor*[62] held otherwise. Thus, the case of *Chin Hooi Nan v Comprehensive Auto Restoration Service Sdn Bhd & Anor*[63] cannot be held as the leading authority to declare that an exclusion clause cannot exclude liability for negligence.[64]

### Legal framework governing exclusion clauses under the Contracts Act 1950[65]

*Doctrine of unconscionability*

**9.17** The preamble to the CA 1950 states that it is an Act relating to contracts and the Act applies throughout Malaysia. The only grounds to challenge a contract is if there is a claim of coercion, undue influence, fraud, misrepresentation or mistake. In *Saad Marwi v Chan Hwan Hua & Anor*[66] the Court of Appeal adopted and applied the English doctrine of inequality of bargaining power. However, this was rejected in the case of *American International Assurance Company Ltd v Koh Yen Bee*.[67] The courts are also reluctant to adopt the doctrine of unconscionability compared to the UK.

**9.18** Although section 16(3)(a) provides that where a person who is in a position to dominate the will of another, enters into a contract with him, and the transaction appears, on the face of it or on the evidence adduced, to be unconscionable, the burden of proving that the contract was not induced by undue influence shall lie upon the person in a position to dominate the will of the other – it should be noted that the term unconscionability is used in the context of undue influence. Hence, the doctrine of unconscionability does not stand on its own. This can be seen in the Federal Court decision of *Datuk Joginder Singh v Tara Rajaratnam*.[68] The word 'unconscionable' was used, but only in the context of the doctrine of undue influence.

*Public policy*

**9.19** At the outset, the term public policy must be understood. Lord Brougham in *Holman v Johnson*[69] defines public policy as the principle which declares that no man can lawfully do that which has a tendency to be injurious to the public.

---

61  [1995] 4 CLJ 84.

62  [2003] 5 MLJ 550.

63  [1995] 1 BLJ 25.

64  Vijayalakshmi Venugopal, 'The Effects of Exclusion Clauses' (Part 1 & 2) (2002) Current Law Journal liii.

65  Hereinafter referred to as CA 1950.

66  [2001] 3 CLJ 98.

67  [2002] 4 CLJ 49.

68  [1983] 2 MLJ 196.

69  [1775–1802] ALL ER Rep 98.

In *Merong Mahawangsa Sdn Bhd & Anor v Dato' Shazryl Eskay b. Abdullah*,[70] the Federal Court had observed that public policy is not static.

There was an opportunity for the courts to test the validity of exclusion clauses on the ground that it is against public policy.[71] Support can also be found in cases from the United States namely *Henningsen v Bloomfield Motors*.[72] Thus, reference should be made to section 24(e) which reads that the consideration or object of an agreement is lawful, unless the court regards it as immoral, or opposed to public policy. However, the argument was rejected in *Wee Lian Construction Sdn Bhd v Ingersoll-Jati Malaysia Sdn Bhd*[73] on the ground that the consideration or object of an agreement which is unlawful and thus against public policy. Reddy J in the Andhra Pradesh High Court, observed in *Ratanchand Hirachand v Askar Nawaz Jung*[74] that in a modern and progressive society with fast changing social values and concepts it becomes more and more imperative to evolve new heads of public policy wherever necessary to meet the demands of new situation. Law cannot afford to remain static.

Hence, in *Lily White v Munusami*,[75] the High Court of Madras held that an exemption clause in a consumer contract was contrary to public policy and hence unenforceable. Since the CA 1950 is based on the Indian Contracts Act 1872, this case should be referred to in interpreting section 24(e). Support can also be found in Canadian cases such as *Tercon Contractors Ltd v British Columbia (Transportation and Highways)*[76] and *Plas-Tex Canada Ltd v Dow Chemical of Canada Limited*.[77] In fact, the validity of public policy is considered as a rationale to address the various problems created by exclusion causes.[78]

**9.20** Nonetheless, even if the argument is accepted, the CA 1950 can be contracted out on the basis of freedom of contract as pointed in *Ooi Boon Leong & Ors v Citibank NA*.[79] Since parties have freedom of contract, courts are usually reluctant to interfere as pointed by Sir George Jassel MR in *Printing and Numerical Registering Company v Simpson*.[80] Hence, the court will not make any improvements on the contract as succinctly put by the court in *Berjaya Time Square Sdn Bhd v M Concept Sdn Bhd*.[81] Be that as it may, Denning LJ in *John*

---

70 [2015] 5 MLJ 619.

71 Visu Sinnadurai, 'Exemption Clause v Public Policy and Inequality of Bargaining Power' (1978) 2 Malayan Law Journal cxxx.

72 75 A.L.R. 2d 1.

73 [2005] 1 MLJ 162.

74 (1991) 3 SCC 67, 77.

75 A.I.R. 1966 Mad.13.

76 2010 SCC 4, [2010] 1 SCR 69.

77 2004 ABCA 309 at paras 54–55, 245 DLR (4th) 650.

78 Krish Maharaj, 'Limits on the Operation of Exclusion Clauses' (2012) 49(3) Alberta Law Review 635–654.

79 [1984] 1 MLJ 222.

80 [1874–75] LR 19.

81 [2010] 1 MLJ 597. See also *Investors Compensation Scheme Limited* v *West Bromwich Building Society* [1998] 1WLR 896.

*Lee & Sons (Grantham) Ltd and Others v Railway Executive*[82] stated that 'above all, there is the vigilance of the common law while allowing for freedom of contract, watches to see that it is not abused'.

### Agreements in restraint of legal proceedings

**9.21** Section 29 provides that every agreement, by which any party thereto is restricted absolutely from enforcing his rights under or in respect of any contract, by the usual legal proceedings in the ordinary tribunals, or which limits the time within which he may thus enforce his rights, is void to that extent. However, there are two exceptions namely where parties agree that any dispute which may arise between them shall be referred to arbitration. Second, where any contract in writing between the Government and any person with respect to an award of a scholarship by the Government wherein it is provided that the discretion exercised by the Government under that contract shall be final and conclusive and shall not be questioned by any court.

**9.22** Section 29 has never been used by the courts to strike down any exclusion clauses from the time the CA was enacted in 1950 until the Federal Court decision of *CIMB Bank Berhad v Anthony Lawrence Bourke & Alison Deborah Essex Bourke*.[83] In this case, the effect of the loan agreement was that the respondents were precluded from claiming any loss or damage and the appellant will not be liable for any amount for loss of income or profit or savings, or any indirect, incidental, consequential, exemplary, punitive or special damages. Thus, the issue was whether this is caught by section 29. There is the patent unfairness and injustice to the respondents had this clause been allowed to deny their claim/rights against the appellants. It is unconscionable on the part of the bank to seek refuge behind the clause and an abuse of the freedom of contract. Hence, any contracts which seek to oust the jurisdiction of the courts are invalid.[84]

**9.23** The approach taken by the Federal Court is commendable. Nevertheless, it is still too early to establish that exclusion clauses can be struck off by use of section 29. This is because the provision does not expressly prohibit exclusion clauses. The court argued that an exclusion clause is a form of a restraint of legal proceedings.

## Legal framework governing exclusion clauses under the Sale of Goods Act 1957[85]

### Exclusion of implied terms

**9.24** The preamble of the Sale of Goods Act (SOGA) 1957 states that it is an Act relating to the sale of goods. The SOGA 1957 governs dealings between a buyer and a seller. It could be a transaction between two businesspersons or

---

82 [1949] 2 All ER 581.
83 Civil Appeal No: 02-105-10/2017(W).
84 Richard A Buckley, *Illegality and Public Policy*, 3rd edn (Sweet & Maxwell 2013).
85 Hereinafter referred to as SOGA 1957.

between a business person and a consumer. Section 4(1) provides that a contract of sale of goods is a contract whereby the seller transfers or agrees to transfer the property in goods to the buyer for a price.

**9.25** The legislature being aware there is inequality of bargaining position between a buyer and a seller, provided protection to the buyer in the form of implied terms as found in section 14 to section 17. This is quite different from the usual meaning of implied terms.[86] The implied terms provide that the buyer shall have title, quiet possession, goods which are free from encumbrance, goods which corresponds with description, goods which are fit for purpose and good which are merchantable quality including goods bought based on the sample. Some of the protections are in the form of implied conditions namely section 14(a) which governs title, section 15 which governs description, section 16(1)(a) which govern fitness for purpose, section 16(1)(b) which governs merchantable quality and section 17 which governs sale by sample. Whereas section 14(b) which governs quiet possession and section 14(c) which governs goods to be free from encumbrance are implied warranties. However due to section 16(1)(a) which reads '… in the course of the seller's business to supply …' and section 16(1)(b) which reads '… a seller who deals in goods of that description …' the implied terms as to fitness for purpose and merchantable quality will only apply if the transaction is between two businesspersons. Hence, it does not apply to private sales.

**9.26** Despite the noble effort taken by the legislature in enacting section 14 to section 17, the SOGA 1957 allows the use of exemption clauses in trade and it is a term most commonly used in standard form contracts. This is evident from section 62 which reads 'where any right, duty or liability would arise under a contract of sale by implication of law, it may be negatived or varied by express agreement or by the course of dealing between the parties, or by usage, if the usage is such as to bind both parties to the contract'. Thus, the implied terms of section 14 to section 17 which are meant to protect the buyer fail to do so. A seller may easily resort to section 62 to exclude his liability for a breach of any of the implied terms. Therefore, it defeats the purpose of granting protection to the buyer if implied terms can be excluded.

### Application of law for the states of Sabah and Sarawak

**9.27** The SOGA 1957 applies to Peninsular Malaysia and not Sabah and Sarawak. Hence reference should be made to section 5(2) CLA. It provides that in all questions or issues which arise or which have to be decided in the States of Sabah and Sarawak with respect to the law concerning any of the matters referred to in subsection (1), the law to be administered shall be the same as would be administered in England in the like case at the corresponding period, if such question or issue had arisen or had to be decided in England, unless in any case

---

86 F R Davies, *Contract*, 5th edn (Sweet & Maxwell 1986) 69.

other provision is or shall be made by any written law. This means that the legal framework governing sale of goods in Sabah and Sarawak is the English Sale of Goods Act 1979.[87]

**9.28** Essentially, section 55(1) SOGA 1979 states that where a right, duty or liability would arise under a contract of sale of goods by implication of law, it may (subject to the Unfair Contract Terms Act (UCTA) 1977)[88] be negatived or varied by express agreement, or by the course of dealing between the parties, or by such usage as binds both parties to the contract. The provision is similar to section 62 SOGA 1957 except that exclusion clauses in a contract of sale of goods are subject to UCTA 1977. The operation of UCTA 1977 in addressing exclusion clauses is dealt with in detail in subsequent sections. At this juncture, suffice to state that exclusion clauses are more likely to be invalid in the states of Sabah and Sarawak due to the UCTA compared to exclusion clauses in Peninsular Malaysia due to the ineffectiveness of section 62 SOGA 1957. Hence, there is no uniform approach to exclusion clauses under the law of sale of goods in Malaysia.

### Legal framework governing exclusion clauses under the Hire-Purchase Act 1967[89]

**9.29** The Hire-Purchase Act (HPA) 1967 is an Act to regulate the form and contents of hire-purchase agreements, the rights and duties of parties to such agreements. Section 1(2) provides that this Act shall apply in respect only of hire-purchase agreements relating to the goods specified in the First Schedule. They are all consumer goods; motor vehicles, namely invalid carriages; motor cycles; motor cars including taxi cabs and hire cars; goods vehicles (where the maximum permissible laden weight does not exceed 2,540 kilograms) and buses, including stage buses. Hence, a hire-purchase agreement could be a consumer or a non-consumer contract.

**9.30** Section 7(1)(a) to (c) implies terms that the hirer should have quiet possession of the goods, title to the goods and that the goods shall be free from encumbrance respectively in order to protect the hirer since there is no equality of bargaining position between the owner and the hirer. Similarly, terms are implied to protect the hirer that the goods shall be of merchantable quality and fit for its purpose as can be seen in section 7(2) and section 7(3) respectively.

**9.31** Essentially, the approach taken to protect a hirer, is the same as the approach taken to protect a buyer in the context of SOGA. Nevertheless, there is a slight difference as regards to the use of exclusion clauses. Section 7(2)(b) and section 7(3) allows the owner to rely on exclusion clauses if the goods are second hand and the owner proves that the hirer has acknowledged in writing that the statement was brought to his notice.

---

87 Hereinafter referred to as SOGA 1979.
88 Hereinafter referred to as the UCTA 1977.
89 Hereinafter referred to as the HPA 1967.

**9.32** Hence, the implied terms under section 7(1)(a)–(c) cannot be excluded. Nonetheless, it is strange that a hirer has better rights under the HPA 1967 compared to a buyer under the SOGA. Rightfully, a buyer should have better rights since he has already purchased the goods.

**9.33** A further difference is that exclusion of implied terms under the SOGA 1957 applies to all type of goods whereas exclusion under the HPA 1967 only applies to second hand goods. Hence, if the goods are new, the hirer has full protection under section 7(2) and (3). Nevertheless, the HPA is silent on the meaning of second hand goods, Hence, even one-day old goods are considered as second hand goods. It is unreasonable to allow an owner to rely on exclusion clauses in such cases and exclude his duty to ensure goods are of merchantable quality. Moreover, a mere initial of signature by the hirer on every page of the hire-purchase agreement does not amount to an acknowledgement of the existence of an exclusion clause in the hire-purchase agreement. It also does not mean that the hirer is made aware of the existence of the exclusion clauses.

## Legal framework governing exclusion clauses under the Consumer Protection Act 1999[90]

### Inadequacy of the Consumer Protection Act (CPA)

**9.34** In 1993, the National Advisory Council for Consumer Protection in Malaysia suggested to adopt the Unfair Contract Terms Act 1977 of the United Kingdom. Hence, the preamble of the CPA 1999 states that it is an Act to provide for the protection of consumers, the establishment of the National Consumer Advisory Council and the Tribunal for Consumer Claims. Moreover, when the CPA 1999 came into effect, it was expected to contain comprehensive provisions to regulate exclusion clauses.[91]

**9.35** However, the CPA 1999 did not address the issue of exclusion clauses in consumer contracts.[92] This is so although the CPA 1999 has been influenced by the legal developments in the UK.[93] Furthermore, the CPA 1999 does not cover all types of services such as healthcare services and services provided by professionals since they are regulated by specific written laws. In these situations, the common law shall apply. Nevertheless, as seen earlier, the common law governing exclusion clauses poses various problems. Hence, persons who are receiving healthcare and professional services are at a disadvantage. Furthermore, the

---

90 Hereinafter referred to as the CPA 1999.

91 Mohamad Fazli Sabri, 'The Development of Consumer Protection Policies in Malaysia' (2014) 4(6) International Journal of Business and Social Research 98.

92 Farhah Abdullah and Shakina Syed Abdul Yusoff, *Corporate Integrity and Accountability: A Story of Exemption Clauses in Consumer Contracts – A Myth or Reality?* 2nd International Conference on Business and Economic Research, 14–16 March 2011, Langkawi, Kedah, Malaysia.

93 Naemah Amin, 'Protecting Consumers Against Unfair Contract Terms in Malaysia: The Consumer Protection (Amendment) Act 2010' (2013) 1 Malayan Law Journal lxxxix.

CPA 1999 only applies to consumer contracts as provided in section 2 CPA 1999 since the objective is to give protection to consumers.[94]

**9.36** However, there is a conflict with section 24B which states that the provisions of this part i.e. Part IIIA CPA 1999 shall apply to all contracts. The concern is whether the legislature intended Part IIIA to apply to all types of contracts regardless of whether they are consumer or non-consumer contracts. If it only applies to consumer contracts then if it is a contract between two business persons, the CPA is inapplicable. The legislature opines that there is an equal bargaining position between the parties. The legislature failed to realise that in some cases the business person could be a small or medium sized industry operating as a sole trader, partnership firm or a small private company owned by family members.

**9.37** Moreover, the CPA 1999 is limited in its application due to section 2 which states that the application of the Act shall be supplemental in nature and without prejudice to any other law regulating contractual relations. Further support can be found in section 24B which provides that without prejudice to the provisions in the Contracts Act 1950, Specific Relief Act 1950, Sale of Goods Act 1957 and the provisions of any other law for the time being in force, the provisions of this Part shall apply to all contracts.

**9.38** Be that as it may, section 6 provides that the provisions of this Act shall have effect notwithstanding anything to the contrary in any agreement. Hence, the CPA 1999 supersedes any attempts made by any party to a contract to exclude the operation of the Act. The provision further states that every supplier and every manufacturer who purports to contract out of any provision of this Act commits an offence. The effect of section 6 can be seen in the decision of the Tribunal for Consumer Claims in *Seng v De Paris Image Sdn Bhd*[95] where the non-recovery clause in the receipt was declared void as it was in breach of section 6. However, section 6 fails to cover a wide range of exclusion clauses which are usually found in standard form contracts.

*Unfair contract terms*

**9.39** In 2010, the legislature amended the CPA 1999 and introduced Part IIIA titled 'Unfair Contract Terms' to address unfair terms in a contract. Nevertheless, the amendment is not free from weaknesses. Section 24A(c) defines an 'unfair term' as a term in a consumer contract which, with regard to all the circumstances, causes a significant imbalance in the rights and obligations of the parties arising under the contract to the detriment of the consumer. Furthermore, section 24D(1)(e) provides that a contract or a term of a contract is substantively unfair if the contract or the term of the contract excludes or restricts

---

94 Adnan Trakic, 'Statutory Protection of Malaysian Consumers Against Unfair Contract Terms: Has Enough Been Done?' (2015) 44(3) Common Law World Review 203.
95 No.TTPM-Q-(P)-18-2010.

liability for breach of express or implied terms of the contract without adequate justification. This shows that an exclusion clause can still be valid if adequate justification is given. This is further provided in section 24E which states that if a contract or a term of a contract excludes or restricts liability, or excludes rights, duties and liabilities, it is for the supplier relying on such exclusion or restriction to prove that it is not without adequate justification.

**9.40** Furthermore, the CPA does not regulate standard form contracts effectively. This can be seen in section 24A(b) which defines a standard form contract as a consumer contract which is drawn up for general use in a particular industry, with no regards to whether the contract differs from the contracts normally used in that industry or not. Therefore, if the exclusion clause is incorporated through standard form contracts which are the same across the industry, the exclusion clause is not procedurally unfair under section 24C. It also means that there can be more than one type of standard form contract in a particular industry if the standard form contracts are for general use. Hence, the question is whether it can still be considered as a standard form contract.

**9.41** Another provision is section 24I which states that the contravention by 'any person' of Part IIIA is an offence. However, it is silent on how it is breached. Additionally, the term 'any person' is unclear as to whether it would be possible for consumers to commit an offence under it.[96] The tribunal in *Che Mohd Hashim Abdullah v Air Asia X Sdn Bhd*[97] stated that a consumer has no bargaining power when purchasing tickets online and Part IIIA can give better protection to consumers in situations where unequal bargaining powers between consumers and suppliers exist.

**9.42** Hence there are two tests to determine whether a term is unfair, namely procedural unfairness as explained in section 24C and substantive unfairness as explained in section 24D.

**9.43** Section 24C(1) provides that a contract or a term of a contract is procedurally unfair if it has resulted in an unjust advantage to the supplier or unjust disadvantage to the consumer on account of the conduct of the supplier or the manner in which or circumstances under which the contract or the term of the contract has been entered into or has been arrived at by the consumer and supplier. Hence, procedural unfairness refers to the process of making a contract.[98]

**9.44** Section 24D(1) provides that a contract or a term of a contract is substantively unfair if the contract or the term of the contract is in itself harsh; is oppressive; is unconscionable; excludes or restricts liability for negligence; or excludes or restricts liability for breach of express or implied terms of the contract without adequate justification. Substantive unfairness concerns the result of the process.

---

96 Azwina Wati Abdull Manaf and Norazuan Binti Amiruddin, *Comparative Study on Law of Unfair Terms of Contract in Malaysia*, 4th International Conference on Advances in Education and Social Sciences, 15–17 October 2018, Istanbul, Turkey.

97 No:TTPM-WPPJ-(P)-10-2011.

98 Farhah Abdullah and Sakina Shaikh Ahmad Yusoff, *Legal Treatment of Exclusion Clauses in Consumer Contracts Malaysia*, International Academic Conference 2015, Terengganu, Malaysia.

**9.45** Nonetheless, the CPA 1999 does not provide a test for determining adequate justification as provided in section 24D(1)(e) and section 24E.

*Guarantees in respect of supply of goods*

**9.46** Section 32(1) provides where goods are supplied to a consumer there shall be implied a guarantee that the goods are of acceptable quality. Section 39 further provides that this Part gives a consumer a right of redress against a supplier of goods where the goods fail to comply with any of the implied guarantees under sections 31 to 37.

**9.47** However, this right can be excluded as can be observed in section 40[99] which provides notwithstanding section 39, there shall be no right of redress against the supplier of goods under this Act in respect of the failure of the goods to comply with the implied guarantee as to acceptable quality where (a) the manufacturer makes a representation in respect of the goods otherwise than by a statement on any packaging or label; and (b) the goods would have complied with the implied guarantee as to acceptable quality if that representation had not been made. What is unclear is the mode of representation which is being used i.e. must it be in writing or could it be verbal through the media, or must an official notification be sent to the Ministry. Making a representation does not guarantee that it has reached the consumers. It is also unclear when the representation should be made. This is because difficulties can arise in cases where consumers have already started using the goods. Furthermore, the question is whether an exclusion clause fits within the scope of a representation. This provision is unacceptable as it allows a manufacturer to make a representation after a contract has been entered into. Rightfully all representations should have been made before a contract is entered into. By allowing a manufacturer do to so, the CPA 1999 does not give opportunity to the consumer to respond to the representations made. There is no opportunity for the consumer to decide whether to enter into a contract as it is too late. In other words, he is not a well-informed consumer.

*Product liability*

**9.48** Part X of the CPA 1999 governs product liability. Section 66 defines the term product as any goods. Section 71 provides that the liability of a person under this Part to a person who has suffered damage caused wholly or partly by a defect in a product, or to a dependent of such a person, shall not be limited or excluded by any contract term, notice or other provision.

**9.49** Section 71 uses the term 'shall' which connotes that one is not permitted to rely on exclusion clauses if there is a defect in a product. This is in contrast to the approach taken by section 40. The issue is whether unacceptable quality

---

99 Nur Rabiatuladawiah Abdul Rahman, 'The Rise and Fall of Caveat Emptor in Malaysian Sale of Goods Contract' (2018) 1(1) Journal of Law & Governance 1.

under section 32 is synonymous to a defect under section 70. Section 32(2)(a)(iii) states that for the purposes of subsection (1), goods shall be deemed to be of acceptable quality if they are free from minor defects. On the other hand, section 71 does not categorise the type of defects into minor and major. Section 67(1) states that subject to subsections (2) and (3), there is a defect in a product for the purposes of this Part if the safety of the product is not such as a person is generally entitled to expect. Hence, defect is linked to safety of the product and not the quality of the product. This shows that defect is based on what an ordinary person will consider. Hence, a manufacturer may exclude his liability if he makes a representation in the form of an exclusion clause as regards to defects which are minor in the sense they are related to quality but not safety. On the other hand if there is a defect and it concerns safety, an exclusion clause can never be valid. Nevertheless, this provision only applies to Part X.

**9.50** Thus, it can be concluded that the CPA 1999 is not comprehensive in addressing exclusion clauses.[100]

### Lessons from the United Kingdom

**9.51** The UK realized the shortcomings of the common law rules in addressing an exclusion clause which has acted to the detriment of consumers. Hence, the Unfair Contract Terms Act 1977[101] and the Unfair Terms in Consumer Contracts Regulations 1999 were enacted. Despite its name, the UCTA 1977 deals with exclusion clauses, and not with terms that are unfair.[102] The Unfair Terms in Consumer Contracts Regulations 1999 is now superseded by the Consumer Rights Act 2015. These laws have invalidated many exclusion clauses by using the 'reasonableness test'. The first case brought up under the regulations was the *Director General of Fair Trading v First National Bank PLC.*[103]

### Unfair Contract Terms Act 1977

**9.52** The preamble of the UCTA states that it is an Act to impose further limits on the extent to which civil liability for breach of contract, or for negligence or other breach of duty, can be avoided by means of contract terms.

100 Sakina Shaik Ahmad Yusoff, Azimon Abdul Aziz and Rahmah Ismail, 'Legislative Control of Exclusion Clauses in Selected Common Law Countries' (2011) 14 Malaysian Journal of Consumer and Family Economics 90; Azimon Abdul Aziz, Sakina Shaik Ahmad Yusoff, Shamsuddin Suhor, Rahmah Ismail, Kartini Aboo Talib and Muhammad Rizal Razman, 'Standard Form Contracts in Consumer Transactions: A Comparative Study of Selected Asian Countries' (2012) 15 Malaysian Journal of Consumer and Family Economics 21.

101 Hereinafter referred to as the UCTA 1977.

102 John Adriaanse, *Construction Contract Law*, 3rd edn (Palgrave Macmillan 2010).

103 [2002] 2 All ER 759.

**9.53** The first case which was brought to the House of Lords after the enactment of the UCTA 1977 was *Photo Production Ltd v Securicor Transport Ltd.*[104] The House of Lords made it clear that they deprecated the use of artificial methods of construction, now that legislative methods were available to strike down unreasonable exclusion clauses. Hence, the court found that the common law Rules of Incorporation and Rules of Construction are not the suitable test to determine the validity of exclusion clauses.

**9.54** The UCTA prevents either absolutely or subject to qualifications the restriction or exclusion of liability by exclusion clauses in contracts. Section 2(1) states that a person can never exclude liability for death or personal injury caused by negligence. Section 1 defines negligence as a breach of any obligation, arising from the express or implied terms of a contract, to take reasonable care or exercise reasonable skill in the performance of the contract or of any common law duty to take reasonable care or exercise reasonable skill (but not any stricter duty). Subsection 2 provides that in the case of other loss or damage, a person cannot so exclude or restrict his liability for negligence except in so far as the term or notice satisfies the requirement of reasonableness. Subsection 3 states where a contract term or notice purports to exclude or restrict liability for negligence a person's agreement to or awareness of it is not of itself to be taken as indicating his voluntary acceptance of any risk.

**9.55** Furthermore, section 3(1) addresses the use of exclusion clauses in standard form contracts. Section 3(2)(a) states that a person cannot exclude his liability for a breach of contract. Section 3(2)(b) does not permit a party to render a different performance from what was contracted or render no performance at all.

**9.56** Moreover, section 6 protects a buyer absolutely against clauses which attempt to exclude liability in cases where there was no title to goods, goods which did not correspond with description, sample, quality or fitness for purpose in sales of goods. Similarly, the provision protects a hirer in the context of hire-purchase agreements. If it is a non-consumer contract, an exclusion clause will only be valid if it satisfies the test of reasonableness as stated in section 6(3).

**9.57** The test of reasonableness is not defined but explained in section 11. It means that the clause must have been a fair and reasonable one to be included having regard to the circumstances which were known to the parties when the contract was made. Guidelines as to what amount to reasonableness is provided in Schedule 2. The courts will look at the strength of the bargaining positions of the parties, whether the customer received an inducement to agree to the term, whether the customer knew or ought reasonably to have known of the existence and extent of the term, whether the term excludes or restricts any relevant liability if some condition is not complied with, whether the goods were manufactured, processed or adapted to the special order of the customer. Nevertheless,

---

104 [1980] AC 827.

cases such as *The Trustees of Ampleforth Abbey Trust v Turner & Townsend Project Management Ltd*[105] and *Allen Fabrications Ltd v ASD Ltd*[106] show that the test is not free from difficulties.

**9.58** The UCTA 1977 'greatly restricts the use of exclusion clauses whereby contracting parties protect themselves from legal liability'. The Act extends beyond consumer protection, since it also operates, within limits, where businessmen contract on standard written terms.[107]

### Consumer Rights Act 2015

**9.59** The Act is aimed to amend the law relating to the rights of consumers and protection of their interests. Attention must be drawn on section 31, section 47, section 57 and section 65.

**9.60** Section 31(1) provides that a term of a contract to supply goods is not binding on the consumer to the extent that it would exclude or restrict the trader's liability arising under section 9 (goods to be of satisfactory quality). A trader cannot contract out of statutory rights and remedies under a digital content contract. Hence, section 47(1) provides a term of a contract to supply digital content is not binding on the consumer to the extent that it would exclude or restrict the trader's liability as regards to digital content to be of satisfactory quality, digital content to be fit for particular purpose, digital content to be as described, other pre-contract information included in contract, or trader's right to supply digital content. Section 57(1) states a term of a contract to supply services is not binding on the consumer to the extent that it would exclude the trader's liability arising under section 49 (service to be performed with reasonable care and skill). Section 65(1) states a trader cannot by a term of a consumer contract or by a consumer notice exclude or restrict liability for death or personal injury resulting from negligence. Subsection (2) states where a term of a consumer contract, or a consumer notice, purports to exclude or restrict a trader's liability for negligence, a person is not to be taken to have voluntarily accepted any risk merely because the person agreed to or knew about the term or notice.

**9.61** The CRA 2015 has certainly lived up to its aim and preamble to protect consumers as can be observed in sections 31, 47, 57 and 65.

### Lessons from Australia

#### Application of common law

**9.62** The distinction between an exemption clause and a limitation clause is irrelevant as the courts apply the same rules of construction to both type of clauses. This was made clear by the High Court in *Darlington Futures Ltd v*

---

105 [2012] EWHC 2137.
106 (2012) EWHC 2213.
107 Patrick Atiyah, *An Introduction to Law of Contract* (Clarendon Press 1977).

*Delco Australia Pty Ltd.*[108] This decision insisted that a natural and ordinary meaning interpretation must be given to determine the validity of exclusion clauses.[109] This makes a lot of sense as ultimately as far as consumers are concerned they are affected regardless of whether it is an exclusion clause or limitation clause. Nevertheless, it does not mean that the English cases are inapplicable in Australia, as can be seen in cases such as *L'Estrange v Graucob,*[110] *Curtis v Chemical Cleaning and Dyeing Co Ltd,*[111] *Parker v South Eastern Railway Co,*[112] *Olley v Marlborough Court Ltd,*[113] *Thornton v Shoe Lane Parking Ltd.*[114]

**9.63** However, additionally there are two rules, namely the deviation rule and main purpose of the contract rule. They are analogous to the four corners rule. The rules rely on grave breach of the contract for its operation. This was considered in *Sydney City Council v West.*[115] The contract for parking a car in a parking station contained an exclusion clause that excluded liability for loss or damage to the car howsoever caused. The car was stolen from the parking station as a result of the defendant's actions. It was held that the defendant could not rely on the exclusion clause because his agent had dealt with the car in a way that went beyond negligence; the agent's actions in releasing the car to the thief was neither authorized nor permitted by the contract. However, the rule will not apply if the language of an exclusion clause is sufficiently explicit as stated in *Nissho Iwai Australia Ltd v Malaysian International Shipping Corp, Berhad*[116] and *Glebe Island Terminals Pty Ltd v Continental Seagram Pty Ltd.*[117] The latter decision was distinguished in *Kamil Exports (Aust) Pty Ltd v NPL (Australia) Pty Ltd*[118] where the clause was not adequate to avoid the application of the deviation rule. It did not protect a deliberate breach of the main object of the contract. Nevertheless, it was effective in protecting a second, non-deliberate breach of that object. Hence, a lot of difficulties[119] arise as a result of the decision of *Darlington Futures Ltd v Delco Australia Pty Ltd.*[120]

---

108 (1986) 68 ALR 385.

109 Robert Bryan Vermeesch and Justice Kevin E Lindgreen, *Business Law of Australia,* 10th edn (Butterworths 2001).

110 [1934] 2 KB 394.

111 [1951] 1 KB 805.

112 [1930] 1 KB 41.

113 [1949] 1 KB 532.

114 [1971] 2 QB 163.

115 (1965) 114 CLR 481.

116 (1989) 167 CLR 219. See also *Glebe Island Terminals Pty Ltd v Continental Seagram Pty Ltd* (1993) 40 NSWLR 206.

117 (1993) 40 NSWLR 206.

118 1 VR (AD) 538.

119 N Richardson, 'Recent Cases' (1990) 64 Australian Law Journal 94. See also Brian Coote, 'Exception Clauses, Deliberate Acts and the Onus of Proof in Bailment Cases' (1997) 12 Journal of Contract Law 169.

120 (1986) 68 ALR 385.

**9.64** Since there were a lot of risks and uncertainties involving exclusion clauses, the government stepped in and resorted to legislation to set out a comprehensive framework to govern exclusion clauses. A term will be considered as unfair if the term does not protect the legitimate interests of the party who would be advantaged by the term.

## Section 68 Trade Practices Act 1974 (Cth)[121]

**9.65** The provision provides that any term of a contract for the supply by a corporation of goods or services to a consumer (including a term that is not set out in the contract but is incorporated in the contract by another term of the contract) that purports to exclude, restrict or modify or has the effect of excluding, restricting or modifying: (a) the application in relation to that contract of all or any of the provisions of this Division; (b) the exercise of a right conferred by such a provision; or (c) any liability of the corporation for breach of a condition or warranty implied by such a provision, is void. Section 68 (2) states that a term of a contract shall not be taken to exclude, restrict or modify the application of a provision of this Division unless the term does so expressly or is inconsistent with that provision. This applies to consumer transactions.

## Sale of Goods Act 1923 (NSW)

**9.66** Section 57 provides for exclusion of implied terms and conditions. It states that where any right, duty or liability would arise under a contract of sale by implication of law, it may be negatived or varied by express agreement, or by the course of dealing between the parties, or by usage, if the usage be such as to bind both parties to the contract. It can be observed that this provision is similar to the Malaysian section 62 Sale of Goods Act 1957.

## Contracts Review Act 1980 (NSW)

**9.67** Section 7(1) provides that where the court finds a contract or a provision of a contract to have been unjust in the circumstances relating to the contract at the time it was made, the court may, if it considers it just to do so, and for the purpose of avoiding as far as practicable an unjust consequence or result, do any one or more of the following: (a) decide to refuse to enforce any or all of the provisions of the contract, (b) make an order declaring the contract void, in whole or in part, (c) make an order varying, in whole or in part, any provision of the contract, (d) in relation to a land instrument, make an order for or with respect to requiring the execution of an instrument that: (i) varies, or has the effect of varying, the provisions of the land instrument, or (ii) terminates or otherwise affects, or has the effect of terminating or otherwise affecting, the operation or

---

121 Hereinafter referred to as the TPA.

effect of the land instrument. Where the court makes an order under subsection (1) (b) or (c), the declaration or variation shall have effect as from the time when the contract was made or (as to the whole or any part or parts of the contract) from some other time or times as specified in the order. Section 7(3) provides that the operation of this section is subject to the provisions of section 19. Hence, if a court considers an exclusion clause to be harsh or unjust, this provision will be invoked.[122]

*Australian Consumer Laws*[123]

**9.68** The Australian Consumer Laws, being Schedule 2 to the Competition and Consumer Act 2010, is a uniform legislation for consumer protection, applying as a law of the Commonwealth of Australia and is incorporated into the law of each of Australia's states and territories. It replaces the TPA 1974. It only applies to consumer transactions.[124]

**9.69** Particular reference should be made to section 24 which provides that a term of a consumer contract is unfair if: (a) it would cause a significant imbalance in the parties' rights and obligations arising under the contract; and (b) it is not reasonably necessary in order to protect the legitimate interests of the party who would be advantaged by the term; and (c) it would cause detriment (whether financial or otherwise) to a party if it were to be applied or relied on. In determining whether a term of a consumer contract is unfair under subsection (1), a court may take into account such matters as it thinks relevant, but must take into account the following: (a) the extent to which the term is transparent; (b) the contract as a whole. Section 24(3) provides that a term is transparent if the term is: (a) expressed in reasonably plain language; and (b) legible; and (c) presented clearly; and (d) readily available to any party affected by the term. Section 24(4) provides that for the purposes of subsection (1)(b), a term of a consumer contract is presumed not to be reasonably necessary in order to protect the legitimate interests of the party who would be advantaged by the term, unless that party proves otherwise. The wordings used are similar to section 24A(c) and section 24C of the Malaysian CPA 1999. Interestingly, section 25 provides examples of the kinds of terms of a consumer contract or small business contract that may be unfair. This is not found in the Malaysian CPA 1999. It is noteworthy that the examples given in section 25 do not limit the operation of section 24. Particularly, reference should be made to section 25(a) which states that a term that permits, or has the effect of permitting, one party (but not another party) to avoid or limit performance of the contract is an unfair term.

---

122 K Tapsell, 'Exemption Clauses, the Contracts Review Act 1980 (NSW) and Personal Injury' (1993) 67 Australian Law Journal 306.

123 Hereinafter referred to as the ACL.

124 Steve Donohoe and Jeremy Coggins, 'Enforceability of Exemption Clauses in Construction Contracts: A Comparative Study of Approaches in England and Australia', in S D Smith and D D Ahiaga-Dagbui (eds), *Procs*, 29th Annual ARCOM Conference, 2–4 September 2013, Reading, UK, Association of Researchers in Construction Management, 739–744.

**9.70** Furthermore, section 64 renders void any term of a contract that purports to exclude, restrict or modify a consumer's rights to rely on the consumer guarantee regime. This is similar to the approach taken by the Malaysian CPA 1999. However, section 64A permits modification of rights in certain circumstances, by allowing a supplier to limit the remedies available to the consumer if, and only if, the contract is for goods or services that are not ordinarily for personal, domestic or household use. Hence, if a business is supplying business type products to another business, the supplier can rely on section 64A. The limits on the remedies include replacement, repair or payment of the cost of replacement or repair (for goods) or supplying the services again or paying for them to be supplied again (for services). Section 64A(3) also imposes a reasonableness test regarding the imposition of the clause, and the supplier bears the onus of proving 'reasonableness'. The test to assess reasonableness is almost identical to that used by the UCTA 1977.

**9.71** The Australian provisions were modelled on the Victorian unfair contract term provisions, which in turn were modelled on the United Kingdom unfair term provisions.[125] Some of the terminologies from the United Kingdom provisions can be seen clearly in the Australian provisions, for example, 'significant imbalance' and 'detriment'.[126]

### The way forward in setting out a proper framework to govern exclusion clauses

**9.72** Based on the experiences in the UK and Australia, there are several alternatives open to Malaysia, if it wishes to set out a comprehensive framework in regulating exclusion clauses. Most importantly, in order for the unfair contract term law to achieve the legislatures' desired outcome of eliminating unfair contract terms, the courts must move away from their traditional focus on the myth of freedom of contract and that consumers are rational.[127]

*Contracts Act 1950*

**9.73** In a consumer contract, it is obvious that there is inequality of bargaining position. This is more so if it is a standard form contract. Hence, the courts should take a stricter view of exclusion clauses and protect the consumer.[128] A legislative framework to govern exclusion clauses is a reform that is very

---

125 Fair Trading Act 1999 (Vic) pt 2B, as repealed by Fair Trading Amendment (Australian Consumer Law)Act 2010 (Vic) s 17.

126 Unfair Terms in Consumer Contracts Regulations 1999 (UK) SI 1999/2083.

127 Alexandra Sims 'Unfair Contract Terms: A New Dawn in Australia and New Zealand?' (2013) 39(3) Monash University Law Review, 739–775.

128 Visu Sinnadurai, 'Exclusion Clauses v Public Policy and Inequality of Bargaining Power' [1978] 2 MLJ cxxx.

much awaited.[129] In *Standard Chartered Bank v Boomland Development Sdn Bhd & 3 Others*[130] and *Wee Lian Construction Sdn Bhd v Ingersoll-Jati Malaysia Sdn Bhd*,[131] the courts held that it was not appropriate to apply the UCTA 1977 in Malaysia unless domestic law permits it. The court further contended that the CA 1950 is sufficient to provide remedies to the aggrieved party. In *Wee Lian Construction Sdn Bhd v Ingersoll-Jati Malaysia Sdn Bhd*,[132] the plaintiff brought an action as the machine purchased became defective after a few months. As the defendant relied on the exclusion clause to deny liability, the plaintiff attempted to invoke the UCTA 1977 which was rejected by the court.

**9.74** Nonetheless, as seen earlier, the CA 1950 does not address the validity of exclusion clauses. Relying on common law to determine validity of exclusion clauses is an outmoded approach. The UK themselves are no longer relying on common law due to the enactment of the UCTA 1977. Furthermore, relying on section 24(e) and section 29 is not a settled principle yet. This is because terms such as public policy and restraint of legal proceedings are still open to interpretation. Hence the CA 1950 should be amended by adding provision(s) on exclusion causes. This should be done particularly under section 24(e) and section 29 as exclusion clauses are against public policy and they oust a court's jurisdiction. In that way, the CA 1950 would be clearer in addressing exclusion clauses. Furthermore, if judicial activism and creativity continues, much hope can be placed on section 24(e) and section 29 to regulate exclusion clauses. In that case, the development will be in tandem with those in India and Canada. After all, the CA 1950 is based on the Indian Contracts Act.

## Sale of Goods Act 1957

**9.75** The first step to be taken is that since Sabah and Sarawak are part of Malaysia, a single legislation should govern contract for the sale of goods. In other words, the SOGA 1957 should be extended to Sabah and Sarawak similar to the approach taken where the SOGA 1957 was extended to Penang and Malacca. Second, section 5(2) CLA 1956 should be repealed. In that case, the SOGA 1979 will not apply to Sabah and Sarawak. Consequently, there will be a single uniform law applicable throughout Malaysia. Third, section 62 should be amended to include the provision '... subject to Consumer Protection Act 1999 ...' just after the words '... it may ...' and before '... be negative ...'. This will be similar to the approach taken by the UK in section 55 SOGA 1979. By doing so, an exclusion clause will not be able to exclude the implied terms which are meant to the protect the buyer in cases where they are procedurally and/or substantially unfair.

---

129 Farhah Abdullah and Sakina Shaik Ahmad Yusoff, 'Consumer Protection on Unfair Contract Terms: Legal Analysis of Exemption Clauses in B2C Transactions in Malaysia' (2018) 8(12) International Journal of Asian Social Science 1097.
130 [1997] 4 AMR 3442.
131 [2005] 1 MLJ 162.
132 Ibid.

## Hire-Purchase Act 1967

**9.76** Section 7(2)(a) should be repealed. It is unfair to exclude the implied terms as to merchantable quality in relation to defects which ought to have been revealed by the examination carried out by the hirer. This is because in most cases, the hirer will only carry out a superficial cursory examination. Hence, the onus should be on the owner to ensure that the goods are of merchantable quality.

**9.77** Moreover, a blanket rule of excluding the implied term as to merchantable quality in cases of second hand goods is also unreasonable. Furthermore, the meaning of second hand varies with the type of goods. For instance, a one-year old car does not have the same life span as a one-year television. Hence, section 7(2)(b)(i) should be amended. The implied term as to merchantable quality should only be allowed to be excluded if it is reasonable. Hence, section 7(2)(b)(i) should incorporate the words '... subject to Consumer Protection Act 1999'. In that case, the clause will only be valid if there is no substantive unfairness.

**9.78** Additionally, section 7(2)(b)(ii) should be repealed. It should no longer be a case where the exclusion clause is effective since the hirer has acknowledged in writing. It must be borne in mind that there is inequality of bargaining position. This is evident even more so in a hire purchase agreement since the hirer is not financially able to buy the goods in cash. In view of Malaysia moving to the direction of being a developed country and creating a consumer friendly environment, the HPA 1967 should operate in favour of the hirer.

## Consumer Protection Act 1999

**9.79** The CPA 1999 should be amended by adding a new Part on exclusion clauses. Alternatively, a specific regulation on exclusion clauses should be made under section 150. In addition, the following must be addressed.

**9.80** It must include healthcare and professionals. This is because as observed earlier, common law is inadequate to address exclusion clauses. It is unfair to treat consumers who ply healthcare and professional services with a different set of laws than other consumers. Since the CPA 1999 is the most recent legislation compared to the CA 1950, SOGA 1957 and HPA 1967, the CPA 1999 should be at the forefront to protect consumers. Hence, section 2(4) should be amended. The terms '... supplemental ... and without prejudice ...' should be removed. In that case, the CPA 1999 will supersede the other legislations in relation to consumer protection. Similarly, section 24B which contain the words '... without prejudice ...' should also be removed.

**9.81** The definition of standard form contract in section 24A(b) should be amended as it covers various types of standard form contracts. A standard form contract is a contract which has already been prepared. The fact that it is being used in the industry does not necessarily mean it will contain fair terms. Hence, fairness of terms in standard form contracts is a question of law and not a question of business.

**9.82** Section 24B should remain as it states that it applies to all contracts. Section 2(1) should be amended whereby the CPA should apply to consumer and non-consumer contracts. In cases where it is a non-consumer contract, the party relying on exclusion clauses should bear the burden of proof as provided in section 24E. In that case, the law is being fair to all parties. The CPA should remove the words '... adequate justification ...' from section 24D(1)(e) as it gives opportunity to a party to provide justification although there is substantive unfairness. Similarly, section 40 should be removed as it is not fair to allow manufacturers to make representations after a contract is entered into. Hence, the duty on the supplier to ensure that the goods are of acceptable quality should be absolute. This will be similar to the approach taken in section 47(1)(a) CRA 2015.

*Specific legislation*

**9.83** Alternatively, instead of reforming the CA 1950, SOGA 1957, HPA 1967 and the CPA 1999, a specific legislation on exclusion clauses with specific provisions on form and content of such clauses should be enacted. This method of regulating exclusion clauses is regarded as the best method for Malaysia, since there are limitations in other legislations, namely the CA 1950, SOGA 1957, HPA 1967 and CPA 1999. Malaysia should take into account the provisions of the UCTA 1977, CRA 2015 and ACL 2010 and merge them into a new legislation to govern exclusion clauses. The new Act should incorporate the suggested reforms that should be made to the CA 1950, SOGA 1957, HPA 1967 and CPA 1999.

**Concluding remarks**

**9.84** The CA 1950, SOGA 1957, HPA 1967 and CPA 1999 have their own way of regulating dealings between contracting parties by providing rights to the disadvantaged party. Nevertheless, they have failed to regulate exclusion clauses effectively. As a result, there is a proliferation of the usage of exclusion clauses in the market. The ones affected the most are consumers followed by small or medium sized industries. The notion of freedom of contract and let the buyer beware is a myth especially in cases of standard form contracts. The judicial activism based on section 24(e) and section 29 CA 1950 should continue if the courts are the hallmarks of justice for consumers. Subordinate courts should take heed of those cases. The legislature should adopt a uniform approach throughout Malaysia in extending the SOGA 1950 to Sabah and Sarawak. Most importantly, it should amend section 62 SOGA 1957 to read that the exclusion clause is subject to the CPA 1999. The HPA 1967 and the CPA 1999 should be amended to address its shortcomings and weaknesses. Reference should be made to the approaches taken in the UK and Australia based on the legislations which have been enacted namely the UCTA 1977, CRA 2015 and ACL 2010. The UK and Australia have long shifted from the common law in determining the validity of exclusion clauses. The way forward in Malaysia is to make significant inroads to the legal framework governing exclusion clauses. Otherwise consumers will be at a disadvantage.

## CHAPTER 10

# Economic duress

## Present state and future development in England, Australia and Malaysia

### *Sri Bala Murugan*

## Introduction

**10.1** The concept of freedom of contract represents the cornerstone of contractual relationships. Under the law, parties are free to agree to terms that pursue their commercial objective. But for many contracts, freedom is assumed because it would be impractical for courts to explore the existence of freedom in every contract case that comes before the courts. The law of contract provides rules and means to show that a party lacks freedom. One such doctrine is the doctrine of duress.

**10.2** There are essentially three forms of duress recognised universally by courts and law. These are duress to person, duress to property and economic duress in each of the jurisdictions examined. While the chapter briefly considers the usual forms of duress (duress to person and property), the chapter will primarily focus on economic duress.

The concept of economic duress is challenging because, unlike the other forms of duress, economic duress concerns pressure not prohibited by law. How do the courts determine a legitimate pressure as duress? What circumstances of factors are relevant for judicial consideration?

**10.3** English law is used as a point of reference in the chapter because, within the Commonwealth countries, the doctrine was developed first under English Common Law. The comparison with Malaysia and Australia is made with the objective to explore the extent the doctrine has been adopted or modified.

## English law

**10.4** In the *Universe Sentinel*,[1] Lord Diplock explained that the use of economic duress in itself is not a tort. However, it could be, depending on the form that it takes.[2] In *The Siboen and The Sibotre*,[3] Kerr J was of the view that

---

1 *Universe Tankships v International Transport Workers Federation (The Universe Sentinel)* [1983] 1 AC 366.

2 Ibid, p. 385.

3 *Occidental Worldwide Investment Corporation v Skibs A/S Avanti, The Sibeon and The Sibotre* [1976] 1 Lloyd's Rep 293.

contracts entered into under compulsion should not be enforced. Nevertheless, Kerr J did stress that where duress was not against the person, the court must be satisfied that such compulsion not only caused another to enter into a contract but also had the effect of overbearing the will to vitiate consent.

**10.5** The existence of protest at the time of duress or shortly after was deemed relevant to decide whether the will was overborne. Lord Scarman in *Pao On v Lau Yiu Long*,[4] also opined that economic duress could render a contract voidable provided coercion of will vitiated consent.[5] In *The Atlantic Baron*,[6] Mocatta J found that a threat to breach contractual obligations without legal justification does amount to economic duress.[7]

**10.6** These cases reflect that courts are open to intervene when there has been illegitimate or unlawful pressure. But willingness is tempered with caution. In *Pao On*, Lord Scarman identified salient factors to determine economic duress, the first being whether there was coercion. If there was, the second element is whether the party coerced did or did not protest at the time the contract was made. Third the courts would also consider the adequacy of the legal remedy available to the party coerced and whether the party concerned took steps to avoid the contract.

**10.7** If a party to the contract were to induce the contract of any kind, whether new or merely one that modifies or amends an existing one, by threat (tortious or one which has criminal elements) it is easy to say that duress caused the contract made.[8] In *Rookes v Barnard*,[9] it was held that the threat which induced the contract was illegal. Lord Devlin found that there was no distinction between a threat made to breach the contract from any other illegal threat.[10] In *Barton v Armstrong*,[11] the Privy Council found that the respondent's threat that he would have the appellant murdered if the appellant did not sign the contractual document was duress.[12]

**10.8** In both cases, the nature of the threats was illegal and so the outcome is unsurprising. For example, in *Barton v Armstrong*, Lord Cross took cognisance of the trial judge's findings that the appellant was in genuine torment after the threats were made.[13] The appellant, arguably, was put into a state that falls within the ambit of common law assault, i.e. conduct creating the apprehension of immediate

---

4 [1979] 3 All ER 65, p. 79.

5 [1980] A.C. 614, p. 636.

6 *North Ocean Shipping Co. Ltd. v Hyundai Construction Co. Ltd (The Atlantic Baron)* [1979] Q.B. 705.

7 Ibid, p. 719.

8 *Barton v Armstrong* [1976] AC 104; *Skeate v Beale* (1840) 11 Ad & E 983; *Thorne v Motor Trade Association* [1937] AC 797, p. 806; Peel E, *Treitel: The Law of Contract*, 14th edn (Sweet & Maxwell 2015) para. 10–002.

9 [1964] AC 1129.

10 Ibid, p. 1209.

11 [1976] AC 104.

12 Ibid, p. 120.

13 Ibid.

personal violence.[14] In *Rookes v Barnard*, the intimidation was found to be tortious. Another case with a similar feature is *D & C Builders v Rees*,[15] where the court refused to uphold a bargain struck to pay less than the agreed sum because the conduct of the party seeking to uphold the bargain was improper.[16]

**10.9** While the issue of duress was not raised in the case, Lord Denning referred to *Rookes v Barnard* in deciding whether a threat to break the contract was acceptable in the circumstances. His Lordship held that no settlement for lesser payment could be reached by intimidation.[17] The approach is in line with the first of two points explained by Thomas Aquinas. Thomas Aquinas had explained where a person promises under oath, two promises arise.[18] The first is to the promisee (legal obligation) and the second is to God (moral obligation). If the promise is extorted by duress, then the promise should not be kept, arguably because it loses its moral as well as legal obligation to be kept.[19]

**10.10** However, the existence of duress is unclear where parties have contracted earlier, but subsequently create a new contract to vary the obligations between them. The change can either relate to means of contractual performance or the value of consideration for the performance of the previous contract.

**10.11** In these circumstances, the question of whether there is duress between the parties is dependent on the nature of pressure exerted by one on the other that leads to the new contract being made. It is also common that the change made is for the benefit of the party accused of exerting pressure to bring about the change.

**10.12** Lessius had observed that 'one compelled by duress is deprived through injury of liberty' of his will to consent.[20] However, it is still accepted that coerced consent is still valid consent.[21] The view that coerced consent is still valid consent can be deduced from Kerr J's view in *The Siboen and The Sibotre* which was that the court must be satisfied that, '...the consent of the other party was overborne by a compulsion to deprive him of any *animus contrahendi*. This would depend on the facts of each case'.[22]

Hence where the circumstances do not provide a clear reflection of duress, the consent is presumed as a matter of fact unless it is disproved. The contract in itself is evidence of consent and more so if the contract has been signed[23] or payment made without further protest. This then leads to an analysis of the conditions required to prove duress in cases of economic duress.

---

14 *Stephens v Myers* (1830) 4 C & P 349.

15 [1966] 2 QB 617.

16 Ibid, p. 626

17 [1966] 2 QB 617 (CA), p. 625.

18 Gordley J, *The Philosophical Origins of Modern Contract Doctrine* (Oxford University Press 1991), p. 83.

19 Ibid. See *Spanish Government v North of England Steamship* (1938) 61 Ll L Rep 44.

20 Gordley J, *The Philosophical Origins of Modern Contract Doctrine* (Oxford University Press 1991), p. 84; Lessius L, *De iustitia et jure* (Paris 1628), lib 2, cap 2, dub 6.

21 Alexander L, 'The Moral Magic of Consent (II)' (1996) 2 Legal Theory 165.

22 [1976] 1 Lloyd's Rep 293, p. 336.

23 *L'Estrange v Groucob* [1934] 2 KB 394.

**10.13** In *The Siboen and the Sibotre*, Kerr J explained that there were two factors to consider.[24] The first was whether the party invoking duress protested at the time the contract was made or shortly after that. The second factor to consider was whether the party relying on duress treated the matter as closed and binding on him or was the matter still open.

**10.14** In the *Evia Luck*,[25] Lord Goff stated that it had been accepted that economic pressure could amount to duress if the pressure is illegitimate and it was a substantial cause leading to the contract made.[26] Lord Goff in the *Evia Luck* on the question of duress explained that three issues arise: first, what constitutes duress; second, the impact of duress on the formation of a contract; and third, the remedial action available to the innocent party.[27]

**10.15** Two deductions can be made from Kerr J's highlighted factors. The first is that where the nature of pressure being illegitimate is unclear, the onus falls on the party invoking duress to show what his actions were after the contract was concluded. These actions would be indicative of whether the party concerned had contracted under compulsion.

**10.16** While the first factor alone would be open to abuse, the second factor considers the speed at which the party who is invoking duress acts to set aside the contract. Hence, the time taken to initiate litigation or terminate the contract is a vital element. If the 'time lapse' is too long, then there is a risk that the contract would be affirmed which would ensure an action for duress fails.

*Illegitimate pressure*

**10.17** In *The Evia Luck*, in deciding whether there was economic pressure, Lord Goff began his analysis by considering whether the alleged threat was allowed or prohibited by statute.[28] If the threat is not prohibited by statute, the issue has to be considered in light of common law. The approach was also adopted by Lord Diplock in *The Universe Sentinel* where he opined that there could be duress if the act constituting duress amounted to a tort.[29] Whether it does depends on existing statutory authority legitimising the tort.

**10.18** The cases illustrate that one should begin analysis in a situation where statutory prohibition is absent. Naturally where statute prohibits an act, which results in contract, it could lead to the contract being illegal. However, when an act is not prohibited, it is difficult to decide whether economic duress arises

---

24 [1976] 1 Lloyd's Rep 293, p. 336.

25 *Dimskal Shipping Co SA v International Transport Workers Federation (The Evia Luck) (No.2)* [1992] 2 A.C. 152.

26 Ibid, p. 165.

27 Ibid, p. 168. See also *Huyton SA v Peter Cremer GmbH & Co* [1999] 1 Lloyd's Rep. 620.

28 *Dimskal Shipping Co SA v International Transport Workers Federation (The Evia Luck) (No.2)* [1992] 2 AC.152, p. 168.

29 *Universe Tankships Inc. of Monrovia v International Transport Workers Federation* [1983] 1 AC 366, p. 385.

when a party does an act which is presumably legal. It would not be far-fetched to say that the act is regarded more as immoral rather than illegal. A further difficulty for the courts is to determine the degree of immorality required to tilt the issue into the realm of duress.

**10.19** In English law, Lord Atkin explained that 'an intimation that a man is going to do what he lawfully may do is not a threat'.[30] As discussed earlier, the threat to breach the contract would not be duress if the person making the threat had a right to do so. It is neither tort of intimidation nor unlawful under contract law if the right exists under the law. For example, such a right may arise if there is a breach of condition of payment for goods or services delivered by the contract.

**10.20** Even if the courts agree there is economic duress by a lawful threat,[31] courts will proceed cautiously. Lord Steyn explained that courts were open to finding duress in 'fields of protected relationships'.[32] However, in 'purely commercial' contexts, a claim for economic duress would be hard to sustain.[33] In commercial contexts, it would be harder to invoke duress if the party who made the threat honestly believed they had justified grounds to make the threat.

**10.21** Further, commercial pressure is common in commercial transactions.[34] It is a fact that commercial pressure drive parties in a business relationship. The fundamental issue is whether pressure originates from one party in the relationship. It is risky and challenging for the courts to decide the nature of pressure as illegitimate because it would interfere with parties' freedom of contract. The party accused of duress could be merely guilty of clever manoeuvring.

**10.22** In *CTN Cash and Carry Ltd v Gallagher Ltd*,[35] the claimants and the defendants contracted for the delivery of a consignment of cigarettes. The claimants were given a credit facility in dealing with the defendants. The defendants sent the consignment to the wrong address. Subsequently, the cigarettes were stolen. The defendants honestly but mistakenly believed that the plaintiffs bore the risk for the consignment and duly sent them an invoice seeking payment. The defendants sought payment of the sum stated on the invoice. If there was a failure to comply, the defendants threatened to withdraw the claimants' credit facility. Since the claimants were dependant on the credit facility, they paid.

**10.23** The Court of Appeal held that the right to withdraw the credit facility under the terms of the credit agreement was lawful. The terms of the agreement between the parties provided for such a right. The court could find nothing unlawful about exercising such a right, and as such there was no duress. It was also recognised that the parties that dealt with each other were trading companies

---

30 *Ware and De Freville Ltd v Motor Trade Association* [1921] 3 KB 40, p.87.
31 *CTN Cash and Carry Ltd v Gallaher Ltd* [1994] 4 All E.R. 714, p. 719.
32 Ibid.
33 Ibid.
34 *Dawson v Bell* [2016] EWCA Civ 96, para [77].
35 [1994] 4 All ER 714.

and not one of supplier and consumer.[36] The defendant was in the position of monopoly. However, Lord Steyn opined that control of such entities is Parliament's responsibility. Lord Steyn further explained that the courts do not recognise the inequality of bargaining power in commercial contracts. Lord Steyn stated that extending the doctrine of duress in commercial contexts

> would be a radical one with far-reaching implications. It would introduce a substantial and undesirable element of uncertainty in the commercial bargaining process. Moreover, it will often enable bona fide settled accounts to be reopened when parties to commercial dealings fall out. The aim of our commercial law ought to be to encourage fair dealing between parties. But it is a mistake for the law to set its sights too highly when the critical inquiry is not whether the conduct is lawful but whether it is morally or socially unacceptable. That is the inquiry in which we are engaged. In my view there are policy considerations which militate against ruling that the defendants obtained payment of the disputed invoice by duress.[37]

The reluctance of the court is twofold here. First, rebutting the presumption of 'equality of bargaining power' was very difficult in the absence of an illegal act. A plea of duress envisages that bargaining is not equal. The CTN case illustrates that even if an entity were a monopoly (which demonstrates superior bargaining power), it does not support the premise that parties are unequal.

**10.24** Second, to delve into such an inquiry would require analysis into the state of mind of the person making the legitimate threat.[38] The party invoking duress must provide evidence to persuade the court there is something unlawful about the way the legal right was exercised.[39]

**10.25** Possibly, one might argue that while the threat made was legal, the way in which the threat was made was illegal. However, it is a very fine line to distinguish between the illegitimate threat and the means used to make the illegitimate threat. Simply put, in the latter, while the threat is legal, the means used to make the threat could be illegitimate. It is subject to evidence to possibly show that the other party is abusing the law or legal process. As such, it may justify a judicial inquiry into the state of mind of the person making the threat. But not otherwise.

**10.26** For example, in *Dawson v Bell*,[40] the claimant and defendant were in a personal relationship as well as directors and shareholders of a company they had formed to produce films for adult entertainment. They were also parties to a shareholder's agreement. A clause in the agreement provided that when the claimant ceased to be a director of the company, he would be deemed to have served a transfer notice concerning his shares in the company. When the parties' intimate relationship came to an end, they had made several other agreements

---

36 *CTN Cash and Carry Ltd v Gallaher Ltd* [1994] 4 All ER 714, p. 717.
37 Ibid, p. 719.
38 Tan D, 'Constructing a Doctrine of Economic Duress' (2002) Const. L.J. 87 at 91.
39 *Norreys v Zeffert* [1939] 2 All ER 187, p. 189.
40 [2016] EWCA Civ 96.

which included another share purchase agreement. Under this agreement, the claimant's shares were transferred to the defendant for £47,500. The claimant then resigned as a director. After the agreements were signed, the defendant failed to make necessary payments under the share purchase agreement. The defendant argued that, without her knowledge, the claimant had overpaid himself £54,000 in dividends from the company. The claimant then subsequently brought an action to recover the sum owed.

**10.27** One of the issues raised was that he was coerced to contract into the share purchase agreement. The claimant sought an order to set aside the share purchase agreement. The argument for duress failed. Tomlinson LJ explained that there was no doubt that the claimant was under pressure to sign the share purchase agreement. However, the issue is whether the claimant succumbed to such pressure. In His Lordship's words, *'being under pressure is not the same as succumbing to it'*.[41] The benefit received by the claimant and the existence of independent legal advice before the agreement being signed showed that the claimant's will was not overborne.

**10.28** In *DSND Subsea Ltd v PGS Offshore Technology AS*,[42] Dyson J identified three ingredients for economic duress. The first was pressure. However, pressure must result in compulsion or lack of practical choice for the victim of duress. Second, the pressure must be illegitimate, and third it has to be a significant cause which induces the victim to contract.[43] However, these ingredients are not exactly a precise analytical tool.[44]

**10.29** The first ingredient focuses on the result of the threat, i.e. the possibility of duress is high because the victim had no practical choice but to accept the new contractual terms.[45] After which Dyson J moved to identify factors acts that could be characterised as illegitimate pressure. These factors include actual or threatened breach of contract, whether the defendant acted in good faith or bad faith, whether there was a realistic and practical alternative for the victim, and whether the victim protested at the time of the contract or whether the victim sought to affirm the contract.[46]

**10.30** These factors aim to ensure pressure exerted is illegitimate. Pressures arising from the 'rough and tumble of normal commercial bargaining' would be insufficient to set the contract aside.[47] It is a tricky situation for the courts because there may be a fine line between illegitimate pressure and commercial manoeuvring or strategy that maximises profit as well as achieves high contractual utility.

---

41 *Dawson v Bell* [2016] EWCA Civ 96, para [34].

42 [2000] BLR 530.

43 *Universal Tanking of Monrovia v ITWF* [1983] AC 336, p. 400, and *Dimskal Shipping Co SA v International Transport Workers Federation (The Evia Luck) (No.2)* [1992] 2 A.C. 152, p. 165.

44 *Adam Opel GmbH v Mitras Automotive (UK) Ltd* [2007] EWHC 3481, para [26].

45 Virgo G, *The Principles of the Law of Restitution*, 3rd edn (Oxford University Press 2015), p. 218.

46 *DSND Subsea Ltd v PGS Offshore Technology AS* [2000] BLR 530, para [131].

47 Ibid.

**10.31** Even if one party has shown behaviour reflective of bad faith in securing modifications from the original contract made, it is difficult to identify it as duress when it is custom within the industry. To interfere with the contract would mean courts are enforcing an element of policy on parties' contractual freedom.[48]

**10.32** In *Carillion Construction Ltd v Felix (UK) Ltd*,[49] a developer hired the claimant for construction of an office building. The claimant then subcontracted with the defendant, and other subcontractors, for design manufacture and supply of cladding. The defendant agreed to complete work in 22 weeks. In light of delays complained of by the claimant, the defendant stated that it was not willing to complete work until the claimant agreed with the final account. The claimant was concerned with the delay because the defendant's delay also delayed other subcontractors hired by the claimant. The developer who hired the claimant also imperilled them to the risk of substantial liquidated damages. In a meeting with the defendant, the defendant put forward a figure for the final account. The claimant believed the final figure to be lower than stated but agreed with the defendant so that work could progress and be completed on time. At the time of the meeting, both parties had their solicitors with them.

**10.33** In this case, Dyson J held that the defendant's threat to withhold deliveries of their work was a breach of contract.[50] Dyson J also found the defendants were not within their contractual rights to withhold delivery of their work.[51] In light of the dilemma that the claimant was in, the claimant did not have practical alternatives other than to agree to the defendant's demands. Therefore, there was economic duress.

**10.34** The *Carillion case* brought Dyson J's factors mentioned in *DSND Subsea* into play. First, there was a lack of choice because the claimant had a deadline to meet under the contract with the developer. In light of that fact, the claimant was compelled to agree with the defendant's demands. The claimant did have an alternative which involved litigation against the defendant for breach of contract as well as to hire another subcontractor. However, this option, while workable in theory, would not have solved the claimant's predicament in practice. The claimant would suffer a high amount of damages and whether these were claimable in subsequent litigation is also doubtful.

**10.35** Considering the uncertainty of whether damages against the subcontractor would have been claimable and damages arising under the contract with the developer, the claimant decided to agree to the demands of the subcontractor. The existence of legal advice at the meeting made little difference. Also, the defendant was not entitled to the demand that they made. However, as noted previously by Lord Scarman cases such as this would be rare.

---

48 *Rock Advertising Ltd v MWB Business Exchange Centres Ltd* [2018] UKSC 24, para [12].
49 (2000) 74 ConLR 144.
50 Ibid, para [36].
51 Ibid, para [37].

**10.36** In *Progress Bulk Carriers Ltd v Tube City IMS LLC*,[52] the owners of a chartered vessel, without the approval of the charterers, chartered the vessel to another. The conduct of the owners placed them in repudiatory breach with the charterers. Instead of accepting the breach and terminating the contract, the charterers accepted assurances given by the owners to find an alternative vessel and that losses suffered would be compensated for. When an alternative vessel was offered, the owners were acceptable to a discounted rate but it also required the charterers to waive claims or losses arising from nominating a substitute vessel. The charterers agreed to the terms so that they could avoid their increasing liabilities to the receiver of the freight.

The court found the charterers to have no practical choice. It was a choice to be made between two evils and the court held that there was economic duress. Cooke J explained that illegitimate pressure could arise from conduct, which is not particularly unlawful. However, it would be an unusual case.[53] He also was of the view that the 'past unlawful act, as well as the threat of a future unlawful act', could amount to economic duress in the right circumstances.[54]

**10.37** In *Progress Bulk*, the conduct by the owners had put the charterers in a precarious position to either accept the discount and substitute the ship or claim for compensation for losses suffered. While the alternative to claiming for losses exists, the consequence to the charterer's business would be dire in the circumstances. Cooke J opined that *'the critical inquiry is not whether the conduct is lawful but whether it is morally or socially unacceptable'*.[55] Both the *Carillion* case and *Progress Bulk* appear to consider the practicality of the choice available to the party claiming duress. Just because choice exists in theory, it does not mean that the choice is practical in the commercial context. In both cases, choice was impractical because the party claiming duress was committed to obligations to a third party, with whom breach was inevitable had they not accepted the demands under duress.

**10.38** In *Times Travel (UK) Ltd v Pakistan International Airlines Corp*,[56] the appellant was the sole operator of direct flights between the UK and Pakistan. The appellant and respondent had a travel agency agreement. The respondent's travel agency business substantially relied on ticket sales for the appellant. Many of the appellant's agents brought litigation to recover unpaid commissions allegedly owed. The appellant had terminated all existing agency agreements by notice and reduced agents' ticket allocations. It offered the agents new contracts providing new terms that any claim on commission should be waived under previous agreements. The respondent accepted the new contract. Subsequently, the respondent brought proceedings to recover commission due under the previous

---

52 [2012] EWHC 273 (Comm).
53 Ibid, para [36].
54 Ibid, para [39].
55 Ibid, para [30] and *CTN Cash and Carry Ltd v Gallaher Ltd* [1994] 4 All ER 714, p. 719.
56 [2019] EWCA Civ 828.

contract. The trial judge at first instance found for the respondent on the ground the economic duress brought about the contract made.

**10.39** While delivering judgment at the Court of Appeal, David Richards LJ stated that none of these cases assisted *Time Travel (UK)*. His Lordship then proceeded to analyse illegitimate pressure. His Lordship observed that the critical issue in the *CTN Cash and Carry* case is whether economic duress could arise when threats made are lawful and with genuine belief.

His Lordship concluded there would be no grounds for economic duress if the threat is grounded in 'genuine belief' as well as reasonable in the circumstances of the case.[57] However, identifying when a threat is made with genuine belief but is unreasonable is rather vague. It was observed, rightly, that there was 'little or no support' to extend economic duress to these circumstances.[58]

**10.40** The reason is that reasonableness is a standard of uncertain content, and it is unclear why it should be used to limit the exercise of a right which is lawful and advanced in good faith.[59] Hence, His Lordship concluded that a lack of reasonable grounds for a threat is insufficient to invoke the doctrine of duress.[60]

**10.41** Post *Time Travel (UK)*, it can be surmised that unreasonable behaviour is insufficient to show there was illegitimate pressure. Illegitimate pressure must originate from some form of an act deemed unlawful. Parties to a contract are assumed to be of equal bargaining power and they should decide what their rights are under the contract.

**10.42** The risk of contracting on some terms disadvantageous to themselves is part and parcel of their freedom of contract. In this context, the question of illegitimate pressure and duress is whether there are grounds to suppose that freedom had been restrained due to some clear and identifiable unlawful act by the other. Mere assumptions of what amounts to reasonable behaviour is not enough to show duress.

*Causation*

**10.43** In *The Evia Luck*, Lord Goff opined that for economic duress to succeed, illegitimate pressure must be a significant cause. In *Huyton SA v Peter Cremer GmbH & Co*,[61] Mance J disagreed with this view. Mance J opined that the minimum test should be the 'but for' test to decide whether the illegitimate pressure caused the agreement to be made.[62] The pressure must have been decisive to induce the other into the contract.

---

57  Ibid, para [70].
58  Ibid, para [73].
59  Ibid, para [106].
60  Ibid, para [113].
61  [1999] 1 Lloyd's Rep 620.
62  Ibid, pp. 636–639; *Kolmar Group AG v Traxpo Enterprises Pvt Ltd* [2010] EWHC 113 (Comm).

**10.44** It is possible that a different test was used in other cases (such as the one suggested by Lord Goff in the *Evia Luck*). In such cases, there are two concurrent causes where 'each otherwise sufficient to ground a claim of relief, in circumstances where each alone would have induced the agreement, so that it could not be said that, but for either, the agreement would not have been made'.[63]

**10.45** For example, in *Pao On v Lau Yiu Long*,[64] it was found that commercial pressure was present, but it was not enough to amount to coercion.[65] Similarly in *B & S Contracts and Design Ltd v Victor Green Publications Ltd*,[66] Kerr LJ explained a threat to breach the contract would amount to duress if the consequence of refusal would be severe and there was no possibility of a legal alternative. In this regard, 'reasonable alternative' should be a practical alternative in the circumstances.

**10.46** For example, in both the *Carillion Construction Ltd* and the *Progress Bulk Ltd* cases, access to legal advice was available to the parties who claimed duress. However, this was of little help on the facts because if parties went to court to claim breach of contract, it would have caused them severe financial loss.

**10.47** In *Dawson v Bell*,[67] it was factually accurate the claimant was under economic pressure to sign the share purchase agreement with the defendant. However, the court recognised that the claimant had legal advice and had time to decide whether the agreement was beneficial to him. The claimant was already shielded under a shareholders' agreement previously signed by the claimant and defendant. As such, in these circumstances, it was held that the claimant was under pressure but could not be said to be compelled to sign the share purchase agreement subsequently.

**10.48** The same factors apply whether the cause is decisive or significant. However, when the argument proposes the cause as significant, the evidence should prove that illegitimate pressure overshadows the other equally probable cause to the contract. In the end, the burden is on the party invoking duress to persuade the courts. *McKendrick* observed that the causal threshold diminishes as the degree of illegitimacy increases.[68]

**10.49** However, as seen in many cases, causation in economic duress is not easy to identify. It is especially tricky when parties have an existing contract between them. When subsequently they proceed to make a new contract to alter the terms, how does one say that illegitimate pressure is the leading cause in the absence of proof of a clear unlawful act by one over the other? As such application of the 'but for' test would be difficult in such a case.

---

63 Ibid, pp. 636–639.
64 [1980] A.C. 614.
65 Ibid, p. 635.
66 [1984] ICR 419, p. 428.
67 [2016] EWCA Civ 96.
68 McKendrick E, *Contract Law: Texts, Cases and Materials*, 5th edn (Oxford University Press 2012), p. 652; *R v A-G for England and Wales* [2003] UKPC 22, para [16].

**10.50** On the other hand, Virgo observed that as long as the test for causation does not confine itself to show pressure was the sole cause for contracting, it is still workable if several factors are considered when applying the 'but for' test.[69] The party alleging duress has the burden to adduce evidence to show they were compelled to contract and subsequently had done sufficiently enough to avoid the contract with reasonable haste because they did not intend to be bound by the contract. This reasoning then leads the court to consider the evidence the party alleging duress puts forth about the pressure that was imposed.

**10.51** The factors for causation explained by Kerr J in *The Siboen and The Sibotre* was further considered in *The Atlantic Baron*.[70] In this case, the defendants were to build a tanker for the plaintiffs. The price was agreed under the contract and was payable in instalments. The first instalment was paid – subsequently, the currency in which the contract was made dropped in value in the international money market. The defendants made demands for a 10% increase in the contract price. They also informed the plaintiffs that the ship would not be built unless their demands were met. At the time the threat was made, the plaintiffs were to proceed with a charter agreement with another party after the ship was completed under the contractually stipulated time. The defendants were unaware of this fact.

**10.52** In light of their circumstance, the plaintiffs informed that they were not legally obligated to pay the additional sum but eventually agreed to pay. The plaintiffs paid the new increased price in four instalments contractually agreed and took delivery of the ship. The plaintiffs then brought an action to recover the additional sum eight months later. But the plaintiffs' action failed.

**10.53** There were two key considerations for Mocatta J's judgment. The first was that the defendants did not have a legal justification for demanding increases in price and threatening to breach the contract. In essence, this leads to the conclusion that there was economic duress. The contract was voidable. Time began to run against the plaintiff with regards to what they would do in light of the excess payment made to the defendants.

**10.54** The second factor was that the defendants waited too long before they brought their case to court. In effect, they had affirmed the contract even though it was found there was duress. The action for duress did not fail because of lack of duress, but rather because the contract had been affirmed and accepted by the plaintiffs' inaction to respond to the duress with expediency and urgency. The implicit affirmation arising from inaction could also arguably negate the allegation of duress. It would not be reasonable to delay avoidance of a contract

---

69 Virgo G, *The Principles of the Law of Restitution*, 3rd edn (Oxford University Press 2015), p. 223.

70 *North Ocean Shipping Co. Ltd v Hyundai Construction Co. Ltd, The Atlantic Baron* [1979] QB 705.

that lacks consent. Therefore, affirmation in essence also negates the allegation of duress itself.

**10.55** The approach is consistent with the Common Law approach towards voidable contracts. If the plaintiffs could avoid the contract in light of the affirmation, it would further confuse the categorisation of duress as a voidable contract. Instead, duress would then be treated as a void contract. Therefore, this marks the difference between lawful act duress and unlawful act duress (which borders with illegality).

**10.56** The factors identified by Lord Scarman in his obiter dictum in the *Pao On* case are essential factors to consider whether the party alleging duress has acted voluntarily or otherwise.[71] Virgo points out that these factors help analyse whether the pressure exerted led to the subsequent contract between the parties.[72] Dyson J had identified these factors as well.[73]

### Australia

**10.57** Under Australian law, duress has traditionally been applied in circumstances where there has been actual violence or threats of violence. The *Barton v Armstrong*[74] case was one of the more notable cases relied on by Australian courts. Similar to the approach by English courts, the Australian courts have been cautious to recognise whether duress can arise where a party to the contract makes threats they are entitled to do. The Australian cases show that where commercial pressure is applied, it would be difficult to sustain a case for duress.

**10.58** In Australia, in order to establish economic duress,[75] the victim must show, first, that there was illegitimate pressure imposed to compel the victim to the transaction. Second, that the victim did not have any reasonable alternative but to agree to the transaction. Third, that the pressure must have caused the victim to agree to the transaction.

**10.59** McHugh J echoed these requirement in *Crescendo Management Pty Ltd v Westpac Banking Corp*,[76] where it was explained that in order to show economic duress one must first show the pressure imposed induced the contract; and second that the pressure went beyond what law would deem as legitimate.[77] It was observed that McHugh J applied the higher standard in deciding that the pressure was a significant cause of the contract.[78]

---

71 Virgo G, *The Principles of the Law of Restitution*, 3rd edn (Oxford University Press 2015), p. 221.

72 Ibid.

73 *DSND Subsea Ltd v PGS Offshore Technology AS* [2000] BLR 530, para [131].

74 [1976] AC 104; (1973) 3 ALR 355.

75 Seddon N, Bigwood R and Ellinghaus M, *Cheshire & Fifoot Law of Contract*, 10th edn (LexisNexis Butterworths, Australian edition 2012), p. 743.

76 (1988) 19 NSWLR 40.

77 Ibid, p. 45.

78 *Westpac Banking Corporation v Cockerill, Dingle & Dingle* (1998) 152 ALR 267, p. 288.

*Illegitimate pressure*

**10.60** The courts are ready to set aside a contract when the threat made is proved to be unlawful. However, when a legitimate threat is made, it presents a difficult question for the courts. The courts recognise that the commercial world can be harsh and 'market players are not expected to behave fairly and reasonably with each other'.[79] In *Queensland Wire Industries Pty Ltd v BHP Co Ltd*,[80] Mown CJ observed that 'competition by its very nature is deliberate and ruthless'.[81]

**10.61** For example, in *Smith v William Charlick*,[82] the economic duress argument failed. In this case, the plaintiff, a miller, bought his supply of wheat from the Wheat Harvest Board. It was recognised that the Board's position was similar to a Government department with discretionary powers. After the plaintiff had paid for wheat that was delivered, the Board demanded additional payment. It argued that it was morally entitled to this payment from the plaintiff even though it did not have a legal basis for such payment.

**10.62** The court decided the plaintiff could not recover the payment made because he had made the payment with full knowledge of all material facts. Even though the Board could cease selling him wheat had the plaintiff withheld payment, it was insufficient to substantiate a claim of duress. Mere commercial pressure could not amount to economic duress.[83] The pressure exerted will be illegitimate if it consists of unlawful threats or unconscionable conduct. The Board, in this case, is in a similar position to that of the appellant in *Times Travel (UK) Ltd v Pakistan International Airlines Corp.*[84] The fact remains, even in Australia, being in a superior position in a commercial relationship could not infer duress. Duress must be proved by showing the demand made was illegitimate and it resulted in the contract made.

**10.63** In *Esso Australia Pty Ltd v The Australian Workers' Union*,[85] Buchanan J explained that 'coercion is the satisfaction of two elements, being: the negation of choice and the use of unlawful, or illegitimate or unconscionable means'.[86] It was further explained that it was not necessary that a person intended to act unlawfully neither is it relevant that they believed that their action would be lawful.

---

79 Seddon N, Bigwood R and Ellinghaus M, *Cheshire & Fifoot Law of Contract*, 10th edn (LexisNexis Butterworths, Australian edition 2012), p. 749.

80 (1989) 167 CLR 177.

81 Ibid, p. 191.

82 (1924) 34 CLR 38.

83 Ibid, p. 70.

84 [2019] EWCA Civ 828.

85 (2016) 258 IR 396.

86 Ibid, para [174]. See also *Finance Sector Union of Australia v Commonwealth Bank of Australia* (2000) 106 FCR 16; 106 IR 158; *Seven Network (Operations) Ltd v Communications, Electrical, Electronic, Energy, Information, Postal, Plumbing and Allied Services Union of Australia* (2001) 109 FCR 378; 106 IR 404; *Fair Work Ombudsman v National Jet Systems Pty Ltd* (2012) 218 IR 436 and *Victoria v Construction, Forestry, Mining and Energy Union* (2013) 218 FCR 172; 239 IR 441).

**10.64** In *Australian Building and Construction Commissioner v Construction, Forestry, Mining, and Energy Union*,[87] the court had to consider economic duress in light of sections 343 and 348 Fair Work Act 2009 (Cth). The concept considered in both provisions involved deciding the test applicable to determine whether a person had been 'coerced' within the meaning of the provisions stated. The approach, it was observed, is consistent with the common law context of coercion, which can be traced back to economic duress.[88]

**10.65** The critical consideration focuses on the act alleged to have imposed pressure. The question to determine is whether the act is unlawful. If legislation permits the act, then doing the act complained of is lawful. In *Smith v William Charlick*, the behaviour of the Board arguably was permitted by the way in which legislation (The Wheat Harvest Act 1917) empowered it. Hence the demand of additional payment in the case could not be treated as duress.

**10.66** However, if it is argued that the conduct alleged as duress fell outside the scope of the provision (by statutory interpretation), then the act could be unlawful. This argument is then dependent on the clarity of the legislative provision as much as the policy behind the legislation. Even if courts can either stretch or narrow the interpretation to aid an allegation of duress, whether they are willing depends on whether the character and purpose of the act would be defeated or preserved. Therefore, even if a particular act is perceived as duress, in most cases it is doubtful courts would agree if it results in the legislation becoming redundant.

**10.67** It follows that even in Australia, proving the nature of pressure being illegitimate is of critical importance. The pressure could be illegitimate if it forced the other to perform an obligation they did not owe.[89] The broader question is whether the pressure must be proved to be wrongful. The conduct, it has been observed, need not fall within recognised categories of wrongdoing.[90] In *Thorne v Kennedy*,[91] the High Court explained that an analysis of duress focuses on the effect of a type of pressure on the person invoking duress to set aside the contract.[92] It was stated that,

> It does not require that the person's will be overborne. Nor does it require that the pressure be such as to deprive the person of any free agency or ability to decide. The person subjected to duress is usually able to assess alternatives and to make a choice. The person submits to the demand knowing 'only too well' what he or she is doing.[93]

---

87 [2017] FCA 157.

88 Ibid, para [46]. See also *Esso Australia Pty Ltd v The Australian Workers' Union* (2016) 258 IR 396, para [194].

89 *Nixon v Furphy* (1925) 25 S.R. (N.S.W.) 151.

90 Seddon N, Bigwood R and Ellinghaus M, *Cheshire & Fifoot Law of Contract*, 10th edn (LexisNexis Butterworths, Australian edition 2012), p. 749.

91 [2017] HCA 49 (2017) 91 ALJR 1260

92 [2017] HCA 49, para [26]. Beatson J, 'Duress by Threatened Breach of Contract' (1976) 92 Law Quarterly Review 496 at 497–498.

93 [2017] HCA 49, para [26]. Reference was made to *Union Pacific Railroad Co v Public Service Commission of Missouri* (1918) 248 US 67, p. 70

The case concerned the validity of a pre-nuptial agreement and a post-nuptial agreement the appellant signed before her wedding to the respondent. The respondent, aged 67, was a wealthy property developer. The appellant, aged 36, lived overseas and was relatively poor by the appellant's standard of living. The appellant and respondent met on an online website for potential brides. After a brief courtship, the appellant and the respondent were to marry. When she came to Australia, it was with minimal possessions, and she was highly dependent on the respondent.

**10.68** The court recognised that, if the relationship ended, the appellant would have nothing. The appellant, as was noted, had been given independent advice about the agreements and was advised not to sign them. Her lawyer's advice to her also showed that the appellant was under significant stress because the wedding would not proceed if she did not sign the agreement. Nettle J viewed the '*test of illegitimate pressure was whether the pressure goes beyond what is reasonably necessary for the protection of legitimate interests*'.[94]

Arguably the respondent's behaviour in the circumstances was lawful. The pre- and post-nuptial agreements were recognised by the law. However, the fact that the appellant was highly dependent on the respondent weighed on the judgment of the court. An additional factor appears to be that even though the agreements were lawful, they were, arguably, disproportionate to the objective they sought to achieve. Nevertheless, the court was of the view that the decision should be based on the doctrine of unconscionability rather than duress.[95] Also, whether the court would readily accept the impairment of consent in business relationships is doubtful. But in some exceptional cases it is possible to posit the view that a permitted act can be unlawful if it went beyond the purpose it intends to achieve.

**10.69** In *Peanut Marketing Board v Cuda*,[96] the defendants had argued that the seed purchase contract with the Board was procured by duress. The defendants alleged that after they had prepared the land for planting when the Board informed them that they would purchase the seed from, and sell their harvest through, the Board. Campbell J found there was no ground for economic duress to succeed because the defendants still had a market for the peanuts supplied by the Board. There was no evidence of economic duress. Sidone observed that if a threat not to contract in the future does not interfere with existing legal right, then an argument for duress could not succeed.[97] However, if it was unlawful to make the threat it would be a different matter.

**10.70** The pressure in *Peanut Marketing Board* is similar to *Thorne*. The party who raises duress is dependent on the other party. The dependence in *Peanut Marketing Board* was grounded on future potential income and earnings. They had no choice but to accept the contract because they needed the income.

---

94  [2017] HCA 49, para [71].
95  Ibid, para [29].
96  (1984) 79 FLR 368.
97  Sidone MP, 'The Doctrine of Economic Duress Part 2' (1996) 14 Aust Bar Rev 114.

The defendants also knew full well the contract they were signing. Even so, the Board's position, similar to *Smith v William Charlick*, could not be said to have done anything unlawful because the Board's act appears to be legislatively permitted. Even if it was considered unconscionable, it could not lead to a successful action for duress.

**10.71** It is clear that in business transactions where parties have an existing contract with each other, economic duress requires proof of illegitimate economic pressure, the result of which is the victim does not have any other available alternative.[98] In existing business relationships, it is the illegitimacy of pressure that affects the quality of consent, not inequality of bargaining power.[99] In *Mitchell v Pacific Dawn Pty Ltd*,[100] the dispute between the parties concerned a settlement agreement between the builder and contractor. The contractor's threat that they will refuse payment unless the builder agrees to a settlement agreement did not amount to duress.The performance of the project undertaken by both parties had stretched both parties financially. It was found the builder delayed the completion of the project for the contractors. As such, the threat made by the contractors was merely a factual statement of their position financially, and the settlement agreement was an opportunity for both parties to walk away from the contract with some payment. The argument that there was duress failed.

**10.72** In *Morgan Stanley Wealth Management Australia Pty Ltd v Detata (No 3)*,[101] the court had to consider whether the defendant procured a settlement contract with the plaintiff by duress. The plaintiff had employed the defendant as a financial adviser. The defendant was given, under his contract of employment, significant retention and incentive payments. If he were to resign, his contract of employment obliged him to repay these sums to the plaintiff. In February 2013, the plaintiff and the defendant entered into a settlement deed whereby they agreed that the defendant's contract of employment would be ended. The defendant agreed to pay the plaintiff a lesser sum in instalments. The defendant defaulted on the instalment payments. The defendant argued that the settlement deed was procured with, among other things, economic duress and ought to be set aside.

**10.73** Banks-Smith J observed that the plaintiff, in this case, did not compel the defendant either leave or stay. Both options were open to the defendant.[102] The court, however, decided that in the circumstances, it was lawful for parties to enter into negotiations and the circumstances of the case did not give rise to economic duress.[103] The defendant was bound by the terms of the contract to make the payments to the plaintiff if he left.

**10.74** In *Detata (No 3)*, the facts reveal the defendant would have to pay a much more significant sum if the terms of defendant's original employment

---

98 *Suncorp-Metway v Nagatsuma* [2019] QSC 016, para [6].
99 *Westpac Corporation v Cockerill* (1998) 152 ALR 267, p. 292.
100 [2011] QCA 98.
101 [2018] WASC 32.
102 Ibid, para [412].
103 Ibid, para [414].

contract were enforced. The settlement deed provided for a lower sum which the plaintiff in the case need not have offered. Further, it was the defendant who proposed the idea of leaving the plaintiff.[104] The compromise that the defendant secured with the plaintiff, it was observed would not have provided the plaintiff with any financial windfall.[105] Banks-Smith J could not find the defendant to be in any disadvantage in the transactions as well as the transaction in itself being fair and reasonable in the circumstances. Given the facts described, it cannot be ignored that either way the plaintiff required the defendant to pay a certain sum to secure release from employment. As such, the fact mentioned puts the plaintiff in a superior position to the defendant. Nevertheless, being a commercial transaction, given the nature of the defendant's social status, illegitimate pressure was not established following true to the approach taken in *Mitchell*. It does go to show regardless of the superior bargaining position of one party, reasonable and fair conduct would negate the existence of duress.

**10.75** With regards to the issue of whether the threat amounts to illegitimate pressure, there were circumstances where the court would have to consider whether the persons who exerted the pressure did so in good or bad faith.[106] On that note, in *Electricity Generation Corporation (t/as Verve Energy) Woodside Energy Ltd*[107] the existence of good faith would not preclude a finding of economic duress with a threatened or actual breach of contract.[108] A threat would also not be illegitimate if the threat could be resisted and its enforceability tested in court.[109]

**10.76** In *Beerens v Bluescope Distribution Pty Ltd*,[110] the appellant argued that the respondent procured the guarantee provided under economic duress. However, the court did observe that instead of making the debt immediately payable, the respondent provided the appellant with credit duration within which the appellant was to settle the debts with the respondent.[111] Further, the law allowed a threat by way of winding up and bankruptcy proceedings, in good faith to persuade the debtor to pay the debt owed.[112] The argument for economic duress failed.

**10.77** The issue of good faith or bad faith will only be an issue if the threat in itself is lawful. Of course, good faith would be irrelevant where the threat is unlawful, in the first place.[113] In this regard, the approach is similar to that taken in *Times Travel (UK) Ltd v Pakistan International Airlines Corp.*[114]

---

104 Ibid, para [398].
105 Ibid, para [407].
106 [2011] QCA 98, para [52].
107 [2013] WASCA 36.
108 Ibid, para [195].
109 *Mackay v National Australia Bank* [1998] 4 VR 677, p. 683, 686–687.
110 [2012] VSCA 209.
111 Ibid, para [41].
112 Ibid, para [48].
113 Ibid, para [46].
114 [2019] EWCA Civ 828.

## Causation

**10.78** The issue of causation has been settled in *Barton v Armstrong*.[115] In *Barton v Armstrong*, the Privy Council decided that threats need only be one of the reasons the victim entered into the contract. Thus, the threat need not be the reason. However, the test in *Barton* ought to be approached with common sense. In *Barton*, the pressure applied came from a threat of murder (clearly an unlawful act). Unless the act complained to be economic duress is unlawful, the test in *Barton* for causation should be applied sparingly.[116] In *Crescendo Management Pty Ltd v Westpac Banking Corp*,[117] McHugh JA explained that it was unnecessary for the victim to prove duress was the sole reason to contract.[118] The burden is on the party applying the pressure to show that it had no impact on the decision of the other party to contract.[119] The respondent, in this case, had done an unlawful and improper act by detaining proceeds of sale belonging to the director of the appellant. However, the unlawful act was found not operative to induce the appellant to enter into the mortgage agreement with the respondent. Therefore, the case of duress was not made out.

**10.79** Similarly, in *Ford Motor Company of Australia Ltd v Arrowcrest Pty Ltd*,[120] it was stated that once illegitimate pressure is proved, it must be such that it compelled the victim to contract.[121] However, in business, it was recognised that parties are 'obliged for good and sufficient commercial reasons to enter into transactions which they would otherwise avoid'. In this case, the court found no evidence that the party alleging duress (Ford Motor) had intended to avoid the contract complained of at the first available opportunity. In this regard, Ford Motor did not appear to be lacking choice. As such, the pressure complained of did not compel Ford Motor to enter into the contract. The argument of duress was held to fail.

**10.80** While illegitimate pressure need not be the leading cause of why a party entered into the contract, it needs to be operative. Even if there may exist other causative reasons for a party crying economic duress to contract, duress must be shown to be the operative cause.[122] Evidence should be led to show that 'but for' the commercial pressure exerted the contract made would not exist.

**10.81** The above-mentioned is not the same as the approach in *Barton*, for *Barton*'s case concerned unlawful conduct. Hence the relaxed causation test would only be applicable where the conduct of the party exerting pressure is shown to be *prima facie* illegal under the law. A possible extension of the doctrine could lie where the way with which the pressure is exercised is unlawful.

115 [1976] AC 104.
116 Seddon N, Bigwood R and Ellinghaus M, *Cheshire & Fifoot Law of Contract*, 10th edn (LexisNexis Butterworths, Australian edition 2012), p. 756.
117 (1988) 19 NSWLR 40.
118 Ibid, p. 46.
119 Ibid.
120 (2003) 134 FCR 522.
121 Ibid, para [163].
122 (1988) 19 NSWLR 40, p. 46.

An extreme example would be where a creditor hires thugs to exert pressure on a debtor for a debt owed. Clearly, the creditor has a right to recover the debt owed. However, the method is unlawful.

## Malaysia

**10.82** Under Malaysian law, much of the rules for the law of contract are found in the Contracts Act 1950. The law in itself is a codification of common law principles found in England before 1950.[123] Nevertheless, the Contracts Act 1950 does not use the term 'duress' within its provisions. Instead the terminology that is used is 'coercion'.

**10.83** Section 14 identifies 'coercion' as one of the recognised categories as a factor that vitiates contract because it negates 'free consent'.[124] Section 19(1) provides that the contract affected by coercion is voidable.[125] The definition for coercion is provided for under section 15. The provision is then followed by an illustration that is intended to guide the application of the law. The illustration refers to contract secured by intimidation.

**10.84** The Penal Code further provides that whether the Penal Code is applicable at the place the contract is made is irrelevant. This means even if the contract is made outside of Malaysia, where the Penal Code is now law, the contract could still be set aside by Malaysian courts if the act in question is associated with coercion under the Penal Code. Hence a party seeking to set aside the contract for coercion, may still do so under section 15

**10.85** However, the word 'coercion' is also found in section 73 of the Contracts Act 1950. The application of the principle of duress is then subject to provision of the Act and how far the courts are willing to extend the principles on economic duress found in other jurisdictions. The subsequent parts of the chapter will first deal with 'coercion' as found in section 15 then proceed to deal with whether 'economic duress' can be imported into section 73 Contracts Act 1950.

### Section 15 Contracts Act 1950

**10.86** Coercion is defined by section 15 of the Contracts Act 1950. Section 15 provides that

'Coercion' is the committing, or threatening to commit any act forbidden by the Penal Code, or the unlawful detaining or threatening to detain, any property, to the prejudice of any person whatever, with the intention of causing any person to enter into an agreement.

---

123 Trakic A, Ramasamy N, Cheah YS, Andrews PL, Murugan SB, Vijayganesh P and Chandran K, *Law for Business*, 2nd edn (Sweet & Maxwell 2018), para 3.022.
124 Sections 10 and 14 of the Contracts Act 1950.
125 Section 19(1) of the Contracts Act 1950.

The question of whether the concept of coercion under section 15 adopts the English principle of economic duress is answered by viewing the provision through a pre-1950 lens of English law. Clearly, economic duress was recognised in English Law more prominently after the decision of *The Universe Sentinel*,[126] in 1983. This reasoning has led the courts to take a restrictive view of whether economic duress is applicable in Malaysia.

**10.87** In order to prove coercion, the nature of the promise made must be shown to be procured by an unlawful 'act' prescribed in the Penal Code or by unlawful detention or threat thereof of property belonging to another. For example, if an agreement is procured by assault[127] or criminal force,[128] the agreement would be caught by section 15 because these are specific offences provided for under the Penal Code. In *Nuri Asia Sdn Bhd v Fosis Corp Sdn Bhd*,[129] the court found that the agreement was tainted by coercion because the victim had been intimidated by the apprehension of violence to sign the agreement. There was evidence that the victim was surrounded and pushed by a number of persons before the agreement was signed.[130]

**10.88** The second category under section 15 requires the party invoking coercion to show that the contract was procured by unlawful detention of property or threats to that effect. The detention or threat could be unlawful under the Penal Code or any other law. For example, in a contract for the sale of goods, the seller must deliver the goods.[131] A seller who extorts additional payment from a buyer who has already paid in full for the goods by detaining or threatening to detain the goods would be committing an unlawful act.[132] The buyer can avoid the agreement to make additional payments.

**10.89** The consequence of section 15 in these cases are direct, if there is evidence to show an act provided for under the Penal Code, followed by causation[133] between the offence and the agreement. It then attracts the inevitable outcome laid in section 19(1) of the Contracts Act 1950. For example, in *Mayland Lending Sdn Bhd v Rossmaizati bt Mohamad*,[134] it was said that evidence of duress could include a police report made about the conduct alleged to be duress.[135] A police report would be the natural response of a person who has

---

126 *Universe Tankships Inc. of Monrovia v International Transport Workers Federation* [1983] 1 AC 366, p. 385.

127 Section 351 of the Penal Code.

128 Section 350 of the Penal Code.

129 [2006]3 MLJ 249.

130 *Nuri Asia Sdn Bhd v Fosis Corp Sdn Bhd* [2006]3 MLJ 249, paras [25] and [27].

131 Section 31 of the Sale of Goods Act 1957.

132 The assumption here is that there aren't any terms in the contract between the buyer and the seller that modifies or vary the duty.

133 In *Perlis Plantations Bhd v Mohammad Abdullah Ang* [1988]1 CLJ 670, pp 675–677, evidence that coercion caused the victim to contract was lacking. The argument for coercion failed.

134 [2015] 7 MLJ 216.

135 Ibid, para [37]. The necessity of a police report had been confirmed in *Soo Lip Hong v Tee Kim Huan* [2006] 2 MLJ 49, para [8].

been put under duress by an unlawful act. The details in the police report will allow the court to determine if an act falling within the Penal Code has taken place.

### Section 73 Contracts Act 1950 and economic duress

**10.90** The other provision under the Contracts Act 1950 which provides for 'coercion' is in section 73. The section deals with a situation where a person has paid money or delivered something to another under coercion or mistake. The consequence of the provision is that where coercion exists, the person receiving the money or thing in question must return it. It is argued that section 73 applies only to a quasi-contractual transaction.[136]

**10.91** The premise, arguably, is that the provision is found in Part VI of the Act which deals with 'Certain Relations Resembling Those Created by Contract'. As such, from a literal interpretation, the provision does not deal with circumstances that create a contractual relationship.[137] Other circumstances dealt with under Part VI under the Act are 'claims for necessaries supplied to persons lacking capacity',[138] 'reimbursement owed to a third party who pays the debt owed by one person',[139] 'compensation for the person who provides service or goods to another not done gratuitously which the other person receives a benefit thereof'[140] and 'the responsibilities of a person who finds goods belonging to another as a bailee'.[141]

**10.92** These quasi-contracts arise from a fictitious promise created by law[142] to impose an obligation on one person to pay another a certain sum of money. The promise to pay is based on natural justice and equity. While English law considers economic duress as pressure vitiating consent, Malaysian courts could approach the issue from the perspective of equity.

**10.93** If so, the concept would fall squarely within the ambit of section 73. The premise of the argument is that if the other person has received a benefit (otherwise he would not have received) by use of economic coercion at the plaintiff's expense, it would be unjust to allow him to retain that benefit.[143] Thus economic duress becomes relevant within the Malaysian statutory framework for contract law.

---

136 Ayus AM, *Law of Contract in Malaysia* (Sweet & Maxwell 2009), p. 18.
137 Ibid.
138 Section 69 of the Contracts Act 1950.
139 Section 70 of the Contracts Act 1950.
140 Section 71 of the Contracts Act 1950.
141 Section 73 of the Contracts Act 1950.
142 Furmston MP, *Cheshire, Fifoot and Furmston's Law of Contract* (Oxford University Press 2017), p. 12. See also *Moses v Macferlan* (1760) 2 Burr 1005.
143 *Wynn Resorts (Macau) SA v Wang Yen Liang* [2017] 11 MLJ 169, para [66].

*A restrictive judicial approach*

**10.94** The economic duress argument has been raised in many cases. In *Chin Nam Bee Development v Tai Kim Choo*,[144] the respondents and the appellants signed a contract for the construction for individual houses. Each respondent signed a sale and purchase agreement with the appellants to purchase each house respectively for $29,500. The appellants subsequently demanded an additional $4,000 from each respondent. The appellants sought to cancel the sale and purchase agreements with the respondents if they did not make the demanded payments. The respondents then brought an action for the return of the $4,000 paid.

**10.95** The judge at first instance found that the payments were not voluntary because they were made under coercion. The issue that arose was whether 'coercion' under section 73 of the Contracts Act 1950 should be given the same meaning as 'coercion' provided for under section 15. If so, the appellants contended that they had not done anything unlawful and therefore the sum paid involuntarily need not be returned. At the High Court, it was explained that the definition of 'coercion' under section 15 and section 73 are different.[145] Section 15, it was reasoned, provided for a statutory definition of coercion which centred on unlawful acts. However, coercion under section 73 should be given its ordinary meaning.[146]

**10.96** The decision in *Chin Nam Bee* provides some avenue to suppose that there would be a potential for the economic duress under the ambit of section 73. If the ordinary meaning is attributed to the provision, then illegitimate pressure in commercial transactions could be included. However, it is merely a possibility and further consideration has been rather cautious.

**10.97** In *Abdul Rashid bin Maidin v Lian Mong Yee*,[147] the Federal Court affirmed the Court of Appeal's decision that coercion under section 73 must be proved before the effects of the provision are invoked.[148] Gopal Sri Ram JCA, in the Court of Appeal,[149] was of the view that section 73 was based on the English case of *Smith v Cuff*.[150] In *Smith*, the plaintiff was placed in a situation of oppression and abject submission.[151] However, in *Abdul Rashid*, the respondent did not show coercion, and as such, the case could not succeed on this ground. The reference to abject submission and oppression required for the applicability of section 73 reflect the nature of pressure required for section 73 application.

**10.98** However, the interpretation of 'oppression' and 'abject submission' was not further explicated. It would have been worthwhile to explore the concepts before deciding the elements did not exist on the facts of the case. However, since the respondents did not offer evidence of coercion, it would

---

144 [1988] 2 MLJ 177.
145 Ibid, p. 118.
146 Ibid, p. 119.
147 [2008] 1 MLJ 469.
148 Ibid, para [5].
149 *Lian Mong Yee v Abdul Rashid bin Maidin* [2001] 4 MLJ 38.
150 (1817) 6 Maule and Selwyn 160.
151 *Lian Mong Yee v Abdul Rashid bin Maidin* [2001] 4 MLJ 38, p. 48.

have been an arduous exercise at the time. In *Smith v Cuff*, Lord Ellenborough CJ observed there was inequality between the parties where one party had applied a high degree of pressure on the other to agree and comply with the terms.[152]

**10.99** 'Abject submission' can be interpreted to apply where one party to the contract has used their position illegitimately to contract with another, who has no choice but to comply with the demands made under the contract. The demands could be unreasonable and any attempt to question them would result in termination of the contract. This arguably could be considered as extorsive behaviour as well But extortive behaviour could be distinguished with the legal right. It is not extorsive behaviour where a party to the contract demands a promise within his legal right unless a wrongful way was used to claim the right. In this sense, section 73 could be interpreted to cover economic duress.

**10.100** In *OCBC Securities (Melaka) Sdn Bhd (Formerly known as Sykt Tan, Chow & Loh Securities Sdn Bhd) v Koh Kee Hua*,[153] the defendant worked with the plaintiff as a remisier. As a condition of employment, the defendant deposited RM65,000 with the plaintiff. In 1991, the defendant joined another securities company. As a condition of release from his current employment, the defendant executed an indemnity in favour of the plaintiff. The issue before the court was that the indemnity agreement was procured under economic duress. Low Hop Bing J considered the question of economic duress by referring to *Pao On v Lau Yiu Long*[154] as a guideline.[155] The judge observed that the courts should be slow to find economic duress unless there is positive evidence to show pressure exerted vitiated consent. The key passage referred to is as follows:

> ...There must be present some factor 'which could in law be regarded as a coercion of his will so as to vitiate his consent.'... In determining whether there was a coercion of will such that there was no true consent, it is material to inquire whether the person alleged to have been coerced did or did not protest; whether, at the time he was allegedly coerced into making the contract, he did or did not have an alternative course open to him such as an adequate legal remedy; whether he was independently advised; and whether after entering the contract he took steps to avoid it...[156]

The judgment adopts an approach, similar to English common law, by virtue of the factors considered. However, the question of economic duress had not been considered further in-depth. The defendant had not led evidence to show there was coercion at the time the parties made the contract. This necessitated the analysis of the factors in *Pao On*. As such, the finding in the case was that the agreement was not procured by duress.

---

152 (1817) 6 Maule and Selwyn 160, p. 166.
153 [2004] 2 MLJ 110.
154 [1980] AC 614; *Pao On v Lau Yiu Long* [1980] AC 614, p. 635.
155 [2004] 2 MLJ 110, paras [16] and [25].
156 Ibid, para [17].

**10.101** In *Teck Guan Trading Sdn Bhd v Hydrotek Engineering (S) Sdn Bhd*,[157] the plaintiff and the first defendant contracted for the sale of round bars. The second and third defendants had given a guarantee for the contract price. The first defendant defaulted on payment. The plaintiff subsequently sent a notice of demand to the second and third defendants. Having received no reply from them, the plaintiff commenced an action against the defendants to recover a sum owed under the contract. The defendants disputed the sum provided by the plaintiff. One of the issues raised was that of coercion. The first defendant argued that after orders were placed and the deposit paid, the plaintiff refused to supply unless the first defendant agreed to a higher price for the round bars. The first defendant argued that they initially resisted but eventually agreed to price stipulated by the plaintiff because they had committed to the production and supply of concrete to third parties. The court held that there was no coercion because the parties freely agreed to the price.

**10.102** Ian Chin J was of the view that the pressure exerted on the first defendant merely amounted to commercial pressure and improper use of dominant bargaining power.[158] Even if the first defendant resisted the plaintiff's new price, it was clear that parties here were dealing at 'arm's length' where the first defendant had threatened the plaintiff with legal action.[159] As such, there was no evidence to suggest that the defendant's will had been dominated.

**10.103** While the court did recognise that there was a dominant use of bargaining power, the mere use of dominant power is not duress. This approach is also similar to that taken in English law. There should be more than the mere use of dominant power because securing the best position in a business relationship is reflective of the concept of freedom of contract in any given circumstances, unless there is a legislative policy to regulate commercial relationship. For example, the relationship between a seller and the consumer buyer.[160]

**10.104** In *Perlis Plantations Bhd v Mohammad Abdullah Ang*,[161] the plaintiff and the defendant contracted to buy land belonging to Kauri in three equal shares with the help of a firm of solicitors. The written 'sale and purchase agreement' was signed between the purchasers and Kaikoura Sdn Bhd. This company was under the control of the plaintiffs and Kauri vendors. The plaintiffs argued that payments were made to Kauri and its solicitors. The defendant agreed to repay a sum with interest to the plaintiffs on or before 15 August 1983 as consideration. The plaintiffs also argued that the defendants had made some payments. Also, the defendant had requested that the remainder be paid in instalments. After three instalments were paid the defendant stopped the payments. While there was evidence that the defendant had given a written acknowledgement to repay the amount to the plaintiffs, it was not given under duress. VC George J

---

157 [1996] 4 MLJ 331; *Emar Sdn Bhd (Under Receivership) v Adigi Sdn Bhd* [1992] 2 MLJ 734.
158 [1996] 4 MLJ 331, p. 339.
159 Ibid, p. 340.
160 See for example the Consumer Protection Act 1999.
161 [1988]1 CLJ 670.

was of the view that in order to plead duress, the defendant should have pleaded the argument within the ambit of section 15 of the Contracts Act 1950. If such a plea were made, it would still fail because there was no room for economic duress within the context of section 15. However, neither did the court explore whether the coercion was a form of economic duress which could fall within the scope of section 73. Indeed, some exploration of the issue could have thrown light on the law.

**10.105** In *Mohd Fariq Subramaniam v Naza Motor Trading Sdn Bhd*,[162] the defendants appointed the plaintiff as a taxi driver for their business. The terms of the agreement provided, among other things, the right of the plaintiff to terminate the agreement upon breach of its terms by the plaintiff. The plaintiff failed to pay his daily rental for the taxi. Subsequently, the defendants repossessed the taxi and sent notice to the plaintiff that the agreement would be terminated. The plaintiff challenged the defendants' right to repossess the taxi. The defendants argued that they had the right under a variation agreement signed after the original agreement. The plaintiff argued that the variation agreement was signed under economic duress. The High Court in determining whether there was economic duress referred to *Pao On v Lau Yiu Long*. It was reasoned that the plaintiff did not protest either before or after the variation agreement was signed.[163] It was factually found that there was no evidence to show that the plaintiff was coerced to sign the agreement.[164] Therefore the argument of duress failed.

**10.106** *Mohd Fariq Subramaniam* is a rare case that discusses the concept of economic duress. However, the High Court precedent is merely persuasive whether the concept is applicable in Malaysian contract law. Further, no appeal arose from this case. It is uncertain how an appellate court would embrace the adoption of the meaning of duress enumerated in *Pao On v Lau Yiu Long*. In light of the Federal Court decision in *Abdul Rashid bin Maidin v Lian Mong Yee*, it is arguable that the decision could be per incuriam. However, it is doubtful whether the outcome of the case would be any different. The plaintiff in *Mohd Fariq Subramaniam* was not put in a situation of 'abject submission'. As such, even if he brought the case under section 73, his argument for duress would equally fail.

**10.107** Clearly, there are legislative hurdles in Malaysian contract law to allow economic duress as a concept. However the question could be addressed if the issue were to be discussed from the perspective of the constitutional power of the courts. The Malaysian Federal Constitution determines the power of the Malaysian courts to decide on legal issues.[165] The Malaysian Federal Constitution also emphasises that the powers of the courts are subject to limitations of, among other

---

162 [1998] 6 MLJ 193. Also made reference to the Singapore case of *Third World Development Ltd v Atang Latief* [1990] 1 MLJ 385.

163 [1998] 6 MLJ 193, p. 201.

164 Ibid.

165 Articles 121(1), 121(1B)(b), 121(2)(c) of the Federal Constitution.

things, federal law, the process of the courts and judges. For many, this presents itself as a hurdle to developing economic duress within Malaysian contract law. Other hurdles often cited are sections 3 and 5, Civil Law Act 1956.

**10.108** Sections 3 and 5 of the Civil Law Act 1956 provide for the application and binding status of English law in Malaysia. English law (legislative, common law or equitable principles) will apply if three conditions within these provisions are fulfilled. The provisions have a cut-off date from which English law does not apply. However, these cut-off dates differ from Peninsular Malaysia, Sabah and Sarawak.[166] Under the second condition, English law can be resorted to only to fill a gap for which Malaysian law does not provide.[167] The third condition provides that even if the principle is adopted, the judge ought to ensure its application is suitable within the context of Malaysian law.[168]

**10.109** In cases of economic duress, more often than not, intervention by the courts is dependent on their will to develop the doctrine. As was discussed, there is a reflection of 'will' in some cases, but in others the 'will' is somewhat lacking. Raja Azlan Shah FJ stated, in essence, the role of the courts is to expound the law and the law must be taken as that provided by the courts even if there are those who will disagree with the decision of the courts.[169] For it is the resulting intellectual discourse that inevitably leads to the formation of doctrine and subsequent legislation to deal with issues such as economic duress.

**10.110** Clearly, there is room for the adoption of economic duress if the courts have the 'will' to adopt and develop the doctrine. There is an opportunity under section 73 of the Contracts Act 1950 (in light of sections 3 and 5 of the Civil Law Act 1950) as there is also opportunity under the inherent jurisdiction of the courts under the Federal Constitution to adopt principle where legislation has not provided a solution. Rather than apply the existing provisions which were not designed to deal with the concept, the courts should take a proactive role.

**10.111** The dominant position and unequal bargaining power are rampant in contemporary commercial dealings. There is room for the courts to determine the policy which requires parties to act fairly with each other to achieve the commercial objective. The doctrine of freedom of contract indeed requires that parties be allowed to contract as they see fit. However, the sanctity of the doctrine should be guarded against bad faith transactions or use of dominant position in the wrong way.

---

166 Trakic A, Ramasamy N, Cheah YS, Andrews PL, Murugan SB, Vijayganesh P and Chandran K, *Law for Business*, 2nd edn (Sweet & Maxwell 2018), paras 3.025–3.026 and 3.032–3.0335.

167 Ibid, para 3.023. See also *Song Bok Yong v Ho Kim Poui* [1968] 1 MLJ 56, *Wee Lian Construction Sdn Bhd v Ingersoll Jati Malaysia Sdn Bhd* [2005] 1 MLJ 162, paras 33–37 and *Aseambankers Malaysia Bhd v Shencourt Sdn Bhd* [2014] 4 MLJ 619, paras 120–121.

168 *Chung Khiaw Bank Ltd v Hotel Rasa Sayang* [1990] 1 MLJ 356 at 361–362. See also the majority decision in *Government of Malaysia v Lim Kit Siang* [1988] 2 MLJ 12.

169 *Loh Kooi Choon v Government of Malaysia* [1977] 2 MLJ 187, p. 189 and *Henry v Geopresco International Ltd* [1975] 2 All ER 702, p. 718.

**Conclusion**

**10.112** The comparison between English, Australian and Malaysian law reveals that the courts approach the concept of duress rigidly and cautiously. The English courts confine the concept within the realm of duress. While the concept began with threats occasioning violence against the person or threats involving property, economic duress has been allowed some room within the doctrine. The more unlawful the threat, the higher the probability there was duress vitiating consent.[170]

**10.113** Nevertheless, it is difficult to suppose that commercial pressure can be generalised to reflect unlawful characteristics. On the other hand, in business, it will be difficult to find contracts where parties genuinely have equal bargaining power, with the exception of consumer contracts. The nature of commerce is that one party to the contract will be in a dominant position. Judges, overall, recognise this as fact.

**10.114** Where economic duress is concerned, the illegitimacy of the act that coerces the other to agree is critical to decide whether a party has used their dominant position in the wrong way. Hence one of the criteria commonly considered is the alternatives available to the party invoking duress. However, such a party to the contract could also find themselves in a lesser position due to market forces, either a change in the market trend or change of government or laws or other similar circumstance. All of which provides pressure, but not pressure which originates from the other party to the contract. In addition, as observed in *Time Travel (UK)*,[171] a party in dominant position or superior bargaining position does not need to be reasonable when making a demand that is lawful.

**10.115** When one party capitalises on an opportunity to secure a better deal from the other, there is no duress unless the act of capitalising on the opportunity was illegitimate, or unlawful.[172] Nevertheless, there is room to consider whether a party in a dominant position has abused its position. The unconscionable act which may constitute illegitimate pressure, could be relatable procedural unconscionability which creates a defect in the bargaining process.[173] At times, a defective bargaining position is found when the party of whom demand has been made has no practical choice but to accept. The practicality of choice consideration was evident in the decisions of *Progress Bulk* and *Carillion*.[174]

---

170 McKendrick E, *Contract Law: Texts, Cases and Materials*, 5th edn (Oxford University Press 2012), p. 652; *R v A-G for England and Wales* [2003] UKPC 22, para [16].

171 See n 60.

172 Willett C, 'Good Faith in Consumer Contracts' in Forte ADM (ed.), *Good Faith in Contract and Property* (Hart Publishing 1999), p. 194.

173 Katz AW, 'Economic Foundations of Contract Law' in Klass G and Letsas G, *Philosophical Foundations of Contract Law* (Oxford University Press 2014), p. 180; Epstein RA, 'Unconscionability: A Critical Reappraisal' (1975) 18 J. Law & Econ. 293.

174 See n 55.

**10.116** From the Australian perspective, the issue of economic duress focusses on unconscionability.[175] In *Equiticorp Finance Ltd v Bank of New Zealand*,[176] Kirby J found that economic duress posed uncertain variables and viewed that it should be considered under the doctrines of undue influence and unconscionability.[177] While the English Courts have been open to explore the degree of illegitimacy required for economic duress to be successful, though uncertain, Australian courts are reluctant to find economic duress as duress.[178]

**10.117** It is because once an 'act' is characterised as illegitimate pressure, the *Barton* test assumes that consent has been vitiated unless rebutted by the party accused of issuing the threat.[179] In addition to being a heavy burden on the party accused of duress, it also sets a precedent which affects the freedom of contract. Arguably, the Australian courts take a practical and middle ground approach to endeavour to find economic duress a new home. However, there are some cases which exhibit special facts. In cases like *Thorne*, even though the person accused of duress had a right, he had gone beyond what was deemed necessary to protect his legal interest. But it should be remembered that *Thorne* was not purely a contract case. Nevertheless, the approach in *Thorne* has potential for doctrine of economic duress by reframing the nature of duress from illegitimate pressure to one of disproportionate pressure.[180] This would align with cases such as *Mitchell* as well.[181]

**10.118** At the other end of the spectrum, Malaysian courts have used legislation, namely the Contracts Act 1950, to defend non-inclusion of economic duress into law, at least at appellate levels. It is either done by deciding that economic duress does not fall within the scope of the provision[182] or not to explore the issue on the ground the party seeking to rely on economic duress did not plead it.[183] While there is some hope under section 73, only when the other party is placed in 'abject submission' could a person rightly claim for economic duress under the provision.[184] However, it is submitted that this view of economic duress is rather narrow. It is indeed narrower than the English approach. The question to be asked then is what is the future for economic duress?

**10.119** The Australian approach appears to be the obvious solution. It has moved such issues into the realm of unconscionability. As such, for Australia economic duress has a home and within this home a role to play. It is arguable

---

175 Seddon N, Bigwood R and Ellinghaus M, *Cheshire & Fifoot Law of Contract*, 10th edn (LexisNexis Butterworths, Australian edition 2012), p. 748.

176 (1993) 32 NSWLR 50.

177 Ibid, paras [106]–[107].

178 Seddon N, Bigwood R and Ellinghaus M, *Cheshire & Fifoot Law of Contract*, 10th edn (LexisNexis Butterworths, Australian edition 2012), p. 757.

179 Ibid.

180 See n 94.

181 See n 100.

182 As seen in *Perlis Plantations Bhd v Mohammad Abdullah Ang* [1988]1 CLJ 670.

183 *OCBC Securities (Melaka) Sdn Bhd (Formerly known as Sykt Tan, Chow & Loh Securities Sdn Bhd) v Koh Kee Hua* [2004] 2 MLJ 110 and *Perlis Plantations Bhd v Mohammad Abdullah Ang* [1988]1 CLJ 670.

184 See *Abdul Rashid bin Maidin v Lian Mong Yee* [2008] 1 MLJ 469.

that unconscionability and good faith are perhaps two sides of the same coin. But comparatively good faith does not concern the legitimacy of the act. Rather it concerns whether a person having the right ought to exercise the right. The same can be said of proportionality. But unlike proportionality, good faith does provide a value judgement of the action to either praise or condemn the act. Proportionality does no such thing, but rather considers the validity of one act in light of a better alternative. If there was a least infringing alternative, the choice of a more infringing one does beg question whether the person who made the choice to do an act had ulterior motive.

**10.120** Another principle which is unexplored in the context of economic duress is the 'arm's length' principle. It has been mentioned somewhat in a few cases. For example, in *Teck Guan Trading Sdn Bhd v Hydrotek Engineering (S) Sdn Bhd*,[185] Ian Chin J decided that the argument for economic duress failed because parties dealt with each other at arm's length when entering into the contract. In *Pao On v Lau Yiu Long*,[186] Lord Scarman made a comment which said that men who have negotiated at 'arm's length' should be held accountable to their promise unless there is duress.[187] While the argument of economic duress is still potentially open, perhaps explicating the 'arm's length' principle could further assist in determining whether illegitimate pressure exists. In *Electricity Generation Corporation (t/as Verve Energy) Woodside Energy Ltd*,[188] Gageler J, in the High Court of Australia, said that commercial parties who deal with each other at arm's length are free to agree on terms each considers to be to their commercial advantage.[189]

**10.121** Where the current factors of duress focus on the illegitimacy of the threat, the question of whether parties dealt with each at arm's length considers how the contract was formed between them. It does not eliminate the question of illegitimate pressure altogether but instead should allow the courts to filter the facts and decide if they should go further to consider at all the pressure exercised. It would resemble the doctrine of negligence somewhat where if a duty of care is not proved, it would be pointless to consider the other elements such as breach, causation and remoteness.

**10.122** In each of the cases named in 10.120, parties were found to have dealt at 'arm's length'. In each of the cases, the argument for economic duress failed. While the reasons why economic duress failed differ, the common denominator between the cases is that evidence showed parties dealt at 'arm's length' and therefore were free to choose whether to pursue the contract they entered. It then follows that if parties had a choice, exercise of a choice to contract on the terms complained of cannot amount to duress. Therefore, the development of the principle could pose possible reinvention into the criteria for economic duress in the future.

---

185 [1996] 4 MLJ 331, p.340.
186 [1990] 1 All ER 512.
187 [1980] AC 614, pp. 634–635; *Williams v Roffey Bros and Nicholls (Contractors) Ltd* [1990] 1 All ER 512, p. 521.
188 [2013] WASCA 36.
189 Ibid, para [53].

**10.123** Another possibility is to consider the principle of proportionality. The principle of proportionality has been widely used in the realm of administrative law as well as the European Convention on Human Rights. Under the respective legal frameworks, the proportionality principle provides that an entity with authority can do no more than necessary to achieve a legitimate aim that the entity is empowered to achieve.[190] Within the context of judicial review, in the UK, proportionality is largely used to decide whether an authority exercising power conferred by an Act of Parliament has done an act which is 'unnecessary' to achieve a legitimate aim and has as a result breached fundamental human rights. Hillaire Barnett observes that the doctrine limits the use of power to an act that is 'proportional to the objective pursued'.[191] Lord Ackner sums up the principle in *ex parte Brind*,[192] in the form of a question when he asked, 'Has the Secretary of State used a sledgehammer to crack a nut?'.

**10.124** The principle of proportionality is also found in Australian administrative law. In *Freitas v Permanent Secretary of Ministry of Agriculture, Fisheries, Lands and Housing*,[193] the court held that while legislation can be used to limit fundamental rights in order to achieve a specific legislative objective. However, the public authority must ensure the measures taken to achieve that objective should not go beyond the ambit of achieving the objective concerned. For example, freedom of speech could be limited by a legislation for the specific purpose of preventing hate speech. However, it would be wrong for a public authority to arrest everyone who has a negative view about a particular religion. They would have to first determine whether that view has fulfilled the elements of the crime provided by legislation. In Malaysia, the Federal Court considered the principle of proportionality in *Alma Nudo Atenza v Public Prosecutor*.[194] The issue of proportionality was considered from the perspective of Article 8, Malaysian Federal Constitution, which provides for equality before the law. In essence, the court explained that the principle of proportionality requires state action to be proportionate to the legislative aim, which is to say, state measures must do no more than necessary to achieve the aim. If the measure goes beyond that which necessary, the measure could be deemed disproportionate to the aim. In most cases where a measure is not proportionate to the legitimate aim, the consequence of the act by the authority would be set aside or quashed. There could be in some instances a claim for damages, but this would likely be rare.

**10.125** There are stark similarities between economic duress and circumstances where the principle of proportionality applies. First, an authority with power to achieve a legislative aim is in a similar position to a party in dominant or superior bargaining power in contract from a relational perspective to the

---

190 Barnett H, *Constitutional and Administrative Law* (Routledge 2013), p. 61.
191 Ibid, p. 616.
192 *R v Secretary of State for the Home Department, ex p Brind* [1991] 1 AC 696.
193 [1999] 1 AC 69.
194 [2019] 4 MLJ 1.

party who must submit to the decision of the authority or demands of the dominant party in the contract. Second, the party subject to the decision or demand, may have no choice or rather lack practical choice in the way the decision or demand affects them. Third, in both circumstances, the act is lawful because it is supported by law that provides the power or right in the circumstances. Fourth, in both cases, the courts do not question whether the party exercising the right or power has the right or power in question. Since the existence of the legal right is accepted in law to exist, the issue before the courts is whether the demand made in the circumstances is proportionate to the aim of exercising the right concerned.

**10.126** For example, in the context of economic duress, it would not be disputed whether a party has the right to threaten breach if the law permits (i.e. the conditions surrounding making such a threat is allowed by law). But rather the courts may question the timing of the threat in light of other options available. If there are other options available which are practical and which do not lead to pressuring the other party to accept, it is possible to argue that the pressure was disproportionate in the circumstances. If so, it could provide a neater justification for economic duress.

**10.127** Taking such an approach duly removes economic duress from the realm of illegitimate pressure and places it within the context of disproportionate pressure. It does not force the judge to make a value judgment about whether the conduct of the party making the demands is good or bad or morally apprehensible. It is considering the options available and determining whether the party in dominant position or superior bargaining power had 'used a sledgehammer to crack a nut'. It also places a burden on the party exerting pressure to explain why other options which were least extortive were not considered or taken in the circumstances. However, the idea requires further study and exploration. First, a parallel must be drawn between the legal frameworks in which proportionality applies and, second, the modifications to the principle must be considered for it to apply well within the context of economic duress. Therefore it so appears, that for the doctrine to apply more widely than it does today, the perspective has to change from illegitimate pressure to something else, be it unconscionability (as Australia has done), 'arms-length principle' or disproportionate pressure (under principle of proportionality).

## CHAPTER 11

# The validity of choice of court agreements in international commercial contracts under the Hague Choice of Court Convention and the Brussels Ia Regulation

*Mukarrum Ahmed\**

## Introduction

**11.1** This chapter will examine the validity of choice of court agreements in international commercial contracts under the Brussels Ia Regulation[1] and the Hague Convention on Choice of Court Agreements (Hague Convention).[2] The central concern of this book is how the law of contract will develop in the years ahead. In this context, choice of court agreements give rise to issues of validity and capacity that require the application of the contract law of a state. In the future, the scope and substance of the choice of law rule governing the substantive validity and/or capacity to enter into a choice of court agreement will be tested before the courts. A wide and independent notion of consent may emerge globally together with a simplified criterion for determining the formal validity of a choice of court agreement. Ultimately, in more doubtful penumbral cases, the advantages of an autonomous approach under the relevant instrument itself

* The author wishes to thank Professor Michael Furmston for his comments on a draft version of this chapter. Email: m.ahmed25@lancaster.ac.uk ORCID: 0000-0002-5451-9348.

1 Council Regulation (EU) 1215/2012 of the European Parliament and of the Council of 12 December 2012 on jurisdiction and the recognition and enforcement of judgments in civil and commercial matters (recast) [2012] OJ L351/1 ('Brussels Ia Regulation'). See, generally, A Briggs, *Private International Law in English Courts* (Oxford University Press 2014); A Dickinson and E Lein (eds), *The Brussels I Regulation Recast* (Oxford University Press 2015); R Fentiman, *International Commercial Litigation*, 2nd edn (Oxford University Press 2015); TC Hartley, *Civil Jurisdiction and Judgments in Europe* (Oxford University Press 2017); M Ahmed, *The Nature and Enforcement of Choice of Court Agreements* (Hart Publishing 2017).

2 Concluded at the 20th Session of the Hague Conference on Private International Law, The Hague, 30 June 2005. See, generally, Permanent Bureau of the Conference, *Convention of 30 June 2005 on Choice of Court Agreements: Text and Explanatory Report by Trevor Hartley and Masato Dogauchi* (HCCH Publications 2013), available at www.hcch.net/upload/expl37final.pdf (accessed 22 May 2019); RA Brand and PM Herrup, *The 2005 Hague Convention on Choice of Court Agreements* (Cambridge University Press 2008); TC Hartley, *Choice of Court Agreements under the European and International Instruments* (Oxford University Press 2013); Ahmed (n 1).

may have to be balanced against applying the choice of law rule which refers a matter to the contract law of a state.

**11.2** The Brussels Ia Regulation is the European Union (EU) regime governing jurisdiction and the recognition and enforcement of judgments in civil and commercial matters that applies from 10 January 2015 to legal proceedings instituted and to judgments rendered on or after that date.[3] The Hague Convention is an emerging international commercial litigation regime, which enforces exclusive choice of court agreements at both the jurisdictional and recognition and enforcement stages. On 1 October 2015, the Hague Convention entered into force in 28 Contracting States, including Mexico and all the Member States of the EU, except Denmark.[4] Singapore ratified the Hague Convention on 2 June 2016 and the Convention applies between Singapore and the other Contracting States from 1 October 2016.[5] The Convention has recently entered into force in Montenegro and Denmark on 1 August 2018 and 1 September 2018 respectively.[6] Post-Brexit, it is likely that the Hague Convention will become a far more significant instrument because it may regulate the enforcement of exclusive choice of court agreements in the future civil judicial relationship between the UK and the EU.[7]

**11.3** It will be argued that the significant lessons learnt from the jurisprudence on choice of court agreements under the EU's Brussels Ia Regulation and its predecessor instruments should not be ignored. Hence, the case law on the Brussels Ia Regulation will serve as a guide when navigating the provisions on the validity of choice of court agreements under the Hague Convention.

**11.4** The chapter will commence by introducing the concept, scope and key provisions of the emergent Hague Convention. This will be followed by an overview of the juridical nature and anatomy of choice of court agreements, which will help contextualise our discussion of the validity of choice of court

---

3 Article 81 of the Brussels Ia Regulation.

4 On 4 December 2014, the Council adopted the decision to approve the Hague Convention on behalf of the European Union (2014/887/EU, [2014] OJ L353/5) after the European Parliament gave its consent to the approval of the Hague Convention by legislative resolution of 25 November 2014 ([2016] OJ C289/78). The Civil Jurisdiction and Judgments (Hague Convention on Choice of Court Agreements 2005) Regulations 2015, SI 2015/1644, have brought the Hague Convention into force in the UK.

5 See A Chong and M Yip, 'Singapore As a Centre for International Commercial Litigation: Party Autonomy to the Fore' (2019) 15 *Journal of Private International Law* 97. In *Ermgassen v Sixcap Financials* [2018] SGHCR 8, the Singapore High Court became the first court to recognise and enforce a judgment under the Hague Convention.

6 See the Hague Conference on Private International law website for the status table in relation to the Convention, available at www.hcch.net/en/instruments/conventions/status-table/?cid=98 (accessed 22 May 2019).

7 See M Ahmed, 'BREXIT and English Jurisdiction Agreements: The Post-Referendum Legal Landscape' (2016) 27 *European Business Law Review* 989, 994–997; G Rühl, 'Judicial Cooperation in Civil and Commercial Matters After Brexit: Which Way Forward?' (2018) 67 *International and Comparative Law Quarterly* 99, 127.

agreements. An assessment of the formal validity of choice of court agreements will reveal that contrary to the CJEU's early and restrictive jurisprudence on the writing requirement for choice of court agreements, the prevailing academic view does not support a strict interpretation of the formal requirements in Article 3(c) of the Hague Convention. Moreover, it will be observed that Article 25(1)(a) of Brussels Ia is capable of subsuming the other formal requirements in Articles 25(1)(b)–(c) and Article 3(c) of the Hague Convention correctly jettisons these other formal requirements. An independent concept of consent distinct from the substantive validity of a choice of court agreement has developed under Article 25 of the Brussels Ia Regulation. It will be argued that a wide and independent notion of consent should also be applied in the context of the Hague Convention. This approach will ensure consistency and coherence of the Hague Convention with the Brussels I regime's existing jurisprudence. Significantly, it will reduce the need to rely on the choice of law rule governing the substantive validity of choice of court agreements, which refers to the law of the chosen forum including its private international law rules. The reference to the private international law rules of the chosen forum indicates that *renvoi* is permitted even though the EU choice of law Regulations on contractual and non-contractual obligations expressly forbid *renvoi*. It will be observed that the unilateral national private international law rules of the Member States and Contracting States will act as an impediment to the sound operation of the choice of law rule as the harmonised Rome I Regulation is inapplicable.[8] Therefore, the choice of law rule on substantive validity may increase the litigation risk in multi-state transactions.[9] The application of the Rome I Regulation will be the optimal solution for the choice of law rule governing substantive validity of choice of court agreements in the Brussels Ia Regulation and the Hague Convention. The choice of law rule on substantive validity should only be relied upon where there is a defect of consent (fraud, misrepresentation, duress or mistake), lack of authority or lack of capacity. Moreover, the need to rely on the choice of law rule governing substantive validity is alleviated because the technique of severability insulates the choice of court agreement by ensuring that only a specific attack on the validity of a choice of court clause will be assailable.

## Concept, scope and key provisions of the Hague Convention

**11.5** This section explains the concept and general scope of the Hague Convention, prior to presenting an outline of its key provisions.

---

8 Regulation (EC) No 593/2008 of the European Parliament and of the Council of 17 June 2008 on the law applicable to contractual obligations (Rome I) OJ L/2008/177/6 ('Rome I Regulation'). Post-Brexit, the UK government intends to retain the Rome I Regulation unilaterally by incorporating it into domestic law. See Rühl (n 7) 123–124.

9 See Fentiman (n 1) Chapter 1, for a definition of 'litigation risk' in multi-state transactions.

## Concept

**11.6** The Hague Convention is designed to create a mandatory international legal regime for the enforcement of exclusive choice of court agreements in commercial transactions and the recognition and enforcement of judgments resulting from proceedings based on such agreements. The Hague Convention operates in parallel with the very successful 1958 New York Convention on the Recognition and Enforcement of Foreign Arbitral Awards.[10] The choice of court agreement provisions in the Brussels Ia Regulation have been aligned with the Hague Convention in order to ensure better coordination and to secure the consistent enforcement of choice of court agreements both within the EU and globally.[11] The rules coordinating conflicts between the private international law regimes of the Hague Convention and the Brussels Ia Regulation form part of an increasingly multi-layered, multilateral and multi-speed regional and international legal order. According to the Hague Convention, the Convention will take precedence over the Brussels Ia Regulation if there is an actual incompatibility between the two instruments but excluding the situations where the parties reside exclusively within EU Member States and where recognition or enforcement of a judgment by an EU court is being sought within the EU.[12]

## Scope

**11.7** The Hague Convention applies to exclusive choice of court agreements in international cases in civil and commercial matters.[13] Consumer and employment contracts are excluded from the scope of the Hague Convention.[14] Together with further exclusions under Article 2(2), this leads to the result that the Hague Convention primarily applies in 'business to business' commercial cases. The Hague Convention only applies in international cases. The definition of what is an international case differs between jurisdictional issues (Chapter II) and

---

10 United Nations Convention on the Recognition and Enforcement of Foreign Arbitral Awards, 10 June 1958, 330 UNTS 4739 ('New York Convention'). Cf R Garnett, 'The Hague Choice of Court Convention: Magnum Opus or Much Ado about Nothing?' (2009) 5 *Journal of Private International Law* 161, 171–173, doubts whether the Hague Convention is a true litigation counterpart of the New York Convention. This may be attributed to the presence of a wider range of excluded subject matter under Article 2 compared to international arbitration, the potentially wider defences to enforcement of agreements (particularly the 'manifest injustice' ground) and the scope for Contracting States to remove certain areas from the Convention under Article 21. Moreover, international arbitration offers advantages to parties relating to the process itself including neutrality, judicial support and arbitral institutions of the seat of arbitration, procedural flexibility, privacy and confidentiality.

11 B Hess, T Pfeiffer and P Schlosser, 'Report on the Application of Regulation Brussels I in the Member States' (Study JLS/C4/2005/03, September 2007) ('Heidelberg Report') [338]–[344], [390], 95–97, 112.

12 Article 26(6) of the Hague Convention; Hartley and Dogauchi (n 2) [267]; Hartley, *Choice of Court Agreements* (n 2) Chapter 6, 121–126.

13 Article 1(1) of the Hague Convention; see Brand and Herrup (n 2) Chapter 4.

14 Article 2(1) of the Hague Convention.

recognition and enforcement issues (Chapter III). For the Hague Convention's jurisdictional rules to apply, a case is international unless the parties are resident in the same Contracting State and the relationship of the parties and all other elements relevant to the dispute, regardless of the location of the chosen court, are connected only with that State.[15] For the purposes of obtaining the recognition and enforcement of a judgment in a Contracting State, it is sufficient that the judgment presented is foreign.[16]

*Key provisions*

**11.8** The basic principles of the Hague Convention can be outlined in a few sentences.[17] The chosen court in an exclusive choice of court agreement shall have jurisdiction to decide a dispute which falls within its purview, unless the agreement is null and void under the law of that state.[18] Any court other than the chosen court shall suspend or dismiss proceedings to which an exclusive choice of court agreement applies.[19] A judgment given by a chosen court shall be recognized and enforced in other Contracting States and recognition and enforcement may be refused only on the grounds specified in the Hague Convention.[20] Article 22 provides an optional fourth basic rule allowing each Contracting State the opportunity to declare that, on the basis of reciprocity, its courts will recognize and enforce judgments given by courts of other Contracting States designated in a non-exclusive choice of court agreement.[21] Article 22 is based on the assumption that some Contracting States may opt for enhanced judicial cooperation beyond the minimum mandatory framework of the Hague Convention.

**11.9** A court designated by a choice of court agreement has no power under the Hague Convention to stay its proceedings on *forum non conveniens* grounds or to stay its proceedings on the basis of the *lis alibi pendens* doctrine.[22] This should be interpreted as the conferral of a right on the parties to invoke the jurisdiction of the chosen court. However, in relation to non-international cases, Article 19 of the Hague Convention allows a Contracting State to declare that its courts will not exercise jurisdiction when, except for the location of the chosen court, there is no connection between that State and

---

15  Article 1(2) of the Hague Convention.

16  Article 1(3) of the Hague Convention.

17  Hartley, *Choice of Court Agreements* (n 2) Chapter 1, 21–22; Brand and Herrup (n 2) Chapter 2, 11–14; Hartley and Dogauchi (n 2) [1].

18  Article 5 of the Hague Convention.

19  Article 6 of the Hague Convention.

20  Article 8 of the Hague Convention.

21  Article 22 of the Hague Convention.

22  Article 5(2) of the Hague Convention; see Brand and Herrup (n 2) Chapter 5, 82–84; RA Brand and SR Jablonski, *Forum Non Conveniens: History, Global Practice, and Future Under the Hague Convention on Choice of Court Agreements* (Oxford University Press 2007) Chapter 9, 208.

the parties or the dispute. Thus, if a declaration pursuant to Article 19 has been made, the possibility of declining jurisdiction effectively trumps the rule in Article 5(2).[23]

## The nature and anatomy of choice of court agreements

**11.10** The substantive and procedural aspects of a choice of court agreement warrant the classification of a 'hybrid' contract.[24] The dual nature of the choice of court agreement is manifested both as a private law contract and via the clause's procedural (jurisdictional) effects. The applicable law of a choice of court agreement reflects this dual classification.

**11.11** Issues of interpretation, formal and substantive validity and enforceability represent the anatomy of a choice of court agreement. There are two distinct aspects of interpretation: whether the clause is 'exclusive' or 'nonexclusive' and whether the scope of the clause applies to the claims raised by the claimant in the proceedings.[25] Formal validity is regulated by the instrument itself (i.e. Hague Convention or the Brussels Ia Regulation), which provides uniform and autonomous rules, whereas substantive validity is subject to the law of the chosen forum including its private international law rules. The enforcement of choice of court agreements is governed by the autonomous rules of the instruments.[26] Under the English common law regime and to the extent permitted by the autonomous system of the instruments,[27] anti-suit injunctions, actions for damages and anti-enforcement injunctions may enforce the breach of a choice of

---

23 Brand and Herrup (n 2) Chapter 5, 84; P Beaumont, 'Hague Choice of Court Agreements Convention 2005: Background, Negotiations, Analysis and Current Status' (2009) 5 *Journal of Private International Law* 125, 149. No party to the Convention has made the Article 19 declaration so far.

24 Ahmed, *Nature and Enforcement of Choice of Court Agreements* (n 1) 37; See also Hartley, *Choice of Court Agreements* (n 2) 4–6, 129–130; B Hess, 'The Draft Hague Convention on Choice of Court Agreements, External Competencies of the European Union and Recent Case Law of the European Court of Justice' in A Nuyts and N Watté (eds), *International Civil Litigation in Europe and Relations with Third States* (Bruylant 2005) 263, 271; Hartley, *Civil Jurisdiction and Judgments in Europe* (n 1) 227.

25 Article 25(1) of Brussels Ia provides an autonomous presumption that the choice of court agreement shall be exclusive unless the parties have agreed otherwise. Cf Article 3(b) of the Hague Convention. In relation to the scope of the clause, the CJEU has confirmed that questions of interpretation are a matter for Member State courts and the applicable national law: See *infra* n 66.

26 Article 31(2) of the Brussels Ia Regulation; Articles 5 and 6 of the Hague Convention.

27 In Case C-159/02 *Turner v Grovit* [2005] ECR I-3565 and Case C-185/07 *Allianz SpA v West Tankers Inc* [2009] 1 Lloyd's Rep 413, the CJEU has held that the legal technique used by the English courts to prevent a party from commencing or continuing proceedings in breach of a jurisdiction or arbitration agreement, the anti-suit injunction, could not be granted in circumstances in which the foreign proceedings are before the courts of another EU Member State and are within the scope of the Brussels I Regulation. See M Ahmed, 'The Enforcement of Settlement and Jurisdiction Agreements and Parallel Proceedings in the European Union: *The Alexandros T* Litigation in the English Courts' (2015) 11 *Journal of Private International Law* 406, 412–415.

court agreement.[28] A stay of proceedings may be granted where a foreign choice of court agreement has been breached by contrary proceedings in the forum.[29] The law of the forum governs remedies for breach of choice of court agreements in the English common law regime.[30]

**11.12** This map of related issues has provided context to our discussion of the validity of choice of court agreements under the Hague Convention and the Brussels Ia Regulation.

## Formal validity and consent in choice of court agreements

**11.13** Both the Brussels Ia Regulation and the Hague Convention prescribe formal requirements that must be satisfied if the choice of court agreement is to be considered valid. Consent is also a necessary requirement for the validity of a choice of court clause.[31] Although formal validity and consent are independent concepts, the two requirements are connected because the very purpose of the formal requirements is to guarantee the existence of consent.[32] If the formal requirements are met, this may be taken to constitute the existence of consent. Alternatively, if the requirements of form are not satisfied, the court may find that there was an absence of consent.

**11.14** The CJEU has referred to the close relationship between formal validity and consent in a number of its decisions. The court has made the validity of a choice of court agreement subject to an 'agreement' between the parties.[33] The Brussels Ia Regulation imposes upon the Member State court the duty of examining whether the clause conferring jurisdiction was in fact the subject of consensus between the parties, which must be clearly and precisely demonstrated.[34] The court has also stated that the very purpose of the formal requirements

---

28 M Ahmed and P Beaumont, 'Exclusive Choice of Court Agreements: Some Issues on the Hague Convention on Choice of Court Agreements and its Relationship with the Brussels I Recast Especially Anti-Suit Injunctions, Concurrent Proceedings and the Implications of BREXIT' (2017) 13 *Journal of Private International Law* 386, 394–408.

29 Ahmed, *Nature and Enforcement of Choice of Court Agreements* (n 1) 2.

30 Cf A Briggs, 'The Unrestrained Reach of an Anti-Suit Injunction: A Pause for Thought' [1997] *Lloyd's Maritime and Commercial Law Quarterly* 90; C Sim, 'Choice of Law and Anti-Suit Injunctions: Relocating Comity' (2013) 62 *International and Comparative Law Quarterly* 703.

31 Case C-322/14 *Jaouad El Majdoub v CarsOnTheWeb.Deutschland GmbH* ECLI:EU:C:2015:334, [26]; Case C-543/10 *Refcomp SpA v Axa Corporate Solutions Assurance SA and Others* ECLI:EU:C:2013:62, [26].

32 *Jaouad El Majdoub* (n 31) [30]; *Refcomp* (n 31) [28].

33 Case C-387/98 *Coreck Maritime GmbH v Handelsveem BV and Others* ECLI:EU:C:2000:606, [13]; Case C-24/76 *Estasis Salotti di Colzani Aimo e Gianmario Colzani s.n.c. v Rüwa Polstereimaschinen GmbH* ECLI:EU:C:1976:177, [7]; Case C-25/76 *Galeries Segoura SPRL v Société Rahim Bonakdarian* ECLI:EU:C:1976:178, [6]; Case C-106/95 *Mainschiffahrts-Genossenschaft eG (MSG) v Les Gravières Rhénanes SARL* ECLI:EU:C:1997:70, [15].

34 Ibid.

imposed by Article 17[35] (now Article 25 of Brussels Ia) is to ensure that consensus between the parties is in fact established.[36]

**11.15** Article 25(1) of the Brussels Ia Regulation allows the parties to agree upon conferring jurisdiction on a Member State court subject to the agreement satisfying the formal validity requirements. The formal validity requirements for choice of court agreements under the Brussels Ia Regulation have evolved over time into their current state.[37] The choice of court agreement must be either:[38]

1. in writing or evidenced in writing;[39]
2. in a form which accords with practices which the parties have established between themselves; or
3. in international trade or commerce, in a form which accords with a usage of which the parties are or ought to have been aware and which in such trade or commerce is widely known to, and regularly observed by, parties to contracts of the type involved in the particular trade or commerce concerned.

**11.16** A party seeking to rely on a choice of court agreement must have a 'good arguable case' that Article 25(1) of Brussels Ia Regulation's formal requirements are satisfied.[40] The formal requirements cannot be overridden or amended by the national law of Member States and Member State law cannot prescribe additional requirements of form.[41]

**11.17** In the CJEU's nascent jurisprudence on the Brussels I regime, the requirement that the choice of court agreement be in writing or evidenced in writing was construed strictly. In addition to the designation of a particular Member State court in writing, consent was also required to be in writing. In *Colzani*, the CJEU required that the contract be signed by both parties and should contain an express reference to the general conditions which contained the choice of court

---

35 Article 17 of the 1968 Brussels Convention on jurisdiction and the enforcement of judgments in civil and commercial matters OJ L 299, 31.12.1972, p 32.

36 Case 313/85 *Iveco Fiat v Van Hool* ECLI:EU:C:1986:423, [5].

37 The present version of the text was finalised when Spain and Portugal acceded to the Brussels Convention in 1989. This version of the text was inherited by the Brussels I Regulation (2001) and the Brussels Ia Regulation (2012). See Hartley, *Civil Jurisdiction and Judgments in Europe* (n 1) Chapter 13.

38 Cf For the formal requirements of an arbitration agreement see section 5 of the English Arbitration Act 1996.

39 As per Article 25(2), any communication by electronic means which provides a durable record of the agreement is treated as 'writing'. A 'click wrap' agreement is 'in writing' for the purposes of Article 25 because the text of the terms and conditions containing the choice of court agreement can be printed and saved before the conclusion of the contract: *Jaouad El Majdoub* (n 31); See A Dickinson, "Click Wrapping' Choice of Court Agreements in the Brussels I Regime' [2016] *Lloyd's Maritime and Commercial Law Quarterly* 15.

40 *Bols Distilleries (t/a as Bols Royal Distilleries) v Superior Yacht Services Ltd* [2006] UKPC 45 (Lord Rodger).

41 Case 150/80 *Elefanten Schuh GmbH v Pierre Jacqmain* ECLI:EU:C:1981:148, [26].

agreement in order to ensure that the other party had really consented and had an opportunity to check the clause by exercising reasonable care.[42]

**11.18** In *Segoura*, the parties entered into an oral contract for the sale of goods where the choice of court agreement was not discussed.[43] However, when the goods were delivered, the seller handed the buyer a document which expressly stated on the front that the sale and delivery were subject to the conditions on the reverse. The choice of court agreement was printed on the reverse amongst the conditions. The CJEU ruled that:[44]

> Even if, in an orally concluded contract, the purchaser agrees to abide by the vendor's general conditions, he is not for that reason to be deemed to have agreed to any clause conferring jurisdiction which might appear in those general conditions.

**11.19** The court said that the position would be different if the oral agreement was part of a continuing trading relationship between the parties and the dealings between the parties as a whole were governed by the general conditions of the party giving the confirmation, and these conditions contained a choice of court agreement. Under these circumstances, it would be contrary to good faith for the recipient of the confirmation to deny that he had agreed to the choice of court agreement.[45]

**11.20** Under Article 25(1)(a) of the Brussels Ia Regulation, it is also possible to have an oral agreement 'evidenced in writing'. In *Berghoefer*, the contract contained a choice of court agreement nominating a French court.[46] However, there was a subsequent oral agreement that the chosen court would be in Germany. A written document setting out what had been agreed was received by the other party but there was no response. The CJEU held that there was a choice of court agreement evidenced in writing.[47] The court also held that it was immaterial that the choice of court agreement was in favour of the party providing the written confirmation.[48]

**11.21** *Prima facie*, it might be difficult to reconcile the decisions in *Segoura* with *Berghoefer*. In *Segoura*, the parties had agreed that the contract would be subject to the vendor's general conditions. The general conditions contained the choice of court agreement but there was no express oral agreement in relation to the choice of court clause. The CJEU adjudicated that this was insufficient. On the other hand, in *Berghoefer* there was an express oral agreement about the choice of court agreement. Once this oral agreement was evidenced in writing, the requirements of the Brussels I regime were satisfied.

---

42 *Colzani* (n 33) [9].
43 *Segoura* (n 33).
44 Ibid, [8].
45 Ibid, [11].
46 Case 221/84 *F. Berghoefer GmbH & Co. KG v ASA SA* ECLI:EU:C:1985:337.
47 Ibid, [14].
48 Ibid.

**11.22** It has been argued that the scope of application of the formal requirements in Article 25(1) of the Brussels Ia Regulation overlap.[49] It appears that Article 25(1)(c) covers Article 25(1)(b) as it is applicable where the parties have previously had business relations. As compared to Article 25(1)(a), the other two formal requirements allow oral agreements on jurisdiction. However, oral agreements are less likely to be encountered in international commerce where parties usually provide objective evidence of their contract through writing. Article 25(1)(a) of the Brussels Ia Regulation is capable of subsuming the other formal requirements, because the decision in *Berghoefer* demonstrates that an oral agreement on choice of court can later be evidenced in writing.[50] The reluctance of the delegations to adopt the other two formal requirements in Article 3(c) of the Hague Convention seems justified.[51]

**11.23** Under the Hague Convention, consent is an essential constituent of a choice of court agreement. The autonomous notion of consent applies independently of the law of any Contracting State and is governed by the Convention itself. However, the legal effect of fraud, mistake, duress and other defects of consent is determined by the law of the Contracting State designated in the choice of court agreement including its private international law rules. This follows from the choice of law rule that a choice of court agreement is invalid if it is null and void under the law of the State of the chosen court.[52] The choice of law rule governing material validity cannot encroach on the rules explicitly laid down in the Convention. As a result, the requirement of the Convention that consent must exist cannot be determined by the law of the State of the chosen court.[53] A distinction may therefore be drawn between the factual existence and the substantive validity of a choice of court agreement.

**11.24** Article 3(c) of the Hague Convention lays down the requirements of form for a choice of court agreement. These formal requirements cannot be overridden or amended and no additional formal requirements can be imposed by the law of a Contracting State.[54]

---

49 P Beaumont and B Yüksel, 'The Validity of Choice of Court Agreements under the Brussels I Regulation and the Hague Choice of Court Agreements Convention' in K Boele-Woelki, T Einhorn, D Girsberger and S Symeonides (eds), *Convergence and Divergence in Private International Law: Liber Amicorum Kurt Siehr* (Eleven International Publishing 2010) 563, 571; PR Beaumont and PE McEleavy, *Anton's Private International Law*, 3rd edn (W Green 2011) 248–249.

50 Ibid.

51 See Hartley, *Civil Jurisdiction and Judgments in Europe* (n 1) 264.

52 Articles 5(1), 6(a) and 9(a) of the Hague Convention.

53 Hartley and Dogauchi (n 2) [94]–[96].

54 Ibid, [110].

**11.25** Article 3(c) of the Hague Convention states:

> [A]n exclusive choice of court agreement must be concluded or documented[55] –
> (i) in writing; or
> (ii) by any other means of communication which renders information accessible so as to be usable for subsequent reference.[56]

**11.26** This is different from the equivalent provision in the Brussels Ia Regulation and needs further analysis. The Hartley and Dogauchi Report explains that where the agreement is in writing, its formal validity is not dependent on it being signed.[57] However, the lack of signature might render it more difficult to prove the existence of the agreement.[58] The Hartley and Dogauchi Report also states that if the agreement is oral and one party puts it into writing, it does not matter if he was the one who benefitted from it because the chosen court was in his country.[59]

**11.27** The prevailing academic authority does not support a strict interpretation of the formal requirements in Article 3(c) of the Hague Convention.[60] Therefore, it would be wrong for courts in the EU Member States and the other Contracting States of the Hague Convention to adhere to the strict interpretation originally given by the CJEU to Article 25(1)(a) of the Brussels Ia Regulation in decisions such as *Colzani* and *Segoura*.[61] A choice of court agreement on the reverse of the contract should suffice, if the other party was aware that it should look at the back of the contract. In similar vein, a choice of court agreement in a separate document given to the other party should suffice if it was aware that it should read it. An express oral agreement prior to a written confirmation should not necessarily be required. An objective test of reasonableness should guide the application of the formal validity provision in the Hague Convention.

---

55 Ibid, [113]: The phrase 'evidenced in writing' in Article 25(1)(a) of the Brussels Ia Regulation was replaced with 'documented in writing'.

56 This provision has the same effect as Article 25(2) of the Brussels Ia Regulation. Both provisions are inspired by Article 6(1) of the UNCITRAL Model Law on Electronic Commerce 1996.

57 Hartley and Dogauchi (n 2) [112].

58 Ibid.

59 Ibid, [114].

60 Hartley, *Civil Jurisdiction and Judgments in Europe* (n 1) 265 notes that a more liberal approach is justified in the Hague Convention because only commercial transactions are covered and controversial matters such as carriage of goods by sea are excluded. See also Brand and Herrup (n 2) 46; Beaumont and McEleavy (n 49) 261.

61 See n 33.

## Substantive validity of choice of court agreements

**11.28**  Article 23 of the Brussels I Regulation did not contain an express provision on the substantive validity of a choice of court agreement.[62] The law of some Member States referred substantive validity of a choice of court agreement to the law of the forum whereas other Member States referred it to the applicable law of the substantive contract.[63] However, the Brussels Ia Regulation applies the law of the *forum prorogatum* (chosen forum) including its choice of law rules to the issue of the substantive validity of a choice of court agreement.[64] Under Article 25(1) the elected court shall have jurisdiction 'unless the agreement is null and void as to its substantive validity under the law of that Member State'.[65] The CJEU has confirmed that questions of interpretation are a matter for Member State courts and the applicable national law.[66]

---

62 Council Regulation (EC) 44/2001 on jurisdiction and the recognition and enforcement of judgments in civil and commercial matters (Brussels I) [2001] OJ L12/1. See Beaumont and McEleavy (n 49) Chapter 8, 249–255; ZS Tang, *Jurisdiction and Arbitration Agreements in International Commercial Law* (Routledge 2014) Chapter 2, 22–25. Briggs (n 1) 251–252 terms the reference to the law of the chosen court including its private international law rules to assess matters of substantive validity as 'retrograde'; A Briggs, *Agreements on Jurisdiction and Choice of Law* (Oxford University Press 2008) 257, advances the view that 'Article 23 does not require, and is not necessarily satisfied by, a contractually-binding agreement on jurisdiction'; A Dickinson, 'Surveying the Proposed Brussels I bis Regulation – Solid Foundations but Renovation Needed' (2010) 12 *Yearbook of Private International Law* 247, 301, contends that a solution to the issue is unnecessary and that the CJEU has already achieved a high level of legal certainty by affirming that the consent of the parties is to be determined solely by reference to the requirements of Article 23 of the Brussels I Regulation. Moreover, Dickinson argues that the new provision should not be used by Member State courts to permit a challenge to the validity of choice of court agreements on grounds which the CJEU has interpreted autonomously, i.e. CJEU jurisprudence should not be reversed; L Merrett, 'Article 23 of the Brussels I Regulation: A Comprehensive Code for Jurisdiction Agreements?' (2009) 58 *International and Comparative Law Quarterly* 545 argues that the requirements of Article 23 are both necessary and sufficient conditions for the material validity of jurisdiction agreements in Brussels I Regulation cases and if any other tool is needed to deal with cases where the jurisdiction agreement itself is directly impeached, a Community notion of good faith is the appropriate way to deal with such cases.

63 See *Heidelberg Report* (n 11) [326], 92.

64 Article 25(1) and Recital 20 of the Brussels Ia Regulation. For an early proposal to the same effect under the Brussels Convention, see AG Slynn in Case 150/80 *Elefanten Schuh GmbH v Pierre Jacqmain* ECLI:EU:C:1981:112, 1697–1698; In Case C-222/15 *Hőszig Kft. v Alstom Power Thermal Services* ECLI:EU:C:2016:224, [47], AG Szpunar examined the scope of the *lex fori prorogatum* rule and suggested that the new formulation does not attempt to reverse the CJEU's case law on the autonomous determination of consent. For a similar argument, see U Magnus and P Mankowski (eds), *Brussels Ibis Regulation* (Verlag Dr Otto Schmidt 2016) 628; Dickinson and Lein (n 1) 298.

65 The phrase 'null and void' might be interpreted to exclude 'voidable' acts. A more accurate and specific provision would not limit the choice of law rule on substantive validity to just 'void' choice of court agreements: See U Magnus, 'Choice of Court Agreements in the Review Proposal for the Brussels I Regulation' in E Lein (ed.), *The Brussels I Review Proposal Uncovered* (BIICL 2012) 83, 93. Cf section 9(4) of the English Arbitration Act 1996 and Article II(3) of the New York Convention.

66 Case C-352/13 *Cartel Damage Claims (CDC) Hydrogen Peroxide SA v Evonik Degussa GmbH and Others* ECLI:EU:C:2015:335, [67]; Case C-214/89 *Powell Duffryn plc v Wolfgang Petereit* [1992] ECR I-01745 [36]–[37]; Case C-269/95 *Francesco Benincasa v Dentalkit Srl* [1997] ECR I-03767 [31]; *Roche Products v Provimi* [2003] EWHC 961 (Comm), [81] (Aikens J).

**11.29** There is a contrary indication in the Hartley and Dogauchi Report of the Hague Convention that most 'consent' questions are governed by the choice of law rules established to determine substantive validity and capacity.[67] However, Beaumont has warned us about the dangers in the argument that issues of consent are governed by either 'the law of the forum – including its choice of law rules'[68] or even the law of the chosen forum including its choice of law rules.[69] It should be noted that in both the Brussels Ia Regulation and the Hague Convention, the general principle of consent applies independently of the law of any Member State or Contracting State and follows autonomously from the instrument itself.[70] The Brussels Ia Regulation and the Hague Convention provide a complete system of rules to determine whether there is a choice of court agreement.[71]

**11.30** The policy basis animating the selection of the law of the chosen court including its choice of law rules is to render the Brussels Ia Regulation compatible with the Hague Convention. The wording of the rules for substantive validity for choice of court agreements in both the instruments is almost identical.[72] This has facilitated the approval of the Hague Convention by the EU and ensures the consistent treatment of issues of substantive validity of choice of court agreements under both the Brussels Ia Regulation and under the Hague Convention.

**11.31** The application of 'substantive validity' should be limited to the contractual validity of the choice of court clause and should not extend to its jurisdictional or procedural effects. It is submitted that subjecting the procedural aspects of the choice of court agreement to the choice of law rule for substantive validity will undermine the fundamental structure of both the Hague Convention and the Brussels Ia Regulation. The national law of a Member State or Contracting State should apply to defects of consent that impair or negate the contractual validity of a choice of court agreement. Procedural issues such as whether a valid choice of court agreement may be incorporated into a contract with a weaker party (consumer or employee) is concerned with its jurisdictional effect. A characterisation issue of contemporary practical relevance relates to whether the perceived incompatibility of asymmetric choice of court agreements with the Brussels Ia Regulation is subject to the choice of law rule regulating substantive validity or the autonomous procedural effect of a choice

---

67 Hartley and Dogauchi (n 2) [94]–[96].

68 Brand and Herrup (n 2) 79. Cf RA Brand, 'The Evolving Private International Law/Private Law Overlap in the European Union' in P Mankowski and W Wurmnest (eds), *Festschrift für Ulrich Magnus* (Dr Otto Schmidt 2014) 371.

69 Beaumont (n 23) 139.

70 Hartley, *Choice of Court Agreements* (n 2) 133; Beaumont (n 23) 139.

71 For the Brussels Ia Regulation, see *Refcomp* (n 31) [21]; Case C-222/15 *Hőszig Kft. v Alstom Power Thermal Services* ECLI:EU:C:2016:525 [29].

72 Article 25(1) of the Brussels Ia Regulation; Article 5(1) of the Hague Convention.

of court agreement.[73] The Hague Convention only applies to exclusive choice of court agreements as opposed to asymmetric choice of court agreements.[74]

**11.32** According to Recital 20 of the Brussels Ia Regulation the reference to the nominated court's law includes both its substantive law and its choice of law rules. Therefore it is clear that the inclusion of *renvoi* within Article 25 is intended and the question whether a choice of court agreement is materially valid is therefore to be ascertained under the substantive law to which the choice of law rules of the Member State of the chosen court refer.[75]

**11.33** Some commentators have questioned whether *renvoi* should be applied in determining the substantive validity of a choice of court agreement.[76] They argue that contractual relations governed by party autonomy should exclude *renvoi* from the application of choice of law rules.[77] The exclusion of *renvoi* from the choice of law regimes of the Rome I[78] and Rome II[79] Regulations is evidence that certainty and predictability may be compromised by the application of *renvoi*. Moreover, the unilateral national private international law rules of the Member States may act as an impediment to the sound operation of the choice of law rule as the harmonised Rome I Regulation is inapplicable. It is argued that the choice of law rule on substantive validity may increase litigation risk in multi-state transactions and should only be relied upon where there is a defect of consent (fraud, misrepresentation, duress or mistake), lack of authority or lack of capacity.[80] It should not extend to issues of contractual enforceability that are extrinsic to the consent or capacity of the parties, such as illegality or public policy.[81]

---

73 M Ahmed, 'The Legal Regulation and Enforcement of Asymmetric Jurisdiction Agreements in the European Union' (2017) 28 *European Business Law Review* 403, 412–413; L Merrett, 'The Future Enforcement of Asymmetric Jurisdiction Agreements' (2018) 67 *International and Comparative Law Quarterly* 37, 51; Fentiman (n 1) 82; Hartley, *Civil Jurisdiction and Judgments in Europe* (n 1) 265; J Strnad, 'Determining the Existence of Consent for Choice-of-Court Agreements under the Brussels I-bis Regulation' (2014) 14 *The European Legal Forum* 113, 117–118.

74 Article 3(a) of the Hague Convention; Minutes No. 3 of the Twentieth Session, Commission II, [2]–[11]; Hartley and Dogauchi (n 2) [106]; See Ahmed, *Nature and Enforcement of Choice of Court Agreements* (n 1) 231. Cf Merrett (n 73) 58.

75 For a discussion of *renvoi*, see L Collins and others (eds), *Dicey, Morris and Collins on the Conflict of Laws* (Sweet & Maxwell 2012) Chapter 4; JJ Fawcett and JM Carruthers, *Cheshire, North and Fawcett: Private International Law* (Oxford University Press 2008) Chapter 5; Beaumont and McEleavy (n 49) Chapter 4, 100–109.

76 B Hess, 'The Brussels I Regulation: Recent Case Law of the Court of Justice and the Commission's Proposed Recast' (2012) 49 *Common Market Law Review* 1075, 1107; P Hay, 'Notes on the European Union's Brussels-I 'Recast' Regulation' (2013) 13 *The European Legal Forum* 1, 3; K Takahashi, 'Damages for Breach of a Choice of Court Agreement: Remaining Issues' [2009] *Yearbook of Private International Law* 73, 85; Briggs (n 1) 252.

77 PE Nygh, *Autonomy in International Contracts* (Oxford University Press 1999) 83–84.

78 Article 20 of the Rome I Regulation.

79 Article 24 of Regulation 864/2007 EC on the law applicable to non-contractual obligations [2007] OJ L199/40 ('Rome II Regulation').

80 Dickinson and Lein (n 1) 297; Magnus and Mankowski (n 64) 630; See also Merrett (n 73) 51.

81 Ibid.

**11.34** However, in some cases it may be unreasonable to apply the substantive law of the *forum prorogatum* to the issue of capacity.[82] The forum chosen by the parties is often due to its neutrality and efficient dispute resolution and the chosen forum may have a tenuous connection with the actual dispute. In such cases it may be preferable to apply the choice of law rules of the chosen forum to determine the capacity of a party to enter into a choice of court agreement. The application of *renvoi* in these cases will lead to the application of a law closely connected to the dispute. In similar vein, where the parties have made a choice of law agreement that differs from the substantive law usually applied before the *forum prorogatum*, *renvoi* to the chosen law should be applied in deference to the principle of party autonomy.[83] In the absence of an express choice of law agreement, the court will have to determine the law applicable to the substantive validity of the choice of court agreement.[84] In this regard, a forum where a choice of court agreement is a strong indication of implied choice of law of the chosen court will be at an advantage compared to a forum where a choice of court agreement is just one of the factors that could determine whether a choice of law has been clearly demonstrated.[85]

**11.35** On the other hand, in the case of other defects of consent, it is not clear how *renvoi* can help in determining the substantive validity of a choice of court agreement. The substantive law of the chosen court may provide an appropriate legal regime to govern such issues, making a reference to the choice of law rules of the chosen court unnecessary. The factors pointing away from the law of the *forum prorogatum* in issues of capacity may not exert the same pull in relation to the other defects of consent. Indeed, the law of a neutral forum may negative any advantage available under a law closely connected to the dispute such as the applicable law of the underlying contract. The doctrines of severability[86] and *Dépeçage*[87] allow the choice of court agreement to be governed by a law separate from the law governing the underlying contract. In fact, a separate law governing the choice of court agreement may ensure the continued validity of such agreements where the entire contract is impeached.

**11.36** Difficult issues of proof of foreign law arise with the application of the doctrine of *renvoi*. Unlike civil law legal systems, foreign law is a question of fact in the English common law.[88] Therefore, the party relying on foreign law is

---

82 T Ratković and Rotar D Zgrabljić, 'Choice-of-Court Agreements under the Brussels I Regulation (Recast)' (2013) 9 *Journal of Private International Law* 245, 258.

83 Beaumont and McEleavy (n 49) Chapter 8, 254–55; See generally M Ahmed, 'The Nature and Enforcement of Choice of Law Agreements' (2018) 14 *Journal of Private International Law* 500.

84 Beaumont and Yüksel (n 49) 576.

85 Recital 12 of the Rome I Regulation. See Briggs (n 1) 541.

86 Article 25(5) of the Brussels Ia Regulation; Article 3(d) of the Hague Convention.

87 See '*Dépeçage*' ('Splitting the applicable law'); see Article 3(1) of the Rome I Regulation and the Rome Convention; Collins (n 75) Chapter 32, 1789–1792; Beaumont and McEleavy (n 49) Chapter 10, 454–455.

88 A Briggs, *The Conflict of Laws*, 3rd edn (Oxford University Press 2013) Chapter 1, 7–13.

required to plead and prove the content of foreign law.[89] When applying the doctrine of *renvoi*, evidence of the foreign rules on *renvoi* and foreign choice of law rules have to be pleaded and proved in the English common law courts.[90] In civil law legal systems, evidence of the foreign choice of law rules will suffice for the application of the doctrine of *renvoi*.[91] However, the inherent advantage of the English common law's pragmatic approach to foreign law is that the parties can choose not to rely on the foreign law by not pleading it.[92] English law as the law of the forum is applied instead.[93] Second, the English courts usually apply English law as a default where the content of the foreign law is not proved.[94] An analogy may be drawn between the parties not relying on the foreign law and a delayed choice of English law to govern the dispute.[95] A flexible approach to proof of foreign law in English courts may help the litigants ignore the doctrine of *renvoi* altogether by not pleading and proving the applicable law.

**11.37** The Rome I Regulation does not apply to choice of court agreements.[96] National choice of law rules will govern the issue of the substantive validity of a choice of court agreement.[97] The lack of harmonisation of national choice of law rules may lead to uncertainty in the determination of the applicable law of the choice of court agreement. For instance, in English law the 'proper law' of the choice of court agreement, which is quite often the applicable law of the underlying contract, applies.[98] The proper law is the term which was used at common law to signify the law by which the validity of the contract is tested, and is used in this context to acknowledge that the identification of the law which governs a choice of court agreement is a matter for the common law rules of the conflict of laws.

**11.38** Although the Rome I Regulation excludes choice of court agreements from its scope, it is argued that the analogical application of the choice of law regime by the law of the forum would result in an optimal solution where the same law governs the validity of the choice of court agreement and the underlying

---

89 Ibid.

90 Hartley, *Choice of Court Agreements* (n 2) Chapter 7, 165–167: reference to the 'foreign court' or 'double *renvoi*' or 'total *renvoi*' theory adopted by England and many other common law countries.

91 Ibid: reference to the 'single *renvoi*' theory adopted by France and Germany.

92 Briggs (n 88).

93 Ibid.

94 Ibid.

95 See Article 3(2) of the Rome I Regulation and the Rome Convention; Collins (n 75) Chapter 32, 1805–1806; Beaumont and McEleavy (n 49) Chapter 10, 455–456.

96 Article 1(2)(e) of the Rome I Regulation; Article 1(2)(d) of the Rome Convention; see M Giuliano and P Lagarde, 'Report on the Convention on the Law Applicable to Contractual Obligations' [1980] OJ C282/1, 11–12; Collins (n 75) Chapter 32, 1788; Beaumont and McEleavy (n 49) Chapter 10, 434–439.

97 *Heidelberg Report* (n 11) [326]–[327], 92.

98 Collins (n 75) Chapter 12, 603–604; D Joseph, *Jurisdiction and Arbitration Agreements and their Enforcement* (Sweet & Maxwell 2010) 182; Briggs (n 88) 231; see *Sulamerica CIA Nacional de Seguros SA and others (Sulamérica) v Enesa Engenharia SA and others (Enesa)* [2012] EWCA Civ 638, [2012] 1 All ER (Comm) 795.

contract.[99] In practice, this would secure a uniform standard for the applicable law rules of choice of court agreements. However, the lingering conceptual problem with this solution is that Article 20 of the Rome I Regulation excludes *renvoi* and Article 25 of the Brussels Ia Regulation has created an applicable law rule which permits *renvoi*.[100] The Hague Principles of Choice of Law in International Commercial Contracts do not address the law governing choice of court agreements.[101] However, the widespread adoption and application of the Hague Principles to choice of court agreements will ensure that the autonomy of the parties as to the applicable law of the choice of court agreement is respected globally irrespective of the forum seised.

**11.39** The Hartley and Dogauchi Report elucidates that 'null and void' applies only to substantive grounds of invalidity.[102] The choice of law rule governing substantive validity should only apply to defects of consent (fraud, misrepresentation, duress or mistake). The choice of law rule cannot override or amend the form requirements in Article 3(c) and leaves no room for the national law of a Contracting State to apply to issues of form. This interpretation of the ambit of the choice of law rule regulating substantive validity is in alignment with the position under the Brussels Ia Regulation.

**11.40** The Hartley and Dogachi Report further states that the law of the chosen court includes the choice of law rules of that Contracting State. Therefore, *renvoi* is permitted. It is submitted that that unilateral national choice of law rules that permit *renvoi* may increase the litigation risk in multi-state transactions and should only be relied upon where there is a defect of consent.[103] The choice of law rule should not extend to issues of contractual enforceability that are extrinsic to the consent or capacity of the parties, such as illegality or public policy.[104] The application of the Rome I Regulation to the choice of law rule governing substantive validity in the courts of Member States (who are

---

99  See Dickinson and Lein (n 1) 297; Magnus and Mankowski (n 64) 629; MH Ballesteros, 'The Regime of Party Autonomy in the Brussels I Recast: The Solutions Adopted for Agreements on Jurisdiction' (2014) 10 *Journal of Private International Law* 291, 299–300; See also SP Camilleri, 'Article 23: Formal Validity, Material Validity or Both?' (2011) 7 *Journal of Private International Law* 297, 313–318. Beaumont and Yüksel (n 49) 576 argue that in the absence of an express or implied choice of law, the court's analysis should not extend to the objective applicable law rules and the court should apply the internal law of the chosen court as *renvoi* has to be applied consistently with party autonomy.

100  Ahmed, *Nature and Enforcement of Choice of Court Agreements* (n 1) 219.

101  Article 1(3)(b) and [1.26] of the Hague Choice of Law Principles and Commentary in Permanent Bureau of the Conference, *The Hague Principles on Choice of Law in International Commercial Contracts* (approved on 19 March 2015), available at https://assets.hcch.net/docs/5da3ed47-f54d-4c43-aaef-5eafc7c1f2a1.pdf (accessed 22 May 2019).

102  Hartley and Dogauchi (n 2) [126].

103  C Kessedjian, 'Commentaire de la refonte du règlement n° 44/2001' (2011) 47 *Revue trimestrielle de droit européen* 117, 126–127 has foreseen that the introduction of a choice of law element into the substantive validity of jurisdiction agreements under Article 25 of Brussels Ia will have the knock-on effect of increasing the number of disputes concerning the validity of such agreements.

104  Dickinson and Lein (n 1) 297; Magnus and Mankowski (n 64) 630; See also Merrett (n 73) 51.

also Contracting States) will result in greater certainty by ensuring decisional harmony regardless of forum.

**11.41** The Hague Convention contains a special choice of law rule on capacity to enter into a choice of court agreement. A choice of court agreement is invalid if one of the contracting parties lacked capacity to conclude it by either the law of the chosen court or the law of the forum. As opposed to the Brussels Ia Regulation, under the Hague Convention, capacity is both an element of essential validity and a separate concept.[105] If the chosen court is seised, the choice of law rule for capacity will not engage as the law of the chosen court and the law of the forum are synonymous. However, if a non-chosen court is seised, the issue of capacity of either party to conclude the choice of court agreement will be referred to both the law of the chosen court and the law of the forum. It should be noted that incapacity under the law of the forum includes the choice of law rules of the forum. Therefore, *renvoi* is permitted and the law of the forum may refer the issue of capacity to its internal law, the law of the chosen court or the law of a third state based on the party's domicile or other personal connecting factor.

## Severability of choice of court agreements

**11.42** Article 25(5) of the Brussels Ia Regulation enshrines the technique of severability by providing that a choice of court agreement which forms part of a wider contract must be treated as a separate agreement.[106] Article 3(d) of the Hague Convention contains an almost identical provision on severability.[107] Severability of choice of court agreements was established by the CJEU jurisprudence prior to its explicit provision in the Brussels Ia Regulation.[108] In *Benincasa v Dentalkit*, the CJEU found that a void contract does not render the choice of court agreement void as well.[109]

---

105 Hartley and Dogauchi (n 2) [150] and [184].

106 The legal basis of the technique of severability may be questioned because as a matter of logic a choice of court agreement should be invalid where the entire contract in which it is situated has been invalidated. However, concerns of a pragmatic nature prevent the choice of court agreement from succumbing to the same fate as the rest of the contractual provisions. Cf *infra* n 110. The pragmatic legal basis of severability may be compared with the concept of the putative applicable law (or 'putative proper law') of the contract, which governs the material validity of the contract (Article 10 of the Rome I Regulation). The putative applicable law is the law that would govern the contract in the event that it was valid in the first place. A logical circularity is involved as the concept of the putative applicable law assumes the very validity of the contract, which it is supposed to ascertain.

107 Cf section 7 of the English Arbitration Act 1996. The technique of severability was confirmed in the English common law by *Fiona Trust and Holding Corp v Privalov* [2007] UKHL 40. See Briggs (n 62) Chapter 3.

108 *Powell Duffryn plc v Wolfgang Petereit* (n 66); *Francesco Benincasa v Dentalkit Srl* (n 66); Case C-159/97 *Trasporti Castelletti Spedizioni Internazionali SpA v Hugo Trumpy SpA* [1999] ECR I-01597.

109 *Francesco Benincasa v Dentalkit Srl* (n 66) [24]–[29]. See also *Trasporti Castelletti Spedizioni Internazionali SpA v Hugo Trumpy SpA* (n 108) [34], [49], [51].

**11.43** The technique of severability serves to insulate the choice of court agreement from the invalidity of the underlying contract. A challenge to the validity of the underlying contract will not on its own impugn the validity of the choice of court agreement. However, a specific attack on the validity of the choice of court agreement may impeach it. The doctrines of severability and *Dépeçage* allow the choice of court agreement to be governed by a law separate from the law governing the underlying contract.[110] In fact a separate law governing the choice of court agreement may ensure the continued validity of such agreements where the entire contract is impugned.[111] The principles of party autonomy and legal certainty provide the justification and legal basis for the technique of severability.

**11.44** The practical application of the technique of severability will mean that issues of the substantive validity of a choice of court agreement will only arise where the validity of a choice of court agreement is specifically challenged. Severability therefore acts as a first line of defence by seeking to prevent any question of the substantive validity of the choice of court agreement from arising in the first place.

### Conclusions

**11.45** It has been observed that the dispensation with the additional formal requirements of a choice of court agreement in the Hague Convention is an application of Occam's razor. What emerges is a simple yet justifiable criterion that the choice of court agreement has to be 'in writing or documented in writing'. The CJEU's nascent jurisprudence on choice of court agreements under the Brussels I regime in *Colzani* and *Segoura* narrowly construed the 'in writing or evidenced in writing' formal requirement. It has been argued that Member State courts and the courts of other Contracting States should disregard this strict interpretation when applying Article 3(c) of the Hague Convention. As a result, a choice of court agreement on the reverse of the contract should suffice, if the other party was aware that it should look at the back of the contract. In similar vein, a choice of court agreement in a separate document given to the other party should suffice if it was aware that it should read it. An express oral agreement

---

110 Cf A narrow conception of severability for arbitration agreements finds support in recent English and commonwealth decisions: The implied choice of law for the arbitration agreement is likely to be the same as the expressly chosen law of the underlying contract. See *Sulamérica v Enesa* (n 98) [26]–[27] (Moore-Bick LJ, with whom Hallett LJ agreed); *BCY v BCZ* [2016] SGHC 249, [49] (Steven Chong J) (Singapore High Court); *National Thermal Power Corporation vs Singer Company And Ors* (1993) AIR 998, [1992] SCR (3) 106 (TK Thommen J) (Supreme Court of India). See also R Nazzini, 'The Law Applicable to the Arbitration Agreement' (2016) 65 *International and Comparative Law Quarterly* 681, 687–689.

111 In *Francesco Benincasa v Dentalkit Srl* (n 66), the application of national substantive law to the validity of the choice of court agreement was dismissed in order to protect the entire contract from being void under that law. The CJEU held that the choice of court agreement served a 'procedural purpose' and was governed by the autonomous provisions of the Brussels Convention.

prior to a written confirmation should not necessarily be required. An objective test of reasonableness should guide the application of the formal validity provision in the Hague Convention.

**11.46** An independent concept of consent has developed under Article 25 of the Brussels Ia Regulation and the corresponding provisions of its predecessor instruments. This notion of consent is distinct from substantive validity and is closely linked to the formal requirements of a choice of court agreement. As a matter of procedure, consent is autonomously governed by the relevant instrument. It has been argued that a wide and independent notion of consent should also be applied in the context of the Hague Convention. This approach will ensure consistency and coherence of the Hague Convention with the Brussels I regime's existing jurisprudence.

**11.47** Significantly, it will reduce the need to rely on the choice of law rule governing the substantive validity of choice of court agreements, which refers to the law of the chosen forum including its private international law rules. The reference to the private international law rules of the chosen forum indicates that *renvoi* is permitted even though the EU choice of law Regulations on contractual and non-contractual obligations expressly forbid *renvoi*. It has been noted that the unilateral national choice of law rules of the Member States may act as an impediment to the sound operation of the choice of law rule. The application of the Rome I Regulation will be the optimal solution for the choice of law rule governing substantive validity under the Brussels Ia Regulation and the Hague Convention. Globally, the widespread adoption and application of the Hague Choice of Law Principles to choice of court agreements will ensure that the autonomy of the parties as to the applicable law of the choice of court agreement is honoured regardless of the forum seised. Otherwise, the choice of law rule on substantive validity may increase the litigation risk in multi-state transactions by creating uncertainty and risking decisional harmony. It has been argued that the scope of the choice of law rule on substantive validity should be narrowly interpreted and only be relied upon where there is a defect of consent (fraud, misrepresentation, duress or mistake), lack of authority or lack of capacity. It should not extend to issues of contractual enforceability that are extrinsic to the consent or capacity of the parties, such as illegality or public policy. Moreover, the need to rely on the choice of law rule governing substantive validity is alleviated because the technique of severability insulates the choice of court agreement by ensuring that only a specific attack on the validity of a choice of court clause will be assailable.

**11.48** In the future, the scope and substance of the choice of law rule governing the substantive validity and/or capacity to enter into a choice of court agreement will be tested before the courts. Ultimately, in more doubtful penumbral cases, the advantages of an autonomous approach under the relevant instrument itself may have to be balanced against applying the choice of law rule which refers a matter to the contract law of a state.

## CHAPTER 12

# De-identification of Islamic finance contracts by the common law courts

## Adnan Trakic

## Introduction

**12.1** The Islamic finance contract is a legal instrument used by the contracting parties in the Islamic finance industry to secure their rights and obligations, and also to ensure smooth enforcement in case of default. It facilitates Islamic financial intermediation in the manner allowed by Shari'ah.[1] Elements which are inconsistent with Shari'ah, such as *riba* (interest), *gharar* (excessive risk or uncertainty) and *maysir* (gambling) must be avoided at all costs. Other than this, for the most part, the conventional common law contract structures have been retained by the Islamic finance industry as far as legal requirements pertaining to documentation and enforceability are concerned. In fact, the law that applies to Islamic finance contracts is the same law that applies to conventional contracts.

**12.2** In *Bank Kerjasama Rakyat Malaysia Bhd v Emcee Corporation Sdn Bhd*,[2] Abdul Hamid Mohamad JCA, delivering the judgment of the Court of Appeal, famously said:

> As was mentioned at the beginning of this judgment the facility is an Islamic banking facility. But that does not mean that the law applicable in this application is different from the law that is applicable if the facility were given under conventional banking. The charge is a charge under the National Land Code. The remedy available and sought is a remedy provided by the National Land Code. The procedure is provided by the Code and the Rules of the High Court 1980. The court adjudicating it is the High Court. So, it is the same law that is applicable, the same order that would be, if made, and the same principles that should be applied in deciding the application.[3]

**12.3** The court noticeably declined to accentuate that this is an Islamic finance contract and that, as such, it should be treated differently from a conventional one. Quite contrarily, the court equated the two in terms of the applicable law and

---

1 Literally, the word 'Shari'ah' means 'the way'. Technically, Shari'ah refers to the legal system of Islam. In this chapter, the word Shari'ah is synonymous with 'Islamic law'.
2 [2003] 1 CLJ 625.
3 Ibid, 629.

reinforced that the remedies available for the breach of a conventional finance contract are equally available when the breach occurs in an Islamic finance contract.[4] This judgment is a strong judicial authority which solidifies the relevance of the conventional common law legal principles to Islamic finance contracts.

**12.4** A mere compliance with conventional laws only, however, may not be sufficient to uphold the validity of Islamic finance contracts as they, unlike their conventional counterparts, must also comply with Shari'ah requirements. If the non-compliance with Shari'ah is tolerated, then how different would they be from the conventional contracts? This chapter wishes to ascertain how the courts of two major common law countries, Malaysia and the UK, have dealt with Shari'ah non-compliance in Islamic finance contracts. The chapter is limited to these two jurisdictions because their courts have adjudicated the highest number of Islamic finance disputes. Furthermore, Malaysia has developed a reputation as the world's leader in Islamic finance, while the UK has been the preferred choice of law and forum in cross-border Islamic finance contracts.[5]

**12.5** The courts' approach in adjudicating Islamic finance disputes has been characterized as either non-interventionist or interventionist.[6] The non-interventionist approach concentrates mainly on compliance with conventional laws thereby ignoring the need to comply with Shari'ah. By doing so, the courts effectively convert what was initially a Shari'ah compliant contract into a conventional, Shari'ah non-compliant contract. The interventionist approach, on the other hand, does the opposite but, arguably, with similar results. The court recognizes the Shari'ah non-compliance as an issue and either interprets Shari'ah while not being competent to do so or delegates the task to Shari'ah scholars. As a result, the Shari'ah compliant contract may also become Shari'ah non-compliant through the decision of a judge or Shari'ah scholars. Both approaches may result in de-identification of the Shari'ah underlying nature of Islamic finance contracts. How this de-identification occurs through both court approaches is explained in this chapter.

### Non-interventionist approach to Islamic finance contracts

**12.6** The non-interventionist approach has been adopted by the courts in the UK, as demonstrated in two landmark Islamic finance cases. *Islamic Investment Company of the Gulf (Bahamas) Ltd v Symphony Gems NV and others* is said to

---

4 It needs to be noted that Abdul Hamid Mohamad JCA later on clarified that the judgment needs to be understood in the proper context. The issue raised in this case was conventional, relating to the validity of the charge. A Shari'ah non-compliance, which is termed as a Shari'ah issue, was not raised in this case. For more details, see Tun Abdul Hamid Mohamad and Adnan Trakic, 'The Adjudication of Shari'ah Issues in Islamic Finance Contracts: Guidance from Malaysia' (2015) 26 *Journal of Banking and Finance Law and Practice* 39, 52.

5 See Julio C Colon, 'Choice of Law and Islamic Finance' (2011) 46 *Texas International Law Journal* 411.

6 See Tun Arifin Bin Zakaria, 'A Judicial Perspective on Islamic Finance Litigation in Malaysia' (2013) 21 *IIUM Law Journal* 143, 156.

be the first Islamic finance dispute decided by the English court.[7] The main issue revolved around a proper construction of a *murabahah* (mark-up sale) contract.[8] The financier, seller (Islamic Investment Company), agreed to provide financing to the purchaser (Symphony Gems) under *murabahah* contract for the acquisition of a large quantity of rough diamonds of assorted varieties. The contract specified that the supplier of the diamonds shall be chosen by the purchaser who will then nominate the same to the financier. The funds were released to the supplier after the financier received the instructions from the purchaser. The diamonds, however, were never delivered to the purchaser which led to the purchaser's subsequent default. The financier then applied for a summary judgment against the purchaser who objected on the basis that there were triable issues in this case. One such issue pertained to an alleged incapacity of the financier to enter into Shari'ah non-compliant agreement in the light of its Memorandum and Articles of Association. The court received reports from two expert witnesses who concluded that the *murabahah* agreement did not comply with Shari'ah. The written record of the case does not state the reasons for the non-compliance but it is believed that the contentious parts were the ones which provided that the sale price is payable to the financier irrespective of whether the diamonds have been delivered to the purchaser, and that the financier is free from all risks associated with the diamonds.[9]

**12.7** Tomlinson J, delivering the judgment of the court, made it very clear that even though he had no reason to doubt the experts' assessment on Shari'ah non-compliance, the contract was not governed by Shari'ah but by English law. As the agreement was enforceable under English law, he ignored Shari'ah non-compliance. By doing so, the learned judge did not only undervalue an important aspect of the agreement, but he also effectively converted what was intended to be an Islamic finance contract into a conventional financing agreement. The decision changed the nature of the contract against the original wishes of the parties. It has never been disputed in this case that the intention of the parties had been to have a contract which shall comply with Shari'ah. This is evidenced by the recital, also known as 'purpose clause', in the *murabahah* agreement which the court mentioned but did not consider. The recital provided the following: 'The Purchaser wishes to deal with the Seller for the purpose of purchasing Supplies (as hereinafter defined) under this Agreement *in accordance with Islamic Shariah*'.[10] This was a clear indication of the parties' wishes to conclude the agreement which must comply with Shari'ah. Even without the recital, the

---

7 [2002] All ER (D) 171 (Feb) (*Symphony Gems*).

8 *Murabahah* is a simple arrangement between a financier and a customer who, due to insufficient funds, is unable to acquire an asset that he wishes to own. The financier purchases the asset and then sells it to the customer on a deferred basis for a marked-up price.

9 Clause 4.4 and 5.7 of the agreement. In a Shari'ah complaint *murabahah* agreement, the sale price only becomes due after the asset has been delivered to the purchaser and the risks associated with the asset, while owned by the financier, ought to be borne by the financier and properly insured. For more details, see Hakimah Yaacob, 'A Critical Appraisal of Islamic Finance Cases, and the Way Forward' (2011) ISRA Research Paper No 19, 8.

10 Ibid (emphasis added).

fact that the parties have concluded an agreement which is called *murabahah*, should be evidence in itself that they intended it to comply with Shari'ah.

**12.8** The blame equally lies with the contracting parties for what appears to be a rather poorly drafted *murabahah* agreement. They seemed to have willingly included in the agreement clauses which did not comply with Shari'ah. Moreover, they specifically indicated that the agreement shall be 'governed by, and shall be construed in accordance with, English law ...' and that 'the courts of England shall have exclusive jurisdiction to hear and determine any suit ...'[11] These clauses appear to be the main reason why Tomlinson J refused to adjudicate the Shari'ah issues raised before him. This raises a related question as to what does English law construction of contract entail. Does English law allow the court to ignore what the parties intended at the time of the conclusion of the agreement? Why did the court not consider the recital? It could be because the recital was in conflict with the express terms of the agreement. Perhaps, if the court mentioned this as the reason for ignoring Shari'ah non-compliance, it would be less contentious as it is a trite law that recitals do not override clear provisions of the agreement.[12] The court could have at least acknowledged this and then decided either way.

**12.9** It is also perplexing why did the court accept and analyze the reports of two expert witnesses if their submissions were not to be considered in the first place. Furthermore, if the recital clarified that the agreement shall be based on Shari'ah and, moreover, the agreement was named *murabahah*, why non-compliance with Shari'ah was not considered as a fundamental breach of contract. Therefore, the court's decision to ignore Shari'ah non-compliance with little explanation for doing so resulted in the de-identification of *murabahah* agreement and its effective conversion into a conventional loan agreement.

**12.10** Another Islamic finance case of great significance decided by the English court was *Shamil Bank of Bahrain v Beximco Pharmaceuticals Limited and others*.[13] The claimant, an Islamic financial institution incorporated in Bahrain, entered into *murabahah* financing agreements with the defendants, pharmaceutical companies incorporated in Bangladesh. After they successfully obtained the financing facility, the defendants defaulted on some of the instalments and the parties thereafter agreed to execute 'exchange agreements' in which the defendants transferred to the claimant certain identified assets that the defendants were entitled to use subject to the payment of a user fee in accordance with *ijarah* (leasing). When the defendants defaulted again, the claimant initiated proceedings for summary judgment.

**12.11** The defendants submitted a number of defenses but the main one pertained to an alleged Shari'ah non-compliance of the *murabahah* and *ijarah* agreements. The governing clause of the agreements stated that 'Subject

---

11 Ibid.
12 For legal effects of recitals to a contract, see *Mackenzie v Duke of Devonshire* (1896) AC 400 and *Toomey Motors v Chevrolet* [2017] EWHC 276 (Comm).
13 [2003] EWHC 2118 (Comm) (*Shamil Bank*).

to the principles of Glorious Sharia'a this agreement shall be governed by and construed in accordance with the laws of England'. This clause, the defendants argued, meant that the agreements needed to comply with both Shari'ah and English law. Consequently, as the *murabahah* and *ijarah* agreements did not comply with Shari'ah, they should have been declared as unenforceable. The alleged non-compliance of the *murabahah* agreement was based on the claim that it was used to fund general working capital and not the purchase of specific goods. As for the *ijarah*, the non-compliance allegedly occurred as the claimant did not take the title, or the right of usufruct to the goods purportedly leased. In other words, both *murabahah* and *ijarah* agreements were merely 'a disguise for an otherwise undocumented interest bearing loan'.[14]

**12.12** The claimant opposed the defendants' submissions stating that the words 'Subject to the principles of Glorious Sharia'a' in the governing law clause did not affect the application of English law and the choice of law. Rather, the words implied that the claimant was determined to conduct its affairs in accordance with Shari'ah principles under the supervision of its own Religious Supervisory Board which certified at the end of each year that transactions of the claimant were Shari'ah compliant. Both parties produced expert witnesses who adduced a considerable amount of evidence in support of their claims.

**12.13** Morison J, delivering the judgment, expressed his skepticism about the defendants' objectives noting that 'No "religious" point was made until the defendants were sued'.[15] He called the Shari'ah non-compliance defence 'a lawyers' construct' by which the party at fault wants to evade earlier undertaken contractual obligations.[16] The non-compliance, somehow, only became apparent after the funds were consumed and after the parties defaulted. In the end, Morison J decided not to consider the alleged Shari'ah non-compliance. He said:

> Looking at the background, it seems to me clear that it cannot have been the intention of the parties that it would ask this secular court to determine principles of law derived from religious writings on matters of great controversy.[17]

**12.14** With respect, it is not clear how Morison J could come to this conclusion when the statement in the agreement explicitly stated that '*Subject to the principles of Glorious Sharia'a* this agreement shall be governed by and construed in accordance with the laws of England'. This clause expressly indicated what the intention of the parties was at the time of contracting. The clause

---

14  Ibid, [15].

15  Ibid, [17].

16  Ibid, [40]. This, unfortunately, seems to be the case in many Islamic finance disputes where Shari'ah non-compliance was raised as an issue in adjudication. Until today, there are no reported cases where the party has returned the funds obtained from the financier because of an alleged non-compliance with Shari'ah. Contrary to that, all cases involving Shari'ah non-compliance defence came about as a result of the financiers' attempt to recover the owed sums after the customers' default.

17  Ibid, [36].

showed that the governing law is English law alone. There is no dispute about that as contract can only be governed by a law of a country and not by a non-state law like Shari'ah.[18] But, the clause also showed that the parties intended the court to do exactly what Morison J claimed the parties could not have intended the court to do and, that is, to uphold Shari'ah compliance of the agreement.

**12.15** Furthermore, the court justified its decision by saying:

> The English court, as a secular court, is not suited to ascertain and determine highly controversial principles of a religious based law and it is unlikely that the parties would be satisfied by any such ruling; that is not what they were wanting by their choice of law clause.[19]

**12.16** It is true that the alleged Shari'ah non-compliance issue was and still remains debatable. The conflicting views of the experts in this case also showed that the issue was controversial. However, a controversy and conflicting views is not something unique to a religious-based law. Morison J could have done what the English court normally does when faced with issues related to a foreign law. This is where expert opinions are particularly useful. Surely, both parties may appoint experts who are likely to adduce evidence in their favour. But, a thorough and careful cross-examination of experts' views should help the court to decide whose evidence is more credible. The court's own additional research on the matter, if necessary, can also be done. As a result, if the decision of the court is controversial and, in the opinion of Shari'ah scholars, wrong, the parties may appeal and the Appellate Court could correct it at a later stage. The due judicial process should determine the issues, regardless of whether they are Shari'ah or conventional. Ignoring them or simply saying that that the court is not a proper forum for their adjudication, for whatever reason, only perpetuates the problem and transforms an Islamic facility into a conventional one.

**12.17** The defendants appealed the decision of Morison J.[20] The main issue on the appeal revolved around the construction of the governing law clause. The appellants (the defendants) maintained that the clause meant that the agreements had to comply with both Shari'ah and English law. Since they did not comply with Shari'ah, they were unlawful, invalid and unenforceable, the appellants claimed. The respondent (the claimant) reiterated again that the impugned agreements did comply with Shari'ah as certified by their internal Religious Supervisory Board. The Court of Appeal considered submissions from expert witnesses from both sides.

---

18 See art 3(1) of the Rome Convention on the Law Applicable to Contractual Obligation 1980 (Rome Convention). See also *American Motorists' Insurance Co v Cellstar Corpn and Another* [2003] EWCA Civ 206.
19 Ibid.
20 See the Court of Appeal decision [2004] EWCA Civ 19.

**12.18** Dr Lau,[21] the respondent's expert, claimed that:

If a bank's Religious Supervisory Board is satisfied that the bank's activities are in accordance with Shari'ah law, that concludes the matter, there being no provision in Bahrain law, or Islamic law generally, for an appeal by a customer of the bank against the Board's rulings and certifications.[22]

**12.19** This is an astonishing claim. Why should the decision of the bank's internal Religious Advisory Board be final and not appealable? More so, when one takes into account that the members of the Religious Advisory Board are appointed by the bank. It is possible that the appointed members could approve products and services which they themselves are not keen on approving because the refusal to do so could result in their replacement with someone else who will comply with the bank's wishes.

**12.20** Khan J,[23] the appellants' expert, responded to the above claim by saying that '...certification by the Board (Bank's Religious Supervisory Board) that the operations of the bank are according to the Sharia would not be a decision binding on any court dealing with the dispute under the law of Sharia. The dispute would fall to be resolved by the court in the light of its own view of the position under Sharia law'.[24]

**12.21** Khan J's statement accurately represents the Shari'ah position on the matter. The court should be the final arbiter in the adjudication of Islamic finance issues, irrespective of whether they are of conventional or Shari'ah nature. The court is adequately equipped to treat any dispute in a fair and just manner, and to be guided by the parties and experts in the decision making process.

**12.22** The appellants cited two authorities to demonstrate that the English court is well-equipped and capable to determine and apply Shari'ah when assisted with expert evidence. First, the decision of Moore-Bick J in *Glencore International AG v Metro Trading International Inc*,[25] where the court, after having been concerned about the meaning and scope of the word *ghasb* (misappropriation), interpreted and applied the term to the facts of the case with the help of expert witnesses. Second, the judgment of Hart J in *Al-Bassam v Al-Bassam*,[26] where the court, assisted by the help of experts, interpreted and applied the Shari'ah principles pertaining to the law of succession. Potter LJ, delivering the judgment of the Court of Appeal, held that both authorities had no relevance to this case. In the former, the choice of law was the law of Fujairah Civil Code which the court was under the obligation to interpret and apply and, in the latter, the court was under the obligation to determine position under the

---

21 The former director of the Centre of Islamic and Middle Eastern Law.

22 Ibid, [29].

23 Former chairman of the Shari'ah Appellate Bench of the Supreme Court of Pakistan.

24 Ibid, [34].

25 [2001] 1 Lloyds Law Rep 284.

26 [202] EWHC 2281 (Ch).

law of succession in Saudi Arabia, the deceased's country of domicile at the date of his death. Potter LJ concluded by saying that 'Neither case was concerned with the construction of a disputed choice of law'.[27]

**12.23** The Court of Appeal was presented here with two choices. First, the easier and less controversial choice, was to distinguish this case from the two cited authorities. Indeed, neither case contained the choice of law issue like the one raised in this case. Based on this point alone, the court had a basis to ignore the judgments and draw the distinction. However, had the court decided not to ignore the judgments and had it considered the methodology applied by the courts in those two cases in dealing with the matters of foreign law such as Shari'ah, it would have had the basis for doing so.

**12.24** The appellants also argued that the governing law clause should be understood as incorporating specific rules of Shari'ah in relation to *murabahah* and *ijarah* agreements. Potter LJ dismissed this proposition explaining that incorporation 'can only sensibly operate where the parties have by terms of their contract sufficiently identified "black letter" provisions of a foreign law or an international code or set of rules'.[28] This point serves as a useful reminder that Shari'ah principles can only be incorporated into a contract if they are specifically identified. A general reference to Shari'ah is not sufficient.

**12.25** The decisions in *Symphony Gems* and *Shamil Bank* do not only attest to the court's deliberate ignorance of Shari'ah non-compliance in Islamic finance contracts but, they also exert, perhaps inadvertently, a significant influence over other common law courts which may follow their precedence. This was certainly the case in a recent Malaysian Court of Appeal decision in *Maybank Islamic Bhd v M-10 Builders Sdn Bhd and Anor*.[29] One of the issues that the court dealt with was whether an Islamic finance contract which did not comply with Shari'ah was legally enforceable if it, nonetheless, complied with the conventional contract laws. This trial court decided that the contract in this case failed to comply with Shari'ah requirements.[30] As a result, the court concluded that the contract was illegal under section 24 of the Contract Act 1950. When the contract is found to be illegal under section 24, it becomes void and unenforceable.[31] The Court of Appeal, however, found that the contract complied with Shari'ah and reversed the trial court's decision. But, the court did not stop there. Rather, it proceeded to answer the question as to whether a contract could be declared illegal only on Shari'ah non-compliance grounds. The court cited the decisions in *Symphony*

---

27 Ibid, [54].

28 Ibid, [51].

29 [2017] 7 CLJ 127.

30 For the High Court decision, see *Maybank Islamic Bhd v M-10 Builders Sdn Bhd and Anor* [2015] 1 SHR 137; [2015] 4 CLJ 526.

31 See s 24 of the Contracts Act 1950 (Malaysia). An agreement is illegal, according to s 24, if the consideration or object of the agreement is either a) forbidden by law, b) of such a nature, that if permitted, it would defeat any law, c) fraudulent, d) involves or implies injury to the person or property of another, e) immoral, or opposed to public policy.

*Gems* and *Shamil Banks* with approval and held that Shari'ah non-compliance of an Islamic finance contract will not affect the validity of the contract under the conventional law.

**12.26** A lesson that could be deduced from these cases is that the compliance with conventional laws seems to be more important than the compliance with Shari'ah. One could also argue, less convincingly though, that the non-compliance with Shari'ah will not have any effect on the validity of the agreement. One may appreciate the difficulties the English court had in dealing with Shari'ah non-compliance issues, but why would the courts in Malaysia discriminate between the non-compliance in the two systems of law which are supposed to run in parallel with each other.[32] An Islamic finance contract is the result of a fusion between the two legal traditions. It should never be considered as either conventional or Shari'ah agreement alone.

**12.27** The courts should recognize that Islamic finance contracts can only exist if they are Islamic. Take away the 'Islamic' part from them and they turn into conventional contracts. So why is it so hard for the court to see that an Islamic finance contract which does not comply with Shari'ah should be declared as illegal? If the same contract were to be in non-compliance with the conventional law, the court would perhaps have no difficulty in declaring it as illegal. This discriminatory treatment of Shari'ah by the courts needs to come to an end if the Islamic finance is to be given a due recognition that it deserves.

## Interventionist approach to Islamic finance contracts

**12.28** The approach of the civil courts in Malaysia to Islamic finance disputes can be characterized as interventionist. Traditionally, the courts in Malaysia have approached Shari'ah non-compliance issues in two ways. The first approach, adopted in a small number of cases, was to decide Shari'ah issues by themselves. At times, this was done discreetly under the pretext that the disputes pertained to contractual interpretation which necessitated the application of civil law and not Shari'ah. There were, however, a few cases where Shari'ah issues were adjudicated by reference to Shari'ah. These judgments, very few in numbers though, attracted criticisms from various parties. The second, more popular approach, was to delegate Shari'ah interpretation and determination to the Shari'ah scholars who have been appointed to serve on the Central Bank of Malaysia Shari'ah Advisory Council (SAC). This approach, though mostly accepted by all the major stakeholders, is also not without controversy. The concerns have been raised around usurpation of judicial power of the court and substantive unfairness in the Shari'ah scholars' rulings. The questions pertaining to Shari'ah compliance of some of the SAC rulings have also been raised. Both of these approaches deserve to be looked at in a more detailed manner below.

---

32 S 27 of the CBMA 2009 states: 'The financial system in Malaysia shall consist of the conventional financial system and the Islamic financial system'.

*Judicial treatment of Shari'ah non-compliance*

**12.29** By the end of 2005, the High Court delivered a judgment in *Affin Bank Bhd v Zulkifli Abdullah.*[33] The case pertained to the quantum of pay under a *bai' bithaman ajil* (deferred payment sale), also known as a BBA Islamic financing facility. Under the BBA arrangement, the plaintiff (bank) purchased a property from the defendant under the Property Purchase Agreement (PPA) and then immediately after that resold the property to the defendant on a deferred basis under the Property Sale Agreement (PSA). The purchase price was the amount of financing requested by the defendant while the sale price consisted of the purchase price and the profits that the bank calculated for the duration of the tenure. The agreed tenure for the payment of monthly instalments was 25 years. The defendant defaulted in paying the monthly instalments after only two years and eight months. The bank then applied for the summary judgment and claimed the balance of the full sale price even though the defendant did not make use of the full tenure. The main issue before the court was whether the provider of an Al-Bai Bithaman Ajil facility can, in the event of default before the end of tenure, claim as part of the sale price or banking selling price the profit margin under the unexpired tenure of the facility.[34]

**12.30** The court could have approached this issue in two ways. It could have framed the issue as a matter of Shari'ah and then referred it to Shari'ah scholars in the SAC to ascertain whether the BBA and the bank's claim of profits for the unexpired tenure under the BBA complied with Shari'ah. However, the court must have known that the bank could have only offered the BBA facility after it had been approved by the SAC as Shari'ah compliant. Therefore, asking the SAC to ascertain whether the BBA complied with Shari'ah after the same SAC had already approved it would not make sense. Abdul Wahab Patail J, delivering the judgment, admitted that he was initially considering making a reference to the SAC on the basis that the issue involved a question of Shari'ah. But, instead, he decided to look at the issue as a matter of 'interpretation and application of the terms of the contractual documents'.[35]

**12.31** The learned judge departed from the literal interpretation of the sale price stated in the PSA and decided that the bank's claim of the profits for the unexpired tenure could not be sustained. The sale price in the PSA, according to the judge, was not a typical sale price paid by a single payment but, rather, it consisted of series of equal monthly instalments. The sale price, thus, represented the bank's purchase price and profit margin calculated with the profit rate applied to the full tenure of the facility. Since the defendant only made use of

---

33 [2006] 1 CLJ 438 (*Affin Bank*).
34 Ibid, 447.
35 Ibid, 448.

part of the tenure, the bank's claim for the full sale price became unreasonable. Abdul Wahab Patail J had this to say:

> The profit margin that continues to be charged on the unexpired part of the tenure cannot be actual profit. It is clearly unearned profit. It contradicts the principle of Al-Bai Bithaman Ajil as to the profit margin that the provider is entitle to. Obviously, if the profit has not been earned it is not profit, and cannot be claimed under the Al-Bai Bithaman Ajil facility.[36]

**12.32** It became apparent that even though the court declined to consider the validity of the BBA from a Shari'ah point of view, it nonetheless, changed the terms of the BBA by reference to the conventional laws on the construction of contracts. The court observed that the intention of the parties was that the sale price of the PSA could only be recovered if the defendant had a full use of the tenure of the facility. This was a risky move as the common law courts have traditionally been reluctant to imply that the parties intended anything different from what has been expressly written in their contract.[37] The change of the sale price by the court brings the element of uncertainty into the price. The price in a typical sale contract must be certain for it to be Shari'ah compliant. The irony is, however, that the judge rewrote the terms of the PSA to make the entire product fair and equitable and, by extension, Shari'ah complaint.

**12.33** The sale contract, arguably, was never meant to be used for the purposes other than a typical sale. In the BBA, the sale contracts are used for financing purposes. When that happens, then they ought to be treated as financing instruments and not as typical sale contracts. When Shari'ah scholars create a product which, according to many Muslim consumers and scholars, is not Shari'ah compliant, then the court may use other, conventional means at its disposal to remedy the unfair outcomes.[38]

**12.34** One year after the decision in *Affin Bank*, the same issue regarding the BBA was raised before the High Court again in *Malayan Banking Bhd v Marilyn Ho Siok Lin*.[39] The defendant, who defaulted 14 months after she received financing under the BBA, argued that the plaintiff (bank) could not be entitled to the profits of RM495,205.64 as those profits were for a period of 20 years or 240 months. David Wong J, who had the benefit of reading the judgment in *Affin Bank*, decided not to consider the issue as a matter of Shari'ah or contractual interpretation, but instead sought assistance from the law of equity.

---

36 Ibid, 450.

37 Banks' right to claim the full sale price in case of premature termination of the BBA facility has been hailed by some scholars as both Shari'ah compliant and in accordance with the contract law. See, for instance, Norhashimah Mohd Yasin, 'Islamic Banking: Case Commentaries involving Al-Bay Bithaman Ajil' [1997] 3 *Malayan Law Journal* cxcii and Mohd Illiayas, 'Islamic Interest-Free Banking in Malaysia: Some Legal Considerations' [1995] 3 *Malayan Law Journal* cxlix.

38 See Adnan Trakic, 'The Unfairness in Islamic Finance Contracts: The Malaysian Case' (2018) 29 *Journal of Banking and Finance Law and Practice* 294.

39 [2006] 7 MLJ 249 (*Marilyn Ho*).

He drew inspiration from Lord Denning LJ's decision in *Stockloser v Johnson*[40] where the seller's forfeiture of all the prior sums paid by instalments, by virtue of a forfeiture clause in the agreement which allowed the seller to do so in the event of default of any instalment payment, was held to be inequitable. David Wong J also remarked that 'the principle of equity is consistent with Islamic teaching'.[41] As a result, the court agreed to reduce the full sale price for the unexpired tenure of the facility as per *Affin Bank's* formula.

**12.35** The court's argument that equity is consistent with Shari'ah is interesting. Why was this statement made and what it means? Does it mean that since the sale price provision in the PSA was inequitable, it was also Shari'ah non-compliant because equity is consistent with Islamic teaching? Furthermore, the court followed the decision in *Affin Bank* 'as an authority for the proposition that it would not be equitable to allow the bank to recover the sale price as defined when the tenure of the facility is terminated prematurely'.[42] This conclusion was reached despite the fact that the court in *Affin Bank* decided the case on the basis of a proper construction of the contract rules and not equity. David Wong J, however, was of the view that *Affin Bank* could also be used as an authority to say that the recovery of full sale price in premature termination of the facility was inequitable.

**12.36** The reference to equity was also made in *Malayan Banking Bhd v Ya'kup bin Oje & Anor.*[43] The issue the court needed to decide was the same as in the two earlier cases. Hamid Sultan JC held that the bank's insistence on the full profits was against the Qur'anic injunction to act with justice and equity. The learned judge did not hesitate to criticize both scholars and Islamic banking institutions who argued that the bank is entitled to full profits in premature termination of the BBA facility. It is surprising to see the extent to which Shari'ah was discussed by the court. More than half of a written judgment dealt with Islamic law jurisprudence on the topics of justice and Shari'ah, prohibition of *riba* (interest) and validity of BBA. In the end, Hamid Sultan JC decided that the BBA agreement could not be interpreted by only looking at what was agreed by the parties, but a due consideration needed to be paid to the principles of equity. In line with that, the court allowed the plaintiff to file an affidavit stating that upon the recovery of the proceeds of sale the defendant will get a substantial rebate taking into account the prevailing market force by banks and meaningful decisions in *Affin Bank* and *Marilyn Ho*.

**12.37** The central issue in all of the three cases pertained to the proper interpretation of the 'sale price' clause in the PSA of the BBA facility. Was this a Shari'ah or conventional issue? The answer to this question matters because if it was a Shari'ah issue, then the proper way to decide it would be to either make

---

40 [1954] 1 QB 476.
41 [2006] 7 MLJ 249, 265.
42 Ibid, 266.
43 [2007] 6 MLJ 389 (*Ya'kup bin Oje*).

a reference to the SAC of the BNM, which at the time when these cases were decided was not mandatory,[44] or to hear evidence from expert witnesses. On the other hand, if the issue pertained to the conventional law matters, as the court decided it did, then the court was entitled to decide it on its own. That raises the question: how to differentiate between Shari'ah and conventional issues? The answer can be found in the Manual issued by the SAC.[45] The Manual is an illustrious practical guide meant to be used by the civil court judges and arbitrators deciding Islamic finance disputes. The Manual was published in 2012. This means that for Islamic finance disputes which had been decided prior to that, like the ones discussed previously, it was left to the judges to decide whether a purported issue was a matter of Shari'ah or conventional law.

**12.38** The apparent lack of clear distinction between Shari'ah and conventional issues led the court in the previous three cases to identify the sale price issue as a contractual issue that can only be remedied by the application of the conventional contract law and equity. The same issue could have been identified as a Shari'ah issue, in which case the court would not be in a position to ascertain the Shari'ah position on its own. The views of the SAC or other Shari'ah scholars would likely convince the court to decide that the reduction of the sale price would lead to *gharar* (uncertainty) which is not allowed in Shari'ah. Therefore, the outcome would have been different.

Judicial reference of Shari'ah non-compliance to Shari'ah scholars

**12.39** In 2009, the Court of Appeal delivered a decision in *Bank Islam Malaysia Bhd v Lim Kok Hoe & Anor and Other Appeals.*[46] This was an appeal from the decision in *Arab-Malaysian Finance Bhd v Taman Ihsan Jaya Sdn Bhd & Ors,*[47] in which the High Court delivered a common judgment for 12 cases concerning the BBA financing facility. The issue before Abdul Wahab Patail J, the same judge who decided *Affin Bank's* case, was once again about the sale price in the BBA. This time, the learned judge decided to be more direct and held that the BBA facility was not in compliance with Shari'ah. This is not to say that he acknowledged that there was a Shari'ah issue to be decided. Rather, he explicitly stated that an Islamic bank, as a licensed entity which is allowed to operate Shari'ah complaint banking business, must, by virtue of Islamic Banking Act 1984 (IBA)[48]

---

44 See s 16B of the repealed Central Bank of Malaysia Act 1958. The word used was 'may' and not 'shall' as stated in the current Central Bank of Malaysia Act 2009.

45 The full name of the Manual is *Manual Rujukan Mahkamah dan Penimbang Tara Kepada Majlis Penasihat Syariah Bank Negara Malaysia* (translated as Manual by which the Court and Arbitrators May Refer Shari'ah Matters to the Shari'ah Advisory Council of Bank Negara Malaysia) 2012 (the Manual). For more information on the Manual, see Tun Abdul Hamid Mohamad and Adnan Trakic, 'The Adjudication of Shari'ah Issues in Islamic Finance Contracts: Guidance from Malaysia' (2015) 26 *Journal of Banking and Finance Law and Practice* 39.

46 [2009] 6 CLJ 22 (*Lim Kok Hoe*).

47 [2008] 5 MLJ 631 (*Taman Ihsan Jaya*).

48 Islamic Banking Act 1984 (IBA) applied to Islamic banking institutions and was repealed by Islamic Financial Services Act 2013 (IFSA).

or Banking and Financial Institutions Act 1989 (BAFIA),[49] ensure its products and services are Shari'ah compliant. In other words, Shari'ah compliance for Islamic banks was mandatory requirement under the conventional banking laws (i.e. IBA and BAFIA). Consequently, the non-compliance with Shari'ah was, at the same time, non-compliance with conventional banking laws.[50]

**12.40** This was perhaps the first decision in which the civil court held unequivocally that an Islamic finance product offered by an Islamic finance provider and approved by its Shari'ah Advisory Board and the SAC, did not comply with Shari'ah. That said, it needs to be noted that the learned judge's proclamation was only a by-product of his deliberation of the conventional banking law issue which pertained to the scope of the Islamic bank's operations. The judge must have been aware, however, that the only way to decide if the Islamic bank was in breach of IBA, was to make a prior finding as to whether the BBA facility offered by the bank complied with Shari'ah. As expected, the decision rattled the Islamic finance industry and attracted criticisms on the basis that it is not proper for a civil court judge, who may have limited expertise in Shari'ah, to make a ruling as to whether an Islamic finance product is allowed under Shari'ah. That decision should be left to competent Shari'ah scholars, so goes the argument. Perhaps the strongest critique came from the Court of Appeal in *Lim Kok Hoe* which eventually reversed the decision.

**12.41** The Court of Appeal held that the learned judge erred in making a comparison between the BBA agreement and the conventional loan facility as the former is a sale transaction while the latter is a loan agreement.[51] The court also disagreed with the equitable interpretation of the sale price by the trial judge. This, according to the court, amounted to rewriting of the contract for the parties which the court should not have done.[52] The court also observed that it is not proper for a civil court judge to decide the Shari'ah matters. This is what Raus Sharif JCA, delivering the judgment of the court, said:

> In this respect, it is our view that judges in civil courts should not take upon themselves to declare whether a matter is in accordance to the Religion of Islam or otherwise. As rightly pointed out by Suriyadi J (as he then was) in *Arab-Malaysia Merchant Bank Bhd v Silver Concepts Sdn Bhd* [2006] 8 CLJ 9 that in the civil court 'not every presiding judge is a Muslim, and even if so, may not be sufficiently equipped to deal with matters, which ulalamak take years to comprehend.' Thus, whether the bank business is in accordance with the Religion of Islam, it needs consideration by eminent jurists who are properly qualified in the field of Islamic jurisprudence.[53]

---

49 Banking and Financial Institutions Act 1989 (BAFIA) applied to Islamic banking divisions within conventional banking institutions and was repealed by Financial Services Act 2013.
50 S 28 of the IFSA provides that Islamic financial institution must ensure Shari'ah compliance.
51 [2009] 6 CLJ 22, 35.
52 Ibid, 36.
53 Ibid, 37.

**12.42** It was believed that this Court of Appeal decision would bring to an end the uncertainty around the sale price clause in the BBA facility and the equitable interpretation of the terms in Islamic finance contracts. However, just one year after *Lim Kok Hoe* was decided, the sale price in the prematurely terminated BBA agreement came to the High Court's attention again in the case of *Bank Islam Malaysia Bhd v Azhar bin Osman and other cases.*[54] The High Court unexpectedly decided not to enforce the sale price in the PSA as it was agreed by the parties but, instead, held that it was an implied term of the contract that the customer was entitled to *ibra'* (rebate) for the unexpired tenure of the agreement. This was, according to the court, implied from the long established customary practice of Islamic banks to grant rebate to their customers in premature termination of the facility. Islamic banks used to claim the full sale price in their statement of claims but, in practice, when the judgment was obtained for the full amount, the rebate was normally given for the unexpired tenure of the facility.[55] The High Court also reinstated the claim from the earlier discussed High Court decisions that the BBA cannot be regarded as a sale transaction simpliciter. Shortly after, however, this decision was reversed by the Court of Appeal in *Bank Islam Malaysia Berhad v Mohd Azmi bin Mohd Salleh.*[56] The Court of Appeal held that the High Court judge erred in stating that the BBA is not a sale contract simpliciter and that the customer is entitled to rebate. The court essentially reinforced the decision in *Lim Kok Hoe.*

**12.43** The situation surrounding the uncertainty around the reference of Shari'ah questions to the SAC prompted the Malaysian Parliament to replace the discretionary reference with the mandatory one. The newly enacted section 56 of the Central Bank of Malaysia Act 2009 (CBMA) replaced the word 'may' with the word 'shall' making the reference to the SAC mandatory for a civil court judge. The ruling made by the SAC pursuant to the reference made under section 56 was made biding on the court under section 57 of the CBMA. Since their enactment in 2009, both sections 56 and 57 have been judiciously applied by the civil court judges. There has not been any case where the court deliberately decided not to follow the mechanism prescribed by the CBMA. There have been, however, a number of cases where the mechanism was challenged on constitutional grounds.

**12.44** A recent landmark judicial decision by the Malaysian Federal Court in *JRI Resources Sdn Bhd v Kuwait Finance House (Malaysia) Bhd; President of Association of Islamic Banking Instituions Malaysia & Anor (Interveners)*[57] is the case on point. The main issue in this case revolved around the validity of

---

54 [2010] 9 MLJ 192 (*Azhar bin Osman*).

55 Abdul Hamid Mohamad and Adnan Trakic, 'Application and Development of Ibra' in Islamic Banking in Malaysia' (2013) *The Law Review* 26, 41.

56 Unreported (Civil Appeal No W-02-609-2010) (*Mohd Azmi bin Mohd Salleh*).

57 [2019] 5 CLJ 569 (*JRI Resources*). See also the Court of Appeal decision in (Civil Appeal No: B-02(IM)(NCVC)-1674-09/2016) and the High Court decision in *Kuwait Finance House (Malaysia) Bhd v JRI Resources Sdn Bhd* [2016] 10 CLJ 435.

an indemnity clause in *ijarah* (leasing) agreement by which the customer voluntarily accepted to indemnify the bank from any major maintenance related costs that may arise in relation to the leased asset. The customer challenged the validity of the indemnity clause on the ground of Shari'ah non-compliance as it is a well-accepted position that one of the requirements for the validity of *ijarah* is that the risk over the asset and major maintenance costs in relation to the asset must be borne by the owner or the lessor which in this case was the bank.[58] The issue was referred to the SAC for ascertainment as per section 56 and the SAC decided that the bank was allowed to transfer the maintenance costs to the customer through voluntary contractual arrangement in the form of an indemnity clause. However, there has been a strong argument that this is not allowed under Shari'ah. This was even confirmed by a reputed Shari'ah scholar who submitted expert evidence to that effect at the trial stage of the case. The mechanism under the CBMA, however, does not allow any other party, including the court and expert witnesses appointed by the parties, to make a decision on Shari'ah non-compliance. Therefore, the decision of the SAC was binding on the court and, by necessary extension, on the parties by virtue of section 57 of the CBMA.

**12.45** The customer challenged the constitutionality of sections 56 and 57 arguing that they usurped the judicial function of the court. The customer also argued that they were effectively denied the right to be heard as the SAC made a decision on the Shari'ah issue without giving the customer right to present its case to the SAC and, on the top of it, its decision was final. If the SAC was only viewed as a statutory expert, then why was the customer not allowed to cross examine the expert. On 10 April 2019, the nine panel Federal Court decided, by a slim majority of five to four, that the provisions were constitutional.

**12.46** This monopoly over Shari'ah pronouncements that the SAC holds may produce some unintended consequences. The customers, for example, may start doubting the Islamicity of Islamic banking and finance products. Their dissatisfaction could be accelerated when they realize that their side of the story cannot be heard by the SAC nor can the SAC's decisions be challenged by the court. Apart from this, the constitutionality of the CBMA mechanism has survived for now, but the thin majority of five to four shows that a substantial part of the judiciary thinks that the mechanism is unconstitutional.

### The way forward

**12.47** It becomes apparent from the preceding discussion that the interventionist approach adopted by the courts in Malaysia is more in line with the spirt and letter of Shari'ah than the approach of the courts in the UK. What is less

---

58 See MY Saleem, 'Islamic Contracts for Financing (Part2)' in A Trakic and HHA Tajuddin (eds), *Islamic Banking and Finance: Principles, Instruments & Operations* (Malaysian Current Law Journal, 2016) 133–134.

apparent, however, is the difference in the approach between the Malaysian High Court and the Court of Appeal. Whose decisions are more in line with the spirit of Shari'ah? An easy answer would be the Court of Appeal approach as it ensures that the Shari'ah matters are only decided by the competent Shari'ah scholars (i.e. the SAC). However, does it mean that the decisions of the High Court in the earlier mentioned cases are not in accordance with Shari'ah just because the civil court judges decided cases according to their own interpretation of Shari'ah? I would argue that what matters is what was decided and not necessarily who decided it. Ironically, the decisions of the High Court judges appear to be more in line with the spirit of Shari'ah then the approach taken by the Shari'ah scholars in Malaysia who have certified as Shari'ah compliant the product which most other Shari'ah scholars around the world view as Shari'ah non-compliant.[59] This is not to say that the civil court judges who have limited knowledge of Shari'ah should be making Shari'ah pronouncements. That function should be left to Shari'ah experts. But, whether a particular Shari'ah expert or a group of experts should have monopoly over interpretation of Shari'ah is the question to which Malaysian Parliament answered in the affirmative by enacting sections 56 and 57 of the CBMA. This monopoly over Shari'ah pronouncements in itself may not be in line with the spirit of Shari'ah.

**12.48** Islam promotes the plurality of thoughts and encourages parties to innovate and consider problems from different angles, provided that the discussion is within the parameters allowed in Islamic jurisprudence. The SAC, as the sole Shari'ah authority in Islamic finance, with all its impressive credentials and expertise, is not infallible. Their approach, at times, has been based on the literal interpretation of the Qur'anic injunction that parties are obliged to fulfil their contractual obligations.[60] That seems to be the fundamental aspect behind the decisions that the sale price in the PSA cannot be changed by the court or that the indemnity clause in the *ijarah* agreement which transfers the risk on to customers must be upheld by the court as agreed by the parties.

**12.49** I would disagree with such a reasoning. This reasoning would make sense if the parties have 'freely' negotiated their contract. However, most of the contracts today concluded between Islamic financial institutions and their customers are standard form contracts where customers have unequal bargaining power. If they refuse to accept certain terms, they would probably be denied the financing that they so desperately require. This is where the Islamic finance contract needs to be looked at in its entirety together with the circumstances

---

59 Three classical schools of thought in Islam, namely Hanafi, Maliki and Hanabali, prohibit the practice of *bai 'inah* (back to back sale) which forms the basis of the BBA facility. Only Shafi' school of thought, to which Malaysia belongs, allows it. Most of the Middle East Shari'ah scholars are of the view that *bai 'inah* is not allowed because of its fictitious nature which is meant to legalese interest. For further details, see A Shaharuddin, 'The Bay' al-'Inah Controversy in Malaysian Islamic Banking' (2012) 26 *Arab Law Quarterly* 499.

60 Qur'an, Chapter 5: 1 where Allah says: 'O ye who believe! fulfil (all) obligations'.

in which it was concluded. A contract or a term of the contract which is substantially unfair simply cannot be Shari'ah compliant even in the case where the Shari'ah scholars have certified it as such. Something unfair and oppressive should not be labeled 'Islamic'. As famous Shari'ah scholar, Ibn Qayyim, observed:

> The Shari'ah is entirely justice, compassion, wisdom, and prosperity. Therefore, any ruling that replaces justice with injustice, mercy with cruelty, prosperity with harm, or wisdom with nonsense, is a ruling that does not belong to the Shari'ah, even if it is claimed to be so according to some interpretations.[61]

**12.50** The solution, in my view, would be to return the judicial power to the courts to handle both Shari'ah and conventional issues in Islamic finance contracts. In the UK, the courts should recognize Shari'ah issues and make decisions after they have heard the expert evidence from both sides. Ignoring Shari'ah on the pretext that the contract is governed only by English law is simply wrong. Nothing prevents the court from considering Shari'ah in the same way it would consider any other foreign laws. In Malaysia, the courts should reclaim back the judicial power over Shari'ah issues in Islamic finance contracts. This is not to say that the civil court judges should be making Shari'ah rulings on their own. The role of the SAC in the resolution of Islamic finance disputes is necessary. But, the SAC cannot be allowed to dictate to the courts how to judge Shari'ah issues. Judging can only be done by judges and not by a non-judicial body such as the SAC. Therefore, sections 56 and 57 which in their current form seem to divest the courts of the judicial power would need to be amended. The SAC must maintain its position as an expert body whose opinions should certainly be sought after by the courts. The SAC should also welcome the parties to cross-examine them in the courts. A further scrutiny of their views by the parties and the deciding judge will only improve the overall outcome in the dispute. If the SAC feels that some of its resolutions ought to be made into laws, then they can, as an independent advisor to the Central Bank of Malaysia, advise the bank to pass these resolutions into standards which will then have the force of law. In this way, the judicial power remains with the courts to apply and interpret the standards while the SAC continues to play a critical role in setting of these standards.

---

61 Ibn al-Qayyim, *I'lam al-Muwaqi'een, Vol. 4*, 1st edn (Dar Ibn al-Jawzi) 337.

# INDEX